ALL THINGS IN CHRIST

EDITED BY VINCENT A. YZERMANS

ALL THINGS IN CHRIST

ENCYCLICALS AND SELECTED DOCUMENTS OF SAINT PIUS X

THE NEWMAN PRESS · 1954 · WESTMINSTER, MARYLAND

Nihil obstat: Gregory Roettger, O.S.B., S.T.D.
Censor librorum

Imprimatur: Peter W. Bartholome, D.D.
Bishop of Saint Cloud, Minnesota

May 29, 1954

Library of Congress Catalog Card Number: 54-7544

Printed in the United States of America

affectionately dedicated

to

My Mother and My Father

Foreword

OUR LORD said that a tree could be judged by the goodness of its fruit; a good tree bears good fruit. The present book of Reverend Vincent Arthur Yzermans, in which are gathered and explained the principal encyclicals and documents of Pius X, clearly demonstrates how beneficent and fertile was the pontificate of this saintly Pontiff. Scarcely forty years after his death, Pius X in this Marian Year has been raised to the honor of the altars with the aureola of sanctity. How fitting it is to recall these encyclicals and documents, the fruit of his pontificate and shining witness to the supernatural wisdom which guided him in his determined efforts for the sanctification of souls and the Christian restoration of society. They are documents full of vitality, repeated in history books, cited in treatises on ecclesiastical discipline, and some even incorporated in the canons of the Church. They came forth from the Chair of Peter, and now, we might say, they resound from heaven.

The entire life of Saint Pius X glows with sanctity. He lived *"in spiritu humilitatis"* (Dan. 3:39), and with apostolic ardor he stirred the flame which was kindled in the Cenacle, a true *"Ignis ardens,"* for the salvation of souls and the honor of the House of God. His first encyclical, *E Supremi Apostolatus* (October 3, 1903), revealed the supernatural spirit which would animate his deeds and writings; it is a characteristic document, outlining the program of his eleven years in the papacy. He begins by recalling the discouragement and terror which seized him as soon as the votes of the 1903 conclave centered upon him. The possibility of being elevated to the Chair of Peter was for Cardinal Sarto something completely unthinkable, and with prayers and tears he did everything to avoid it. Finally, enlightened and raised in spirit by Him who strengthens, he accepted the burden of Sovereign Pontiff with one purpose in mind—*"instaurare omnia in Christo*—to re-establish all things in Christ" (Eph. 1:10).

But how was so vast a program to be actuated? He realized the inefficacy of purely human remedies as he saw before him a panorama of desolation effected by widespread dissensions and increasing apostasy from God. In another document also recorded in this volume, *Acerbo Nimis* (April 15, 1905), Pius X declares with grief-stricken heart that the cause of rampant moral evils is ignorance of religion. The only remedy, therefore, is to return to Christ, to Him who came to save mankind. He invites everyone of good will to renew his faith and hope in Christ and begs that "Christ be formed" (Gal. 4:19) in each member of the clergy and laity that both may be able to co-operate in the program.

In this collection are gathered the principal appeals of the Holy Father to the clergy and laity. The saintly Pontiff on every occasion insisted on the urgent necessity "to re-establish all things in Christ" and he continued to recall this motto in his principal decrees. He did so in his *Motu proprio* of the codification of Canon Law, *Arduum Sane Munus.* The disciplinary laws of the Church were to be reordered, examined and "collected into one body," and for this arduous task he proposed one guiding principle, namely, that for each canon the supreme law was to be the good of souls. That occurred at the beginning of his pontificate, March 19, 1904. The very same motto is brought into relief again in documents written to awaken religious fervor, as, for example, the encyclical *Ad Diem Illum* (February 2, 1904), with which he invited the faithful to celebrate the golden jubilee of the proclamation of the dogma of the Immaculate Conception in much the same way as the reigning Pontiff has called us to commemorate its centenary with this Marian Year. In this document he ardently urges devotion to the Mother of God and points out that she is also our Mother, from whose hands we have received Christ and through whom we are united to Him.

In this collection the goal has been to gather especially those documents in which the Sovereign Pontiff addressed the clergy and laity to obtain their collaboration in his announced program of Christian restoration. Among them is found the exhortation *Haerent Animo* (August 4, 1908), on the occasion of his golden sacerdotal jubilee. It is like a harmonious bell calling ecclesiastics to a consideration of the loftiness of the priesthood and its inherent duties, a simple yet profound document, instructive and paternal, destined to survive through the years. Among the documents directed to the faithful, two, in the mind of Pius X, were basic for the hoped-for re-establishment and were cherished by him. One was the decree *Sacra Tridentina Synodus* (December 20, 1905), inviting the faithful to frequent Communion; the other, *Quam Singulari* (August 8, 1910), fixing the age of children for First Communion. Even the young will contribute to the restoration of all things in Christ if in their years of innocence they are joined to Christ with bonds of love, grow in holiness, and in union with Christ diffuse their candor in a salutary way. The Eucharist is the bread of the soul, Pius X tells us, and, like bread, we have constant need of it. He reminds us that we are weak and inclined to evil and that the Eucharist is the medicine and antidote. He points out that to receive Communion worthily only two things are necessary, the grace of God and a good intention. It is evident that the reality of these words of advice never diminishes; they are for all time.

Saint Pius X noted that "to restore all things in Christ" has always been the motto of the Church in her work. The Church lives on faith in God and on works of charity. This book shows how priests and laity must make their contribution to the life of the Mystical Body of Christ of which we are all members. It is a saintly Sovereign Pontiff who speaks to us, and the ways of the saints are the ways of God. May this fine volume carry his inspiring message to many hearts.

AMLETO GIOVANNI CICOGNANI
Archbishop of Laodicea
Apostolic Delegate

Washington, D. C.
June 6, 1954

Preface

IT WOULD seem presumptuous even to attempt composing a preface to the works of a saint. To bring forth the writings of a modern saint who steered the Barque of Peter through one of the most severe storms in history and, what is more, to edit, revise, and comment upon the very documents which have so deeply impressed the spirit of the Church in the twentieth century is doubly a task that calls for the highest degree of courage. By the very office he exercises, however, an editor must have courage. From the very beginning, this work was providential; its completion now also seems to be a work of Providence.

This volume contains thirteen encyclical letters of Saint Pius X, as well as ten documents selected from the three thousand three hundred and twenty-two that came forth from Rome under the guidance of this "universal Pastor of Christendom." Though they are but a handful, I believe that these documents portray the depth and extent of his desire that "when in every city and village God's law is faithfully observed, reverence shown for sacred things, the Sacraments frequented and the ordinances of a Christian life carried out. . . . We need labor no further in re-establishing all things in Christ." Even a casual glance at these writings will convince the reader that Saint Pius' words were, according to Pope Pius XII, "now as a thunderclap or a sword, now as a soothing balm. They carried a message which deeply impressed and influenced the whole Church and reached out beyond. His words had a power that was irresistible, not only because of the depth of meaning contained in them, but still more because of the intimate love which filled his heart. One felt that here was a shepherd who lived in God and with God, whose only wish was to lead his sheep and lambs to God."

In preparing these documents for publication my guiding principle was the following advice of Mr. Hilaire Belloc:

> Transmute boldly: render the sense by the corresponding sense without troubling over the verbal difficulties in your way. Where such rendering of sense by corresponding sense involves considerable amplification, do not hesitate to amplify for fear of being verbose. . . . Sometimes, even, a whole passage must be thus transmuted, a whole paragraph thrown into a new form, if we would justly render the sense of the original; and the rule should stand that, after having grasped as exactly as possible all that

> the original stands for, with the proportion between its various parts, the distinction between what is emphasized and what is left on a lower plane, we should say to ourselves, not "How shall I make this foreigner talk English?" but "What would an Englishman have said to express the same?" *That* is translation. *That* is the very essence of the art: the resurrection of an alien thing in a native body; not the dressing of it up in native clothes but the giving to it of native flesh and blood.

In view of that principle an editor necessarily becomes subject to Monsignor Knox's observation that one "cannot be a translator without being, to some extent, an interpreter; and the ways of the Catholic interpreter are not always plain and easy."

When setting out on this work, therefore, I drew up the following directives.

1. *Introductory paragraphs.* Each encyclical letter is prefaced with a few introductory remarks of a historical and analytical nature to give the reader the setting of the message as well as a thumbnail sketch of its content. The ten selected documents, however, which are for the most part very brief and deal with disciplinary and practical measures, are preceded only by a short introduction of a very general character.

2. *Paragraphs and sentences.* When clarity demanded it, the long Latin paragraphs and sentences were divided into two, or sometimes three, distinct paragraphs and sentences. This aids in "the resurrection of an alien thing in a native body." Nevertheless, for the convenience of the scholar who wishes to compare the translation with the original the paragraphs are so numbered as to correspond with the original Latin and Italian paragraphs.

3. *Marginal titles.* Again for the sake of clarity marginal titles have been inserted for each paragraph. These will help in following the train of thought more closely and will simplify the reading of each encyclical letter.

4. *Text.* With the exception of those documents which are taken from other works and acknowledged elsewhere, the original texts as found in the *Acta Sanctae Sedis* and the *Acta Apostolicae Sedis* were closely examined along with the translation issued upon their initial publication in either the *American Catholic Quarterly Review* or the *Catholic University Bulletin.* After this examination the English text was rendered as attractively and effectively as possible. In that task the editor could not be "a translator without being, to some extent, an interpreter."

5. *Bibliography.* The references placed in the bibliography are those books and articles which aided me in understanding the encyclical letters and the other documents. Naturally, some are more useful than others. All of them are included, however, for the sake of the reader who may desire to do

more extensive study. Along with these references is the original source of each document and, when possible, the source of a previous translation.

* * * * * *

I am most deeply grateful to my Ordinary, the Most Reverend Peter W. Bartholome, D.D., for the constant counsel, assistance, and encouragement he has shown me during the preparation of this volume. Its merit is, to a large extent, a tribute to his paternal interest and support.

I also extend my expression of gratitude to Sister M. Claudia Carlen, I.H.M., who has been an unfailing source of consultation and inspiration; Very Reverend Paul F. Tanner, for his editorial assistance and advice; Reverend Benjamin Stein, O.S.B., for his kindness and assistance in letting me use the facilities of Saint John's Abbey Library; Reverend Joseph LaManna, for his translation from the Italian of the encyclical letter *Il Fermo Proposito;* Messrs. Walter and Alphonse Matt, for their encouragement and advice; Very Reverend John Van den Bosch, O.S.C., Reverend Ferdinand Falque and Reverend David Dillon, S.T.D., for examining the manuscript and offering many useful suggestions; Sister M. Redempta, O.S.F., for typing the manuscript; and my brother priests at Saint Mary's Cathedral for their assistance in parochial duties.

In the early morning of August 20, 1914, Saint Pius X uttered his last words: "Together in One—all things in Christ." These words have been adopted as the title of this volume of the writings of him whose all-consuming desire was "to restore all things in Christ." That this work of restoration, so wisely inaugurated by Saint Pius X, may progress until the face of the earth is renewed for the glorious coming of Christ the King is the prayer of every earnest Christian, as it is also the purpose of this volume.

VINCENT A. YZERMANS

Feast of the Immaculate Conception, 1953
Saint Cloud, Minnesota

Acknowledgments

I wish to thank the following publishers for permission to use documents which have appeared in books bearing their imprint:

Burns, Oates & Washbourne, Ltd., for the encyclical *Pascendi* from *The Doctrines of the Modernists;*

Dial Press, for the *Motu Proprio Doctoris Angelici* from Jacques Maritain's *The Angelic Doctor;*

Grail Press, for the apostolic letter *Quoniam in Re Biblica* from *Rome and the Study of Scripture,* and the apostolic exhortation *Haerent Animo* from *A Papal Symposium on the Priesthood;*

Saint Anthony Guild Press, for the encyclical *Acerbo Nimis* and the decrees *Sacra Tridentina* and *Quam Singulari* from *Catechetical Documents of Pope Pius X;*

The Confraternity of Christian Doctrine, for use of the Confraternity Edition of the *New Testament* for all New Testament quotations.

V. A. Y.

Contents

PART TWO—SELECTED DOCUMENTS

Part One

ENCYCLICAL LETTERS

CHAPTER 1

E Supremi Apostolatus *October 4, 1903, The Restoration of All Things in Christ*

AS SOON as Giuseppe Sarto, the Patriarch of Venice, assumed the honor of the Papacy the world was eager to discover his program. The world had heard little of this man until that memorable August 4 when, in spite of his pleading and tears, his colleagues among the Cardinals chose him to be the two hundred and fifty-ninth successor to Saint Peter as Bishop of Rome.

The press of the time, secular as well as Catholic, the diplomatic corps attached to the Vatican, the whole Catholic world wondered how this man, said to be of little learning and lacking in diplomatic skill, would be able to carry on the glorious achievements of his Predecessor, Leo XIII.

On October 4, three short months following his elevation, Saint Piux X set up his program in this his first encyclical letter on the restoration of all things in Christ.

He prefaces his program by recalling what to him must have been the saddest day of his life—his election to the papal dignity (section 1). He pays tribute to the memory of Leo XIII and describes the state of human society as godless (2). Then, dispelling all human fear and casting aside all worldly prudence, he goes on to state in unmistakable terms his guiding purpose: "Relying on the power of God in the work entrusted to Us, We proclaim that We have no other program in the Supreme Pontificate than that 'of re-establishing all things in Christ,' so that 'Christ may be all things and in all'" (3).

After considering the vehemence and totality of the attacks waged by the enemies of God, he calls upon his brothers in the episcopacy to labor zealously and ceaselessly in this apostolate of restoring all things in Christ (4–10). He exhorts them to foster a Christlike clergy because they "are destined by the duty of their vocation to form Him in others." Therefore he admonishes them to "consider your seminary as the delight of your heart" and direct it according to the provisions of the Council of Trent (11–12).

He recalls the necessity of teaching Christian doctrine and invites the laity to share in this total work of restoration, since "God recommended everyone to be solicitous for his neighbor's welfare" (13–15).

Finally he sets forth the objective of his program in no less intelligible terms. "When in every city and village God's law is faithfully observed, reverence is shown for sacred things, the Sacraments are frequented and the ordinances of a Christian life carried out, then, Venerable Brethren, We need labor no further in re-establishing all things in Christ." Already in his first encyclical he gave promise that he would be as renowned for his interior reform of the Church as Leo XIII was for his diplomatic genius.

Upon its publication the encyclical was received with much the same awe as filled the diplomatic corps after its first audience with the newly-elected Pontiff.

"What under the sun," asked the Russian minister, "is there in him that exercises so powerful an attraction?"

After a long, awkward silence the Portuguese ambassador ventured a reply, "Since no one has answered the question of what his attraction is, I shall try. Is it perhaps his sanctity?"

E Supremi Apostolatus *Encyclical Letter of Our Holy Father Pius X to the Patriarchs, Primates, Archbishops, Bishops and Other Ordinaries in Peace and Communion with the Apostolic See*

VENERABLE BRETHREN, HEALTH AND THE APOSTOLIC BLESSING:

Reluctance to accept the papal honor. 1. In addressing you for the first time from the Chair of the Supreme Apostolate to which We have been elevated by the inscrutable designs of God, it is necessary to remind you how We strove with many tears and earnest prayers to evade this formidable burden of the Pontificate. Although We are unequal in merit with Saint Anselm, it seems that We may truly make Our Own his words of lamentation when, against his will and in spite of his struggles, he was constrained to receive the honor of the episcopate. We can truthfully bring forth those same proofs of grief which he invokes in his own behalf to show Our Own dispositions of mind and will when We submitted to the most serious charge of feeding the flock of Christ. "My tears are witnesses," he wrote, "as well as the sounds and moanings of my anguished heart, such as I never remember having come from me in any sorrow before that day on which the great misfortune of the Archbishopric of Canterbury fell upon me. Those who gazed on my face that day could not fail to perceive how I, in color more like a dead than a living man, was pale for amazement and alarm. I have previously resisted, in all truth, as far as I could, my election—or rather, the violence inflicted upon me. Now, however, whether I like it or not, I am forced to confess that God's judgments opposed greater and greater resistance to my own efforts, and I see no way of escaping them. Vanquished as I am, therefore, by the violence not of men, but of God (against which there is no providing), after praying as long as I could and striving as much as I could that this chalice should if possible pass from me without drinking of it, I realize now that there is nothing left for me but to set aside my personal feelings and desires and resign myself entirely to the design and will of God."

Tribute to Pope Leo XIII. 2. Numerous and most weighty reasons were not lacking to justify Our resistance. We considered Ourself altogether unworthy, because of Our insignificance, to be named to the honor of the Pontificate and be designated to succeed him who, ruling the Church most wisely for nearly twenty-six years, was adorned with such loftiness of mind and lustre of every virtue that he gained the admiration even of his adversaries and by his glorious achievements made his name venerable for all ages.

A godless society today. Again, passing over many other motives, We were terrified beyond all else by the disastrous state of human society today. Who can fail to see that at the present time society is suffering more than in any past age from a terrible and radical malady which, while developing every day and gnawing into its very being, is dragging it to destruction? You understand, Venerable Brethren, this disease is apostasy from God. Truly nothing is more allied with ruin, according to the saying of the Prophet: "For, behold, they that go away from thee, shall perish." [1] We saw, therefore, that in virtue of the ministry of the Pontificate which was to be entrusted to Us, We must hasten to find a remedy for this great evil. Thus We considered as addressed to Us the Divine Command: "Lo, I have set thee this day over the nations, and over kingdoms, to root up, and to pull down, and to waste and to destroy, and to build and to plant." [2] Nevertheless, realizing Our weakness, We recoiled in terror from a task as urgent as it is arduous.

Program of Pontificate. 3. However, since it has so pleased the Divine Will to raise Our lowliness to such sublime power, We take courage in Him who strengthens Us. Relying on the power of God in the work entrusted to Us, We proclaim that We have no other program in the Supreme Pontificate than that "of re-establishing all things in Christ," [3] so that "Christ may be all things and in all."[4] Of course, there will be some who, measuring divine things by human standards, will seek to discover Our secret aims, distorting them for earthly purposes and political designs. In order to banish all such vain delusions for them, We repeat for their sake that We neither wish to be and, with the Divine assistance, never shall be anything else before human society than the minister of God, with whose authority We are invested. The interests of God shall be Our interests. For these We are resolved to spend all our strength and Our very life. Should anyone, therefore, ask Us for a sign that would reveal Our intention, We will give this and no other: "To re-establish all things in Christ."

Assistance of the Hierarchy. 4. We receive great strength in undertaking this glorious task in the knowledge that We shall have all of you, Venerable Brethren, as generous co-operators. If We doubted that fact We should have to regard you unjustly as either unconscious or heedless of that sacrilegious war which is now almost universally being stirred up and fomented against God. Truly "the nations are in tumult and the people devise vain things"[5] against their Creator. More and more frequently God's enemies cry out: "Depart from us."[6] As might be expected, We find extinguished among the majority of men all respect for the Eternal God and no regard paid in manifestations of public and private life to the Supreme Will. On the contrary, every effort and artifice is employed to blot out the memory and the knowledge of God.

Banishment of God. 5. Considering all these things, there is good reason to fear that this great perversity may be the foretaste and perhaps the beginning of those evils reserved for the last days, and the "son of perdition,"[7] of whom the Apostle speaks, may already be in the world. In very truth, We cannot think otherwise in virtue of the audacity and wrath employed everywhere in persecuting religion, in combating the dogmas of faith, in the firm determination of uprooting and destroying all relations between man and the Divinity. Moreover, and according to the same Apostle this is the distinguishing mark of the Antichrist, with unlimited boldness man has put himself in place of God, exalting himself above all that is called God. He has done this in such a way that although he cannot utterly extinguish in himself all knowledge of God, he has condemned God's majesty and made the universe a temple in which he himself is to be adored. "He sits in the temple of God and gives himself out as if he were God."[8]

God will be victorious. 6. No one of sound mind can doubt the outcome of this contest between man and the Most High. By abusing his liberty, man can violate the right and the majesty of the Creator of the universe, but the victory will ever be with God. In fact, in the very moment when man, under the delusion of his triumph, rises up with most audacity, defeat is knocking at the door. We are assured of this in the Sacred Scripture by God Himself.

Seemingly unmindful of His strength and greatness, He "overlooks the sins of men," [9] but swiftly, after these apparent retreats, "aroused like a mighty man that has been overcome by wine," [10] "he shall break the heads of his enemies," [11] that all may know "that God is king of all the earth," [12] "that the Gentiles may know themselves to be but men." [13]

Time for work and prayer. 7. All these things, Venerable Brethren, We believe with unshakable faith and expect to come to pass. This, however, does not prevent Us, according to each one's individual ability, from bending every effort to hasten the work of God. This we can achieve not merely by praying assiduously, "Arise, O Lord, let not man be strengthened," [14] but, more important still, by openly professing in word and deed God's supreme dominion over man and all things, in order that His right to command and His authority may be fully realized and respected.

Desire for peace. This work falls upon our shoulders not only as a natural duty but because of our common interest. Who can avoid, Venerable Brethren, being appalled and afflicted when he beholds, in the course of a justly extolled progress in civilization, the greater part of mankind fighting among themselves so fiercely that one would think strife is universal? The desire for peace is assuredly harbored in every heart. Everyone ardently seeks it. But peace without God is absurd. When God is absent, justice departs; and once justice is banished, vain is the hope for peace. "And the work of justice shall be peace." [15] We are well aware that there are many who, in their desire for peace (that is to say, the tranquillity of order), band themselves into societies and parties which they call parties of order. Hope and labor lost! There is only one party of order capable of restoring peace amid all this turmoil, and that is the party of God. This party, therefore, we must promote and draw as many followers as possible into its ranks if we are really urged by the love of peace.

Restoration through Christ. 8. Venerable Brethren, no matter how much we try, only through Jesus Christ shall we succeed in calling men back to the majesty and empire of God. "No one," the Apostle admonishes us, "can lay other foundation than that which has been laid, which is Christ Jesus." [16] It is, We repeat, Christ alone, "whom the Father has made holy and sent into the world," [17] "the brightness of his glory and the image of his substance," [18] true God and true man, without whom nobody can know God with knowledge for salvation, "nor does anyone know the Father except the Son, and him to whom the Son chooses to reveal him." [19] It follows, therefore, to re-establish all things in Christ and to lead men back to submission to God is one and the same aim. We must therefore labor to bring men back to the dominion of Christ, and when this is accomplished, we shall have then have brought them back to God. When We say God, We do not mean that inert being heedless of all things human which the materialists have devised, but the true and living God, one in nature, triune in person, Creator of the world, most wise Ordainer of all things, most just Lawgiver, Who punishes the wicked and rewards the virtuous.

The Church is the Way to Christ. 9. You see, then, Venerable Brethren, that We and you have the duty of bringing human society, now estranged from the wisdom of Christ, back to the discipline of the Church. Then the Church will subject it to Christ, and Christ to God. If We, through the goodness of God Himself, bring this task to a happy issue, We shall be filled with joy to see evil give place to good and hear with gladness "a loud voice in heaven saying, 'Now has come the salvation and strength and the kingdom of our God, and the authority of his Christ.'"[20] If, however, Our desire to obtain this end is to be fulfilled, We must use every means and bend every effort to bring about the total disappearance of that enormous and detestable wickedness so characteristic of our time—the substitution of man for God. Once this is accomplished, We must restore the sacred laws and counsels of the Gospel to their ancient position of honor. We must boldly proclaim the truths taught by the Church, such as her teachings on the sanctity of marriage, the education and discipline of youth, the possession and use of property, and the duties that men owe to those who rule the State. Finally, We must restore equilibrium between the different classes of society according to Christian precept and custom. In submitting Ourselves to the manifestations of the Divine Will, We resolved to aim at these objectives during Our Pontificate, and We shall labor without ceasing to attain them. It remains for you, Venerable Brethren, to confirm Our efforts by your own holiness, knowledge and experience, and especially by your zeal for the glory of God, with no other aim than that Christ may be formed in all.

Solicitude for priests. 11. The means to be employed in attaining this great end are so obvious that it seems superfluous to mention them. Let your first care be to form Christ in those who are destined by the duty of their vocation to form Him in others. We refer to priests, Venerable Brethren. All those who are stamped with the seal of the priesthood must realize that they have the same mission to the people among whom they live as that which Paul proclaimed he received in these tender words: "My dear children, of whom I am in labor again, until Christ is formed in you!"[21] How will they be able to exercise this duty if they are not first clothed with Christ themselves, and so clothed with Christ as to be able to say with the same Apostle: "It is now no longer I that live, but Christ lives in me,"[22] "For to me to live is Christ."[23] Even though everyone is included in the exhortation "to advance towards the perfect man, in the measure of the age of the fullness of Christ,"[24] it is principally addressed to him who exercises the sacerdotal ministry. He is therefore called another Christ, not merely by the communication of power, but especially because he imitates His works. He should therefore bear stamped upon himself the image of Christ.

Pastoral care over seminaries. 12. This being so, Venerable Brethren, you see the great care you must exercise in forming the clergy in holiness. All other tasks must yield to this one. Your greatest diligence, therefore, will be directed towards the right government and ordering of your seminaries, so that they may flourish both in sound doctrine and upright morals. Look upon your seminary as the delight of your heart and on its behalf neglect none of those provisions which the Council of Trent has prescribed with admirable forethought. When the time arrives for calling the youthful candidates to holy orders, do not forget Paul's words to Timothy: "Do not lay hands hastily upon anyone." [25] Bear carefully in mind that as a general rule the faithful will be such as are those whom you call to the priesthood. Therefore do not listen to private interests of any kind, but have at heart only God, the Church, and the eternal welfare of souls, so that, as the Apostle admonishes, "you will not be a partner in other men's sins." [26]

Vigilance over young priests. Furthermore, be most solicitous for young priests who have just left the seminary. From the bottom of Our heart We urge you to draw them often close to you, in order to enkindle them and inspire them so that they may aspire only after God and the salvation of souls. Rest assured, Venerable Brethren, that on Our part We shall exercise the greatest diligence in preventing members of the clergy from being drawn into the snares of a certain new and fallacious science, which does not savor of Christ but with masked and cunning arguments strives to open the door to the errors of rationalism and semi-rationalism. The Apostle warned Timothy to be on his guard against this when he wrote: "Guard the trust and keep free from profane novelties in speech and the contradictions of so-called knowledge, which some have professed and have fallen away from the faith." [27] This, however, does not prevent Us from esteeming those young priests worthy of praise who dedicate themselves to useful studies in every branch of learning so they can better prepare themselves for the defense of truth and the refutation of calumnies which the enemies of the faith may hurl at the Truth. Nevertheless, We cannot conceal, on the contrary, We proclaim in the most open manner that Our preference is, and ever shall be, for those who, while cultivating ecclesiastical and literary erudition, totally dedicate themselves to the welfare of souls through the exercise of the ministrations proper to a priest zealous for the Divine Glory. "I have great sadness and continuous sorrow in my heart" [28] because Jeremias' lamentation is so applicable in our times: "The little ones have asked for bread, and there was none to break it unto them." [29] Among the clergy there is no end to the lists of those who, following their own preferences, devote their energies to works that have an apparent rather than a real solidarity. Not so numerous, however, are those who, following the example of Christ, make their own the words of the prophet: "The Spirit of the Lord is upon me; because, he has anointed me; to bring good news to the poor he has sent me, to proclaim to the captives release, and sight to the blind." [30]

Ignorance breeds indifference. Who can fail to see, Venerable Brethren, that whenever men follow reason and liberty religious instruction will be the principal means of restoring the empire of God in their souls? How many there are who hate Christ and detest the Church and the Gospel more through ignorance than malice! Concerning these people it may be well said: "These men deride whatever they do not know." [31] This is the case not only among the poorer classes, who are therefore more easily led astray, but even among the more cultured classes who have had the advantage of a general education. The result is that great numbers lose their faith. It is not true that progress, but ignorance, in knowledge extinguishes the faith. The more ignorance prevails, the greater is the havoc wrought by incredulity. For this reason Christ commanded the Apostles: "Go, therefore, and make disciples of all nations." [32]

Charity above all things. 13. In order that the desired fruit may be derived from this apostolate and zeal for teaching (and that Christ may be formed in all), it must be remembered, Venerable Brethren, that no means is more efficacious than charity, for "the Lord is not in the earthquake." [33] It is utter folly to think that one can draw souls to God by bitter zeal. On the contrary, more harm than good is accomplished by harshly taunting men with their faults and bitterly reproving them for their vices. Even though the Apostle counseled Timothy to "reprove, entreat, rebuke" he took pains to add "with all patience." [34] Christ has left us many clear examples of this. "Come to me," we find Him saying, "come to me, all you who labor and are burdened, and I will give you rest." [35] By those who labor and are burdened He meant none other than those who are slaves of sin and error. What gentleness was shown by the Divine Master! What tenderness, what compassion, towards all kinds of misery! Isaias has marvelously described His heart in the following words: "I have given my spirit upon him. He shall not cry . . . neither shall his voice be heard abroad. The bruised reed he shall not break, and smoking flax he shall not quench." [36] This charity, "patient and kind," [37] we should show even to those who are hostile and persecute us. "We are reviled," Saint Paul cried out, "and we bless, we are persecuted and we bear it, we are maligned and we entreat." [38] Perhaps they only seem to be worse than they really are. Their association with others, their preconceived opinions, the counsel and advice of others and a false sense of shame have dragged them into the company of the wicked. Nevertheless their wills are not so depraved as their actions would lead people to believe. Who can prevent Us from hoping that the flame of Christian charity might dispel the darkness of their minds and lead them into the light and peace of God? Perhaps the fruits of Our labors will be slow in coming; but charity wearies not with waiting. Charity knows that God looks to the good intention and not the results of effort.

Work for the laity. 14. It is Our mind, Venerable Brethren, that in this total, arduous work of restoring the human race to Christ you and your clergy should have assistance. We know that God recommended everyone to be solicitous for his neighbor's welfare.[39] Not only priests, but all the faithful without exception must be concerned about the interests of God and souls. This care must be exercised, not according to their own views, but always under the guidance and command of the bishops. No one in the Church but you has been commissioned to preside, to teach, to direct. "Take heed to yourselves and to the whole flock in which the Holy Spirit has placed you as bishops, to rule the Church of God." [40]

Benefits of Catholic organizations. For a long time now Our Predecessors have approved and blessed those Catholics who have banded together into societies of various kinds and have always remained religious in their purpose. We, too, unhesitantly shower Our praise upon these institutions as We earnestly desire to see them propagate and flourish far and wide in both rural and urban areas. But We desire that the primary purpose of all these associations will be to maintain constancy in the practice of the Christian life among their members. It would be of little avail to discuss questions with great subtlety or discourse with great eloquence on rights and duties when it is all dissociated from practice. Our times demand action; but action which consists in faithfully and zealously observing the divine law and precepts of the Church, in frankly and openly professing religion, in unselfishly exercising every kind of charitable work. The illustrious example of such an army of soldiers of Christ will be much more effective in attracting men than the most sublime words and dissertations. Then, when human respect is banished and prejudices and doubts dispelled, greater numbers will be won over to Christ. These, in turn, will become promoters of His knowledge and love, the road to true and lasting happiness. When in every city and village God's law is faithfully observed, reverence shown for sacred things, the Sacraments frequented and the ordinances of a Christian life carried out, then, Venerable Brethren, We need labor no further in re-establishing all things in Christ. Such a work will not only realize the attainment of eternal salvation but also will contribute in large measure to the temporal welfare and advantage of civil society. When We arrive at this state of affairs, the wealthy classes will be more just and charitable to the lowly, and the latter will be capable of bearing with more tranquility and patience the trials of a very hard lot. Then the citizens will follow not the whims of lust, but the dictates of law; then reverence and love will be deemed a sacred duty towards those that govern "for there exists no authority except from God." [41] What more can be expected? Finally it will be evident to all that the Church, instituted by Christ, must enjoy full and entire liberty, free from all external domination. In demanding that liberty, We are defending not only the sacred rights of religion, but also have in mind the welfare and safety of all nations. It still remains true that "godliness is profitable in all respects" [42] and especially when it is strong and flourishing the "people shall sit in the beauty of peace." [43]

Exhortation to pray. 15. May God, "who is rich in mercy," [44] favorably hasten this restoration of the human race in Christ Jesus, for "there is question not of him who wills nor of him who runs, but of God showing mercy." [45] "In a contrite heart and humble spirit" [46] and with continual and urgent prayer let us, Venerable Brethren, ask this of Him through the merits of Jesus Christ. Let us also turn to the most powerful intercession of the Divine Mother—and as We address this letter to you on that day set aside for commemorating the Holy Rosary, We ordain and confirm all Our Predecessor's prescriptions in regard to the dedication of the present month to the august Virgin by the public recitation of the Rosary in all churches—and We further exhort that appeal be addressed, as intercessors before God, to the most pure Spouse of Mary, the Patrons of the Catholic Church, and the holy Princes of the Apostles, Peter and Paul.

Apostolic Blessing. 16. In order that all these things may come to pass, Our ardent desire be fulfilled, and everything be prosperous with you, We call down upon you the most bountiful gifts of divine grace. Now as a testimony of the most tender charity in which We embrace you and all the faithful entrusted to Our care, We impart with all the affection in the Lord, the Apostolic Blessing upon you, Venerable Brethren, as well as upon your clergy and your people.

Given at Saint Peter's, Rome, on the fourth day of October, 1903, in the first year of Our Pontificate.

PIUS X, POPE

REFERENCES

1. Ps. 72:27.
2. Jer. 1:10.
3. Eph. 1:10.
4. Col. 3:11.
5. Ps. 2:1.
6. Job 21:14.
7. II Thess. 2:3.
8. II Thess. 2:4.
9. Wisd. 11:24.
10. Ps. 77:65.
11. Ps. 67:22.
12. Ps. 46:8.
13. Ps. 9:21.
14. Ps. 9:20.
15. Is. 32:17.
16. I Cor. 3:11.

17. John 10:36.
18. Heb. 1:3.
19. Matt. 11:27.
20. Apoc. 12:10.
21. Gal. 4:19.
22. Gal. 2:20.
23. Phil. 1:21.
24. Eph. 4:13.
25. I Tim. 5:22.
26. *Ibid.*
27. I Tim. 6:20–21.
28. Rom. 9:2.
29. Lam. 4:4.
30. Luke 4:18–19.
31. Jude 1:10.
32. Matt. 28:19.
33. III Kings 19:11.
34. II Tim. 4:2.
35. Matt. 11:28.
36. Is. 42:1–3.
37. I Cor. 13:4.
38. I Cor. 4:12–13.
39. Ecclus. 17:12.
40. Acts 20:28.
41. Rom. 13:1.
42. I Tim. 4:8.
43. Is. 32:18.
44. Eph. 2:4.
45. Rom. 9:16.
46. Dan. 3:39.

CHAPTER 2

Ad Diem Illum *February 2, 1904, The Jubilee of the Definition of the Immaculate Conception*

ON DECEMBER 7, 1903, Saint Pius X had published a decree concerning the indulgences granted during the jubilee year of the definition of the dogma of the Immaculate Conception. Anyone acquainted with the holy Pontiff knew that he would not let the occasion of so important a celebration pass with such scant attention. This anticipation was speedily fulfilled.

On February 2, 1904, Saint Pius X published his second encyclical letter, *Ad Diem Illum,* on the golden jubilee of the definition of the dogma of the Immaculate Conception of the Mother of God. Those who knew the tremendous devotion Saint Pius X had for the Blessed Virgin were not at all surprised that he began his encyclical with a tribute of filial love for his heavenly Queen. "Why, Venerable Brethren," he asks, "can we not rightfully hope that today when we renew the remembrance of the Immaculate Virgin, though separated by half a century, an echo of that holy joy will resound in our souls, and that those magnificent demonstrations of that distant day of faith and love toward the august Mother of God will be repeated? In truth, Our desire for this is inflamed by the devotion, united with supreme gratitude for favors received, which We have always cherished toward the Blessed Virgin."

First of all, then, this encyclical letter is an act of homage and love that the Father of Christendom offers as a child to his Blessed Mother on her anniversary. That homage and love, moreover, prompted the profound act of gratitude which the Pope offers his Lady by making the jubilee indulgence customarily offered by a newly-elected Pontiff a jubilee indulgence in honor of the Immaculate Conception of Mary. For that reason he writes: "That the gift of heavenly graces may help us more plentifully than usual to combine the imitation of the Most Blessed Virgin with the honors shown her . . . and that thus We may more easily attain the aim of restoring all things in Christ, We have decreed, after the example of Our Predecessors at the beginning of their pontificates, to grant to the Catholic world an extraordinary indulgence in the form of a Jubilee."

Devotion to Mary, however, is not the primary purpose of this encyclical. Four short months previously Saint Pius X had made known that "to restore all things in Christ" was the object of his pontificate. Now in this encyclical he would carry that objective a step further. "For Us, the chief reason why the fiftieth anniversary of the proclamation of the Immaculate Conception of the Mother of God should arouse a singular fervor in the Christian people is to restore all things in Christ. . . . For who does not know that there is no surer or easier way than Mary for uniting all persons with Christ . . ." He then sets out to explain the reason why Mary is the surest and easiest way to Christ. In that purpose we find the significance of this encyclical, for, although it is written to commemorate the golden jubilee of the Immaculate Conception definition, a great part of it (4–16) concerns the doctrine of Mary, the Mediatrix of All Grace. That, however, is neither so startling nor amazing as would appear at first sight.

Pope Leo XIII had repeatedly referred to Mary as Mediatrix of All Grace in at least three encyclicals. The patristic references to Mary's mediatory role were during this period a matter of extensive research in many theological quarters. Such interest did not escape the attention of Saint Pius X. Since the encyclical letter is the ordinary vehicle of papal teaching, he used this occasion to teach the role of Mary as Mediatrix of All Grace.

After showing that Mary, since she is the Mother of Christ, is Mother also of the members of Christ (4–8), he brings forth three reasons why Mary is called our Co-Redemptrix. First, she united her sufferings with Christ's for the salvation of the world. Secondly, she truly offered her Divine Son to our Heavenly Father as she stood beneath the Cross. Finally, she offered her sufferings, especially those experienced during the Passion and the Death of Christ, together with His, for the salvation of the world (9).

From the fact that Mary is our Co-Redemptrix the Pope draws out the doctrine that Mary is our Mediatrix (10). Since she is our Mediatrix, Saint Pius X explains why we should have devotion to her (11–12), illustrating by example how Mary can increase the virtues of all her children (13–20).

Finally he promulgates the Jubilee (21), granting a plenary indulgence to all the faithful, provided the conditions he lays down be fulfilled (22–26). He concludes with the Apostolic Benediction.

As is immediately evident, this document is no mere pious expression of Marian devotion. Today this encyclical ranks as one of the most emphatic papal documents concerning the Blessed Virgin Mary as Mediatrix of All Grace.

Ad Diem Illum *Encyclical Letter of Our Holy Father Pius X to the Patriarchs, Primates, Archbishops, Bishops and Other Ordinaries in Peace and Communion with the Apostolic See*

VENERABLE BRETHREN, HEALTH AND THE APOSTOLIC BLESSING:

The Jubilee of the Immaculate Conception. 1. Within a few months the hands of time will again bring to our minds the recollection of a most happy day. Fifty years ago, Our Predecessor, Pius IX, a Pontiff of most holy memory, surrounded by many Cardinals and Bishops, pronounced and promulgated with the authority of the infallible magisterium as a truth revealed by God that the Most Blessed Virgin Mary was free from all stain of original sin in the first instant of her conception. Everyone knows how the faithful throughout the whole world received this promulgation and welcomed it with sentiments of public joy and congratulations. As a matter of fact, no man living today can recall any more universal or more unanimous expression of affection toward the venerable Mother of God or the Vicar of Jesus Christ.

Cause for universal joy. Venerable Brethren, although we are separated by half a century from that event, can we not also rightfully hope that if we recall the glory of the Immaculate Virgin today the same holy joy will, like an echo from the past, resound in our souls? Can we not rightfully hope that those previous magnificent demonstrations of faith and love toward the venerable Mother of God will be repeated? We ardently desire to achieve these same effects because of the devotion We have always had for the Blessed Virgin as well as Our deep gratitude to her for the favors We have received. A certain pledge that Our desires will be fulfilled is the ever ready and willing zeal of all Catholics to show their love and honor for the great Mother of God. Moreover, We believe that Our desire is accentuated by the fact that We seem to be able, by a kind of secret instinct, to perceive the fulfillment of these great expectations in a short time. Pius, Our Predecessor, and all the Bishops were of the opinion (surely not without reason) that this holy joy and love and faith toward the venerable Mother of God would result from the solemn promulgation of the dogma of the Immaculate Conception.

Favors granted through Mary. 2. Many, however, complain that these effects have not as yet been realized. They make the words of Jeremias their own: "We looked for peace, and no good came; for a time of healing, and behold fear." [1] Such persons are men of little faith. They neither perceive the designs of God nor evaluate them in the light of truth. Who can number the secret gifts of grace that God has bestowed upon His Church during these fifty years through the intercession of the Blessed Virgin? If these secret gifts are overlooked, how can one ignore the Vatican Council, which convened at such an appropriate time; or the definition of papal infallibility, which was providentially proclaimed in order to break the onrushing flood of errors; or, finally, that singularly novel devotedness of the faithful from every class and every nation for the Vicar of Christ? Behold, also, the marvellous manifestation of God's providence during the lengthly Pontificates of Our two Predecessors, Pius and Leo, who ruled the Church with such great holiness during a most turbulent period. Another effect is those wonderful apparitions at Lourdes, where the Virgin showed herself soon after Pius IX proclaimed that by Catholic faith we must believe that Mary was free from the original stain. At that time those immense and magnificent temples to the Immaculate Mother of God were built in which miracles occur daily through the intercession of the Mother of God. These splendid arguments should be enough to shatter the incredulity of our days.

Cause for universal hope. We are the witnesses of all these great benefits God has granted through the loving intercession of the Virgin throughout the fifty years that are now coming to an end. Can we not now hope that "our salvation is nearer than when we came to believe"? Our hope should be all the firmer today, since experience teaches us that in the plan of divine Providence liberation is close at hand whenever evil reaches a climax. "Her time is near at hand, and her days shall not be prolonged. For the Lord will have mercy on Jacob, and will yet chose out of Israel." [2] Therefore we have hope that we too shall soon exclaim: "The Lord hath broken the staff of the wicked . . . The whole earth is quiet and still: it is glad and hath rejoiced." [3]

To Christ through Mary. 3. However, Our chief reason, Venerable Brethren, for commemorating the fiftieth anniversary of the proclamation of the Immaculate Conception of the Mother of God is the fact that it should enkindle an ardent zeal in the Christian people for *restoring all things in Christ.* This, you know, was the program We proposed in Our first encyclical letter. Mary is the surest and easiest means for uniting all persons with Christ and obtaining through Him the perfect adoption of sons. In such a way we become holy and immaculate in the sight of God. To Mary it was said: "Blessed is she who has believed, because the things promised her by the Lord shall be accomplished." [4] The promise was that she would conceive and bring forth the Son of God. Consequently, she received in her womb Him Who is by nature Truth Itself in order that, "having been begotten in a new order and a new nativity . . . even though invisible in Himself, He might become visible in our flesh."[5] Therefore, since the Son of God made Man is "the author and finisher of faith," we must recognize His Most Holy Mother as the partaker and, as it were, the custodian, of the divine mysteries. We must acknowledge that, after Christ, she is the noblest foundation on which is built the house of faith for all ages.

We receive Christ through Mary. 4. God could most certainly have given us the Redeemer of the human race and the Founder of the Faith in another way than through the Virgin. However, since Divine Providence willed that the God-Man should come to us through Mary, who conceived Him by the Holy Spirit and bore Him in her womb, we can now receive Christ only from the hands of Mary. For that reason, almost every time Holy Scripture foretells the grace that is to appear among us, the Redeemer of mankind is associated with His Mother. The Lamb Who is the Ruler of the world, will be seen—but from the rock of the desert. The flower will spring forth—but from the root of Jesse. Adam saw none other than Mary crushing the serpent's head, and so he dried the tears the curse brought to his eyes. When Noah was enclosed in the ark of salvation, when Abraham was hindered from slaying his son, when Jacob saw the ladder and the angels ascending and descending it, when Moses was dumfounded at the sight of the burning bush, when David danced and sang while escorting the ark of God, when Elias looked at the little cloud rising out of the sea—one and all, they were contemplating Mary. Second only to Christ, Mary is seen as the image and truth of prophecies.

Mary is our teacher of Christ. 5. The Virgin, and chiefly she, has opened the way for us to acquire knowledge of Christ. In preference to all others, she alone was united to Jesus for thirty years in the intimacy of domestic life. Who better than His Mother could fathom the wondrous mysteries of the origin and childhood of Christ and, above all, that mystery (which is the beginning and foundation of faith) of the assumption of the human nature? Mary not only preserved and meditated in her heart on the events that occurred at Bethlehem and in the Lord's Temple at Jerusalem but also shared the very thoughts and secret desires of Christ. Rightly, then, may she be said to have lived the very life of her Son. No one ever knew Christ so profoundly as she knew Him. No one can ever be a more competent guide and teacher in the knowledge of Christ.

Mary is the Dispenser of Christ's Life. 6. Consequently, as We have already mentioned, no one is better qualified than the Virgin for uniting men with Christ. If, as Christ said, "this is everlasting life, that they may know thee, the only true God, and him whom thou hast sent, Jesus Christ,"[6] and if the life-giving knowledge of Christ is acquired from Mary, then in like manner we can more easily obtain through Mary the life of which Christ is the source and beginning.

Mary is generous. 7. If we devote only a little time to the many reasons why this Most Holy Mother is most eager to give us these excellent gifts, our hopes will undoubtedly soar to the heights.

Mary is Mother of the physical body of Christ. 8. Is not Mary Christ's Mother? Therefore she is also our Mother. Everyone must unhesitatingly believe that Jesus, the Word made flesh, is also the Saviour of the human race. As the God-Man He assumed a body composed like any other man's body. As Saviour of our race, however, He had a certain spiritual—or, as they say, mystical—body. This latter is the society of those who believe in Christ. "We, the many, are one body in Christ." [7] The Virgin conceived the Eternal Son of God not only that He might be made man, assuming His human nature from her, but also in order that He might be the Saviour of men through the nature assumed from her. For this reason the angel said to the shepherds: "Today in the town of David a Savior has been born to you, who is Christ the Lord." [8] Therefore in the one and same womb of His most chaste Mother Christ simultaneously assumed human flesh and united to Himself a spiritual body composed of those "who are to believe in Him."

Mary is Mother of the Mystical Body of Christ. It can, therefore, be rightly stated that while Mary was bearing in her womb the Saviour, she also bore all those whose life was contained in the Saviour's life. All of us, then, who are united with Christ and are, as the Apostle says, "members of his body, made from his flesh and from his bones," [9] have come forth from the womb of Mary as the body is united to its head. Hence, in a spiritual and mystical sense, we are called the children of Mary and she is our Mother. "The Mother in spirit . . . but truly the Mother of the members of Christ, who we are." [10]

Mary's efforts for union. Since the Most Blessed Virgin is both the Mother of God and the Mother of men, she undoubtedly spares no pains to bring it about that Christ, "the head of his body, the Church," [11] infuse His gifts into us, His members, and, above all, that we might know and "live through him." [12]

Mary is Our Co-Redemptrix. 9. Moreover, the Most Holy Mother of God had the honor of "having supplied the substance of her flesh to the Only-begotten Son of God, who was to be born of the human race," [13] and by this flesh the Victim for the salvation of mankind was prepared. Over and above this, however, she was entrusted with the task of rearing and nourishing this Victim. Finally, at the appointed hour, hers was the task of offering It on the altar. The result was a continuous union of life and labor between the Son and the Mother. Thus the Prophet's words can be applied with equal merit to both of them: "My life is wasted with grief and my years in sighs."[14] Finally, when the Son's last hour arrived, "there stood by the Cross of Jesus his Mother." She was not merely occupied in contemplating the cruel spectacle. She was also rejoicing that "her Only-begotten Son was being offered for the salvation of the human race. She suffered so much together with Him that, if it had been possible, she would have been more than willing to bear all the torments that her Son suffered."[15] Through this community of suffering and intention between Christ and Mary "she merited to become in a most noble manner the Reparatrix of the fallen world."[16] As a result of this, she is the Dispenser of all the gifts that Jesus acquired for us by His death and Blood.

Mary, the Dispenser of Christ's Gifts. 10. We do not deny that the distribution of these gifts belongs by strict and proper right to Christ. They are the fruit He alone acquired for us by His Death. He is in His own right the Mediator between God and man. However, that community of suffering and sorrow between the Mother and her Son (which We have already described) has merited the venerable Virgin to be "with her Only-begotten Son the most powerful Mediatrix and Conciliatrix of the whole world."[17] Christ, therefore, is the source, "and of his fullness we have all received."[18] "From him the whole body (being closely joined and knit together through every joint of the system . . .) derives its increase to the building up of itself in love."[19] Mary, however, as Saint Bernard rightly observes, is "the channel"[20] or the neck which unites the Body to the Head and through which the Head sends power and a strength into the Body. "For she is the neck of our Head, through which all spiritual gifts are communicated to His Body."[21] This should make it clear that We are certainly very far from attributing to the Virgin the power of producing supernatural grace. Only God can do that. However, she surpasses all creatures in holiness and in the degree of her union with Christ. She was chosen by Christ to be His associate in the work of human salvation. She has, therefore, merited for us congruously (*de congruo*), as they say, what Christ has merited for us condignly (*de condigno*). She is the principal Minister of the graces to be distributed. He has "taken his seat at the right hand of the Majesty on high,"[22] and Mary as Queen stands at His right hand. "She is the safest refuge and the most trustworthy helper of all who are in danger. Under her guidance, patronage, kindness and protection nothing is to be feared or abandoned."[23]

Mary is inseparable from her Son. 11. After laying down these principles, let Us now return to Our purpose. We have justly and rightly affirmed that Mary was the constant companion of Jesus from the home in Nazareth to the summit of Calvary; that she knew better than anyone else the secrets of His heart; that she distributes, by maternal right, the treasures of His merits. Where else, then, can we find a greater or more secure helper in arriving at the knowledge and love of Christ? The wretched condition of those who, either through diabolical deceit or false opinions, boldly refuse the Virgin's help is a striking proof of that truth. They are miserable and unhappy. Under the pretext of honoring Christ, they neglect Mary. They do not realize that *the Child is found only with His Mother Mary.*

Celebrations will foster devotion. 12. Surely, Venerable Brethren, you know how true that statement is. Our intention, therefore, is that all these celebrations now being prepared throughout the world for honoring the Most Holy Virgin will especially be directed to that end. The most desirable and pleasing honor we can pay Mary is properly knowing and loving Jesus Christ. Let the faithful, therefore, solemnize this occasion in their churches. Let the cities celebrate and rejoice in these festivities. Such things do much in fostering devotion. However, if the consent of the will does not inspire and accompany these events we shall have mere formalities which are only a semblance of religion. When the Virgin beholds such formalities she can justly employ Christ's words in rebuking us: "This people honors me with their lips, but their heart is far from me." [24]

Mary will teach us obedience. 13. A true devotion to the Mother of God is one that springs from the heart. Thus, bodily actions, if separated from the acts of the soul, are worthless and useless. The united actions of soul and body must strive to make us obedient in all things to Mary's divine Son. If that love is real which unites wills, our will must certainly be united with the Most Holy Mother's in this total dedication of ourselves to Christ the Lord. For that reason the Virgin Most Prudent speaks to us today in the same manner she spoke to the servants at the marriage in Cana: "Do whatever he tells you." [25] Now, Christ's command is simply this: "If thou wilt enter into life, keep the commandments." [26] Everyone, then, can be certain that if his devotion to the Most Blessed Virgin does not keep him from sinning and does not inspire him with the desire of abandoning his evil ways, his devotion is deceptive and false since it does not produce in him the effects it should.

Mary herself was obedient. 14. The dogma of the Immaculate Conception of the Mother of God clearly confirms this fact in yet another way. We will pass over Catholic tradition, which, as a source of truth, is equal in merit to Sacred Scripture. Still there is the belief in the Immaculate Conception of the Virgin Mary that appears in every age to be so completely in agreement with the Christian sense that it seems to be implanted and innate in the souls of the faithful. Denis the Carthusian gives the reason for this in the following words: "We shrink in horror from even thinking that the Woman who was to crush the head of the Serpent should ever have been crushed by him; that the Mother of the Lord should ever have been the child of the devil." [27] It is repugnant to the mind of the Christian people even to think that the holy, undefiled and innocent flesh of Christ could have been assumed in the womb of the Virgin from flesh which even for a moment had the slightest stain. The reason for this is simply that God and sin are infinite opposition. Thus Catholics throughout the world have always felt that it was only fitting that the Son of God, "who washed us from our sins in his blood," before assuming human nature, owed it to Himself to preserve, by a singular grace and privilege, His Virgin Mother free from all stain of original sin in the first instant of her conception.

Mary's children must be holy. Because God so thoroughly detests sin, He willed that the future Mother of His Son should in no way be subject to any kind of stain. More than that, by a most singular gift granted through the merits of Christ, He preserved her from that hereditary stain which marks all the children of Adam. Everyone, then, who sincerely desires to win Mary's favor by his homage must amend his sinful and corrupt habits and subdue the passions which turn him toward forbidden things.

Mary reproduces Christ in us. 15. Moreover, if anyone desires (and we all should so desire) to make his devotion to Mary worthy and in every way perfect, he will make progress by trying to imitate her example. God's law is that anyone desiring to attain eternal happiness must reproduce in his life the image of Christ's patience and sanctity. "For those whom he has foreknown he has also predestined to become conformed to the image of his Son, that he should be the firstborn among many brethren." [28] Our weakness, however, can all too easily cause us to be frightened by this Exemplar's majesty. Divine Providence, therefore, has given us another model. This model, who is the Mother of God, is at one and the same time closer to our weakness and also the most perfect reproduction of Christ's image that can be found in human nature. In this regard Saint Ambrose says: "Mary was of such a nature that her life can teach every one." Then he rightly concludes: "Let Mary's virginity and life be shown to us like a picture, and in it, as in a mirror, we will see the reflection of the beauty of chastity and the loveliness of virtue." [29]

Mary will teach us all virtues. 16. It is no more than right to expect that the children should imitate the virtues of their Most Holy Mother. We especially desire that the faithful cultivate the principal virtues of faith, hope and charity toward God and man—those virtues that can be called the nerves and sinews of Christian wisdom. The Virgin was full of the splendor of them throughout her life, but it shone most brilliantly when she stood beside her dying Son. All the while Jesus is being crucified and rebuked by blasphemies "because he has made himself Son of God," [30] with unshaken constancy she acknowledges and worships His divinity. She lays His dead body in the sepulchre, yet she does not doubt that He will rise again. Moreover, her ardent love for God makes her a sharer and companion of Christ's sufferings together with Him. Forgetful of her own sorrow, she unites herself with

Christ in asking pardon for the very executioners who audaciously cry out: "His blood be on us and on our children." [31]

The Immaculate Conception and original sin. 17. Now, it might seem that We have abandoned Our purpose in writing. However, the Immaculate Conception of the Virgin will greatly help us in preserving and rightly developing these virtues. The enemies of the Faith begin their attack by spreading many serious errors which weaken the very faith of many. They deny that man ever fell through sin and was cast down from his primeval dignity. They say, therefore, that original sin and its consequent evils (namely, the vitiation of all men of all time, the introduction of evil among mortal men and the need of a Redeemer) are nothing but fables. Once these things are assumed it is easy to see why Christ, the Church, grace and the supernatural order are excluded. In a word, the whole structure of faith is shaken.

Mary, Protectress of Authority. On the other hand, if people believe and profess that in the first moment of her conception the Virgin Mary was free from all stain, they must also admit the existence of original sin, the redemption of mankind by Christ, the Gospel, the Church, and even the law of suffering. These truths will root up and destroy any kind of *rationalism* or *materialism* that exists. Christian wisdom will then have the honor of being the protector and defender of truth. Over and above this, however, the Faith's enemies today commonly employ the vice of refusing, and openly refusing, to pay any reverence or obedience to the authority of the Church. In fact, they refuse to respect all human authority, thinking that thereby they can more easily tear the Faith out of men's hearts. There is the beginning of anarchism, which is the most dangerous threat to both the natural and the supernatural orders. Even this disease, however, which destroys both civil and Christian society, is stamped out by the dogma of the Immaculate Conception of the Mother of God. This doctrine compels us to recognize that power of the Church which demands intellectual as well as voluntary submission. Because of this intellectual submission the Christian people sing to the Mother of God: "Thou art all fair, O Mary, and there is no original stain in thee." [32] For this reason the Church rightly attributes the destruction of all heresies in the whole world to the venerable Virgin alone.

Mary, Defender of Faith. 18. If, as the Apostle states, faith is nothing but "the substance of things to be hoped for," [33] everyone will readily admit that the Immaculate Conception of the Virgin confirms our faith and strengthens our hope. This is especially clear when we consider that the Virgin was exempt from original sin because she was to be the Mother of Christ. In such a way the hope of eternal happiness was revived in our souls.

Mary, Teacher of Charity. 19. Besides charity to God, however, contemplation of the Immaculate Virgin arouses in us the desire to keep sacred

Christ's personal command of loving one another as He loved us. The Apostle John speaks of the vision with which God favored him in these words: "A great sign appeared in heaven: a woman clothed with the sun, and the moon was under her feet, and upon her head a crown of twelve stars." [34] Everyone knows that this woman was the image of the Virgin Mary, who, in giving birth to our Head, remained inviolate. "And being with child," the Apostle continues, "she cried out in her travail and was in the anguish of delivery." [35] John saw the Most Holy Mother of God enjoying beatitude and at the same time travailing in a certain mysterious childbirth. What kind of a birth was this? It was the birth of all of us who, while being exiles here below, are not yet brought forth into the perfect love of God and eternal happiness. The fact that the heavenly Virgin labors in childbirth shows her loving desire to watch over us and through unceasing prayer complete the number of the elect.

Mary, Guide of the erring. 20. We earnestly desire that everyone in the world who is called a Christian will draw near to this love of the Virgin during this time when we honor the Mother of God in a more solemn manner. The persecution of Christ and the most holy religion He founded is now raging bitterly and fiercely. At this present time, therefore, there is a serious danger that many will be deceived by the increasing number of errors and ultimately abandon the Faith. "Therefore let him who thinks he stands take heed lest he fall." [36] More than that, let us all humbly beg God through the intercession of the Mother of God that those who have fallen from the path of truth may repent. Experience has taught us that such prayers, when motivated by charity and supplemented by the intercession of the holy Virgin, have never been in vain. The Church will always be attacked, "for there must be factions, so that those who are approved may be made manifest among you." [37] The Virgin, however, will always assist us in even the most difficult of trials; she will always continue the battle she has been waging ever since her conception. Thus every day we can say: "Today the head of the ancient serpent was crushed by her." [38]

Promulgation of the Jubilee. 21. At the beginning of their pontificates Our Predecessors have customarily granted an extraordinary Jubilee Indulgence. Following their example, We also have decreed that the Catholic world be granted an extraordinary Indulgence in the form of a Jubilee. We have done this, first of all, in order that, by the gift of heavenly graces, we may most abundantly receive the help we need to imitate the Most Blessed Virgin and pay her greater honor (as we shall do especially during this year). In such a way we should be able to attain more easily the goal of *restoring all things in Christ.*

Conditions of the Jubilee Indulgence. 22. Confiding in the mercy of Almighty God and in the authority of the Blessed Apostles Peter and Paul, and in virtue of the power of binding and loosing which, unworthy though We are, the Lord has given Us, We grant a plenary indulgence of all their sins to all the faithful of both sexes who live in this Our beloved city or who make a pilgrimage to it. Furthermore, this can be gained only by those who, from the first Sunday of Lent (February 21) to the feast of Corpus Christi inclusively (June 2), shall visit one of the four patriarchal basilicas three times. There they must spend some time in beseeching God for the liberty and exaltation of the Catholic Church and this Apostolic See, for the wiping out of heresy and the conversion of all who are in error, for the concord of Christian princes and the peace and unity of all the faithful, and for Our Own intention. Within the aforementioned period and outside of the days excluded in the Lenten Indult, they must also fast one day, using only meager fare, and after confessing their sins receive the Most Holy Sacrament of the Eucharist. Everyone else living anywhere outside this city, and within the time mentioned above or during a space of three months, even not continuous, to be appointed definitely by the Ordinaries according to the convenience of the faithful, but before December 8—every one of these who shall three times visit the Cathedral church, if there be one, or, if not, the parish church, or, in its absence, the principal church, and shall devoutly fulfill the same works We have already mentioned, shall also be able to gain the Jubilee Indulgence. At the same time We permit this Indulgence, which can be gained only once, to be applicable to the suffering souls who have passed from this life united in charity with God.

The Indulgence for travelers. 23. Moreover, We allow travelers by land or sea to gain the same indulgence immediately on their return home, provided they perform the works already indicated.

Faculties for confessors. 24. We grant confessors, approved by their own Ordinaries, the faculties of commuting the above works enjoined by Us to other works of piety. This concession shall be applicable not only to religious of both sexes, but to anyone who cannot perform the works prescribed. We also grant the faculties to dispense from Communion those children who have not yet been admitted to the sacred Table.

Privilege of selecting any priest. 25. Moreover, each and every one of the faithful, both laity and clergy, diocesan and religious, of all orders and institutes, even those calling for special mention, have Our permission and power, for this purpose only, to select any priest, diocesan or religious, among those actually approved (which faculty may also be used by nuns, novices and other women living in the cloister, provided the confessor they select be one approved for nuns), by whom, when they have confessed to him within the prescribed time with the intention of gaining the present Jubilee Indulgence and of fulfilling all the other requirements, they may be absolved on only this occasion and only in the forum of conscience from any excommunication, suspension and every other ecclesiastical sentence and censure pronounced or inflected for any cause by law or by a judge, including those reserved to the Ordinary, to Us, or to the Apostolic See, even in cases reserved in a special manner to anybody and to Us and to the Apostolic See. They may also be absolved from all sins or transgressions, even those reserved to the Ordinaries, to Us, or to the Apostolic See, on condition, however, that a salutary penance be enjoined together with the other prescriptions of the law, and, in the case of heresy, after the renunciation and retraction of error, as is required by law. Likewise, such priests may further commute to other pious and salutary works all vows, even those taken under oath and reserved to the Apostolic See (except those of chastity, of religion, and of obligations which have been assumed by third parties). In the case of such penitents, even religious, or those in sacred orders, such confessors may dispense from all secret irregularities contracted solely by violation of censures affecting the exercise of their orders and promotion to higher orders.

Other Indulgences retained. 26. Besides this, We are happy to add that We permit and decree that everyone during this time of Jubilee still has the privilege of gaining all other Indulgences, including plenary Indulgences, which have been granted by Our Predecessors or by Ourselves.

Mary, Cause of our Hope. 27. Before concluding, Venerable Brethren, We wish to mention once more Our great hope, which has to a large extent motivated this work. In granting this extraordinary favor of the Jubilee under the auspices of the Immaculate Virgin, We hope that large numbers of those who are unhappily separated from Jesus Christ will return to Him and that the love of virtue and zeal for religion will be renewed in the hearts of the Christian people. Fifty years ago, when Pius, Our Predecessor, proclaimed that we must hold as an article of faith that the Most Blessed Mother of God was free from all sin, it seemed, as We have already said, that an incredible abundance of grace descended upon the earth. This renewed confidence in the Virgin Mother of God everywhere stimulated the people to the practice of their ancient religion. What is there to stop us from hoping for even greater blessings in the future? We are certainly passing through calamitous times. Well might We make Our Own the Prophet's lamentation: "For there is no truth, and there is no mercy, and there is no knowledge of God in the land. Cursing and lying and killing and theft and adultery have overflowed." [39] Yet in the midst of this deluge of evil the Virgin Most Merciful stands before us like a rainbow. She is the peace-maker between God and man: "I will set my bow in the clouds, and it shall be the sign of a covenant between me, and between the earth." [40] Although the storm rages and the sky grows dark as night, let no one be alarmed. "The bow shall be in the clouds and I shall see it, and shall remember the everlasting covenant." [41] "And there shall no more be waters of a flood to destroy all flesh." [42] If we trust Mary as we should, especially now when celebrating her Immaculate Conception with greater joy and devotion, we shall come to see even now that she is the Virgin Most Powerful "who with virginal foot crushed the head of the serpent." [43]

Apostolic Blessing. 29. As a pledge of these graces and, lovingly in the Lord, We impart the Apostolic Blessing to you, Venerable Brethren, and to your people.

30. Given at Saint Peter's, Rome, on the second day of February, 1904, in the first year of Our Pontificate.

Pius X, Pope

REFERENCES

1. Jer. 8:15.
2. Is. 14:1.
3. *Ibid.*, 14:5, 7.
4. Luke 1:45.
5. St. Leo the Great, *Serm.* 2, *De Nativ. Domini, c.* 2.
6. John 17:3.
7. Rom. 12:5.
8. Luke 2:11.
9. Eph. 5:30.
10. St. Augustine, *De S. Virginitate, c.* 6.
11. Col. 1:18.
12. I John 4:9.
13. Venerable Bede, *I, iv, In Luc., c.* 11.
14. Ps. 30:11.
15. St. Bonaventure, *I Sent. d.* 48, *ad Litt. dub.*, 4.
16. Eadmerus, *De Excellentia Virg. Mariae, c.* 9.
17. Pius IX, bull *Ineffabilis Dei.*
18. John 1:16.
19. Ephes. 4:16.
20. St. Bernard, *Serm. de temp., in Nativ. B.M., De Aquaeductu, n.* 4.
21. St. Bernardine of Siena, *Quadrag. De Evangelio aeterno, Serm. I, a.* 3, *c.* 3.
22. Heb. 1:3.
23. Pius IX, bull *Ineffabilis Dei.*
24. Matt. 15:8.
25. John 2:5.
26. Matt. 19:17.
27. Denis the Carthusian, 3 *Sent. d.* 3, *q.* 1.
28. Rom. 8:29.
29. St. Ambrose, *De Virginibus, I,* 2, *c.* 2.
30. John 19:7.
31. Matt. 27:25.
32. Gradual of the Mass of the Feast of the Immaculate Conception.
33. Heb. 11:1.
34. Apoc. 12:1.
35. Apoc. 12:2.
36. I Cor. 10:12.
37. I Cor. 11:19.
38. Magnificat Antiphon of the Office of the Immaculate Conception.
39. Osee 4:1–2.
40. Gen. 9:13.
41. Gen. 9:16.
42. Gen. 9:15.
43. Office of the Immaculate Conception.

CHAPTER 3

Iucunda Sane *March 12, 1904, The Thirteenth Centenary of Pope Saint Gregory the Great*

IT IS difficult to determine the beginning of Saint Pius' devotion to Saint Gregory the Great. It would seem that as a young seminarian, devoted to the Church's Sacred Chant, Giuseppe Sarto had a great devotion to this first restorer of the chant that bears his name. The parallel between the two is easy to trace. Both were lovers of simplicity; both were men of profound humility; both were tireless laborers in the school of the Lord's service; both were elevated against their wills to the honor of the Supreme Apostolate; both engaged in the same work of "restoring all things in Christ." That devotion spanned the centuries and prompted Saint Pius X to write his third encyclical letter on the thirteenth centenary of the death of Saint Gregory the Great.

This is the first of the three commemorative encyclical letters of Saint Pius X. In itself, the encyclical on Saint Gregory was prompted by no other motive than that which the Pope himself expresses in his introductory paragraph: "Amid the almost innumerable cares of Our apostolic ministry, amid the many anxieties the government of the Universal Church thrusts on Our shoulders, amid the constant care which We must manifest to the best of Our ability toward you, Venerable Brethren, who have been given a share in Our Apostolate, as well as the faithful committed to your care, We believe that a very special providence of that God Who "killeth and maketh alive . . . humbleth and he exalteth" ordained that We should fix Our gaze at the beginning of Our Pontificate upon this most holy and illustrious Predecessor, the pride and glory of the Church. We have, to be sure, great confidence in his intercession before God. We find Our strength renewed in recalling the sublime maxims by which he ruled and the holy virtues which he practiced."

The sequence of the letter follows easily. First, a rapid sketch of the times and life of Gregory (2–6), a description of the nature of the Church and the dangers she faces in the present day (7–16), a summons for mankind to return to God and for Christians to labor for this restoration (17–23), the means the bishop should employ in working out this restoration through his priests according to Gregory's ideals (24–30), and finally the ability of the Church to meet the demands of the present age (31–37).

Over and above the excellent sketch the encyclical gives of Saint Gregory and his work, there are three points of special interest. The first is the restatement of Church-State relations in paragraph ten. When compared with Leo XIII's classic statement of the matter in his encyclical *Immortale Dei,* the two fit as hand in glove. When one further considers that Saint Pius is merely quoting Saint Gregory, the continuity of the Church's teaching on the question is all the more obvious.

The second point is the emphatic condemnation of the new "science falsely so called." Saint Pius X goes to the very root of the error when he states its fundamental principle in the following words: "This error denies the supernatural order and thus carries with it the denial of both divine intervention in the order of creation and in the government of the world as well as the possibility of miracles." Before the completion of his first year in the Chair of Peter, Saint Pius X realized that his task would be to enlighten men's minds "by continually preaching truth" and refute errors "by the principles of a true and solid philosophy and theology which employs genuine progress in historical criticism."

Both points, however, would be treated in further detail in succeeding years. The problem of Church and State would be the theme of the three encyclical letters to the French and the one to the Portuguese, and the "new knowledge," called Modernism, would be the subject of *Pascendi Domini gregis.*

The third point is mentioned only in passing, but is nonetheless clearly and unmistakably expressed. What would remain a point of discussion in many circles until Pope Pius XII definitely taught it in his encyclical on the Mystical Body of Christ, Saint Pius X already declared in 1904 in this encyclical. In *Mystici Corporis Christi* Pope Pius XII wrote concerning the birth of the Church as follows: "That He [Christ] completed His work on the gibbet of the Cross is the unanimous teaching of the holy Fathers who assert that the Church was born from the side of our Saviour on the Cross like a new Eve, mother of all the living." This same truth Saint Pius X stated in this encyclical in the following words: "The Church . . . remains today radiant with eternal youth and strong with the same primitive force she possessed as she issued forth from the Heart of Christ dying on the Cross."

We have said, in drawing a parallel between Gregory and Pius, that both were men of profound humility. In describing Gregory's character Saint Pius X pointed out the former's outstanding virtues. Little did he realize that the virtues he ascribes to Gregory were the same virtues which moved all who came in contact with Pius to call him *"Il Santo"*—"such as his knowledge of affairs, his ability to bring his undertakings to a successful completion, his truly wonderful prudence down to the least details, his constant vigilance and his endless solicitude. Never did he push himself forward as one invested with strength and power like the great ones of the world." Such is the affinity that binds God's saints together!

Iucunda Sane *Encyclical Letter of Our Holy Father Pius X to the Patriarchs, Primates, Archbishops, Bishops and other Ordinaries in Peace and Communion with the Apostolic See*

VENERABLE BRETHREN, HEALTH AND THE APOSTOLIC BLESSING:

Thirteenth Centenary of Saint Gregory. 1. Exceedingly great is the joy that fills Our soul, Venerable Brethren, when We recall "that great and incomparable man,"[1] Pope Gregory I, as We begin the solemn celebration of the thirteenth centenary of his death. Amid the almost innumerable cares of Our apostolic ministry, amid the many anxieties the government of the Universal Church thrusts on Our shoulders, amid the constant care which We must manifest to the best of Our ability towards you, Venerable Brethren, who have been given a share in Our Apostolate as well as the faithful committed to your care, We believe that a very special providence of that God who "killeth and maketh alive . . . humbleth and he exalteth"[2] ordained that We should fix Our gaze at the beginning of Our Pontificate upon this most holy and illustrious Predecessor, the pride and glory of the Church. We have, to be sure, great confidence in his intercession before God. We find Our strength renewed in recalling the sublime maxims by which he ruled and the holy virtues which he practiced. So great, so deep, and so permanent was the impress he left on God's Church by the power of his word and the fruitfulness of his example that both his contemporaries and posterity have rightly called him "Gregory the Great." The truth of the inscription on his tomb has endured throughout the centuries: "He shall live everywhere eternally by his countless good works."[3] For that reason those who imitate his admirable example shall be able, with the help of divine grace, to carry out their duties inasmuch as the infirmity of human nature will allow.

Times in which Gregory lived. 2. It is superfluous to repeat here what everyone knows from public documents. When Gregory entered upon the

Supreme Pontificate public affairs had attained chaotic proportions. The ancient civilization was practically extinct. The barbarian nations had invaded the crumbling Roman Empire. Italy was abandoned by the Byzantine emperors and made the prey of the wandering Lombards. They carried destruction by fire and sword wherever they went and left in their wake only desolation and death. This very city, threatened from without by its enemies and tried from within by the scourges of pestilence, floods and famines, was reduced to such a miserable state that the chief problem was how to preserve the spark of life not only in its citizenry but also in the countless refugees who fled here for shelter. Here one found men and women from every station in life: bishops and priests hurrying about, carrying the sacred vessels snatched from the piles of plunder; monks and innocent spouses of Christ seeking safety here by fleeing from the enemy's swords or brutal men's sacrilegious attacks. Gregory himself describes the Church of Rome as "an old, woefully battered ship, with water seeping in on all sides and joints, beaten by the daily stress of the storm, rotten and threatening shipwreck." [4] But God raised up a pilot with a firm hand whom He placed at the helm. This pilot not only brought the ship safely to port despite the raging seas but also preserved her from future storms.

Gregory, savior of Italy. 3. Marvellous beyond words is the work he accomplished during his reign of little more than thirteen years! He restored Christian living in all its aspects, rekindling the devotion of the faithful, the observance of the monks, the discipline of the clergy and the pastoral solicitude of the bishops. He was "the most prudent father of the family of Christ," [5] simultaneously preserving and increasing the patrimony of the Church as well as coming to the aid of impoverished people, Christian society and individual churches, each according to its needs. "Having been made God's consul," [6] he extended his fruitful activity far beyond the walls of Rome solely for the welfare of civilized society. He fearlessly withstood the unjust claims of the Byzantine emperors; he shattered the audacity and curbed the shameless extortions of the governors and imperial administrators. He was the public defender of social justice. He tamed the ferocity of the Lombards, going out to the very gates of Rome to meet Agulfus and inducing him to lift the siege of the city, as Leo the Great had previously dealt with Attila. Through his ceaseless prayer and dexterous diplomacy, that dreaded nation settled down and adopted an established form of government. Then it entered into the Catholic fold through the influence of his daughter in Christ, the pious queen Theodolinda. Gregory is, then, rightly called the savior and liberator of that Italy which he himself calls "his own land." [7]

Gregory, founder of the Middle Ages. Through his incessant pastoral care the embers of heresy were extinguished in Italy and Africa, ecclesiastical life was restored in France, the Visigoths in Spain were welded together as one nation by means of the conversions already begun among them, and the true faith of Christ was brought to the illustrious English nation, which, "set out on the rim of the world, had previously persisted in the worship of woods and stones." [8] At the news of this precious conquest Gregory's heart, like the heart of a father for his most beloved son, overflowed with joy. He attributed its success to Jesus the Redeemer. For the love of Christ, he himself testified, "we seek our unknown brothers in Britain, and through His grace we find those whom we seek." [9] The gratitude of the English people toward the holy Pontiff was expressed in the titles they conferred on him: "our Master," "our Doctor," "our Apostle," "our Pope," "our Gregory." They considered themselves the seal of his apostolate. In a word, so salutary and fruitful was his work that its very memory has impressed the minds of all those who followed him. Especially was this true during the Middle Ages, which breathed the very atmosphere he created, were nourished by the words he uttered, and directed their whole pattern of living according to the example he established. The happy result was the birth of a Christian social civilization in place of the previous Roman civilization which had passed into oblivion.

Gregory, man of humility. 4. This change was brought about by the right hand of the Most High. It is only right to state, as Gregory himself did, that only God could work such wonders in him. What he wrote to the monk Saint Augustine concerning the conversion of England can be applied to all his apostolic labors: "Who else could accomplish such things but Him who said: 'My father works even until now, and I work'? [10] To show the world that its conversion depended not on the wisdom of men, but upon His Own power, He chose unlearned men to be the preachers He would send into that world. In our days he has done the same thing, choosing weak men to perform wondrous deeds among the English people." [11] Today, however, We can see many qualities which the holy Pontiff's humility hid from his own eyes, such as his knowledge of affairs, his ability to bring his undertakings to a successful completion, his truly wonderful prudence down to the least details, his constant vigilance and his endless solicitude. Never did he push himself forward as one invested with strength and power like the great ones of the world. He refrained from using the lofty titles of his pontifical dignity, preferring rather to call himself "the servant of the servants of God," and he was the first to adopt that title. He chose neither profane science nor "the persuasive words of wisdom," [12] neither the cunning of politics nor any scheme of social restoration, no matter how skillfully studied, prepared and executed. He did not even—and this is striking—establish a vast program of apostolic endeavor to be gradually realized. On the contrary, We know that he was so preoccupied with the approaching end of the world that he gave himself little time for thoughts of marvellous exploits. He was delicate and fragile of body. Several times his sickness brought him to the very threshold of death. Yet he possesed an incredible intellectual energy which was continually being replenished by his living faith in the infallible words and divine promises of Christ. Boundless was his confidence in the supernatural power with which God endowed the Church for the successful accomplishment of her divine mission in the world.

Aim of Gregory's life. 5. His words and works reveal the constant purpose of his life, namely, to preserve within himself and arouse in others a lively faith and trust, continually doing as much good as possible while awaiting the divine judgment.

Gregory's determination. 6. This purpose filled him with the firm determination to utilize the abundant wealth of supernatural means God left the Church for the salvation of souls. Such means were the infallible teaching of revealed truth, the preaching of this same teaching to the whole world, the sacraments which either bring or increase life in souls, and finally the grace of prayer uttered in Christ's name assuring heaven's protection.

Indestructibility of the Church. 7. Venerable Brethren, these memories constantly fill Us with inexpressible comfort. As We look out from the Vatican, We, like Gregory, have serious reasons for fear. The storms come up as quickly as the number of enemies join together and advance against us. At the same time We are as much deprived of human aid to ward off the former as We are to meet the shock of the latter. When We recall, however, the spot on which We stand and on which this Pontifical See has been established, We feel perfectly secure on the rock of Holy Church. "For who does not know," Saint Gregory wrote to Eulogious, the Patriarch of Alexandria, "that holy Church is built on the firmness of the Prince of the Apostles, who received his name because of firmness of mind, since he was called Peter from the word 'rock'?" [13] Never throughout the course of the ages has supernatural power been lacking in the Church; never have the promises of Christ failed. They remain as powerful today as they were when they filled the heart of Gregory with consolation. Rather, having withstood the test of time and the change of circumstances and events, they possess even greater assurance.

The Church is unassailable. 8. Kingdoms and empires have faded; time after time nations have toppled under the weight of years. Yet the Church, indefectible by her essence and united by an indissoluble tie with her Heavenly Spouse, remains today radiant with eternal youth and strong with the same primitive force she possessed as she issued forth from the Heart of Christ dying on the Cross. Powerful men of the world have attacked her. They have vanished, yet she remains. Countless philosophical systems, of every possible form, have taken sides against her, claiming to be her masters, boasting to have destroyed her teaching and demolished her dogmas of faith by proving their absurdity. One after the other, however, they have passed into oblivion. But all the while the light of truth shines forth from Peter's rock as brilliant as on the day Jesus first kindled it by His appearance in the world and sustained it with His divine words: "Heaven and earth will pass away, but my words will not pass away." [14]

The Church, sure road to salvation. 9. Strengthened by this faith and established firmly on this rock, We are deeply aware of the tremendous duties that the Primacy demands of Us. At the same time, however, conscious of the strength the Divine Will instills, We await with the greatest calm the moment when the voices shall be scattered to the four winds that now so vainly boast that the Church is doomed, her doctrines are obsolete, and she must now choose between a godless science and godless civilization or disappear from human society. In the midst of such a din, following the example of Saint Gregory, We must remind all, great and small, that if they wish to be saved, if they wish to follow the right road of reason, to be nourished on the truth, to find peace and happiness in this life, then they must look to this Church.

Church-State relations. 10. For this reason, We make the holy Pontiff's words Our Own: "Turn your steps toward this unshakable rock on which our Saviour has established the Universal Church; in such a way he who is sincere in his heart will not be led along devious paths." [15] Only love for and union with the Church "unite what is divided, restore order where there is confusion, temper inequalities, and bring an end to imperfections." [16] We must always remember that "nobody can wisely govern temporalities who does not know how to deal with spiritualities; thus the peace of the states depends on the peace of the Church." * From this it follows that there must be a perfect harmony between the civil and the ecclesiastical power, since both are ordained by God to support each other. For this reason "Heaven has granted some to have power over all men in order that those who wish to lead a good life may be aided, that the road to heaven may be widened, and that earthly kingdoms be subject to the kingdom of heaven." [18]

Gregory, defender of Church rights. 11. These principles were the source of Gregory's indomitable courage, which, with the help of God, We shall strive to imitate. Above all else We are determined to preserve the rights and privileges of the Roman See in good condition. We are the guardian and defender of these before God and men. For this reason Gregory wrote as follows to the Patriarchs of Alexandria and Antioch: Whenever the rights of the Church are in question "we must show to the point of death that we prefer nothing (notwithstanding any personal and private interests) to the common good." [19] Again he wrote the Emperor Maurice: "Who-

* See the *Motu Proprio* on Church music, p. 199.

ever boastfully stands stiff-necked against God Almighty or the statutes of the Fathers, as I trust in the same Almighty God I shall not bend my neck to him, not even by force of the sword."[20] Finally, to the Deacon Sabinianus he wrote: "I am prepared rather to die than to let the Church decline in these days. Since you know me so well, you know that I am very patient; but when I make up my mind to endure no more, then I joyfully face danger."[21]

A new civilization is born. 12. Such were the fundamental principles Pope Gregory proclaimed; such were the principles they heard who listened to him. Since both princes and people obeyed his words, the world was recalled to the path leading to true salvation. More than that, the world entered a new civilization which was noble and beneficent because it was founded upon the most certain dictates of reason and moral discipline, and breathed a new vigor supplied from divinely revealed truth and the evangelical maxims.

The Church, the source of life. 13. Even though the people of those days were ignorant and lacking culture, they were nonetheless eager for life. And this they could receive only from Christ through the Church: "I come that they may have life, and have it more abundantly."[22] By all means they had this life and had it abundantly, since only from the Church does the supernatural life come. This supernatural life embraces and strengthens all the powers of life even in the natural order. "If the root is holy, so also are the branches," Saint Paul told the Gentiles, "and . . . thou, being a wild olive, art grafted in their place, and hast become a partaker of the stem and fatness of the olive tree."[23]

Total attack against the Church. 14. Today the world enjoys a light resplendent with Christian culture, and from this point of view it cannot for a moment be compared with the days of Gregory. Yet it seems that the world has grown weary of that life, even though that life has been and still remains the principal and frequently the only source of all its past and present merits. Not only does the present age, like a useless branch, cut itself off from the stem (as happened in past ages in the case of heresies and schisms), but it lays the axe to the very root of the stem (which is the Church), striving to drain out the sap of life so that its ruin will be certain and it will never bloom again.

Denial of the supernatural order. 15. This error is the principal one at the present time. In fact, it is the source from which all the others flow. It is the reason why so many men are forfeiting their eternal salvation and the cause of many of the evils afflicting religion which We lament today as well as the many more We fear will come about if it is not remedied. This is the error which denies the supernatural order, and thus carries with it the denial of both divine intervention in the order of creation and in the government of the world as well as the possibility of miracles. In such a way the very foundation of the Christian religion is shaken. Men boldly call in question the arguments proving the existence of God. With unprecedented audacity they deny (and accordingly contradict the first principles of reason) the invincible force of the proof that effects ascend to their cause (who is God) and the notion of His infinite attributes. "For since the creation of the world his invisible attributes are clearly seen—his everlasting power also and divinity—being understood through the things that are made."[24] Thus the door is opened to other serious errors, as repugnant to right reason as they are dangerous to good morals.

False science and false critics. 16. This falsely assumed negation of the supernatural principle is the characteristic of an equally false knowledge and has actually become the postulate of an equally false historical criticism. Thus anything related to the supernatural order, either as belonging to, constituting, presupposing or merely finding its explanation in it, is erased without further investigation from the pages of history. In such a way it treats the divinity of Christ Jesus, His incarnation through the operation of the Holy Spirit, His resurrection from the dead by His own power, and in general all the dogmas of our Faith. Once science sets out on this false road, no laws of criticism can restrain it. Whatever displeases it or whatever it believes is contradictory to the pre-established theses it seeks to demonstrate, it capriciously cancels from the holy books. Destroy the supernatural order, and the history of the Church's origin must be built on quite another foundation. Such innovators, therefore, so twist the meaning of historical documents that these no longer represent what their authors meant but what the innovators want them to say.

Recall to true philosophy. 17. Many are so fascinated by this flourish of erudition parading before them as well as the seemingly convincing power of the proofs brought forth that they either lose their faith or feel it has been seriously shaken. Others, who are firm in faith, say the science of criticism is destructive. If that be so, it is not through its own fault, for when rightly applied it can be most useful for honest inquiry. Both those who are shaken in their faith and those who condemn the science of criticism fail to see that it begins with a false hypothesis, namely, a specious science which logically leads to false conclusions. Given a false philosophical principle, everything flowing from it is vitiated. These errors, however, will be uprooted only when the mode of attack is changed. Those who err must be compelled to abandon the field of criticism in which they consider themselves authorities and return to the camp of true philosophy. Their errors are only the result of abandoning true philosophy.

The materialists are "foolish." 18. In the meantime We are deeply pained to have to apply to such brilliant men the rebuke Saint Paul addressed to those who would not rise from earthly things to invisible things. They "became vain in their reasonings, and their senseless minds have been darkened. For while professing to be wise, they have become fools." [25] Foolish, by all means, is the word for him who devours his intellectual ability in building on sandy ground.

All authority comes from God. 19. No less serious is the danger that threatens the moral lives of individuals and society from this denial of the supernatural. If you destroy the principle that there is a Divinity beyond this visible world, nothing is more evident than the fact that unbridled passions of the lowest and vilest kind will be unleashed and minds enslaved by them will run riot among disorders of every imaginable kind. "Therefore," Saint Paul continues, "God has given them up in the lustful desires of their heart to uncleanness, so that they dishonor their own bodies among themselves." [26] Venerable Brethren, you fully realize how the plague of depravity rages on all sides. Likewise you realize that whenever the civil government fails to make use of the means offered by the supernatural order, it is unable to check the plague in any way. Nor will civil authority ever be able to prevent other evils as long as it forgets or denies that all authority comes from God. In such a case the only restraint a government can apply is force; but force can neither be constantly applied nor is it always available. A people suffering from a hidden disease soon becomes displeased with everything. They proclaim the right to act as they please, they stir up rebellions and, trampling on all rights, human and divine, they provoke revolutions within the State. Take away God, and all respect for civil laws and all regard for even the most necessary institutions disappear. Take away God, and justice is spurned and that liberty arising from the natural law is trodden underfoot. Take away God, and men will destroy the very structure of the family, the primary and indispensable foundation of the whole social structure. Consequently it is very difficult during these days so hostile to Christ to apply the powerful remedies for the orderly government of the people with which the Redeemer endowed His Church.

Christ, the Cornerstone of human society. 20. There is, moreover, no salvation for the world except in Christ, "for there is no other name under heaven given to men by which we must be saved." [27] We must, therefore, return to Christ. We must prostrate ourselves at His feet in order to hear words of eternal life from His divine mouth. Only He can show us the road to restoration; only He can teach us the truth; only He can restore our life. Only He can truthfully say: "I am the way, and the truth, and the life." [28] Once again men have tried to get along without Him, and, just as the Apostle Peter rebuked Jesus' executioners, so men today have also begun to build up an edifice after rejecting the cornerstone. Then the building they have raised up crumbles and topples on their heads, crushing all the builders.

Jesus, however, remains forever the cornerstone of human society. Once again events bear witness to the truth that without Him there is no salvation. "This is 'The stone that was rejected by you, the builders, which has become the corner-stone.' Neither is there salvation in any other." [29]

The primacy of prayer. 21. All this, Venerable Brethren, makes it clear how absolutely necessary it is for all of us to strive vigorously to revive this supernatural life in all the departments of human society by using every available means. We must revive this life both in the poor workingman who earns his daily bread by the sweat of his brow, toiling from morning till night, as well as in the great ones of the world who govern the destinies of nations. Above all, we must pray, publicly and privately, imploring the merciful Lord to come to our aid with His powerful assistance. Like the Apostles who were struggling against the storm, we must constantly cry out: "Lord, save us! we are perishing!" [30]

Action also is demanded. 22. But this is not enough. Gregory rebuked a bishop who, loving spiritual solitude and prayer, failed to enter the battlefield in defense of the Lord's cause with these words: "The title of bishop which he bears is an empty one." [31] And rightly so, for men's intellects are enlightened by continually preaching truth, and errors are best refuted by the principles of a true and solid philosophy and theology which employs genuine progress in historical criticism. It is even more necessary, however, that the moral maxims taught by Jesus Christ be deeply impressed on everyone's mind. Then everybody will learn to conquer himself, to curb the passions of the mind, to stifle pride, to live in obedience to authority, to love justice, to practice charity toward everyone, to temper the bitterness of social inequality with Christian love, to detach the heart from worldly goods, to live contented with the state Providence has placed upon him while striving to better it through the fulfillment of his duties, and to thirst for the future life with the hope of eternal reward. Above all, however, these principles must penetrate deep into everyone's heart in order that true and solid piety will take root there. Then everyone, as men and as Christians, will fulfill the duties of his state both in word and deed. Then everyone will approach the Church and her ministers with filial confidence in order to obtain pardon for his sins, receive the grace of the Sacraments, and regulate his life according to the norms of Christian morality.

Action must flow from charity. 23. We must, moreover, unite the charity of Christ to all these principal duties of the sacred ministry. When charity moves us, there will be no affliction that escapes our attention, no tears that will not be dried by our hands, no need that will not be relieved by us. Let us dedicate ourselves totally to this kind of charity. Let personal interests surrender to it. Let our personal affairs bend before it. Let us make ourselves "all things to all men" [32] to win all men to the truth. If needs be, let us surrender our life itself, following the example of Christ, Who placed this duty on the shoulders of the Church's pastors: "The good shepherd lays down his life for his sheep." [33] These precious admonitions are found in the pages of the writings Gregory left us. They are, however, expressed in a far more powerful manner in many examples of his admirable life.

Charity must be based on truth. 24. All this necessarily follows from the nature of the principles of Christian revelation as well as from the intrinsic nature of Our Apostolate. You can plainly see, then, Venerable Brethren, how they err who think they are rendering service to the Church and reaping fruit in the salvation of souls when they, out of human prudence, try to be liberal in granting concessions to a science falsely so called. They are deceived in thinking they can win over those in error more easily. As a matter of fact, they themselves are in constant danger of being lost. Truth is one; it cannot be divided. It remains forever, free from the vicissitudes of time. "Jesus Christ is the same, yesterday and today, yes, and forever." [34]

The Apostolate excludes human prudence. 25. They also seriously err who, while laboring in behalf of the people and especially in defending the cause of the poor classes, strive above all else to improve their material conditions. At the same time, however, they remain indifferent to their spiritual welfare and the duties they must fulfill as Christians. Sometimes they do not even hesitate to pass over the fundamental principles of the Gospel, fearing that otherwise the people will refuse to hear and follow them. By all means prudence demands that one proceed gradually in laying down the truth when dealing with men who are strangers to us and separated from God. "Before using the steel," Gregory said, "let the wounds be treated with a gentle hand." [35] But this carefulness, if proposed as a rule of constant and everyday action, would sink to mere human prudence—all the more so, since this procedure seems to overlook that divine grace which sustains the sacerdotal ministry and is given to all the faithful of Christ in order that our words and actions may find entrance into men's hearts. Gregory did not understand this prudence either in his preaching of the Gospel or in his many wonderful works for the alleviation of misery. He always did what the Apostles had done. When they went out into the world to introduce to it the name of Christ, they repeated the saying: "We, for our part, preach a crucified Christ—to the Jews indeed a stumbling block and to the Gentiles foolishness." [36] If ever there was a period of history in which human prudence offered the only expedient for obtaining something from a world altogether unprepared to accept a doctrine so new, so repugnant to human passions, so opposed to the flourishing civilization of the Greeks and Romans, then it was most certainly during the time of the preaching of the Faith. The Apostles, however, disdained such prudence, because they clearly understood God's command: "It pleased God, by the foolishness of our preaching, to save those who believe."[37] As it was then, so it is today. This foolishness "to those who are saved, that is, to us, . . . is the power of God."[38] The scandal of the Cross, as in the past, will in the future supply us with the most powerful of all weapons. Now, as in the past, we shall find our victory in this sign.

Pastoral care. 26. This weapon, however, will lose much of its power, Venerable Brethren, or be altogether useless in the hands of men unaccustomed to an interior Christian life, or uneducated in the school of true and solid piety, or not thoroughly aflame with zeal for the glory of God and the extension of His Kingdom. So deeply did Gregory feel this that he exercised the greatest diligence in creating bishops and priests who were animated by the desire of working solely for the glory of God and the salvation of souls. This was the purpose of his book *Pastoral Care,* in which he gathered together prescriptions concerning the formation of the clergy and the government of bishops. These rules are as suitable for our time as they were for his. As an "argus of light," says his biographer, "his pastoral solicitude extended throughout the whole world,"[39] searching out and correcting the vices and negligences of the clergy. In fact, he trembled at the very thought that barbarism and immorality might gain a foothold among the clergy. He was deeply moved and did not rest whenever he heard of some infraction of the disciplinary laws of the Church. He would immediately issue an admonition and correction, sometimes threatening the transgressors with canonical penalties, sometimes immediately applying these penalties himself, and sometimes, casting aside delay and human respect, removing the unworthy from their offices.

Maxims to govern the true apostle. 27. He tried to instill among the clergy the principles which we frequently come across in his writings. The following quotations are some examples of these maxims: "With what assurance can one take on the role of interceding for the people with God, without the knowledge of being in His favor by reason of the merits of one's life?"[40] "If, then, in his practice ailments still thrive in him, with what presumption does he hasten to heal the afflicted while he carries a sore on his own face!"[41] What results can be expected in the work of saving souls if the apostles "belie in their conduct what they teach by words"?[42] "A man who is debased by his own guilt must not intercede for the faults of others."[43]

Gregory's ideal of a true priest. 27. Here is the picture that Gregory paints of the true priest. "He must die to all passions of the flesh and by now lead a spiritual life. He must have put aside worldly prosperity; he must fear no adversity, desire only what is interior. He must be a man whose aims are not thwarted by a body out of perfect accord through frailty, nor by any contumacy of the spirit. He is not led to covet the goods of others, but is generous in giving of his own. He is quickly moved by a compassionate heart to forgive, yet never so diverted from perfect rectitude as to forgive beyond what is proper. He does no unlawful act himself while deploring those of others, as if they were his own. In the affection of his own heart he sympathizes with the frailties of others, and so rejoices in the good done by his neighbor, as though the progress made were his own. In all that he does he sets an example so inspiring to all others, that in their regard he has no cause to be ashamed of his past. He so studies to love as to be able to water the dry hearts of others with the streams of instruction imparted. By his practice and experience of prayer he has learned already that he can obtain from the Lord what he asks for."[44]

The evil of imprudent priests. 28. Behold how seriously, Venerable Brethren, a bishop must consider in the presence of God the matter of laying hands on a young levite! Let him never dare—either as a personal favor to anybody or under pressure from others—let him never dare, Gregory says, to promote anyone to Sacred Orders whose life and actions do not give evidence of his worthiness.[45] Only after much thought should he entrust the works of the apostolate into the hands of newly ordained priests. If they do not first prove their worth under the watchful eyes of more prudent priests; if there is not abundant evidence of their probity, their inclination for spiritual exercises, their prompt obedience to the regulations suggested by ecclesiastical custom or experience or imposed by those whom "the Holy Spirit has placed as bishops, to rule the Church of God"[46]—if there is no such evidence, they will perform the sacerdotal ministry not for the salvation but the ruin of the people of Christ. They would then arouse discord and subtle rebellion, giving the world cause to believe that the sad spectacle of division has entered into the flock. The truth of the matter is, however, that such deplorable incidents spring from the pride and obstinacy of only a few. Let such as stir up discord be removed from every office. The Church has no need of such apostles. They are, in fact, not the apostles of Christ Crucified: they are apostles of themselves.

Gregory and the Lateran Council. 29. We can still picture before our mind's eye Gregory, surrounded by a great number of bishops from all parts of the world, presiding over the Lateran Council. How true are the words that flow from his lips on the duties of the clergy! How great is the fire that consumes his heart with zeal! His words are lightning-bolts rending the perverse, scourges striking the indolent, flames of divine love gently embracing the fervent. Take up and read, Venerable Brethren, and have your clergy, especially during the annual retreat, read and meditate upon that marvellous homily of the holy Pontiff.

The Church needs good priests. 30. Among other things, he sadly exclaims, "Behold, the world is full of priests, but rare indeed is the worker who rests in the hands of God. It is true that we assume the priestly office; but the obligations of the office we do not fulfill."[47] How powerful do you think the Church would be today if she could count a worker for every priest? What results do you think you could see if the supernatural life the Church instills in souls would be diligently cultivated by all? While he lived, Gregory succeeded in arousing the spirit of energetic action. The force of that impulse which Gregory initiated was so great that it was kept alive throughout the succeeding ages. The Middle Ages are stamped with what we may call the Gregorian imprint. They inherited most of their institutions from him, such as their ecclesiastical government, their many forms of charitable and philanthropic social institutions, their principles of perfect Christian asceticism and monasticism, their rules governing the Sacred Liturgy and Sacred Music.

The Church appeals to every age. 31. The times have truly changed. Yet, as We have more than once repeated, nothing is changed in the life of the Church. Her Divine Founder endowed her with the power of supplying every age, no matter how different, with everything necessary not only for the spiritual welfare of souls (which is the direct object of her mission) but also everything that advances the cause of true civilization, since this flows as a natural consequence of that same mission.

Grace enhances nature. 32. The Church is the depository of truths of the supernatural order and these, in turn, necessarily foster everything that is true, good and beautiful in the order of nature. The further these truths are traced back to the supreme principle of truth, goodness and beauty (who is God), the more effectively will the natural order prosper.

Revelation guides natural reason. 33. Human science is greatly enriched by revelation, for the latter opens new horizons and makes truth more easily seen by the former. It opens the true road for investigation and protects it from errors of application and methodology. In such a manner the lighthouse points out many things which otherwise would remain unseen, all the while sending out flashes to avoid the rocks on which the ship might go aground.

God Himself is our Model. 34. The Divine Redeemer proposed as our supreme Model of perfection in the matter of moral discipline His Heavenly Father [48]—in other words, Divine Goodness Itself. Can we not see by that act the mighty impulse given to the more perfect observance of the natural law inscribed in our hearts, thereby aiding the welfare of the individual, the family, and society? In such a way the ferocity of the barbarians was transformed into gentleness, women were freed from subjection, slavery was curbed, order was restored between the various classes of society through reciprocal dependence, justice was recognized, true liberty of souls proclaimed, and social and domestic peace assured.

The Church is mother of the arts. 35. Finally, the more the arts are modeled on God, the supreme Exemplar of beauty from Whom all natural beauty flows, the more they withdraw from the vulgar and approach the spiritual concept from which they receive their vigor and vitality. How beneficent has been the practice of making the arts the handmaids of divine worship! Thus everything worthy of God by reason of its richness, goodness, and elegance of form is offered to Him. In Our special *Motu Proprio* on Sacred Music and the Restoration of the Roman Chant according to the ancient tradition We recently spoke on this subject.* What We have said concerning the Chant can equally be applied to the other arts, each in its own sphere, such as painting, sculpture, and architecture. The Church has ever been lavish in inspiration and encouragement toward all such great creations of genius. Fed on this sublime ideal, men build magnificent temples where, in the house of God, as if in their own homes, they lift up their hearts to heavenly things amid the treasures of every beautiful art during sacred ceremonies performed to the accompaniment of the sweetest music.

Exhortation to Restoration. 36. All these benefits, We repeat, Gregory spared no pains to secure for his own age as well as for all succeeding ages. They can still be accomplished in our time not only because of the intrinsic value of the principles that should guide us but also because of the means we have at our disposal. During this time which is given us to maintain a firm stand and be instructed in the proper means at our disposal, let us, relying on the grace of God, zealously protect the remaining good things while restoring in Christ [49] everything that has unfortunately lapsed from the right rule.

Prayer of Saint Gregory. 37. It gives Us great pleasure to conclude this letter with the same words Gregory used to conclude his memorable exhortation in the Lateran Council: "These things, Brethren, you should carefully consider and urge your neighbor to do likewise. Prepare to render to God the fruit of the ministry which you have taken upon your shoulders. The matters we have called to your attention will be fulfilled better through prayer than through discourse. Let us pray: O God, who hast deigned to appoint us pastors over the people, grant, we beseech Thee, that we may be in Thy sight what we are said to be by men." [50]

Apostolic Blessing. 38. While trusting that God will graciously hear Our prayer through the intercession of the holy Pontiff, Gregory, as a pledge of heavenly favor and in token of our paternal good will, We impart to you, Venerable Brethren, and to your clergy and people, Our Apostolic Blessing.

39. Given at Saint Peter's, Rome, on March 12, 1904, the feast of Saint Gregory I, Pope and Doctor of the Church, in the first year of Our Pontificate.

PIUS X, POPE

* See pp. 199–206.

REFERENCES

1. *Roman Martyrology*, September 3.
2. I Kings 2:6–7.
3. *Vita Gregorii*, 4:68.
4. *Registrum*, 1:4; to John, the Bishop of Constantinople.
5. *Vita Gregorii*, 2:51.
6. Inscription on the tomb of Saint Gregory the Great.
7. *Registrum*, 5:36 (40); to the Emperor Maurice.
8. *Ibid.*, 8:29 (30); to Eulogius, the Bishop of Alexandria.
9. *Ibid.*, 11:36 (28); to Augustine, the Bishop of Britain.
10. John 5:17.
11. *Registrum*, 11:36 (28).
12. I Cor. 2:4.
13. *Registrum*, 7:37 (40).
14. Matt. 24:33.
15. *Registrum*, 8:24; to Sabinianus the Bishop.
16. *Ibid.*, 5:58 (53); to Virgilius the Bishop.
17. *Ibid.*, 5:37 (20); to the Emperor Maurice.
18. *Ibid.*, 3:61 (65); to the Emperor Maurice.
19. *Ibid.*, 5:41 (43).
20. *Ibid.*, 5:37 (20).
21. *Ibid.*, 5:6 (4:47).
22. John 10:10.
23. Rom. 11:16–17.
24. Rom. 1:20.
25. Rom. 1:21–22.
26. Rom. 1:24.
27. Acts 4:12.
28. John 14:6.
29. Acts 4:11–12.
30. Matt. 8:25.
31. *Registrum*, 6:63 (30). Cf. *Pastoral Care*, 1:5.
32. I Cor. 9:22.
33. John 10:11.
34. Heb. 13:8.
35. *Registrum*, 5:44 (18); to John the Bishop.
36. I Cor. 1:23.
37. *Ibid.*, 1:21.
38. *Ibid.*, 1:18.
39. *Vita Gregorii*, 2:65.
40. *Pastoral Care*, 1:20. All references to *Pastoral Care* are taken from the translation in the Ancient Christian Writers Series, by Henry Davis, S. J., Newman Press, Westminster, Md., 1950.
41. *Ibid.*, 1:9.
42. *Ibid.*, 1:2.
43. *Ibid.*, 1:11.
44. *Ibid.*, 1:10.
45. *Registrum*, 5:63 (58).
46. Acts 20:28.
47. Homily on the Gospel at the Lateran Council, no. 3.
48. Matt. 5:48.
49. See Eph. 1:10.
50. Homily on the Gospel at the Lateran Council, no. 18.

CHAPTER 4

Acerbo Nimis *April 15, 1905, The Teaching of Christian Doctrine*

RIGHTLY has Saint Pius X been called the "Pope of Christian Doctrine." Throughout his priestly life, from his days as curate of Tombolo, when he gathered the children of the village about him for catechetical instruction, to the days when as Pastor of the Church of Rome he taught the faithful of Rome in the Court of Saint Damasus on Sunday afternoons, he was, from first to last, the "Pope of the Catechism." Those unacquainted with Saint Pius X would say it was impossible for one and the same man to pen the tender *Acerbo Nimis* and the terrible *Pascendi.* Yet his simplicity was so penetrating that he knew the subject of both letters was the same—Christian doctrine.

Acerbo Nimis was the result of long years of pastoral experience combined with a world-wide vision. Tombolo, Salzano, Terviso, Mantua, Venice and Rome were all centers of personal experience which convinced Saint Pius X "that the chief cause of the present indifference and, as it were, infirmity of soul, and the serious evils that result from it, is to be found above all in ignorance of things divine." The threatening separation of Church and State in France, the labor dispute in Germany, the condition of the Church in Portugal, the dearth of clergy in mission countries were all world-wide problems that further convinced Saint Pius X "that there are large numbers of Christians in our own time who are entirely ignorant of those truths necessary for salvation." That firm conviction brought forth the encyclical letter on the teaching of Christian doctrine.

It is composed of an introduction, treating of the evils of present-day society and showing how Christian doctrine, as the light of men's intellects and the strength of men's wills, is the chief means "by which we are raised up to God and joined with Him in the practice of virtue" (1–6). It continues by showing from conciliar legislation and papal documents that the duty of catechetical instructions rests primarily upon the shoulders of all pastors of souls (7–11). Then, lest anyone be content with merely a weekly homily on the Gospel, it points out the distinction between the homily and the instruction (12–13); and as a motive for action, it shows the importance of catechetical instruction and the dignity of the catechist (14–18). In concluding, it promulgates six laws for the universal Church in regard to the education of all the faithful (19–24) and pleads for universal cooperation in the immediate and proper execution of these laws (25–27).

Saint Pius X, in his exalted place in the heavenly court, must surely look down with pleasure upon the hierarchy of the American Church, for they have heard his plea and have carried and continue to carry it into execution: "Venerable Brethren . . . it now rests with you to put it into prompt and complete execution in your respective dioceses, and by the power of your authority to see to it that these prescriptions of Ours be not neglected or, what amounts to the same thing, that they be not carried out carelessly or superficially."

Contrary to the opinion of some that Saint Pius X was merely "a simple country pastor," he was truly, as Pope Pius XII called him, the "Defender of the Faith." One writer put it in the following words: "It was the special mission of Pope Pius X, in a time of great material comfort, to recall a complacent generation to the stark realities of the creed, and, in retrospect, the world has been driven to an understanding of the vital importance of doctrine. While Pius X was Pope, Lenin, in his penurious exile, and with few followers, was almost alone in sharing with the Catholics a flaming conviction that it was much more important to get the doctrine right and prevent it from being perverted than to attract large numbers of adherents. A man who looks out on the world today, where all power is of the masses, can no longer deny that true doctrine is, in fact, vital, because doctrine is the source of motive and action, and popular sovereignty is neither the same thing as wisdom and justice, nor a guarantee of them." *

* *The Tablet,* 197:431.

Acerbo Nimis* *Encyclical Letter of His Holiness Pope Pius X to the Patriarchs, Primates, Archbishops, Bishops and Other Ordinaries in Peace and Communion with the Apostolic See*

VENERABLE BRETHREN, HEALTH AND THE APOSTOLIC BLESSING:

Ignorance breeds indifference. 1. At this very troublesome and difficult time, the hidden designs of God have conducted Our poor strength to the office of Supreme Pastor, to rule the entire flock of Christ. The enemy has, indeed, long been prowling about the fold and attacking it with such subtle cunning that now, more than ever before, the prediction of the Apostle to the elders of the Church of Ephesus seems to be verified: "I know that . . . fierce wolves will get in among you, and will not spare the flock."[1] Those who still are zealous for the glory of God are seeking the causes and reasons for this decline in religion. Coming to a different explanation, each points out, according to his own view, a different plan for the protection and restoration of the kingdom of God on earth. But it seems to Us, Venerable Brethren, that while we should not overlook other considerations, We are forced to agree with those who hold that the chief cause of the present indifference and, as it were, infirmity of soul, and the serious evils that result from it, is to be found above all in ignorance of things divine. This is fully in accord with what God Himself declared through the Prophet Osee: "And there is no knowledge of God in the land. Cursing and lying and killing and theft and adultery have overflowed: and blood hath touched blood. Thereafter shall the land mourn, and everyone that dwelleth in it shall languish."[2]

Effects of religious ignorance. 2. It is a common complaint, unfortunately too well founded, that there are large numbers of Christians in our own time who are entirely ignorant of those truths necessary for salvation. And when we mention Christians, We refer not only to the masses or to those in the lower walks of life—for these find some excuse for their ignorance in the fact that the demands of their harsh employers hardly leave them time to take care of themselves or of their dear ones—but We refer to those especially who do not lack culture or talents and, indeed, are possessed of

* *Acerbo Nimis* was translated by Joseph Collins, S.S., D.D., Ph.D., and appears in *Catechetical Documents of Pope Pius X* (Paterson, N. J., St. Anthony Guild Press). (The marginal titles have been added by the editor.)

abundant knowledge regarding things of the world but live rashly and imprudently with regard to religion. It is hard to find words to describe how profound is the darkness in which they are engulfed and, what is most deplorable of all, how tranquilly they repose there. They rarely give thought to God, the Supreme Author and Ruler of all things, or to the teachings of the faith of Christ. They know nothing of the Incarnation of the Word of God, nothing of the perfect restoration of the human race which He accomplished. Grace, the greatest of the helps for attaining eternal things, the Holy Sacrifice and the Sacraments by which we obtain grace, are entirely unknown to them. They have no conception of the malice and baseness of sin; hence they show no anxiety to avoid sin or to renounce it. And so they arrive at life's end in such a condition that, lest all hope of salvation be lost, the priest is obliged to give in the last few moments of life a summary teaching of religion, a time which should be devoted to stimulating the soul to greater love for God. And even this as too often happens only when the dying man is not so sinfully ignorant as to look upon the ministration of the priest as useless, and then calmly faces the fearful passage to eternity without making his peace with God. And so Our Predecessor, Benedict XIV, had just cause to write: "We declare that a great number of those who are condemned to eternal punishment suffer that everlasting calamity because of ignorance of those mysteries of faith which must be known and believed in order to be numbered among the elect." [3]

Intellect is the guide to holiness. 3. There is then, Venerable Brethren, no reason for wonder that the corruption of morals and depravity of life is already so great, and ever increasingly greater, not only among uncivilized peoples but even in those very nations that are called Christian. The Apostle Paul, writing to the Ephesians, repeatedly admonished them in these words: "But immorality and every uncleanness or covetousness, let it not even be named among you, as become saints; or obscenity or foolish talk." [4] He also places the foundation of holiness and sound morals upon a knowledge of divine things—which holds in check evil desires: "See to it therefore, brethren, that you walk with care: not as unwise but as wise . . . Therefore, do not become foolish, but understand what the will of the Lord is." [5] And rightly so. For the will of man retains but little of that divinely implanted love of virtue and righteousness by which it was, as it were, attracted strongly toward the real and not merely apparent good. Disordered by the stain of the first sin, and almost forgetful of God, its Author, it improperly turns every affection to a love of vanity and deceit. This erring will, blinded by its own evil desires, has need therefore of a guide to lead it back to the paths of justice whence it has so unfortunately strayed. The intellect itself is this guide, which need not be sought elsewhere, but is provided by nature itself. It is a guide, though, that, if it lack its companion light, the knowledge of divine things, will be only an instance of the blind leading the blind so that both will fall into the pit. The holy king David, praising God for the light of truth with which He had illumined the intellect, exclaimed: "The light of Thy countenance, O Lord, is signed upon us." [6] Then he described the effect of this light by adding: "Thou hast given gladness in my heart," gladness, that is, which enlarges our heart so that it runs in the way of God's Commandments.

Christian Doctrine enlightens the intellect. 4. All this becomes evident on a little reflection. Christian teaching reveals God and His infinite perfection with far greater clarity than is possible by the human faculties alone. Nor is that all. This same Christian teaching also commands us to honor God by faith, which is of the mind, by hope, which is of the will, by love, which is of the heart; and thus the whole man is subjected to the supreme Maker and Ruler of all things. The truly remarkable dignity of man as the son of the heavenly Father, in Whose image he is formed, and with Whom he is destined to live in eternal happiness, is also revealed only by the doctrine of Jesus Christ. From this very dignity, and from man's knowledge of it, Christ showed that men should love one another as brothers, and should live here as becomes children of light, "not in revelry and drunkenness, not in debauchery and wantonness, not in strife and jealousy." [7] He also bids us to place all our anxiety and care in the hands of God, for He will provide for us; He tells us to help the poor, to do good to those who hate us, and to prefer the eternal welfare of the soul to the temporal goods of this life. Without wishing to touch on every detail, nevertheless is it not true that the proud man is urged and commanded by the teaching of Christ to strive for humility, the source of true glory? "Whoever, therefore, humbles himself . . . he is the greatest in the kingdom of heaven." [8] From that same teaching we learn prudence of the spirit, and thereby we avoid prudence of the flesh; we learn justice, by which we give to every man his due; fortitude, which prepares us to endure all things and with steadfast heart suffer all things for the sake of God and eternal happiness; and, last of all, temperance through which we cherish even poverty borne out of love for God, nay, we even glory in the cross itself, unmindful of its shame. In fine, Christian teaching not only bestows on the intellect the light by which it attains truth, but from it our will draws that ardor by which we are raised up to God and joined with Him in the practice of virtue.

Intellect moves the will to action. 5. We by no means wish to conclude that a perverse will and unbridled conduct may not be joined with a knowledge of religion. Would to God that facts did not too abundantly prove the contrary! But We do maintain that the will cannot be upright nor the conduct good when the mind is shrouded in the darkness of crass ignorance. A man who walks with open eyes may, indeed, turn aside from the right path, but a blind man is in much more imminent danger of wandering away. Furthermore, there is always some hope for a reform of perverse conduct so long as the light of faith is not entirely extinguished; but if lack of faith is added to depraved morality because of ignorance, the evil hardly admits of remedy, and the road to ruin lies open.

Christian living follows Christian Doctrine. 6. How many and how grave are the consequences of ignorance in matters of religion! And on the other hand, how necessary and how beneficial is religious instruction! It is indeed vain to expect a fulfillment of the duties of a Christian by one who does not even know them.

Duty of Pastors. 7. We must now consider upon whom rests the obligation to dissipate this most pernicious ignorance and to impart in its stead the knowledge that is wholly indispensable. There can be no doubt, Venerable Brethren, that this most important duty rests upon all who are pastors of souls. On them, by command of Christ, rest the obligations of knowing and of feeding the flocks committed to their care; and to feed implies, first of all, to teach. "I will give you pastors according to my own heart," God promised through Jeremias, "and they shall feed you with knowledge and doctrine."[9] Hence the Apostle Paul said: "Christ did not send me to baptize, but to preach the gospel,"[10] thereby indicating that the first duty of all those who are entrusted in any way with the government of the Church is to instruct the faithful in the things of God.

Dignity of the teacher. 8. We do not think it necessary to set forth here the praises of such instruction or to point out how meritorious it is in God's sight. If, assuredly, the alms with which we relieve the needs of the poor are highly praised by the Lord, how much more precious in His eyes, then, will be the zeal and labor expended in teaching and admonishing, by which we provide not for the passing needs of the body but for the eternal profit of the soul! Nothing, surely, is more desirable, nothing more acceptable to Jesus Christ, the Saviour of souls, Who testifies of Himself through Isaias: "To bring good news to the poor he has sent me."[11]

Priestly holiness and learning. 9. Here then it is well to emphasize and insist that for a priest there is no duty more grave or obligation more binding than this. Who, indeed, will deny that knowledge should be jointed to holiness of life in the priest? "For the lips of the priest shall keep knowledge."[12] The Church demands this knowledge of those who are to be ordained to the priesthood. Why? Because the Christian people expect from them knowledge of the divine law, and it was for that end that they were sent by God. "And they shall seek the law at his mouth; because he is the angel of the Lord of hosts."[13] Thus the bishop speaking to the candidates for the priesthood in the ordination ceremony says: "Let your teaching be a spiritual remedy for God's people; may they be worthy fellow-workers of our order; and thus meditating day and night on His law, they may believe what they read, and teach what they shall believe." [14]

Parish priests must teach. 10. If what We have just said is applicable to all priests, does it not apply with much greater force to those who possess the title and the authority of parish priests, and who, by virtue of their rank and in a sense by virtue of a contract, hold the office of pastors of souls? These are, to a certain extent, the pastors and teachers appointed by Christ in order that the faithful might not be as "children, tossed to and fro and carried about by every wind of doctrine devised in the wickedness of men," but that practicing "the truth in love," they may, "grow up in all things in him who is the head, Christ." [15]

Teaching is their primary duty. 11. For this reason the Council of Trent, treating of the duties of pastors of souls, decreed that their first and most important work is the instruction of the faithful.[16] It therefore prescribes that they shall teach the truths of religion on Sundays and on the more solemn feast days; moreover during the holy seasons of Advent and Lent they are to give such instruction every day or at least three times a week. This, however, was not considered enough. The Council provided for the instruction of youth by adding that the pastors, either personally or through others, must explain the truths of religion at least on Sundays and feast days to the children of the parish, and inculcate obedience to God and to their parents. When the Sacraments are to be administered, it enjoins upon pastors the duty to explain their efficacy in plain and simple language.

Holiness and instruction. 12. These prescriptions of the Council of Trent have been summarized and still more clearly defined by Our Predecessor, Benedict XIV, in his Constitution *Etsi minime*. "Two chief obligations," he wrote, "have been imposed by the Council of Trent on those who have the care of souls: first, that of preaching the things of God to the people on the feast days; and second, that of teaching the rudiments of faith and of the divine law to the youth and others who need such instruction." Here the wise Pontiff rightly distinguishes between these two duties: one is what is commonly known as the explanation of the Gospel and the other is the teaching of Christian doctrine. Perhaps there are some who, wishing to lessen their labors, would believe that the homily on the Gospel can take the place of catechetical instruction. But for one who reflects a moment, such is obviously impossible. The sermon on the holy Gospel is addressed to those who should have already received knowledge of the elements of faith. It is, so to speak, bread broken for adults. Catechetical instruction, on the other hand, is that milk which the Apostle Peter wished the faithful to desire in all simplicity like newborn babes.

The task of the catechist. 13. The task of the catechist is to take up one or other of the truths of faith or of Christian morality and then explain it in all its parts; and since amendment of life is the chief aim of his instruction, the catechist must needs make a comparison between what God commands us to do and what is our actual conduct. After this, he will use examples appropriately taken from the Holy Scriptures, Church history, and the lives of the saints—thus moving his hearers and clearly pointing out to them how they are to regulate their own conduct. He should, in conclusion, earnestly exhort all present to dread and avoid vice and to practice virtue.

Primary of catechetical instruction. 14. We are indeed aware that the work of teaching the Catechism is unpopular with many because as a rule it is deemed of little account and for the reason that it does not lend itself easily to the winning of public praise. But this in Our opinion is a judgment based on vanity and devoid of truth. We do not disapprove of those pulpit orators who, out of genuine zeal for the glory of God, devote themselves to defense of the faith and to its spread, or who eulogize the saints of God. But their labor presupposes labor of another kind, that of the catechist. And so if this be lacking, then the foundation is wanting; and they labor in vain who build the house. Too often it happens that ornate sermons which receive the applause of crowded congregations serve but to tickle the ears and fail utterly to touch the hearts of the hearers. Catechetical instruction, on the other hand, plain and simple though it be, is the word of which God Himself speaks through the lips of the prophet Isaias: "And as the rain and the snow come down from heaven, and return no more thither, but soak the earth and water it, and make it to spring and give seed to the sower and bread to the eater: so shall my word be, which shall go forth from my mouth. It shall not return to me void, but it shall do whatsoever I please and shall prosper in the things for which I sent it."[17] We believe the same may be said of those priests who work hard to produce books which explain the truths of religion. They are surely to be commended for their zeal, but how many are there who read these works and take from them a fruit commensurate with the labor and intention of the writers? The teaching of the Catechism, on the other hand, when rightly done, never fails to profit those who listen to it.

Supernatural motives for the catechist. 15. In order to enkindle the zeal of the ministers of God, We again insist on the need to reach the ever-increasing numbers of those who know nothing at all of religion, or who possess at most only such knowledge of God and Christian truths as befits idolaters. How many there are, alas, not only among the young, but among adults and those advanced in years, who know nothing of the chief mysteries of faith; who on hearing the name of Christ can only ask? "Who is he . . . that I may believe in him?"[18] In consequence of this ignorance, they do not consider it a crime to excite and nourish hatred against their neighbor, to enter into most unjust contracts, to do business in dishonest fashion, to hold the funds of others at an exorbitant interest rate, and to commit other iniquities no less reprehensible. They are, moreover, ignorant of the law of Christ which not only condemns immoral actions but also forbids deliberate immoral thoughts and desires. Even when for some reason or other they avoid sensual pleasures, they nevertheless entertain evil thoughts without the least scruple, thereby multiplying their sins above the number of the hairs of the head. These persons are found, we deem it necessary to repeat, not merely among the poorer classes of the people or in sparsely settled districts, but also among those in the higher walks of life, even, indeed, among those puffed up with learning, who, relying upon a vain erudition, feel free to ridicule religion and to "deride whatever they do not know." [19]

God's grace demands man's cooperation. 16. Now, if we cannot expect to reap a harvest when no seed has been planted, how can we hope to have a people with sound morals if Christian doctrine has not been imparted to them in due time? It follows, too, that if faith languishes in our days, if among large numbers it has almost vanished, the reason is that the duty of catechetical teaching is either fulfilled very superficially or altogether neglected. It will not do to say, in excuse, that faith is a free gift of God bestowed upon each one at Baptism. True enough, when we are baptized in Christ, the habit of faith is given, but this most divine seed, if left entirely to itself, by its own power, so to speak, is not like the mustard seed which "grows up . . . and puts out great branches." [20] Man has the faculty of understanding at his birth, but he also has need of his mother's word to awaken it, as it were, and to make it active. So too, the Christian, born again of water and the Holy Spirit, has faith within him, but he requires the word of the teaching Church to nourish and develop it and to make it bear fruit. Thus wrote the Apostle: "Faith then depends on hearing, and hearing on the word of Christ"; [21] and to show the necessity of instruction, he added, "How are they to hear, if no one preaches?" [22]

Restore catechetical instruction. 17. What We have said so far demonstrates the supreme importance of religious instruction. We ought, therefore, to do all that lies in our power to maintain the teaching of Christian doctrine with full vigor, and where such is neglected, to restore it; for in the words of Our Predecessor, Benedict XIV, "There is nothing more effective than catechetical instruction to spread the glory of God and to secure the salvation of souls." [23]

Regulations to be universally observed. 18. We, therefore, Venerable Brethren, desirous of fulfilling this most important obligation of Our Teaching Office, and likewise wishing to introduce uniformity everywhere in so weighty a matter, do by Our Supreme Authority enact the following regulations and strictly command that they be observed and carried out in all dioceses of the world.

One hour weekly instruction for youth. 19. I. On every Sunday and holy day, with no exception, throughout the year, all parish priests and in general all those having the care of souls, shall instruct the boys and girls, for the space of an hour from the text of the Catechism on those things they must believe and do in order to attain salvation.

Preparation for the Sacraments. 20. II. At certain times throughout the year, they shall prepare boys and girls to receive properly the Sacraments of Penance and Confirmation, by a continued instruction over a period of days.

Lenten Eucharistic instruction. 21. III. With a very special zeal, on every day in Lent and, if necessary, on the days following Easter, they shall instruct with the use of apt illustrations and exhortations the youth of both sexes to receive their First Communion in a holy manner.

The Confraternity of Christian Doctrine. 22. IV. In each and every parish the society known as the Confraternity of Christian Doctrine is to be canonically established. Through this Confraternity, the pastors, especially in places where there is a scarcity of priests, will have lay helpers in the teaching of the Catechism, who will take up the work of imparting knowledge both from a zeal for the glory of God and in order to gain the numerous Indulgences granted by the Sovereign Pontiffs.

Release-time religious instruction. 23. V. In the larger cities, and especially where universities, colleges and secondary schools are located, let classes in religion be organized to instruct in the truths of faith and in the practice of Christian life the youths who attend the public schools from which all religious teaching is banned.

Adult catechetical instruction. 24. VI. Since it is a fact that in these days adults need instruction no less than the young, all pastors and those having the care of souls shall explain the Catechism to the people in a plain and simple style adapted to the intelligence of their hearers. This shall be carried out on all holy days of obligation, at such time as is most convenient for the people, but not during the same hour when the children are instructed, and this instruction must be in addition to the usual homily on the Gospel which is delivered at the parochial Mass on Sundays and holy days. The catechetical instruction shall be based on the Catechism of the Council of Trent; and the matter is to be divided in such a way that in the space of four or five years, treatment will be given to the Apostles' Creed, the Sacraments, the Ten Commandments, the Lord's Prayer and the Precepts of the Church.

Bishops are to carry out these regulations. 25. Venerable Brethren, We decree and command this by virtue of Our Apostolic Authority. It now rests with you to put it into prompt and complete execution in your respective dioceses, and by the power of your authority to see to it that these prescriptions of Ours be not neglected or, what amounts to the same thing, that they be not carried out carelessly or superficially. That this may be avoided, you must exhort and urge your pastors not to impart these instructions without having first prepared themselves in the work. Then they will not merely speak words of human wisdom, but "in simplicity and godly sincerity,"[24] imitating the example of Jesus Christ, Who, though He revealed "things hidden since the foundation of the world,"[25] yet spoke "all . . . things to the crowds in parables, and without parables . . . did not speak to them."[26] We know that the Apostles, who were taught by the Lord, did the same; for of them Pope Saint Gregory wrote: "They took supreme care to preach to the uninstructed simple truths easy to understand, not things deep and difficult."[27] In matters of religion, the majority of men in our times must be considered uninstructed.

Necessity of teacher's preparation. 26. We do not, however, wish to give the impression that this studied simplicity in imparting instruction does not require labor and meditation—on the contrary, it demands both more than any other kind of preaching. It is much easier to find a preacher capable of delivering an eloquent and elaborate discourse than a catechist who can impart a catechetical instruction which is praiseworthy in every detail. No matter what natural facility a person may have in ideas and language, let him always remember that he will never be able to teach Christian doctrine to children or to adults without first giving himself to very careful study and preparation. They are mistaken who think that because of inexperience and lack of training of the people the work of catechizing can be performed in a slipshod fashion. On the contrary, the less educated the hearers, the more zeal and diligence must be used to adapt the sublime truths to their untrained minds; these truths, indeed, far surpass the natural understanding of the people, yet must be known by all—the uneducated and the cultured—in order that they may arrive at eternal happiness.

Plea for united effort. 27. And now, Venerable Brethren, permit Us to close this letter by addressing to you these words of Moses: "If any man be on the Lord's side, let him join with me."[28] We pray and entreat you to reflect on the great loss of souls due solely to ignorance of divine things. You have doubtless accomplished many useful and most praiseworthy works in your respective dioceses for the good of the flock entrusted to your care, but before all else, and with all possible zeal and diligence and care, see to it and urge on others that the knowledge of Christian doctrine pervades and imbues fully and deeply the minds of all. Here, using the words of the Apostle Peter, We say, "According to the gift that each has received, administer it to one another as good stewards of the manifold grace of God."[29]

Apostolic Blessing. 28. Through the intercession of the Most Blessed Immaculate Virgin, may your diligent efforts be made fruitful by the Apostolic Blessing which, in token of Our affection and as a pledge of heavenly favors, We wholeheartedly impart to you and to your clergy and people.

29. Given at Rome, at Saint Peter's, on the fifteenth day of April, 1905, in the second year of Our Pontificate.

PIUS X, POPE

REFERENCES

1. Acts 20:29.
2. Osee 4:1–3.
3. *Instit.,* 27:18.
4. Eph. 5:3–4.
5. Eph. 5:15–16.
6. Ps. 4:7.
7. Rom. 13:13.
8. Matt. 18:4.
9. Jer. 3:15.
10. I Cor. 1:17.
11. Luke 4:18.
12. Mal. 2:7.
13. *Ibid.*
14. Roman Pontifical.
15. Eph. 4:14, 15.
16. *Sess. V, cap.* 2, *De Reform.; Sess. XXII, cap.* 8; *Sess. XXIV, cap.* 4 & 7, *De Reform.*
17. Is. 55:10–11.
18. John 9:36.
19. Jude 10.
20. Mark 4:32.
21. Rom. 10:17.
22. *Ibid.,* 14.
23. Constitution, *Etsi minime,* 13.
24. II Cor. 1:12.
25. Matt. 13:35.
26. *Ibid.,* 34.
27. *Morals,* I, 17, *cap.* 26.
28. Ex. 32:26.
29. I Pet. 4:10.

CHAPTER 5

Il Fermo Proposito *June 11, 1905, Catholic Action in Italy*

"ONE DAY when he was talking with a group of cardinals the Pope asked what they thought was the thing most necessary at the present time to save society.

" 'To build Catholic schools,' said one; 'To multiply churches,' said another, but the Pope shook his head at both answers, and also at a third suggestion, 'To increase the clergy.'

" 'No, no,' he said. 'What is most necessary at the present time is to have in every parish a group of laymen who are at the same time virtuous, well-instructed, determined, and really apostolic.' " *

The above incident which Miss Burton so charmingly relates is legendary to all acquainted with Saint Pius X. It also serves as an illustration of his purpose in writing the encyclical letter *Il Fermo Proposito.* Although it will be another Pius who will merit the title of "the Pope of Catholic Action," it will remain the glory of Saint Pius X that he was the first Supreme Pontiff to clarify the term "Catholic Action" and write "by far the longest and most detailed pronouncement on the subject which any Pope had ever written."

Those who would say that Saint Pius X was concerned only with spiritualities and "in other respects set the clock back" † have not had the opportunity of studying such documents as this chiefly because they have been so little known in English-speaking countries. Upon examining *Il Fermo Proposito,* however, one will immediately discern how far ahead of his time Saint Pius X really was in matters of social doctrine. Moreover, when his encyclical is placed alongside the *Motu Proprio* of December 18, 1903, ‡ and read with that latter document in mind, Saint Pius X stands in company

* Katherine Burton, *The Great Mantle* (New York, Longmans, Green and Co., 1950), pp. 179–180.

† John P. McKnight, *The Papacy, A New Appraisal* (New York, Rinehart & Co., Inc., 1952), p. 208.

‡ See pp. 207–211.

with Leo XIII and Pius XI as one of the great social teachers of modern times.

The encyclical calls for little explanation, so easily does its message read. After a somewhat lengthy introduction in which the Pope recalls his interest in Catholic Action, its definition, extension, and field of activity (1–10), he sets out to discuss the conditions Catholic Action imposes (11–12), its objectives (13–19) and its nature (20–23). He concludes by pointing out the relation of the clergy to Catholic Action (24–26) and appeals to the Bishops "to render an inestimable service to the cause" by their exhortations and paternal interest.

Two points stand out in the encyclical above all others. First, Saint Pius' insistence on the necessity of a well trained laity for this apostolate: "To carry it out rightly one must have divine grace, and the apostle receives it only if he is united to Christ. Only when he has formed Jesus Christ in himself shall he more easily be able to restore Him to the family and society. Therefore, all who are called upon to direct or dedicate themselves to the Catholic cause must be sound Catholics, firm in faith, solidly instructed in religious matters, truly submissive to the Church and especially to this supreme Apostolic See and the Vicar of Jesus Christ." Secondly, he lays down the requirement which must be joined to all their activity: " 'To restore all things in Christ' has always been the Church's motto, and it is especially Our Own during these fearful moments through which we are now passing. 'To restore all things'—not in any haphazard fashion, but 'in Christ'; and the Apostle adds, 'both those in the heavens and those on the earth.' "

Of special mention is Saint Pius X's idea of Catholic Action. The *Social Justice Review* (March, 1947) calls attention to *Il Fermo Proposito* with reference to the definition of Catholic Action which Pope Pius XII gave in his letter (*Siamo lieti*) to Cardinal Piazza. In the latter document Pope Pius XII defined Catholic Action in the following words: "Catholic Action is not an exclusive group, but a friendly legion of citizens who have made their own the maternal intention of the Church to redeem all, and to guarantee to society that irreplaceable and indispensable leaven of true culture." § One paper, the *Catholic News* of Port of Spain, Trinidad, called attention to this "new definition" of Catholic Action. If it was new at all, however, it was so only in the sense that it returned to the original idea of Catholic Action as in the mind of Saint Pius X. In *Il Fermo Proposito* the holy Pope defines Catholic Action in the following words: "The field of Catholic Action is extremely vast. In itself it does not exclude anything, in any manner, direct or indirect, which pertains to the divine mission of the Church. Accordingly

§ *Discorsi e Radiomessagi,* VIII (Rome, Tipografia Poliglotta Vaticana, 1947), pp. 465–469.

one can plainly see how necessary it is for everyone to cooperate in such an important work, not only for the sanctification of his own soul, but also for the extension and increase of the Kingdom of God in individuals, families, and society. . . ."

Il Fermo Proposito is timely. Beyond a shadow of a doubt it would be most worth while if all those engaged in the modern apostolate of "restoring all things in Christ" would take it in hand for serious study and meditation "so that divine grace may cause it to grow and prosper in a short time."

Il Fermo Proposito *Encyclical Letter of His Holiness Pope Pius X to the Bishops of Italy*

VENERABLE BRETHREN, HEALTH AND THE APOSTOLIC BLESSING:

United effort of Head and members. 1. The firm purpose and desire which We resolved upon at the beginning of Our Pontificate to consecrate all the energy which the good Lord deigns to grant Us in the work of restoring all things in Christ, reawakens in Our heart a great trust in the all powerful grace of God. Without that grace We can neither plan nor undertake anything great or fruitful for the good of souls here below. At the same time, however, We feel more than ever the need of being upheld unanimously and constantly in this venture both by you, Venerable Brethren, called to participate in Our pastoral office, as well as by all the clergy and faithful committed to your care. Truly, all of us in the Church are called to form that unique Body, whose Head is Christ; "closely joined," as the Apostle Paul teaches, "and knit together through every joint of the system according to the functioning in due measure of each single part." [1] In such a way the Body increases and gradually perfects itself in the bond of charity. Now, if in this work of "building up the body of Christ" [2] it is Our primary duty to teach, to point out the correct way to follow, to propose the means to be used, to admonish and paternally exhort, it is also the duty of Our beloved children, dispersed throughout the world, to heed Our words, to carry them out first of all in their own lives, and to aid in their effective fulfillment in others, each one according to the grace of God received, according to his state in life and duties, and according to the zeal which inflames his heart.

His interest in Catholic Action. 2. Here We wish to recall those numerous works of zeal for the good of the Church, society, and individuals under the general name of "Catholic Action," which by the grace of God flourish throughout the world as well as in Our Italy. You well know, Venerable Brethren, how dear they are to Us and how fervently We long to see them strengthened and promoted. Not only have We spoken to not a few of you on many occasions as well as to their special representatives in Italy when they presented Us with the homage of their devotion and filial affection, but We have also published, or have had published by Our authority, various acts of which you already know. It is true that some of these, as the circumstances—truly sorrowful for Us—demanded, were directed at removing obstacles which hindered the progress of Catholic Action and caused great harm, by undisciplined tendencies, to the common good. For that reason We hesitated to offer a paternal word of comfort and encouragement to all throughout the world, in order that, only after We had removed as much as We possibly could all dangers throughout the world, the good would be able to increase and spread abroad. We are now, therefore, very happy to do so by this present letter in order to encourage everyone, for We are certain that Our words will be heard in a spirit of docility and obeyed by all.

Universality of Catholic Action. 3. The field of Catholic Action is extremely vast. In itself it does not exclude anything, in any manner, direct or indirect, which pertains to the divine mission of the Church. Accordingly one can plainly see how necessary it is for everyone to cooperate in such an important work, not only for the sanctification of his own soul, but also for the extension and increase of the Kingdom of God in individuals, families, and society; each one working according to his energy for the good of his neighbor by the propagation of revealed truth, by the exercise of Christian virtues, by the exercise of the corporal and spiritual works of mercy. Such is the conduct worthy of God to which Saint Paul exhorts us, so as to please Him in all things, bringing forth fruits of all good works, and increasing in the knowledge of God. "May you walk worthily of God and please him in all things, bearing fruit in every good work and growing in the knowledge of God." [3]

The Church, Guardian of civilization. 4. Over and above spiritual goods, however, there are many goods of the natural order over which the Church has no direct mission, although they flow as a natural consequence from her divine mission. The light of Catholic revelation is of such a nature that it diffuses itself with the greatest brilliance on every science. The force of the evangelical counsels is so powerful that it strengthens and firmly establishes the precepts of the natural law. The fruitfulness of the doctrine and morality taught by Jesus Christ is so limitless that providentially it sustains and promotes the material welfare of the individual, the family, and society. The Church, even in preaching Jesus Christ crucified, "stumbling-block and foolishness to the world," has become the foremost leader and protector of civilization. She brought it wherever her apostles preached. She preserved and protected the good elements of the ancient pagan civilizations, disentangling from barbarism and educating for a new civilization the peoples who flocked to her maternal bosom. She endowed every civilization, gradually, but with a certain and always progressive step, with that excellent mark which is today universally preserved. The civilization of the world is Christian. The more completely Christian it is, the more true, more lasting and more productive of genuine fruit it is. On the other hand, the further it draws away from the Christian ideal, the more seriously the social order is endangered. By the very nature of things, the Church has consequently become the guardian and protector of Christian society. That fact was universally recognized and admitted in other periods of history. In truth, it formed a solid foundation for civil legislation. On that very fact rested the relations between Church and State; the public recognition of the authority of the Church in those matters which touched upon conscience in any manner, the subordination of all the laws of the State to the Divine laws of the Gospel; the harmony of the two powers in securing the temporal welfare of the people in such a way that their eternal welfare did not suffer.

A godless society. 5. We have no need to tell you, Venerable Brethren, what prosperity and well-being, what peace and harmony, what respectful subjection to authority and what excellent government would be obtained and maintained in the world if one could see in practice the perfect ideal of Christian civilization. Granting, however, the continual battle of the flesh against the spirit, darkness against light, Satan against God, such cannot be hoped for, at least in all its fullness. Hence, raids are continually being made on the peaceful conquests of the Church. The sadness and pain these cause is accentuated by the fact that society tends more and more to be governed by principles opposed to that very Christian ideal, and is even in danger of completely falling away from God.

Civilization must be restored in Christ. 6. This fact, however, is no reason to lose courage. The Church well knows that the gates of hell will not prevail against her. Furthermore, she knows that she will be sorely afflicted; that her apostles are sent as lambs among wolves; that her followers will always bear the brunt of hatred and contempt, just as her Divine Founder received hatred and contempt. So the Church advances unafraid, spreading the Kingdom of God wherever she preaches and studying every possible means she can use in regaining the losses in the Kingdom already conquered. "To restore all things in Christ" has always been the Church's motto, and it is especially Our Own during these fearful moments through which we are now passing. "To restore all things"—not in any haphazard fashion, but "in Christ"; and the Apostle adds, "both those in the heavens and those on the earth."[4] "To restore all things in Christ" includes not only what properly pertains to the divine mission of the Church, namely, leading souls to God, but also what We have already explained as flowing from that divine mission, namely, Christian civilization in each and every one of the elements composing it.

Objectives of lay action. 7. Since We particularly dwell on this last part of the desired restoration, you clearly see, Venerable Brethren, the services rendered to the Church by those chosen bands of Catholics who aim to unite all their forces in combatting anti-Christian civilization by every just and lawful means. They use every means in repairing the serious disorders caused by it. They seek to restore Jesus Christ to the family, the school and society by re-establishing the principle that human authority represents the authority of God. They take to heart the interests of the people, especially those of the working and agricultural classes, not only by inculcating in the hearts of everybody a true religious spirit (the only true fount of consolation among the troubles of this life) but also by endeavoring to dry their tears, to alleviate their sufferings, and to improve their economic condition by wise measures. They strive, in a word, to make public laws conformable to justice and amend or suppress those which are not so. Finally, they defend and support in a true Catholic spirit the rights of God in all things and the no less sacred rights of the Church.

Catholic Action is servant of the Church. 8. All these works, sustained and promoted chiefly by lay Catholics and whose form varies according to the needs of each country, constitute what is generally known by a distinctive and surely a very noble name: "Catholic Action," or the "Action of Catholics." At all times it came to the aid of the Church, and the Church has always cherished and blessed such help, using it in many ways according to the exigencies of the age.

New means for new times. 9. In passing it is well to remark that it is impossible today to re-establish under the same form all the institutions which have been useful and even the only effective ones in past centuries, so numerous are the radical transformations that time introduces into society and public life, and so numerous the new needs which changing circumstances keep producing. But the Church in its long history and on every occasion has wisely shown that she possesses the marvellous power of adapting herself to the changing conditions of civil society. Thus, while preserving the integrity and immutability of faith and morals and upholding her sacred rights, she easily bends and accommodates herself to all the unessential and accidental circumstances belonging to various stages of civilization and to the new requirements of civil society.

Outline of what will follow. 10. "Godliness," says Saint Paul, "is profitable in all respects, since it has the promise of the present life as well as of that which is to come." [5] Even though Catholic Action changes in its external forms and in the means that it adapts, it always remains the same in the principles that direct it and the noble goal that it pursues. In order that Catholic Action may reach its goal, it is important to consider at this point the conditions it imposes, its nature and its goal.

The apostle must be a man of virtue. 11. Above all, one must be firmly convinced that the instrument is of little value if it is not adapted to the work at hand. In regard to the things We mentioned above, Catholic Action, inasmuch as it proposes to restore all things in Christ, constitutes a real apostolate for the honor and glory of Christ Himself. To carry it out right one must have divine grace, and the apostle receives it only if he is united to Christ. Only when he has formed Jesus Christ in himself shall he more easily be able to restore Him to the family and society. Therefore, all who are called upon to direct or dedicate themselves to the Catholic cause must be sound Catholics, firm in faith, solidly instructed in religious matters, truly submissive to the Church and especially to this supreme Apostolic See and the Vicar of Jesus Christ. They must be men of real piety, of manly virtue, and of a life so chaste and fearless that they will be a guiding example to all others. If they are not so formed it will be difficult to arouse others to do good and practically impossible to act with a good intention. The strength needed to persevere in continually bearing the weariness of every true apostolate will fail. The calumnies of enemies, the coldness and frightfully little cooperation of even good men, sometimes even the jealousy of friends and fellow workers (excusable, undoubtedly, on account of the weakness of human nature, but also harmful and a cause of discord, offense and quarrels)—all these will weaken the apostle who lacks divine grace. Only virtue, patient and firm and at the same time mild and tender, can remove or diminish these difficulties in such a way that the works undertaken by Catholic forces will not be compromised. The will of God, Saint Peter wrote the early Christians, is that by your good works you silence the foolish. "For such is the will of God, that by doing good you should put to silence the ignorance of foolish men."[6]

The field of Catholic Action. 12. It is also important to define clearly the works which the Catholic forces must energetically and constantly undertake. These works must be of such evident importance that they will be appreciated by everybody. They must bear such a relation to the needs of modern society and be so well adapted to moral and material interests, especially those of the people and the poorer classes, that, while arousing in promoters of Catholic Action the greatest activity for obtaining the important and certain results which are to be looked for, they may also be readily understood and gladly welcomed by all. Since the serious problems of modern social life demand a prompt and definite solution, everyone is anxious to know and understand the different ways in which these solutions can be put into practice. Discussions of one kind or another are more and more numerous and rapidly published by the press. It is, therefore, of the greatest importance that Catholic Action seize the present moment and courageously propose its own solution, strengthening it by means of solid propaganda which at the same time will be active, intelligent, disciplined and organized against all erroneous doctrine. The goodness and justice of Christian principles, the true morality which Catholics profess, their evident unconcern for their own welfare while wishing nothing but the supreme good of others, and their open and sincere ability to foster better than all others the true economic interests of the people—these qualities cannot fail to make an impression on the minds and hearts of all who hear them, and to swell their ranks so as to form a strong and compact corps, capable of boldly resisting the opposing current and of commanding the respect of their enemies.

Objective of Catholic Action. 13. Our Predecessor, Leo XIII, of blessed memory, has pointed out, especially in that memorable encyclical *Rerum Novarum* and in later documents, the object to which Catholic Action should be particularly devoted, namely, *the practical solution of the social question according to Christian principles.* Following these wise rules, We Ourselves in Our *Motu Proprio* of December 18, 1903, concerning Popular Christian Action—which in itself embraces the whole Catholic social movement—We Ourselves have laid down fundamental principles which should serve as a practical rule of action as well as a bond of harmony and charity. On these documents, therefore, and within their most holy and necessary scope, Catholic Action, although varied and multiple in form while directed toward the same social good, must be regulated and united.

Union born of common understanding. 14. In order that this social action may continue and prosper by a necessary union of the various activities comprising it, Catholics above all must preserve a spirit of peace and harmony which can come only from a unity in understanding. On this point there cannot exist the least shadow or peradventure of a doubt, so clear and obvious are the teachings handed down by this Apostolic See, so brilliant is the light which most illustrious Catholics of every country have spread by their writings, so praiseworthy is the example of Catholics of other countries who, because of this harmony and unity of understanding, in a short time have reaped an abundant harvest.

Union of the Catholic forces. 15. To arrive at this end, in some places several of these praiseworthy works have called into being an institution of a general character which goes by the name of the "Popular Union." Experience has shown that this has been most effective. The purpose of the Popular Union has been to gather all Catholics, and especially the masses, around a common center of doctrine, propaganda, and social organization. Since, in fact, it answers a need felt in almost every country and its constitution is founded upon the very nature of things, it cannot be said to belong any more to one nation than another, but is suitable to every place where the same needs are present and the same dangers arise. Its extremely popular character causes it to be most desirable and acceptable. It neither disturbs nor hinders the work of existing institutions but, on the contrary, increases their strength and efficiency. Because of its strictly personal organization, it spurs individuals to enter particular institutions, training them to perform practical and useful work, and uniting them all together in one common aim and desire.

Praise for the Italian Popular Union. 16. Once the social center is thus established, all other institutions of an economic character concerned in various ways with the social problem will find themselves spontaneously united by their common end. At the same time, however, they will preserve their own individual structure, and in providing various needs they will still remain within the boundaries which their sphere of influence demands. At this point We are pleased to express Our satisfaction with the great good which in this regard has already been accomplished in Italy, and We feel certain that, with the help of God, much more will be done by this kind of zeal in the future to strengthen and increase the good already accomplished. The work of the Catholic Congresses and Committees is of singular merit, thanks to the intelligent activity of those capable men who plan and direct them. Such economic centers and unions, however, as We have previously stated at the end of the above-mentioned Congresses, must continue to carry on in the same way and under the same expert direction.

Catholic Action must use all means. 17. For Catholic Action to be most effective it is not enough that it adapt itself to social needs only. It must also employ all those practical means which the findings of social and economic studies place in its hands. It must profit from the experience gained elsewhere. It must be vitally aware of the conditions of civil society, and the public life of states. Otherwise it runs the risk of wasting time in searching for novelties and hazardous theories while overlooking the good, safe and tried means at hand. Again, perhaps it may propose institutions and methods belonging to other times but no longer understood by the people of the present day. Or, finally, it may go only half way, failing to use, in the measure in which they are granted, those civil rights which modern constitutions today offer all, and therefore also Catholics. In particular, the present constitution of states offers indiscriminately to all the right to influence public opinion, and Catholics, with due respect for the obligations imposed by the law of God and the precepts of the Church, can certainly use this to their advantage. In such a way they can prove themselves as capable as others (in fact, more capable than others) by cooperating in the material and civil welfare of the people. In so doing they shall acquire that authority and prestige which will make them capable of defending and promoting a higher good, namely, that of the soul.

Civil rights in Italy. 18. These civil rights are of various kinds, even to the extent of directly participating in the political life of the country by representing the people in the legislative halls. Most serious reasons, however, dissuade Us, Venerable Brethren, from departing from that norm which Our Predecessor, Leo XIII, of blessed memory, decreed during his Pontificate. According to his decree it was universally forbidden in Italy for Catholics to participate in the legislative power. Other reasons equally grave, however, founded upon the supreme good of society which must be preserved at all costs demand that in particular cases a dispensation from the law be granted especially when you, Venerable Brethren, recognize the strict necessity of it for the good of souls and the interests of your churches, and you request such a dispensation.

Obligation follows privilege. 19. This concession places a duty on all Catholics to prepare themselves prudently and seriously for political life in case they may be called to it. Hence it is of the utmost importance that the same activity (previously so praiseworthily planned by Catholics for the purpose of preparing themselves by means of good electoral organization for the administrative life of common and provincial councils) be extended to a suitable preparation and organization for political life. This was already recommended by the Circular of December 3, 1904, issued by the general Presidency of Economic Works in Italy. At the same time the other principles which regulate the conscience of every true Catholic must be inculcated and put into practice. Above all else he must remember to be and to act in every circumstance as a true Catholic, accepting and fulfilling public offices with the firm and constant resolution of promoting by every means the social and economic welfare of the country and particularly of the people, according to the maxims of a truly Christian civilization, and at the same time defending the supreme interests of the Church, which are those of religion and justice.

Catholic Action demands a united effort. 20. Such, Venerable Brethren, are the characteristics, the aim and conditions of Catholic Action, considered in its most important function, namely, the solution of the social question. For that reason it demands the most energetic attention of all the Catholic forces. By no means, however, does this exclude the existence of other activities nor does it mean that other organizations should not flourish and be promoted, for each one is directed to different particular goods of society and of the people. All are united in the work of restoring Christian civilization under its various aspects. These works, rising out of the zeal of particular persons, spreading throughout many dioceses, are sometimes grouped into federations. Since the end they foster is praiseworthy, the Christian principles they follow solid, and the means they adopt just, they are to be praised and encouraged in every way. At the same time, they must be permitted a certain freedom of organization (since it is impossible for so many people to be formed in the same mould and placed under the same direction). Organization, therefore, must arise spontaneously from the works themselves, otherwise it will only be an ephemeral building of fine architecture, but lacking a solid foundation and therefore quite unstable. Particular characteristics of different people must also be taken into consideration. Different uses, different tendencies are found in different places. It is of primary importance that the work be built on a good foundation of solid principles and maintained with earnestness and constancy. If this is the case, the method used and the form the various works take will be accidental.

Congresses will aid the cause of unity. 21. In order to renew and increase in all the Catholic works necessary enthusiasm; in order to offer an occasion for the promoters and members of these works to see each other and become better acquainted; in order to strengthen the bond of charity, to inspire one another with a greater zeal for fruitful activity, and to provide for the greater solidity and propagation of the works themselves, it will be very useful from time to time to hold general and particular Congresses of Italian Catholics, according to the norms already laid down by this Holy See. These Congresses, however, must be a solemn manifestation of the Catholic Faith and a festival of mutual harmony and peace.

Catholic Action is subordinate to the Bishop. 22. We must touch, Venerable Brethren, on another point of extreme importance, namely, the relation of all the works of Catholic Action to ecclesiastical authority. If the teachings unfolded in the first part of this letter are thoughtfully considered it will be readily seen that all those works which directly come to the aid of the spiritual and pastoral ministry of the Church and which labor religiously for the good of souls must in every least thing be subordinated to the authority of the Church and also to the authority of the Bishops placed by the Holy Spirit to rule the Church of God in the dioceses assigned to them. Moreover, the other works which, as We have said, are primarily designed for the restoration and promotion of true Christian civilization and which, as explained above, constitute Catholic Action, by no means may be considered as independent of the counsel and direction of ecclesiastical authority, especially since they must all conform to the principles of Christian faith and morality. At the same time it is impossible to imagine them as in opposition, more or less openly, to that same authority. Such works, however, by their very nature, should be directed with a reasonable degree of freedom, since responsible action is especially theirs in the temporal and economic affairs as well as in those matters of public administration and political life. These affairs are alien to the purely spiritual ministry. Since Catholics, on the other hand, are to raise always the banner of Christ, by that very fact they also raise the banner of the Church. Thus it is no more than right that they receive it from the hands of the Church, that the Church guard its immaculate honor, and that Catholics submit as docile, loving children to this maternal vigilance.

Insubordination in Italy. 23. For these reasons it is evident how terribly wrong those few were who in Italy, and under Our very eyes, wanted to undertake a mission which they received neither from Us nor from any of Our Brethren in the episcopate. They promoted it not only without due homage to authority but even openly against the will of that authority, seeking to rationalize their disobedience by foolish distinctions. They said that they were undertaking their cause in the name of Christ; but such a cause could not be Christ's since it was not built on the doctrine of the Divine Redeemer. How truly these words apply: "He who hears you, hears me; and he who rejects you, rejects me."[7] "He who is not with me is against me; and he who does not gather with me scatters." This is a doctrine of humility, submission, filial respect. With extreme regret We had to condemn this tendency and halt by Our authority this pernicious movement which was rapidly gaining momentum. Our sorrow was increased when We saw many young people of excellent character and fervent zeal and capable of performing much good if properly directed, and who are also very dear to Us, carelessly attracted to such an erroneous program.

A danger to the clergy. 24. While pointing out the true nature of Catholic Action, Venerable Brethren, We cannot minimize the grave danger to which the clergy may find themselves exposed because of the conditions of the time. They may attach such importance to the material interests of the people that they will forget those more important duties of the sacred ministry.

The priest and Catholic Action. 25. The priest, raised above all men in order to accomplish the mission he has from God, must also remain above all human interests, all conflicts, all classes of society. His proper field of action is the Church. There, as ambassador of God, he preaches the truth, teaching along with respect for the rights of God respect also for the rights of every creature. In such a work he neither exposes himself to any opposition nor appears as a man of factions, ally to one group and adversary to others. In such a way he will not place himself in the danger of dissimulating the truth, of keeping silence in the conflict of certain tendencies, or of irritating exasperated souls by repeated arguments. In all these cases he would fail in his real duty. It is unnecessary to add that while treating so often of material affairs he may find himself obligated to perform tasks harmful to himself and to the dignity of his office. He may take part in these associations, therefore, only after mature deliberation, with the consent of his Bishop, and then only in those cases when his assistance will be free from every danger and will be obviously useful.

Catholic Action helps the clergy. 26. This does not diminish his zeal. The true apostle must make himself "all things to all men"[9] in order to save all. Like the Divine Redeemer, he ought to be moved with compassion, "seeing the crowds . . . bewildered and dejected, like sheep without a shepherd."[10] By means of the printed and spoken word, by direct participation in the above-mentioned cases, he can labor on behalf of the people according to the principles of justice and charity by favoring and promoting those institutions which propose to protect the masses from the invasion of Socialism, saving them at the same time from both economic ruin and moral and religious chaos. In this way the assistance of the clergy in the works of Catholic Action has a truly religious purpose. It will then not be a hindrance, but rather a help, to the spiritual ministry by enlarging its sphere and multiplying its results.

Catholic Action, a source of comfort. 27. You see now, Venerable Brethren, how much We have desired to explain and inculcate these principles concerning Catholic Action which is to be sustained and promoted in Italy. It is not sufficient to point out the good; it also must be put into practice. Your own exhortations and paternal interest will render an inestimable service to the cause. Although the beginnings are humble, as is the case in all beginnings, divine grace will cause it to grow and prosper in a short time. All Our children who dedicate themselves to Catholic Action should once again listen to the advice which arises so spontaneously from Our heart. Amid the bitter sorrows which daily surround Us, We will say with Saint Paul, "if . . . there is any comfort in Christ, any encouragement from charity, any fellowship in the Spirit, any feelings of mercy, fill up my joy by thinking alike, having the same charity, with one soul and one mind. Do nothing out of contentiousness or out of vainglory, but in humility let each one regard the others as his superiors, each one looking not to his own interests but to those of others. Have this mind in you which was also in Christ Jesus."[11] Let Him be the beginning of all your undertakings: "Whatever you do in word or in work, do all in the name of the Lord Jesus Christ."[12] Let Him be the end of your every word: "For from him and through him and unto him are all things. To him be the glory forever."[13] On this day which is so reminiscent of that when the Apostles, full of the Holy Spirit, went out of the Cenacle to preach to the world the Kingdom of Christ, may the power of that same Spirit descend upon all of you. "May He bend whatever is rigid, inflame whatever has grown cold, and bring back whatever has gone astray."[14]

Apostolic Blessing. 28. May the Apostolic Blessing which We impart from the bottom of Our heart to you, Venerable Brethren, and your clergy and the Italian people, be a sign of divine favor and a pledge of Our very special affection.

29. Given at Saint Peter's, Rome, on the Feast of Pentecost, June 11, 1905, the second year of Our Pontificate.

Pius X, Pope

REFERENCES

1. Eph. 4:16.
2. Eph. 4:12.
3. Col. 1:10.
4. Eph. 1:10.
5. I Tim. 4:8.
6. I Pet. 2:15.
7. Luke 10:16.
8. Luke 11:23.
9. I Cor. 9:22.
10. Matt. 9:36.
11. Phil. 2:1–5.
12. Col. 3:17.
13. Rom. 11:36.
14. *Veni Sancte Spiritus,* Sequence of the Mass of Pentecost.

CHAPTER 6

Tribus Circiter *April 5, 1906, The Mariavites of Poland*

WITHOUT a doubt none of the public documents of Saint Pius X so openly reveals his paternal heart as *Tribus Circiter*. It deals with the age-old problem of extremes that Mother Church frequently meets on her journey through time. At one time it may be the Manicheans, at another the Illuminati. For Saint Pius X it was the Mariavites, or Mystic Priests, of Poland.

The encyclical is clear and to the point. After describing the organization, works, insubordination and folly of the Mariavites (1–5), Saint Pius X tells how he dealt kindly with their representatives because "We felt that the priests in question were blinded more from ignorance and delusion than conscious pride" (6). In spite of his clemency and their promise of amendment, the Mariavites remained obstinate in their disobedience toward their Bishops, for "their profession of fidelity to the Vicar of Christ . . . has no value if they continue to violate the authority of their Bishops" (7–11). For the welfare of the Church, therefore, the Pope once again confirms "that decree in which the Mariavite society, unlawfully and invalidly founded, is entirely suppressed, and We now declare it suppressed and condemned" (12–14).

As simply and directly as that, Saint Pius X met the problem. He minced no words; he concealed nothing. He simply let the truth speak for itself.

Although the encyclical deals with a particular problem in a particular country, its message has universal value. Every country, at one time or another, has its societies similar to the Mariavites: people desiring to be "more Catholic than the Church," people proclaiming that the Church "has fallen from Truth and Justice and therefore had been abandoned by the Holy Spirit," people demanding that "they are to be free from all restrictions of ecclesiastical or human law and customs, and every other ecclesiastical and human power."

In such circumstances and with such people Saint Pius X teaches us how to conduct ourselves. Perhaps in the back of his mind was the great Ciceronian dictum quoted by his predecessor, Leo XIII: "The first law of history is, not to dare to utter falsehood; the second, not to fear to speak the truth; and, moreover, no room must be left for suspicion of partiality or prejudice."

Moreover, he was not unfamiliar with the obligations of Christian charity. *Tribus Circiter* breathes an air of sympathetic, understanding, paternal charity. Although he was forced to act as a pastor charged with the task of driving the wolves away from the flock, Saint Pius X was never for a moment unconscious of his commitment as the universal father, bound to receive the prodigal with open arms and fatherly tenderness.

Tribus Circiter is a literary counterpart of the incident Cardinal Merry del Val relates as an example of the Pope's "fatherly affection." Perhaps this was the very case the Cardinal alludes to; at any rate, it was similar.

"I can well remember how one morning the Holy Father confided to me that he was about to receive in audience a person who had very grievously erred and had betrayed his sacred duty. It was a sad story. The Pope's direct intervention had become inevitable, for the delinquent had thrown off all restraint and seemed little inclined to repent or accept correction. I found His Holiness looking very sad and tired. He acknowledged to me that he had spent a restless night thinking over the approaching interview and the necessity of his speaking with the utmost severity. He was however determined to carry the matter through, he said, but it would cost him a great deal, for he realized what a blow it would undoubtedly be for the unfortunate culprit. 'Say a Hail Mary for me, Eminence,' he added, 'in order that God may bless this audience and that the poor fellow may not rebel and force me to go further.'

"A few hours later the Holy Father was beaming with joy. 'Do you know, all went well,' he exclaimed, with a smile. 'The unhappy man ended by acknowledging the truth of all I said. I did not spare him, but, thank God, he has submitted and now we must do what we can to help him on.'" *

* Cardinal Merry del Val, *Memories of Pope Pius X* (Westminster, Newman Press, 1951), p. 31.

Tribus Circiter *Encyclical Letter of Our Holy Father Pius X to Our Venerable Brethren, the Archbishop of Warsaw and the Bishops of Plotsk and Lubin among the Poles*

VENERABLE BRETHREN, HEALTH AND THE APOSTOLIC BLESSING:

The Mariavites. 1. About three years ago the Apostolic See was properly informed that some of your diocesan priests, especially among the junior clergy, had founded without the permission of their lawful superiors a kind of pseudomonastic society, known as the *Mariavites,* or *Mystic Priests.* The members of this society have gradually turned away from the right road and the obedience they owe their Bishops, whom the Holy Spirit has placed to rule the Church of God, and seem to have become a law unto themselves.

Head of the Mariavites. 2. Without the least hesitation they unreservedly entrusted themselves to a certain woman who, they say, is most holy, marvellously endowed with heavenly gifts, divinely enlightened about many things, and providentially given to a world about to perish. They obey every wish of this woman.

Works of the Mariavites. 3. Relying on an alleged mandate from God and purely on their own initiative, they engage indiscriminately in promoting frequent exercises of piety among the people, especially adoration of the Most Blessed Sacrament and the practice of frequent Communion. (When rightly carried out, this is a very commendable work.) At the same time, however, they level very serious charges against every priest or Bishop who ventures to express any doubt about the sanctity and divine election of this woman, or show any ill-feeling toward the society of the Mariavites. Conditions reached such a peak that there was reason to fear that many of the faithful in their delusion were about to abandon their lawful pastors.

Insubordination of the Mariavites. 4. Accordingly, upon the advice of Our Venerable Brethren, the Cardinals of the General Inquisition, as you are well aware, We had a decree issued on September 4, 1904, suppressing the above-mentioned society of priests, and commanding them to have absolutely nothing to do with this woman. The priests in question, however, notwithstanding the fact that they signed a document expressing their subjection to the authority of their Bishops and that perhaps they did, as they say they did, partly break off relations with this woman, still, they did not abandon their undertaking and sincerely renounce the condemned association. Rather, they condemned your counsels and restraints. Many of them signed an audacious declaration rejecting communion with their Bishops. In more than one place, they incited the deluded people to drive away their lawful pastors. Over and above all that, like the enemies of the Church, they asserted that she had fallen from Truth and Justice, and therefore had been abandoned by the Holy Spirit. They further say that they alone, the Mariavite priests, are divinely called to instruct the faithful in true piety.

Petition of the Mariavites. 5. That is not all. A few weeks ago two of these priests, Roman Prochniewski and Joannes Kowalski, came to Rome. The latter is recognized, in virtue of some kind of delegation from this woman, as the superior by all the members of the society. In a petition they say was written under the express command of Our Lord Jesus Christ, both of them asked the Supreme Pastor of the Church, or the Congregation of the Holy Office in his name, to issue a document expressed in the following words: "Maria Francesca (the woman mentioned above) has been made most holy by God. She is the mother of mercy for all men called and elected to salvation by God in these days. All Mariavite priests are commanded by God to promote throughout the world devotion to the Most Blessed Sacrament and the Blessed Virgin Mary of Perpetual Help. In this work they are to be free from all restrictions of ecclesiastical or human law and customs, and every other ecclesiastical and human power. . . ."

The action of the Pope. 6. After reading these words We felt that the priests in question were blinded more from ignorance and delusion than conscious pride. They were, We felt, like the false prophets of whom Ezechiel wrote: "They see vain things and they foretell lies, saying: The Lord saith: whereas the Lord hath not sent them. And they have persisted to confirm what they have said. Have you not seen a vain vision and spoken a lying divination? And you say: The Lord saith: whereas I have not spoken."[1] Receiving them mercifully, We urged them to forget the folly of vain revelations and sincerely conform their lives and actions to the salutary authority of their superiors. We exhorted them to hasten the return of Christ's faithful to the safe path of obedience and reverence toward their pastors. Finally, Venerable Brethren, We asked them to let the vigilance of the Apostolic See and other competent authorities confirm those pious customs which would be most suitable for a greater increase of the Christian life in the many parishes of your dioceses. At the same time that same vigilance would take care to admonish those priests found guilty of abusively or contemptuously speaking about devout practices and exercises approved by the Church. We were deeply moved when the two priests, touched by Our paternal kindness, threw themselves at Our feet and expressed their firm resolve to fulfill Our wishes with filial devotion. Our hope that these deceived sons had sincerely abandoned their past delusions and returned to the right road increased when they handed Us the following written statement:[2]

Statement of the Mariavites. 7. "Always ready to fulfill the will of

God, which His Vicar has now made known to us [these are their words], we most sincerely and joyfully revoke our letter of the first of February of the present year to the Archbishop of Warsaw in which we declared ourselves separated from him. Moreover, we most sincerely and with the greatest joy profess that we always wish to be united to our Bishops, and especially the Archbishop of Warsaw, to that extent which Your Holiness commands us. Furthermore, since we are representatives of all the Mariavites, we make this profession of complete obedience and subjection not only in the name of all the Mariavites but also of all the Adorers of the Most Blessed Sacrament. We make this profession especially in the name of the Mariavites of Plotsk who, for the same reason as the Mariavites of Warsaw, gave their Bishop a declaration of separation from him. All of us without exception, therefore, prostrate at the feet of Your Holiness, professing over and over again our love and obedience to the Holy See and especially Your Holiness, and most humbly ask pardon for any pain we may have caused Your paternal heart. Finally, we declare that we shall immediately begin to work unceasingly in restoring peace between the people and the Bishops. In fact, we can affirm that this peace will very soon be a reality."

Hope for improvement. 8. It was a source of great joy for Us, therefore, to rest in the belief that these sons whom We so graciously pardoned would give evidence of their promises as soon as they returned to Poland. For that reason, Venerable Brethren, since they professed complete obedience to your authority, We immediately advised you to receive them and their companions mercifully, and, if their actions agreed with their promises, to grant them once again the faculties for exercising their sacerdotal ministry according to the law.

Recalcitrance of the priests. 9. Events, however, belied that hope. We have learned from recent documents that they have again opened their minds to deceitful revelations. Further, since their return to Poland, they have not only refused to tender you, Venerable Brethren, that respect and obedience they promised, but they have actually written their companions a letter quite contrary to truth and genuine obedience.

Authority of the Episcopacy. 10. Their profession of fidelity to the Vicar of Christ, however, has no value if they continue to violate the authority of their Bishops. As Our Predecessor of holy memory, Leo XIII, wrote in his letter of December 17, 1888, to the Archbishop of Turin, "the Bishops are the most noble part of the Church inasmuch as by divine right they teach and rule men. Whoever, therefore, resists them, or obstinately refuses to obey them sets himself apart from the Church. . . . On the other hand, to judge or criticize the acts of Bishops is in no manner the prerogative of individuals but, rather, a duty that falls within the province of their higher authorities, and especially the Supreme Pontiff, since Christ charged him to feed not only His lambs but also His sheep throughout the world. At most, in matters of serious complaint it is permitted to refer the whole case to the Roman Pontiff. Zeal for the common good demands that this be done prudently and moderately, and not clamorously or abusively. By the latter way dissension and hostility are either created or certainly increased."[3]

Their acts belie their words. 11. Thus the exhortation Father Joannes Kowalski addressed to his companions in error in behalf of peace is idle and deceitful as long as he persists in his foolish talk and incitements to rebellion against legitimate pastors, boldly violating the commands of the Bishops.

Suppression of the Mariavites. 12. Therefore, in order that the faithful of Christ and all the so-called Mariavite priests who are in good faith may no longer be led astray by the delusions of the above-mentioned woman and Father Joannes Kowalski, We once again confirm that decree in which the Mariavite society, unlawfully and invalidly founded, is entirely suppressed, and We now declare it suppressed and condemned. Furthermore, We proclaim that prohibition still remains in force which forbids all priests (excepting the one whom the Bishop of Plotsk shall prudently deputize as her confessor) to have anything to do with that woman on any pretext.

Directions for the Bishops. 13. We earnestly exhort you, Venerable Brethren, to embrace with paternal charity the priests who have erred as soon as they sincerely repent. When they have proven themselves truly worthy, do not refuse to take them under your direction once again and let them perform their priestly duties. If (God forbid!) they reject your exhortations and persevere in their contumacy, then it will be Our duty to deal with them severely. Strive to lead the faithful of Christ, who now labor under a pardonable delusion, back to the right path. In your dioceses foster those practices of piety, either recently or long since approved in many documents issued by the Apostolic See. Do this zealously since now, through the blessings of God, your priests can perform their ministry and the faithful imitate the piety of their forefathers.

Apostolic Blessing. 14. As a promise of heavenly gifts and a testimony of Our paternal affection, We impart most lovingly in the Lord to you, Venerable Brethren, and all the clergy and people committed to your care and vigilance the Apostolic Blessing.

15. Given at Saint Peter's, Rome, on April 5, 1906, in the third year of Our Pontificate.

PIUS X, POPE

REFERENCES

1. Ezech. 13:6–7.
2. On February 20, of that year.
3. Cf. *ASS,* 21:321 ff.

CHAPTER 7

Pieni L'Animo *July 28, 1906, The Clergy in Italy*

UNDOUBTEDLY no thought so constantly preoccupied the attention of Saint Pius X as the necessity of a holy and wholesome clergy. Every encyclical letter alludes to the clergy, the need of a holy clergy, the work of a zealous clergy. His solicitude for the clergy is climaxed on the occasion of his own golden sacerdotal jubilee in his personal exhortation to the clergy, *Haerent Animo.*

On July 28, 1906, he addressed his eighth encyclical to his brothers in the Episcopacy on the dangers besetting the Italian clergy. After pointing out "the spirit of *insubordination* and *independence* displayed here and there among the clergy" (1–2), Saint Pius X immediately sets out to explain what things must be done in order to "prevent the evil where fortunately it has not yet appeared." Therefore, in order "to destroy this evil seed which carries with it such destructive consequences" the Bishops must exercise "the most delicate caution and the greatest exactitude in selecting those who are to receive the sacerdotal honor" (3–4). They must guard and foster "most solicitously the proper conduct of the seminaries," putting into practice previously given instructions (5–7). They must follow the norms established by the Holy See in judging "those to whom you will entrust the ministry of the divine word" (8–9). They must watch lest the junior clergy use Popular Christian Action as the means for "advocating exemption from every bond of legitimate authority" (10–11). Finally, they must be vigilant over those priests engaged in writing and publishing, as well as those in social work (12–13). In conclusion, "making this a matter of conscience for the Bishops," he imparts the Apostolic Blessing (14).

At the time of its publication *Pieni L'Animo* was considered in many quarters as one more piece of evidence of the intransigence of the Papacy. Saint Pius X was accused of being "reactionary," of undoing the twenty-five years of Leonine diplomacy and intellectuality, of failing to reconcile the Church and the modern world. For the most part the Catholic press was as silent during all this time as the liberal press was vociferous.

One American churchman, however, wisely saw through the Pope's action. Writing in the *North American Review,* Archbishop John Ireland made the following observation:

"*'Modernita'* is a wide-ranged term; it shelters many living things, some clean, others unclean. By itself the term is no clearing-house certificate for all freightage which it may have labelled. This, nothing more, was intended by Pius X in his Encyclical *'Pieni d'animo'* [*sic*] addressed largely to the younger Italian clergy. New recruits must neither lead the army, nor be trusted by themselves at a distance from its lines. In their ambition to do new things, as befitting a new age, priests are, at times, exposed to the temptation to do things mischievous—'novitá malsana': they must be cautious. 'Progressive civilization'—a term to be spoken with care, lest tares sprout up under its shadow and the good grain be smothered by the rankness of their growth. To what is truly 'progressive civilization' the Catholic Church opposes no objection; she gathers into her bosom 'the old and the new'—'nova et vetera': but she will ever look beneath the name before she makes 'the new' her own, before she serves it up as wholesome food to her children." *

Another Catholic writer of the time saw a direct relation between *Arduum Sane* and *Pieni L'Animo.* "Apart from this clearance of the way by simplifying the code of laws which are to counteract the evils in the Church, Pius X has adopted a policy which goes straight to the root of the actual reform. He begins the change at home by a close examination of the conditions

* "The Pontificate of Pius X," by Archbishop John Ireland, in *North American Review,* 184:244.

of the Church in Italy. One is involuntarily reminded of his illustrious namesake Pius IV in the early days of the Council of Trent. That Pontiff had pledged himself in a letter to his saintly young nephew, Cardinal Charles Borromeo, that he would be assiduous *'per restituire la chiesa cattolica al suo pristino candore.'* " †

Saint Pius X intended to do precisely the same thing. If *Pieni L'Animo* was a rebuke to the offenders, it was at the same time an assurance to the observers. Moreover, it was an integral part of his program of restoration. If "all things" were to be restored "in Christ," there was no better and no easier place to begin than among those that are called to be the closest to Christ and the Vicar of Christ.

† "The Sovereign Pontiff to His Bishops," in *The American Ecclesiastical Review,* 35:338.

Pieni L'Animo *Encyclical Letter of Our Holy Father Pius X to His Venerable Brethren, the Archbishops and Bishops of Italy*

Venerable Brethren, Health and the Apostolic Blessing:

Pastoral concern over his subjects. 1. Our soul is fearful of the strict rendering that We shall one day be called upon to make to Jesus Christ, the Prince of Pastors, concerning the flock He entrusted to Our care. We pass each day with great solicitude in preserving as much as possible the faithful from the dangerous evils that afflict society at the present time. Therefore, We consider addressed to Us the words of the Prophet: "Cry, cease not, lift up thy voice like a trumpet." [1] Accordingly, sometimes by speech and sometimes by letter We constantly warn, beseech, and censure, arousing, above all, the zeal of Our Brethren in the Episcopate so that each one of them will exercise the most solicitous vigilance in that portion of the flock over which the Holy Spirit has placed him.

Novel theories among the clergy. 2. The cause which now moves Us to raise Our voice is of very serious importance. It demands all the attention of your mind and all the energy of your pastoral office to counteract the disorder which has already produced the most destructive effects. If this disorder is not radically removed with a firm hand, even more fatal consequences will be felt in the coming years. In fact, Venerable Brethren, We have letters, full of sadness and tears, from several of you, in which you deplore the spirit of *insubordination* and *independence* displayed here and there among the clergy. Most assuredly, a poisonous atmosphere corrupts men's minds to a great extent today, and the deadly effects are those which the Apostle Saint Jude formerly described: "These men also defile the flesh, disregard authority, deride majesty." [2] That is to say, over and above the most degrading corruption of manners there is also an open contempt for authority and for those who exercise it. What overwhelms Us with grief, however, is the fact that this spirit should creep into the sanctuary even in the least degree, infecting those to whom the words of Ecclesiasticus should most fittingly be applied: "Their generation, obedience and love." [3] This unfortunate spirit is doing the damage especially among young priests, spreading among them new and reprehensible theories concerning the very nature of obedience. In order to recruit new members for this growing troop of rebels, what is even more serious is the fact that such maxims are being more or less secretly propagated among youths preparing for the priesthood within the enclosure of the seminaries.

Obedience especially demanded of priests. 3. We therefore consider it Our duty, Venerable Brethren, to appeal to your conscience to see that you do not spare any effort and with a firm hand and constant resolve you do not hesitate to destroy this evil seed which carries with it such destructive consequences. Never forget that the Holy Spirit has placed you to rule. Remember Saint Paul's command to Titus: "Rebuke with all authority. Let no one despise thee." [4] Be firm in demanding that obedience from your priests and clerics which is a matter of absolute obligation for all the faithful, and constitutes the most important part of the sacred duty of priests.

Care in ordaining men. 4. Take the proper means necessary for the diminution of these quarrelsome souls. Bear well in mind, Venerable Brethren, the Apostle's warning to Timothy: "Do not lay hands hastily upon anyone." [5] In fact, haste in admitting men to Sacred Orders naturally opens the way to a *multiplication of people* in the sanctuary *who do not increase joy*. We know that there are cities and dioceses where, far from there being any reason to lament the dearth of clergy, the clergy greatly exceed the needs of the faithful. Venerable Brethren, what reason is there for imposing hands so frequently? In those places where the lack of clergy is no sufficient reason for haste in so important a matter and the clergy are more numerous than the requirements demand, nothing excuses from the most delicate caution and the greatest exactitude in selecting those who are to receive the sacerdotal honor. The eagerness of the aspirants is no excuse for haste. The priesthood that Jesus Christ instituted for the salvation of souls is by no means a human profession or office which anyone desiring it for any reason can say he has a right to receive. Therefore, let the Bishops call young men to sacred orders, not according to the desires or pretexts of the aspirants, but, as the Council of Trent prescribes, according to the needs of the dioceses. In this task they can select only those who are really suitable and dismiss those who have inclinations contrary to the priestly vocation. The most dangerous of these inclinations are a disregard for discipline and that pride of mind which fosters it.

Episcopal care over the seminaries. 5. In order that young men who display qualities suitable for the sacred ministry may not be lacking, Venerable Brethren, We wish to insist most earnestly on what We have already frequently pointed out. That is to say, you have a very serious obligation before God of guarding and fostering most solicitously the proper conduct of the seminaries. Your priests will be as you have trained them. The letter of

December 8, 1902, which Our most prudent Predecessor addressed to you as a testament from his long Pontificate is very important.[6] We desire to add nothing new to it; We shall merely remind you of the rules it lays down. We especially recommend the immediate execution of Our orders, published through the Sacred Congregation of Bishops and Regulars, on the concentration of the seminaries especially for the study of philosophy and theology. In this way the great advantage resulting from the separation of the major and minor seminaries and the no less great advantage of the necessary instruction of the clergy will be secured.

Directives for the seminaries. 6. Let the seminaries be jealously guarded in order that a proper atmosphere will be maintained. Let them always be destined *exclusively* for preparing youths, not for civil careers, but for the noble vocation of being ministers of Christ. Let philosophy, theology, and the related sciences, especially Sacred Scripture, be studied along the lines of pontifical directives: according to the teaching of Saint Thomas which Our venerable Predecessor so often recommended, and We Ourselves recommended in the Apostolic Letter of January 23, 1904.[7] Therefore, let the Bishops exercise the most prudent vigilance towards the professors' teachings. Let them recall those who run after certain dangerous novelties to their sense of duty. If they do not profit from these warnings, let them be removed—cost what it may—from their teaching position. Young clerics are forbidden to frequent the universities unless the Bishops think there are very good reasons and necessary precautions have been taken. Seminarians are absolutely forbidden to take part in external activities. Accordingly, We forbid them to read newspapers and periodicals, excepting, in the case of the latter, those with solid principles and which the Bishop deems suitable for their study. Let discipline continue to be fostered with renewed vigor and vigilance. Finally, in every seminary there must be a spiritual director. He is to be a man of extraordinary prudence and experienced in the ways of Christian perfection. With untiring zeal he must train the young men in solid piety, the primary foundation of the spiritual life. Venerable Brethren, if these rules are conscientiously and religiously followed they will be your sure guarantee of seeing a clergy growing up around you which will be your joy and your crown.

Importance of these directives. 7. If these instructions are not observed, the problem of insubordination and independence which We now lament will be even more aggravated by some of the younger clergy and cause even more harm. This is especially so since those who are subject to this reprobate spirit are not lacking, and, abusing the sacred office of preaching, they are its outspoken promoters and apostles, to the detriment and scandal of the faithful.

Vigilance over preaching. 8. On July 31, 1894, Our Predecessor, through the Sacred Congregation of Bishops and Regulars, called the Bishops' attention to this very serious problem.[8] The regulations and norms set up in that Pontifical document We now affirm and renew, commanding the Bishops to form their conscience according to it, lest the words of the Prophet Nahum might be applied to any of them: "Thy shepherds have slumbered." [9] No one can have the faculty of preaching "unless he first be approved of in life, knowledge and morals." [10] Priests of other dioceses should not be allowed to preach unless they have testimonial letters from their own Bishop. Let the subject of their sermons be that which the Divine Saviour indicated when He said: "Preach the gospel [11] . . . teaching them to observe all that I have commanded you." [12] Or, according to the Council of Trent, "announcing to them the vices they should avoid and the virtues they should follow in order to escape eternal punishment and attain heavenly glory." [13] Therefore, let those arguments better suited to journalistic campaigns and lecture halls be completely banished from the holy place. Let moral preaching be preferred to sermons which are, to say the least, fruitless. Let the preacher speak "not in the persuasive words of wisdom, but in the demonstration of the Spirit and of power." [14] The principal source, therefore, from which preaching will derive its strength will be the Sacred Scriptures, understood not according to the private judgment of minds very frequently blinded by passions, but according to the traditions of the Church and the interpretations of the holy Fathers and Councils.

Preaching and the Episcopal Office. 9. According to these rules, Venerable Brethren, you should judge those to whom you will entrust the ministry of the divine word. Whenever you find any of them departing from these rules, being more concerned with their own interests than those of Jesus Christ and more anxious for worldly applause than the welfare of souls, warn and correct them. If that proves insufficient, be firm in removing them from an office for which they have proven themselves unworthy. You should be especially diligent in employing this vigilance and severity since the ministry of preaching belongs in a special way to you, and is one of the chief functions of the Episcopal Office. Whoever outside your rank preaches, he does so only in your name and in your place. It follows, therefore, that you are always responsible before God for the way in which the bread of the divine word is distributed to the faithful. In order to remove all responsibility from Our shoulders, We notify and command all Ordinaries to discontinue or suspend, after charitable warnings, any preacher, be he secular or regular, and even if it be during a course of sermons, who does not completely obey the regulations laid down in the above-mentioned Instruction of the Congregation of Bishops and Regulars. Better by far would it be if the faithful were satisfied with the simple homilies and explanations of the Catechism their parish priests offer them than to attend sermons that do more harm than good.

Popular Christian Action and the clergy. 10. Another field where the junior clergy find a wide scope and great stimulus for maintaining and advocating exemption from every bond of legitimate authority is the so-called Popular Christian Action. This action, Venerable Brethren, is not in itself reprehensible, nor by its nature does it lead to contempt of authority. Many, however, misunderstanding its nature, have voluntarily abandoned the rules laid down for its promotion by Our Predecessor of immortal memory.

Renewal of past instructions. 11. You are aware that We are referring to the Instruction on Popular Christian Action which, by command of Leo XIII, the Sacred Congregation of Extraordinary Ecclesiastical Affairs issued on January 27, 1902, and which was sent to each one of you to carry out in your dioceses.[15] For Our part, We maintain and, with the fullness of Our power, We renew these instructions with each and every one of their regulations. Similarly We confirm and renew all the orders We issued in the *Motu Proprio* of December 18, 1903, on Popular Christian Action [16] along with the Circular Letter dated July 28, 1904, of Our beloved son, the Cardinal Secretary of State.[17]

Regulations governing the press. 12. Concerning the founding and directing of newspapers and periodicals, the clergy must faithfully follow Article 42 of the Apostolic Constitution *Officiorum,* namely, "Clerics are forbidden to direct newspapers or periodicals without the previous consent of the Ordinaries." [18] Similarly, without the previous consent of the Ordinary, no cleric can publish any kind of writing, be it concerned with a religious, moral, or merely technical subject. Before the founding of circles and societies their rules and constitutions must be examined and approved by the Ordinary. No priest or cleric can lecture on Popular Christian Action or any other subject without the permission of the Ordinary of the place. Language which might inspire aversion for the higher classes is, and can only be regarded as, altogether contrary to the true spirit of Christian charity. Likewise, all terms smacking of an unhealthy novelty in Catholic publications are condemnable, such as those deriding the piety of the faithful, or pointing out *a new orientation of the Christian life, new directions of the Church, new aspirations of the modern soul, a new social vocation of the clergy,* or a new Christian civilization.

The social work of the clergy. While it is a very praiseworthy thing for the clergy, and especially the younger clergy, to go to the people, nevertheless, they must proceed in this matter with due obedience to authority and the commands of their ecclesiastical superiors. In devoting themselves according to this submission to the cause of Popular Christian Action, their noble duty must be "to rescue the children of the people from ignorance of spiritual and eternal things, encouraging them by their kindness to live honestly and virtuously; to strengthen adults in the faith, fortifying them in the practice of the Christian life by removing all contrary influences; to foster among the Catholic laity those institutions which are really instrumental in improving the moral and material welfare of the masses; and above all, to defend the principles of evangelical justice and charity, applying equally to everyone the rights and duties of civil society. . . . Let them, moreover, be ever mindful that even among the people the priest should inviolately preserve his noble character as a minister of God, being placed at the head of his brethren for their salvation.[19] In devoting himself to the people should he do anything contrary to the dignity of the priesthood or ecclesiastical duties or discipline, he must be rebuked." [20]

The clergy and secular societies. 13. Moreover, Venerable Brethren, in order to erect an effective bulwark against this extravagance of thought and extension of the spirit of independence, by Our authority, We absolutely forbid all clerics and priests to give their names in the future to any society that does not have Episcopal approbation. In a very special manner, under penalty of exclusion from Sacred Orders for clerics and suspension *ipso facto a divinis* for priests, We forbid them to become members of the National Democratic League, whose program was issued from Roma-Torrette on October 20, 1905. Its statutes were published the same year by the Provisional Committee of Bologna without the name of their author.

Apostolic Blessing. 14. Being concerned about the present state of the Italian clergy and the importance of the subject, the solicitude of Our Apostolic Office demanded Us to issue these directives. We must now once again arouse your zeal, Venerable Brethren, in order that these arrangements and regulations will be quickly and fully carried out in your dioceses. Prevent the evil where fortunately it has not yet appeared. Suppress it immediately where it is beginning to spring up. Wipe it out with a firm and resolute hand where unfortunately it has already ripened. Making this a matter of conscience for you, We pray that God will fill you with the spirit of prudence and necessary firmness. For that reason, from the bottom of Our heart, We impart to you the Apostolic Blessing.

15. Given at Saint Peter's, Rome, on July 28, 1906, the third year of Our Pontificate.

PIUS X, POPE

REFERENCES

1. Is. 58:1.
2. Jude 8.
3. Ecclus. 3:1.
4. Titus 2:15.
5. I Tim. 5:22.
6. Cf. *ASS*, 35:257 ff.

7. Cf. *ASS,* 36:467 ff.
8. Cf. *ASS,* 27:162 ff.
9. Nahum 3:18.
10. Council of Trent, *Sess. V, c.* 2, *De Reform.*
11. Mark 16:15.
12. Matt. 28:20.
13. *Loc. cit.*
14. I Cor. 2:4.
15. Cf. *ASS,* 34:401 ff.
16. Cf. *ASS,* 36:339 ff.
17. Cf. *ASS,* 37:19 ff.
18. January 25, 1897. Cf. *ASS,* 30:39 ff.
19. St. Gregory the Great, *Pastoral Care,* 2:7.
20. Encyclical letter of Pope Leo XIII, *Fin dal principio,* December 8, 1902. Cf. *ASS,* 35:257 ff.

CHAPTER 8

Pascendi Dominici Gregis *September 8, 1907, The Doctrines of the Modernists*

ON JULY 3, 1907, Saint Pius X had published the decree *Lamentabili sane.* Just as the *Errorum syllabus* of Pope Pius IX condemned the errors of Liberalism, so the sixty-five propositions of the decree of 1907 condemned the errors of the Modernists. Although the former was accompanied by the encyclical *Quanta cura* of Pope Pius IX, the latter stood alone for two months. But then, on September 8, 1907, Saint Pius X published what has remained without a doubt his most famous encyclical letter, *Pascendi dominici gregis.*

Even a cursory glance at the encyclical *Pascendi* is enough to impress one with the erudition of its author. If up until its publication the intelligentsia considered the Bishop of Rome as merely "a simple country pastor," *Pascendi* was evidence of his profound wisdom. If today there still remain some who hold the same opinion, by all means nothing will so quickly dispel their ignorance as a study of this document. The genius of the great Archbishop of Saint Paul immediately perceived its significance. "The Encyclical of Pius," he wrote, "is the defense of God in the heavens and at the same time of the intellect in man." *

Pascendi, moreover, reveals the Saint's love for doctrine. When calling him "the Pope of Christian Doctrine" we immediately picture him as the loving pastor of Rome instructing the people who flocked into the Court of Saint Damasus to hear his Sunday catechetical explanations. Undoubtedly such is the manner in which he would love to have us recall his memory. Doctrine, however, embraces more than catechetics; it strikes deep into the ground of divine revelation, sacred tradition, and conciliar decisions. If the water is polluted in its source, the whole stream will be infected. If dogma suffers, so also will catechetics. In the encyclical of September 8, 1907, Saint Pius X purifies the waters of everlasting life which he had commanded to be

* "The Dogmatic Authority of the Papacy," by Archbishop John Ireland, in *The North American Review,* 187:490.

poured out to all in the encyclical of April 15, 1904. *Pascendi* is the assurance of the effectiveness of *Acerbo Nimis*. In both, this "Pope of the Catechism" proves his love for doctrine. With the simplicity of the truly wise he guarded sacred doctrine both in its source as well as along its journey.

Modernism was the cause of *Pascendi*. In this encyclical Saint Pius X labels it "the synthesis of all heresies." Hilaire Belloc calls it "an attempt to reconcile opposites." He then proceeds to give the following illustration:

> It has its roots, therefore, in the increasingly unreasoning speculations of Protestant Germany, and it was stamped throughout with that which the plain man will always call (when he talks English) "sentiment"—that is, the desire to have your cake and to eat it too: nay, worse, the fatuous illusion that you *can* have your cake and eat it too.†

Archbishop Ireland describes its origin in the following words:

> The starting-point of Modernism is the assumption that, of itself, human reason is powerless to establish either the existence of God as a transcendent reality, or the divinity of the mission and person of Christ. With some it is adherence to the Kantian system of Philosophy, which teaches that the human reason does not reach beyond "phenomena" or appearances of things, that "noumena" or realities back of appearances totally escape its grasp of vision. With others, it is what they term the weakness and insufficiency of intellectual proofs, available in favor either of natural religion or of Christian revelation. In both cases the conclusion is the same: intellectualism is abandoned as a basis of religion. Another basis must be sought: it is found in the inner sense and experience of the soul, in its cravings for life, in its motives of action. Feeling is substituted for reason: subjective emotion for intellectual assent. ‡

Mr. Belloc explains a basic Modernist belief in the following manner:

> . . . here is one characteristic tenet of Modernism if tenet it can be called: it would be less kind and more truthful to call it one characteristic sentiment—that the Lord was God in a kind of a way because He was a Man Who was so good and so wise that He stretched up to and mixed with the Divine. As against that statement you might use any one of the methods to be used against sentiment. The method used by Pius X was that of restating clear doctrine. It is dogma . . . that the Word was made Flesh. Not that the Flesh in some painful and muddled sort of a fashion, agreeable to the dwellers by the Baltic Plain, managed to get more or less in touch with the Word. §

An examination of the encyclical itself, however, will be the best ex-

† "The Reign of Pope Pius X," by Hilaire Belloc, in *The Tablet,* 197:433.
‡ John Ireland, *art. cit.* p. 491.
§ Hilaire Belloc, *art. cit.,* p. 433.

planation of those Modernistic teachings professed by such men as the Protestant R. J. Campbell and the Catholic George Tyrrell in England, and the Protestant Harnack and the Catholic Loisy on the Continent. It remains the undying glory of Saint Pius X that he first explained Modernism as a logical whole in order to condemn it all the more forcefully.

After an introduction recalling the duty of the "office divinely committed to Us of feeding the Lord's flock" (1–4), Saint Pius X divides the encyclical into these three main parts:

I. Analysis of Modernist Teaching (5–39);
II. The Causes of Modernism (40–43);
III. The Remedies (44–56).

In analyzing the teachings of Modernism he discusses the following Modernist teachings: agnosticism (6), vital immanence (7–8), deformation of religious history (9–10), the religious sense (11), the origin, nature, symbolism and evolution of dogma (12–14); the Modernist as believer (15–18), as theologian (19–28), as historian and critic (29–34), as apologist (35–37), and as reformer (38–39). The causes of Modernism are pride (40), ignorance (41–42), and temerity (43). The remedies needed are a return to Scholasticism (45–47), prudence in calling men to Orders (48–49), vigilance over publications and congresses (50–54), and the erection of diocesan vigilance committees (55).

Modernism grew best in the darkness of the night. The encyclical *Pascendi* struck a lethal blow by exposing it to the piercing rays of the sun of Truth. Mr. Belloc has summarized the contest in the following brilliant passage:

> There is to any thinking man here the most violent contrast in the world. North and South lie upon one line, but North is the contradiction of South, and so plain a truth was saved under Pius X by no process more subtle or more violent than its statement in the clearest terms. It was odd that so powerful a weapon should have seemed to so many at the time so weak. It was mortal. Modernism is dead—and how quickly it was killed! And what a long business it usually is to kill stupidity. ||

|| *Ibid.*

Pascendi Dominici Gregis* *Encyclical Letter of Our Holy Father Pope Pius X to the Patriarchs, Primates, Archbishops, Bishops and Other Ordinaries in Peace and Communion with the Apostolic See*

VENERABLE BRETHREN, HEALTH AND THE APOSTOLIC BLESSING:

Duty of the Apostolic See. 1. One of the primary obligations assigned by Christ to the office divinely committed to Us of feeding the Lord's flock is that of guarding with the greatest vigilance the deposit of the faith delivered to the saints, rejecting the profane novelties of words and the gainsaying of knowledge falsely so called. There has never been a time when this watchfulness of the supreme pastor was not necessary to the Catholic body, for owing to the efforts of the enemy of the human race, there have never been lacking "men speaking perverse things," [1] "vain talkers and seducers," [2] "erring and driving into error." [3] It must, however, be confessed that these latter days have witnessed a notable increase in the number of the enemies of the Cross of Christ, who, by arts entirely new and full of deceit, are striving to destroy the vital energy of the Church, and, as far as in them lies, utterly to subvert the very Kingdom of Christ. Wherefore We may no longer keep silence, lest We should seem to fail in Our most sacred duty, and lest the kindness that, in the hope of wiser counsels, We have hitherto shown them, should be set down to lack of diligence in the discharge of Our office.

Necessity of immediate action. 2. That We should act without delay in this matter is made imperative especially by the fact that the partisans of error are to be sought not only among the Church's open enemies; but, what is to be most dreaded and deplored, in her very bosom, and are the more mischievous the less they keep in the open. We allude, Venerable Brethren, to many who belong to the Catholic laity, and, what is much more sad, to the ranks of the priesthood itself, who, animated by a false zeal for the Church, lacking the solid safeguards of philosophy and theology, nay more, thoroughly imbued with the poisonous doctrines taught by the enemies of the Church, and lost to all sense of modesty, put themselves forward as re-

* This translation of *Pascendi Dominici Gregis* is taken from *The Doctrines of the Modernists,* published in London by Burns, Oates & Washbourne, Ltd. (The marginal titles have been supplied by the editor.)

formers of the Church; and, forming more boldly into line of attack, assail all that is most sacred in the work of Christ, not sparing even the Person of the Divine Redeemer, whom, with sacrilegious audacity, they degrade to the condition of a simple and ordinary man.

Characteristics of the Modernists. 3. Although they express their astonishment that We should number them amongst the enemies of the Church, no one will be reasonably surprised that We should do so, if, leaving out of account the internal disposition of the soul, of which God alone is the Judge, he considers their tenets, their manner of speech, and their action. Nor indeed would he be wrong in regarding them as the most pernicious of all the adversaries of the Church. For, as We have said, they put into operation their designs for her undoing, not from without but from within. Hence, the danger is present almost in the very veins and heart of the Church, whose injury is the more certain from the very fact that their knowledge of her is more intimate. Moreover, they lay the axe not to the branches and shoots, but to the very root, that is, to the faith and its deepest fibres. And once having struck at this root of immortality, they proceed to diffuse poison through the whole tree, so that there is no part of Catholic truth which they leave untouched, none that they do not strive to corrupt. Further, none is more skilful, none more astute than they, in the employment of a thousand noxious devices; for they play the double part of rationalist and Catholic, and this so craftily that they easily lead the unwary into error; and as audacity is their chief characteristic, there is no conclusion of any kind from which they shrink or which they do not thrust forward with pertinacity and assurance. To this must be added the fact, which indeed is well calculated to deceive souls, that they lead a life of the greatest activity, of assiduous and ardent application to every branch of learning, and that they possess, as a rule, a reputation for irreproachable morality. Finally, there is the fact which is all but fatal to the hope of cure that their very doctrines have given such a bent to their minds, that they disdain all authority and brook no restraint; and relying upon a false conscience, they attempt to ascribe to a love of truth that which is in reality the result of pride and obstinacy.

Previous attempts have failed. Once indeed We had hopes of recalling them to a better mind, and to this end We first of all treated them with kindness as Our children, then with severity; and at last We have had recourse, though with great reluctance, to public reproof. It is known to you, Venerable Brethren, how unavailing have been Our efforts. For a moment they have bowed their head, only to lift it more arrogantly than before. If it were a matter which concerned them alone, We might perhaps have overlooked it; but the security of the Catholic name is at stake. Wherefore We must interrupt a silence which it would be criminal to prolong, that We may point out to the whole Church, as they really are, men who are badly disguised.

Division of the encyclical. 4. It is one of the cleverest devices of the Modernists (as they are commonly and rightly called) to present their doctrines without order and systematic arrangement, in a scattered and disjointed manner, so as to make it appear as if their minds were in doubt or hesitation, whereas in reality they are quite fixed and steadfast. For this reason it will be of advantage, Venerable Brethren, to bring their teachings together here into one group, and to point out their interconnection, and thus to pass to an examination of the sources of the errors, and to prescribe remedies for averting the evil results.

The Modernist personality. 5. To proceed in an orderly manner in this somewhat abstruse subject, it must first of all be noted that the Modernist sustains and includes within himself a manifold personality; he is a philosopher, a believer, a theologian, an historian, a critic, an apologist, a reformer. These roles must be clearly distinguished one from another by all who would accurately understand their system and thoroughly grasp the principles and the outcome of their doctrines.

Agnosticism. 6. We begin, then, with the philosopher. Modernists place the foundation of religious philosophy in that doctrine which is commonly called *Agnosticism.* According to this teaching human reason is confined entirely within the field of *phenomena,* that is to say, to things that appear, and in the manner in which they appear: it has neither the right nor the power to overstep these limits. Hence it is incapable of lifting itself up to God, and of recognizing His existence, even by means of visible things. From this it is inferred that God can never be the direct object of science, and that, as regards history, He must not be considered as an historical subject. Given these premises, everyone will at once perceive what becomes of *Natural Theology,* of the *motives of credibility,* of *external revelation.* The Modernists simply sweep them entirely aside; they include them in *Intellectualism,* which they denounce as a system which is ridiculous and long since defunct. Nor does the fact that the Church has formally condemned these portentous errors exercise the slightest restraint upon them. Yet the Vatican Council has defined, "If anyone says that the one true God, our Creator and Lord, cannot be known with certainty by the natural light of human reason by means of the things that are made, let him be anathema"; [4] and also, "If anyone says that it is not possible or not expedient that man be taught, through the medium of divine revelation, about God and the worship to be paid Him, let him be anathema"; [5] and finally, "If anyone says that divine revelation cannot be made credible by external signs, and that therefore men should be drawn to the faith only by their personal internal experience or by private inspiration, let him be anathema." [6] It may be asked, in what way do the Modernists contrive to make the transition from *Agnosticism,* which is a state of pure nescience, to scientific and historic *Atheism,* which is a doctrine of positive denial; and consequently, by what legitimate process of reasoning, they proceed from the fact of ignorance as to whether God has in fact intervened in the history of the human race or not, to explain this history, leaving God out altogether, as if He really had not intervened. Let him answer who can. Yet it is a fixed and established principle among them that both science and history must be atheistic: and within their boundaries there is room for nothing but *phenomena;* God and all that is divine are utterly excluded. We shall soon see clearly what, as a consequence of this most absurd teaching, must be held touching the most sacred Person of Christ, and the mysteries of His life and death, and of His Resurrection and Ascension into Heaven.

Vital immanence. 7. However, this *Agnosticism* is only the negative part of the system of the Modernists: the positive part consists in what they call *vital immanence.* Thus they advance from one to the other. Religion, whether natural or supernatural, must, like every other fact, admit of some explanation. But when natural theology has been destroyed, and the road to revelation closed by the rejection of the arguments of credibility, and all external revelation absolutely denied, it is clear that this explanation will be sought in vain outside of man himself. It must, therefore, be looked for *in* man; and since religion is a form of life, the explanation must certainly be found in the life of man. In this way is formulated the principle of *religious immanence.* Moreover, the first actuation, so to speak, of every vital phenomenon—and religion, as noted above, belongs to this category—is due to a certain need or impulsion; but speaking more particularly of life, it has its origin in a movement of the heart, which movement is called a *sense.* Therefore, as God is the object of religion, we must conclude that faith, which is the basis and foundation of all religion, must consist in a certain interior sense, originating in a need of the divine. This need of the divine, which is experienced only in special and favorable circumstances, cannot of itself appertain to the domain of consciousness, but is first latent beneath consciousness, or, to borrow a term from modern philosophy, in the *subconsciousness,* where also its root lies hidden and undetected.

The need of the Divine. It may perhaps be asked how it is that this need of the divine which man experiences within himself resolves itself into religion? To this question the Modernist reply would be as follows: Science and history are confined within two boundaries, the one external, namely, the visible world, the other internal, which is consciousness. When one or other of these limits has been reached, there can be no further progress, for beyond is the *unknowable.* In presence of this *unknowable,* whether it is outside man and beyond the visible world of nature, or lies hidden within the subconsciousness, the need of the divine in a soul which is prone to religion excites—according to the principles of *Fideism,* without any previous advertence of the mind—a certain special sense, and this sense possesses, implied within itself both as its own object and as its intrinsic cause, the divine *reality* itself, and in a way unites man with God. It is this *sense* to which Modernists give the name of faith, and this is what they hold to be the beginning of religion.

The Modernist's revelation. 8. But we have not yet reached the end of their philosophizing, or, to speak more accurately, of their folly. Modernists find in this *sense* not only faith, but in and with faith, as they understand it, they affirm that there is also to be found *revelation*. For, indeed, what more is needed to constitute a revelation? Is not that religious sense which is perceptible in the conscience, revelation, or at least the beginning of revelation? Nay, is it not God Himself manifesting Himself, indistinctly, it is true, in this same religious *sense,* to the soul? And they add: Since God is both the object and the cause of faith, this revelation is at the same time *of* God and *from* God, that is to say, God is both the Revealer and the Revealed.

Religious consciousness and faith. From this, Venerable Brethren, springs that most absurd tenet of the Modernists, that every religion, according to the different aspect under which it is viewed, must be considered as both natural and supernatural. It is thus that they make consciousness and revelation synonymous. From this they derive the law laid down as the universal standard, according to which *religious consciousness* is to be put on an equal footing with revelation, and that to it all must submit, even the supreme authority of the Church, whether in the capacity of teacher, or in that of legislator in the province of sacred liturgy or discipline.

Deformation of religious history. 9. In all this process, from which, according to the Modernists, faith and revelation spring, one point is to be particularly noted, for it is of capital importance on account of the historico-critical corollaries which they deduce from it. The *unknowable* they speak of does not present itself to faith as something solitary and isolated; but on the contrary in close conjunction with some phenomenon, which, though it belongs to the realms of science or history, yet to some extent exceeds their limits. Such a phenomenon may be a fact of nature containing within itself something mysterious; or it may be a man, whose character, actions, and words cannot, apparently, be reconciled with the ordinary laws of history. Then faith, attracted by the *unknowable* which is united with the phenomenon, seizes upon the whole phenomenon, and, as it were, permeates it with its own life. From this two things follow. The first is a sort of *transfiguration* of the phenomenon, by its elevation above its own true conditions, an elevation by which it becomes more adapted to clothe itself with the form of the divine character which faith will bestow upon it. The second consequence is a certain *disfiguration*—so it may be called—of the same phenomenon, arising from the fact that faith attributes to it, when stripped of the circumstances of place and time, characteristics which it does not really possess; and this takes place especially in the case of the phenomena of the past, and the more fully in the measure of their antiquity. From these two principles the Modernists deduce two laws, which, when united with a third which they have already derived from agnosticism, constitute the foundation of historic criticism. An example may be sought in the Person of Christ. In the Person of Christ, they say, science and history encounter nothing that is not human. Therefore, in virtue of the first canon deduced from agnosticism, whatever there is in His history suggestive of the divine must be rejected. Then, according to the second canon, the historical Person of Christ was *transfigured* by faith; therefore everything that raises it above historical conditions must be removed. Lastly, the third canon, which lays down that the Person of Christ has been *disfigured* by faith, requires that everything should be excluded, deeds and words and all else, that is not in strict keeping with His character, condition, and education, and with the place and time in which He lived. A method of reasoning which is passing strange, but in it we have the Modernist criticism.

The religious sense. 10. It is thus that the *religious sense,* which through the agency of *vital immanence* emerges from the lurking-places of the subconsciousness, is the germ of all religion, and the explanation of everything that has been or ever will be in any religion. This *sense,* which was at first only rudimentary and almost formless, under the influence of that mysterious principle from which it originated, gradually matured with the progress of human life, of which, as has been said, it is a certain form. This, then, is the origin of all, even of supernatural religion. For religions are mere developments of this *religious sense.* Nor is the Catholic religion an exception; it is quite on a level with the rest; for it was engendered, by the process of *vital immanence,* and by no other way, in the consciousness of Christ, who was a man of the choicest nature, whose like has never been, nor will be. In hearing these things we shudder indeed at so great an audacity of assertion and so great a sacrilege. And yet, Venerable Brethren, these are not merely the foolish babblings of unbelievers. There are Catholics, yea, and priests too, who say these things openly; and they boast that they are going to reform the Church by these ravings! The question is no longer one of the old error which claimed for human nature a sort of right to the supernatural. It has gone far beyond that, and has reached the point when it is affirmed that our most holy religion, in the man Christ as in us, emanated from nature spontaneously and of itself. Nothing assuredly could be more utterly destructive of the whole supernatural order. For this reason the Vatican Council most justly decreed: "If anyone says that man cannot be raised by God to a knowledge and perfection which surpasses nature, but that he can and should, by his own efforts and by a constant development, attain finally to the possession of all truth and good, let him be anathema." [7]

The intellect and religious sense. 11. So far, Venerable Brethren, there has been no mention of the intellect. It also, according to the teaching of the Modernists, has its part in the act of faith. And it is of importance to see how. In that *sense* of which We have frequently spoken, since *sense* is not knowledge, they say God, indeed, presents Himself to man, but in a manner so confused and indistinct that He can hardly be perceived by the believer. It is therefore necessary that a certain light should be cast upon this sense so that God may clearly stand out in relief and be set apart from it. This is the task of the intellect, whose office it is to reflect and to analyse; and by means of it, man first transforms into mental pictures the vital phenomena which arise within him, and then expresses them in words. Hence the common saying of Modernists: that the religious man must *think* his faith. The mind then, encountering this *sense,* throws itself upon it, and works in it after the manner of a painter who restores to greater clearness the lines of a picture that have been dimmed with age. The simile is that of one of the leaders of Modernism. The operation of the mind in this work is a double one: first, by a natural and spontaneous act it expresses its concept in a simple, popular statement; then, on reflection and deeper consideration, or, as they say, *by elaborating its thought,* it expresses the idea in *secondary* propositions, which are derived from the first, but are more precise and distinct. These *secondary* propositions, if they finally receive the approval of the supreme magisterium of the Church, constitute *dogma.*

The origin of dogma. 12. We have thus reached one of the principal points in the Modernist's system, namely, the origin and the nature of dogma. For they place the origin of dogma in those primitive and simple formulas, which, under a certain aspect, are necessary to faith; for revelation, to be truly such, requires the clear knowledge of God in the consciousness. But dogma itself, they apparently hold, strictly consists in the *secondary* formulas.

The nature of dogma. To ascertain the nature of dogma, we must first find the relation which exists between the *religious formulas* and the *religious sense.* This will be readily perceived by anyone who holds that these *formulas* have no other purpose than to furnish the believer with a means of giving to himself an account of his faith. These formulas therefore stand midway between the believer and his faith; in their relation to the faith they are the inadequate expression of its object, and are usually called *symbols;* in their relation to the believer they are mere *instruments.*

Dogmas are symbols. Hence it is quite impossible to maintain that they absolutely contain the truth: for, in so far as they are *symbols,* they are the images of truth, and so must be adapted to the religious sense in its relation to man; and as *instruments,* they are the vehicles of truth, and must therefore in their turn be adapted to man in his relation to the religious sense. But the object of the *religious sense,* as something contained in the *absolute,* possesses an infinite variety of aspects, of which now one, now another, may present itself. In like manner he who believes can avail himself of varying conditions. Consequently, the formulas which we call dogma must be subject to these vicissitudes, and are, therefore, liable to change. Thus the way is open to the intrinsic *evolution* of dogma. Here we have an immense structure of sophisms which ruin and wreck all religion.

Evolution of dogma. 13. Dogma is not only able, but ought to evolve and to be changed. This is strongly affirmed by the Modernists, and clearly flows from their principles. For among the chief points of their teaching is the following, which they deduce from the principle of *vital immanence,* namely, that *religious formulas,* if they are to be really *religious* and not merely intellectual speculations, ought to be living and to live the life of the *religious sense.* This is not to be understood to mean that these formulas, especially if merely imaginative, were to be invented for the religious sense. Their origin matters nothing, any more than their number or quality. What is necessary is that the *religious sense*—with some modification when needful —should vitally assimilate them. In other words, it is necessary that the *primitive formula* be accepted and sanctioned by the heart; and similarly the subsequent work from which are brought forth the *secondary formulas* must proceed under the guidance of the heart. Hence it comes that these formulas, in order to be living, should be, and should remain, adapted to the faith and to him who believes. Wherefore, if for any reason this adaptation should cease to exist, they lose their first meaning and accordingly need to be changed. In view of the fact that the character and lot of dogmatic formulas are so unstable, it is no wonder that Modernists should regard them so lightly and in such open disrespect, and have no consideration or praise for anything but the religious sense and for the religious life. In this way, with consummate audacity, they criticise the Church, as having strayed from the true path by failing to distinguish between the religious and moral sense of formulas and their surface meaning, and by clinging vainly and tenaciously to meaningless formulas, while religion itself is allowed to go to ruin. "Blind" they are, and "leaders of the blind" puffed up with the proud name of science, they have reached that pitch of folly at which they pervert the eternal concept of truth and the true meaning of religion; in introducing a new system in which "they are seen to be under the sway of a blind and unchecked passion for novelty, thinking not at all of finding some solid foundation of truth, but despising the holy and apostolic traditions, they embrace other and vain, futile, uncertain doctrines, unapproved by the Church, on which, in the height of their vanity, they think they can base and maintain truth itself." [8]

The Modernist as believer. 14. Thus far, Venerable Brethren, We have considered the Modernist as a philosopher. Now if We proceed to consider him as a believer, and seek to know how the believer, according to Modernism, is marked off from the philosopher, it must be observed that, although the philosopher recognises the *reality of the divine* as the object of faith, still this *reality* is not to be found by him but in the heart of the believer, as an object of feeling and affirmation, and therefore confined within the sphere of phenomena; but the question as to whether in itself it exists outside that feeling and affirmation is one which the philosopher passes over and neglects. For the Modernist believer, on the contrary, it is an established and certain fact that the reality of the divine does really exist in itself and quite independently of the person who believes in it. If you ask on what foundation this assertion of the believer rests, he answers: In the personal *experience* of the individual. On this head the Modernists differ from the Rationalists only to fall into the views of the Protestants and pseudo-mystics. The following is their manner of stating the question: In *the religious sense* one must recognise a kind of intuition of the heart which puts man in immediate contact with the *reality* of God, and infuses such a persuasion of God's existence and His action both within and without man as far to exceed any scientific conviction. They assert, therefore, the existence of a real experience, and one of a kind that surpasses all rational experience. If this experience is denied by some, like the Rationalists, they say that this arises from the fact that such persons are unwilling to put themselves in the moral state necessary to produce it. It is this *experience* which makes the person who acquires it to be properly and truly a believer.

Destruction of one, true religion. How far this position is removed from that of Catholic teaching! We have already seen how its fallacies have been condemned by the Vatican Council. Later on, we shall see how these errors, combined with those which we have already mentioned, open wide the way to Atheism. Here it is well to note at once that, given this doctrine of *experience* united with that of *symbolism,* every religion, even that of paganism, must be held to be true. What is to prevent such experiences from being found in any religion? In fact, that they are so is maintained by not a few. On what grounds can Modernists deny the truth of an experience affirmed by a follower of Islam? Will they claim a monopoly of true experiences for Catholics alone? Indeed, Modernists do not deny, but actually maintain, some confusedly, others frankly, that all religions are true. That they cannot feel otherwise is obvious. For on what ground, according to their theories, could falsity be predicated of any religion whatsoever? Certainly it would be either on account of the falsity of the *religious sense* or on account of the falsity of the formula pronounced by the mind. Now the *religious sense,* although it may be more perfect or less perfect, is always one and the same; and the intellectual formula, in order to be true, has but to respond to the *religious sense* and to the believer, whatever be the intellectual capacity of the latter. In the conflict between different religions, the most that Modernists can maintain is that the Catholic has more truth because it is more vivid, and that it deserves with more reason the name of Christian because it corresponds more fully with the origins of Christianity. No one will find it unreasonable that these consequences flow from the premises. But what is most amazing is that there are Catholics and priests, who, We would fain believe, abhor such enormities, and yet act as if they fully approved of them. For they lavish such praise and bestow such public honor on the teachers of these errors as to convey the belief that their admiration is not meant merely for the persons, who are perhaps not devoid of a certain merit, but rather for the sake of the errors which these persons openly profess and which they do all in their power to propagate.

Religious experience and tradition. 15. There is yet another element in this part of their teaching which is absolutely contrary to Catholic truth. For what is laid down as to *experience* is also applied with destructive effect to *tradition*, which has always been maintained by the Catholic Church. Tradition, as understood by the Modernists, is a communication with others of an *original experience,* through preaching by means of the intellectual formula. To this formula, in addition to its *representative* value they attribute a species of *suggestive* efficacy which acts firstly in the believer by stimulating the *religious sense,* should it happen to have grown sluggish, and by renewing the *experience* once acquired, and secondly, in those who do not yet believe by awakening in them for the first time the *religious sense* and producing the *experience.* In this way is religious experience spread abroad among the nations; and not merely among contemporaries by preaching, but among future generations both by books and by oral transmission from one to another. Sometimes this communication of religious experience takes root and thrives, at other times it withers at once and dies. For the Modernists, to live is a proof of truth, since for them life and truth are one and the same thing. Thus we are once more led to infer that all existing religions are equally true, for otherwise they would not survive.

Faith and science. 16. We have proceeded sufficiently far, Venerable Brethren, to have before us enough, and more than enough, to enable us to see what are the relations which Modernists establish between faith and science—including, as they are wont to do under that name, history. And in the first place it is to be held that the object-matter of the one is quite extraneous to and separate from the object-matter of the other. For faith occupies itself solely with something which science declares to be for it *unknowable.* Hence each has a separate scope assigned to it: science is entirely concerned with phenomena, into which faith does not at all enter; faith, on the contrary, concerns itself with the divine, which is entirely unknown to science. Thus it is contended that there can never be any dissension between faith and science, for if each keeps on its own ground they can never meet and therefore never can be in contradiction. And if it be objected that in the visible world there are some things which appertain to faith, such as the human life of Christ, the Modernists reply by denying this. For though such things come within the category of phenomena, still in as far as they are *lived* by faith and in the way already described have been by faith *transfigured* and *disfigured,* they have been removed from the world of sense and transferred into material for the divine. Hence should it be further asked whether Christ has wrought real miracles, and made real prophecies, whether He rose truly from the dead and ascended into Heaven, the answer of agnostic science will be in the negative and the answer of faith in the affirmative—yet there will not be, on that account, any conflict between them. For it will be denied by the philosopher as a philosopher speaking to philosophers and considering Christ only in His *historical reality;* and it will be affirmed by the believer as a believer speaking to believers and considering the life of Christ as *lived again* by the faith and in the faith.

Faith subject to science. 17. It would be a great mistake, nevertheless, to suppose that, according to these theories, one is allowed to believe that faith and science are entirely independent of each other. On the side of science that is indeed quite true and correct, but it is quite otherwise with regard to faith, which is subject to science, not on one but on three grounds. For in the first place it must be observed that in every religious fact, when one takes away the *divine reality* and the *experience* of it which the believer possesses, everything else, and especially the *religious formulas,* belongs to the sphere of phenomena and therefore falls under the control of science. Let the believer go out of the world if he will, but so long as he remains in it, whether he like it or not, he cannot escape from the laws, the observation, the judgments of science and of history. Further, although it is contended that God is the object of faith alone, the statement refers only to the *divine reality,* not to the *idea* of God. The latter also is subject to science which, while it philosophizes in what is called the logical order, soars also to the absolute and the ideal. It is therefore the right of philosophy and of science to form its knowledge concerning the idea of God, to direct it in its evolution and to purify it of any extraneous elements which may have entered into it. Hence we have the Modernist axiom that the religious evolution ought to be brought into accord with the moral and intellectual, or as one whom they regard as their leader has expressed it, ought to be subject to it. Finally, man does not suffer a dualism to exist in himself, and the believer therefore feels within him an impelling need so to harmonise faith with science that it may never oppose the general conception which science sets forth concerning the universe.

Thus it is evident that science is to be entirely independent of faith, while on the other hand, and notwithstanding that they are supposed to be strangers to each other, faith is made subject to science. All this, Venerable Brethren, is in formal opposition to the teachings of Our predecessor, Pius IX, where he lays it down that: "In matters of religion it is the duty of philosophy not to command but to serve, not to prescribe what is to be believed, but to embrace what is to be believed with reasonable obedience, not to scrutinise the depths of the mysteries of God, but to venerate them devoutly and humbly." [9]

The Modernists completely invert the parts, and of them may be applied the words which another of Our predecessors, Gregory IX, addressed to some theologians of his time: "Some among you, puffed up like bladders with the spirit of vanity, strive by profane novelties to cross the boundaries fixed by the Fathers, twisting the meaning of the sacred text . . . to the philosophical teaching of the rationalists, not for the profit of their hearer but to make a show of science . . . these men, led away by various and strange doctrines, turn the head into the tail and force the queen to serve the handmaid." [10]

The methods of Modernists. 18. This will appear more clearly to anybody who studies the conduct of Modernists, which is in perfect harmony with their teachings. In their writings and addresses they seem not unfrequently to advocate doctrines which are contrary one to the other, so that one would be disposed to regard their attitude as double and doubtful. But this is done deliberately and advisedly, and the reason of it is to be found in their opinion as to the mutual separation of science and faith. Thus in their books one finds some things which might well be approved by a Catholic, but on turning over the page one is confronted by other things which might well have been dictated by a rationalist. When they write history they make no mention of the divinity of Christ, but when they are in the pulpit they profess it clearly; again, when they are dealing with history they take no account of the Fathers and the Councils, but when they catechise the people, they cite them respectfully. In the same way they draw their distinctions between exegesis which is theological and pastoral and exegesis which is scientific and historical. So, too, when they treat of philosophy, history, and criticism, acting on the principle that science in no way depends upon faith, they feel no especial horror in treading in the footsteps of Luther [11] and are wont to display a manifold contempt for Catholic doctrines, for the Holy Fathers, for the Ecumenical Councils, for the ecclesiastical magisterium; and should they be taken to task for this, they complain that they are being deprived of their liberty. Lastly, maintaining the theory that faith must be subject to science, they continuously and openly rebuke the Church on the ground that she resolutely refuses to submit and accommodate her dogmas to the opinions of philosophy; while they, on their side, having for this purpose blotted out the old theology, endeavor to introduce a new theology which shall support the aberrations of philosophers.

The Modernist as theologian. 19. At this point, Venerable Brethren, the way is opened for us to consider the Modernists in the theological arena—a difficult task, yet one that may be disposed of briefly. It is a question of effecting the conciliation of faith with science, but always by making the one subject to the other. In this matter the Modernist theologian takes exactly the same principles which we have seen employed by the Modernist philosopher—the principles of *immanence* and *symbolism*—and applies them to the believer. The process is an extremely simple one. The philosopher has declared: *The principle of faith is immanent;* the believer has added: *This principle is God;* and the theologian draws the conclusion: *God is immanent in man.* Thus we have *theological immanence.* So, too, the philosopher regards it as certain that *the representations of the object of faith are merely symbolical;* the believer has likewise affirmed that *the object of faith is God in himself;* and the theologian proceeds to affrm that: *The representations of the divine reality are symbolical.* And thus we have *theological symbolism.* These errors are truly of the gravest kind and the pernicious character of both will be seen clearly from an examination of their consequences. For, to begin with *symbolism,* since symbols are but symbols in regard to their objects and only instruments in regard to the believer, it is necessary first of all, according to the teachings of the Modernists, that the believer does not lay too much stress on the formula, as formula, but avail himself of it only for the purpose of uniting himself to the absolute truth which the formula at once reveals and conceals, that is to say, endeavors to express but without ever succeeding in doing so. They would also have the believer make use of the formulas only in as far as they are helpful to him, for they are given to be a help and not a hindrance; with proper regard, however, for the social respect due to formulas which the public magisterium has deemed suitable for expressing the common consciousness until such time as the same magisterium shall provide otherwise. Concerning *immanence* it is not easy to determine what Modernists precisely mean by it, for their own opinions on the subject vary. Some understand it in the sense that God working in man is more intimately present in him than man is even in himself; and this conception, if properly understood, is irreproachable. Others hold that the divine action is one with the action of nature, as the action of the first cause is one with the action of the secondary cause; and this would destroy the supernatural order. Others, finally, explain it in a way which savors of pantheism, and this, in truth, is the sense which best fits in with the rest of their doctrines.

The principle of Divine permanence. 20. With this principle of *immanence* is connected another which may be called the principle of *divine per-*

manence. It differs from the first in much the same way as the private *experience* differs from the *experience* transmitted by tradition. An example illustrating what is meant will be found in the Church and the sacraments. The Church and the sacraments, according to the Modernists, are not be regarded as having been instituted by Christ Himself. This is barred by agnosticism, which recognises in Christ nothing more than a man whose religious consciousness has been, like that of all men, formed by degrees; it is also barred by the law of immanence, which rejects what they call external *application;* it is further barred by the law of evolution, which requires, for the development of the germs, time and a certain series of circumstances; it is finally, barred by history, which shows that such in fact has been the course of things. Still it is to be held that both Church and sacraments has been founded *mediately* by Christ. But how? In this way: All Christian consciences were, they affirm, in a manner virtually included in the conscience of Christ as the plant is included in the seed. But as the branches live the life of the seed, so, too, all Christians are to be said to live the life of Christ. But the life of Christ, according to faith, is divine, and so, too, is the life of Christians. And if this life produced, in the course of ages, both the Church and the sacraments, it is quite right to say that their origin is from Christ and is divine. In the same way they make out that the Holy Scriptures and the dogmas are divine. And in this, the Modernist theology may be said to reach its completion. A slender provision, in truth, but more than enough for the theologian who professes that the conclusions of science, whatever they may be, must always be accepted! No one will have any difficulty in making the application of these theories to the other points with which We propose to deal.

Dogma and the Sacraments. 21. Thus far We have touched upon the origin and nature of faith. But as faith has many branches, and chief among them the Church, dogma, worship, devotions, the Books which we call "sacred," it concerns us to know what the Modernists teach concerning them. To begin with dogma, We have already indicated its origin and nature. Dogma is born of a sort of impulse or necessity by virtue of which the believer elaborates his thought so as to render it clearer to his own conscience and that of others. This elaboration consists entirely in the process of investigating and refining the primitive mental *formula,* not indeed in itself and according to any logical explanation, but according to circumstances, or *vitally* as the Modernists somewhat less intelligibly describe it. Hence it happens that around this *primitive* formula *secondary* formulas, as We have already indicated, gradually continue to be formed, and these subsequently grouped into one body, or one doctrinal construction, and further sanctioned by the public magisterium as responding to the common consciousness, are called dogma. Dogma is to be carefully distinguished from the speculations of theologians which, although not alive with the life of dogma, are not without their utility as serving both to harmonise religion with science and to remove opposition between them, and to illumine and defend religion from without, and it may be even to prepare the matter for future dogma. Concerning worship there would not be much to be said, were it not that under this head are comprised the sacraments, concerning which the Modernist errors are of the most serious character. For them the sacraments are the resultant of a double impulse or need—for, as we have seen, everything in their system is explained by inner impulses or necessities. The first need is that of giving some sensible manifestation to religion; the second is that of expressing it, which could not be done without some sensible form and consecrating acts, and these are called sacraments. But for the Modernists, sacraments are bare symbols or signs, though not devoid of a certain efficacy—an efficacy, they tell us, like that of certain phrases vulgarly described as having caught the popular ear, inasmuch as they have the power of putting certain leading ideas into circulation, and of making a marked impression upon the mind. What the phrases are to the ideas, that the sacraments are to the religious sense, that and nothing more. The Modernists would express their mind more clearly were they to affirm that the sacraments are instituted solely to foster the faith—but this is condemned by the Council of Trent: *If anyone say that these sacraments are instituted solely to foster the faith, let him be anathema.*[12]

The Holy Scriptures. 22. We have already touched upon the nature and origin of the Sacred Books. According to the principles of the Modernists they may be rightly described as a summary of *experiences,* not indeed of the kind that may now and again come to anybody, but those extraordinary and striking experiences which are the possession of every religion. And this is precisely what they teach about our books of the Old and New Testament. But to suit their own theories they note with remarkable ingenuity that, although experience is something belonging to the present, still it may draw its material in like manner from the past and the future inasmuch as the believer by memory *lives* the past over again after the manner of *the present,* and lives the future already by anticipation. This explains how it is that the historical and apocalyptic books are included among the Sacred Writings. God does indeed speak in these books through the medium of the believer, but according to Modernist theology, only by *immanence* and *vital permanence.* We may ask, what then becomes of inspiration? Inspiration, they reply, is in nowise distinguished from that impulse which stimulates the believer to reveal the faith that is in him by words or writing, except perhaps by its vehemence. It is something like that which happens in poetical inspiration, of which it has been said: There is a God in us, and when he stirreth he sets us afire. It is in this sense that God is said to be the origin of the inspiration of the Sacred Books. The Modernists moreover affirm concerning this inspiration, that there is nothing in the Sacred Books which is devoid of it. In this respect some might be disposed to consider them as more orthodox than certain writers in recent times who somewhat restrict inspiration, as, for instance, in what have been put forward as so-called *tacit citations*. But in all this we have mere verbal conjuring. For if we take the Bible, according to the standards of agnosticism, namely, as a human work, made by men for men, albeit the theologian is allowed to proclaim that it is divine by *immanence,* what room is there left in it for inspiration? The Modernists assert a general inspiration of the Sacred Books, but they admit no inspiration in the Catholic sense.

The Church. 23. A wider field for comment is opened when we come to what the Modernist school has imagined to be the nature of the Church. They begin with the supposition that the Church has its birth in a double need; first, the need of the individual believer to communicate his faith to others, especially if he has had some original and special experience, and secondly, when the faith has become common to many, the need of the *collectivity* to form itself into a society and to guard, promote, and propagate the common good. What, then, is the Church? It is the product of the *collective conscience,* that is to say, of the association of individual consciences which, by virtue of the principle of *vital permanence,* depend all on one first believer, who for Catholics is Christ. Now every society needs a directing authority to guide its members towards the common end, to foster prudently the elements of cohesion, which in a religious society are doctrine and worship. Hence the triple authority in the Catholic Church, *disciplinary, dogmatic, liturgical.* The nature of this authority is to be gathered from its origin, and its rights and duties from its nature. In past times it was a common error that authority came to the Church from without, that is to say directly from God; and it was then rightly held to be *autocratic.* But this conception has now grown obsolete. For in the same way as the Church is a vital emanation of the collectivity of consciences, so too authority emanates vitally from the Church itself. Authority, therefore, like the Church, has its origin in the religious conscience, and, that being so, is subject to it. Should it disown this dependence it becomes a tyranny. For we are living in an age when the sense of liberty has reached its highest development. In the civil order the public conscience has introduced popular government. Now there is in man only one conscience, just as there is only one life. It is for the ecclesiastical authority, therefore, to adopt a democratic form, unless it wishes to provoke and foment an intestine conflict in the consciences of mankind. The penalty of refusal is disaster. For it is madness to think that the sentiment of liberty, as it now obtains, can recede. Were it forcibly pent up and held in bonds, the more terrible would be its outburst, sweeping away at once both Church and religion. Such is the situation in the minds of the

Modernists, and their one great anxiety is, in consequence, to find a way of conciliation between the authority of the Church and the liberty of the believers.

Relation of Church and State. 24. But it is not only within her own household that the Church must come to terms. Besides her relations with those within, she has others with those who are outside. The Church does not occupy the world all by herself; there are other societies in the world, with which she must necessarily have dealings and contact. The rights and duties of the Church towards civil societies must, therefore, be determined, and determined, of course, by her own nature, that, to wit, which the Modernists have already described to us. The rules to be applied in this matter are clearly those which have been laid down for science and faith, though in the latter case the question turned upon the *object,* while in the present case we have one of *ends.* In the same way, then, as faith and science are alien to each other by reason of the diversity of their *objects,* Church and State are strangers by reason of the diversity of their ends, that of the Church being spiritual while that of the State is temporal. Formerly it was possible to subordinate the temporal to the spiritual and to speak of some questions as *mixed,* conceding to the Church the position of queen and mistress in all such, because the Church was then regarded as having been instituted immediately by God as the author of the supernatural order. But this doctrine is today repudiated alike by philosophers and historians. The State must, therefore, be separated from the Church, and the Catholic from the citizen. Every Catholic, from the fact that he is also a citizen, has the right and the duty to work for the common good in the way he thinks best, without troubling himself about the authority of the Church, without paying any heed to its wishes, its counsels, its orders—nay, even in spite of its rebukes. For the Church to trace out and prescribe for the citizen any line of action, on any pretext whatsoever, is to be guilty of an abuse of authority, against which one is bound to protest with all one's might. Venerable Brethren, the principles from which these doctrines spring have been solemnly condemned by Our predecessor, Pius VI, in his Apostolic Constitution *Auctorem fidei.*[13]

The Church's Magisterium. 25. But it is not enough for the Modernist school that the State should be separated from the Church. For as faith is to be subordinated to science as far as phenomenal elements are concerned, so too in temporal matters the Church must be subject to the State. This, indeed, Modernists may not yet say openly, but they are forced by the logic of their position to admit it. For granted the principle that in temporal matters the State possesses the sole power, it will follow that when the believer, not satisfied with merely internal acts of religion, proceeds to external acts—such for instance as the reception or administration of the sacraments—these will fall under the control of the State. What will then become of ecclesiastical authority, which can only be exercised by external acts? Obviously it will be completely under the dominion of the State. It is this inevitable consequence which urges many among *liberal* Protestants to reject all external worship—nay, all external religious fellowship, and leads them to advocate what they call *individual* religion. If the Modernists have not yet openly proceeded so far, they ask the Church in the meanwhile to follow of her own accord in the direction in which they urge her and to adapt herself to the forms of the State. Such are their ideas about *disciplinary* authority. But much more evil and pernicious are their opinions on *doctrinal* and *dogmatic* authority. The following is their conception of the magisterium of the Church: No religious society, they say, can be a real unit unless the religious conscience of its members be one, and also the formula which they adopt. But this double unity requires a kind of common mind whose office is to find and determine the formula that corresponds best with the common conscience; and it must have, moreover, an authority sufficient to enable it to impose on the community the formula which has been decided upon. From the combination and, as it were, fusion of these two elements, the common mind which draws up the formula and the authority which imposes it, arises, according to the Modernists, the notion of the ecclesiastical magisterium. And, as this magisterium springs, in its last analysis, from the individual consciences and possesses its mandate of public utility for their benefit, it necessarily follows that the ecclesiastical magisterium must be dependent upon them, and should therefore be made to bow to the popular ideals. To prevent individual consciences from expressing freely and openly the impulses they feel, to hinder criticism from urging forward dogma in the path of its necessary evolution, is not a legitimate use but an abuse of a power given for the public weal. So too a due method and measure must be observed in the exercise of authority. To condemn and proscribe a work without the knowledge of the author, without hearing his explanations, without discussion, is something approaching to tyranny. And here again it is a question of finding a way of reconciling the full rights of authority on the one hand and those of liberty on the other. In the meantime the proper course for the Catholic will be to proclaim publicly his profound respect for authority, while never ceasing to follow his own judgment. Their general direction for the Church is as follows: that the ecclesiastical authority, since its end is entirely spiritual, should strip itself of that external pomp which adorns it in the eyes of the public. In this, they forget that while religion is for the soul, it is not exclusively for the soul, and that the honor paid to authority is reflected back on Christ who instituted it.

The evolution of doctrine. 26. To conclude this whole question of faith and its various branches, we have still to consider, Venerable Brethren, what the Modernists have to say about the development of the one and the other.

First of all they lay down the general principle that in a living religion everything is subject to change, and must in fact be changed. In this way they pass to what is practically their principal doctrine, namely, *evolution*. To the laws of evolution everything is subject under penalty of death—dogma, Church, worship, the Books we revere as sacred, even faith itself. The enunciation of this principle will not be a matter of surprise to anyone who bears in mind what the Modernists have had to say about each of these subjects. Having laid down this law of evolution, the Modernists themselves teach us how it operates. And first, with regard to faith. The primitive form of faith, they tell us, was rudimentary and common to all men alike, for it had its origin in human nature and human life. Vital evolution brought with it progress, not by the accretion of new and purely adventitious forms from without, but by an increasing perfusion of the religious sense into the conscience. The progress was of two kinds: *negative,* by the elimination of all extraneous elements, such, for example, as those derived from the family or nationality; and *positive,* by that intellectual and moral refining of man, by means of which the idea of the divine became fuller and clearer, while the *religious sense* became more acute. For the progress of faith the same causes are to be assigned as those which are adduced above to explain its origin. But to them must be added those extraordinary men whom we call prophets—of whom Christ was the greatest—both because in their lives and their words there was something mysterious which faith attributed to the divinity, and because it fell to their lot to have new and original *experiences* fully in harmony with the religious needs of their time. The progress of dogma is due chiefly to the fact that obstacles to the faith have to be surmounted, enemies have to be vanquished, and objections have to be refuted. Add to this a perpetual striving to penetrate ever more profoundly into those things which are contained in the mysteries of faith. Thus, putting aside other examples, it is found to have happened in the case of Christ; in Him that divine something which faith recognised in Him was slowly and gradually expanded in such a way that He was at last held to be God. The chief stimulus of the evolution of worship consists in the need of accommodation to the manners and customs of peoples, as well as the need of availing itself of the value which certain acts have acquired by usage. Finally, evolution in the Church itself is fed by the need of adapting itself to historical conditions and of harmonising itself with existing forms of society. Such is their view with regard to each. And here, before proceeding further, We wish to draw attention to this whole theory of *necessities* or *needs,* for beyond all that we have seen, it is, as it were, the base and foundation of that famous method which they describe as historical.

Tradition and progress. 27. Although evolution is urged on by needs or necessities, yet, if controlled by these alone, it would easily overstep the boundaries of tradition, and thus, separated from its primitive vital principle, would make for ruin instead of progress. Hence, by those who study more closely the ideas of the Modernists, evolution is described as a resultant from the conflict of two forces, one of them tending towards progress, the other towards conservation. The conserving force exists in the Church and is found in tradition; tradition is represented by religious authority, and this both by right and in fact. By right, for it is in the very nature of authority to protect tradition: and in fact, since authority, raised as it is above the contingencies of life, feels hardly, or not at all, the spurs of progress. The progressive force, on the contrary, which responds to the inner needs, lies in the individual consciences and works in them—especially in such of them as are in more close and intimate contact with life. Already we observe, Venerable Brethren, the introduction of that most pernicious doctrine which would make of the laity the factor of progress in the Church. Now it is by a species of covenant and compromise between these two forces of conservation and progress, that is to say between authority and individual consciences, that changes and advances take place. The individual consciences, or some of them, act on the collective conscience, which brings pressure to bear on the depositaries of authority to make terms and to keep to them.

The Modernist complex. With all this in mind, one understands how it is that the Modernists express astonishment when they are reprimanded or punished. What is imputed to them as a fault they regard as a sacred duty. They understand the needs of consciences better than anyone else, since they come into closer touch with them than does the ecclesiastical authority. Nay, they embody them, so to speak, in themselves. Hence, for them to speak and to write publicly is a bounden duty. Let authority rebuke them if it pleases—they have their own conscience on their side and an intimate experience which tells them with certainty that what they deserve is not blame but praise. Then they reflect that, after all, there is no progress without a battle and no battle without its victims; and victims they are willing to be like the prophets and Christ Himself. They have no bitterness in their hearts against the authority which uses them roughly, for after all they readily admit that it is only doing its duty as authority. Their sole grief is that it remains deaf to their warnings, for in this way it impedes the progress of souls, but the hour will most surely come when further delay will be impossible, for if the laws of evolution may be checked for a while they cannot be finally evaded. And thus they go their way, reprimands and condemnations notwithstanding, masking an incredible audacity under a mock semblance of humility. While they make a pretence of bowing their heads, their minds and hands are more boldly intent than ever on carrying out their purposes. And this policy they follow willingly and wittingly, both because it is part of their system that authority is to be stimulated but not dethroned, and because it is necessary for them to remain within the ranks of the Church in order that they may gradually transform the collective conscience. And in saying this, they fail to perceive that they are avowing that the collective conscience is not with them, and that they have no right to claim to be its interpreters.

Previous condemnation of Modernism. 28. It is thus, Venerable Brethren, that for the Modernists, whether as authors or propagandists, there is to be nothing stable, nothing immutable in the Church. Nor, indeed, are they without forerunners in their doctrines, for it was of these that Our predecessor Pius IX wrote: "These enemies of divine revelation extol human progress to the skies, and with rash and sacrilegious daring would have it introduced into the Catholic religion as if this religion were not the work of God but of man, or some kind of philosophical discovery susceptible of perfection by human efforts." [14] On the subject of revelation and dogma in particular, the doctrine of the Modernists offers nothing new. We find it condemned in the Syllabus of Pius IX, where it is enunciated in these terms: "Divine revelation is imperfect, and therefore subject to continual and indefinite progress, corresponding with the progress of human reason"; [15] and condemned still more solemnly in the Vatican Council: "The doctrine of the faith which God has revealed has not been proposed to human intelligences to be perfected by them as if it were a philosophical system, but as a divine deposit entrusted to the Spouse of Christ to be faithfully guarded and infallibly interpreted. Hence also that sense of the sacred dogmas is to be perpetually retained which our Holy Mother the Church has once declared, nor is this sense ever to be abandoned on plea or pretext of a more profound comprehension of the truth." [16] Nor is the development of our knowledge, even concerning the faith, barred by this pronouncement; on the contrary, it is supported and maintained. For the same Council continues: "Let intelligence and science and wisdom, therefore, increase and progress abundantly and vigorously in individuals, and in the mass, in the believer and in the whole Church, throughout the ages and the centuries—but only in its own kind, that is, according to the same dogma, the same sense, the same acceptation." [17]

Further examination of Modernism. 29. We have studied the Modernist as philosopher, believer, and theologian. It now remains for us to consider him as historian, critic, apologist, and reformer.

The Modernist as historian. 30. Some Modernists, devoted to historical studies, seem to be deeply anxious not to be taken for philosophers. About philosophy they profess to know nothing whatever, and in this they display remarkable astuteness, for they are particularly desirous not to be suspected of any prepossession in favor of philosophical theories which would lay them open to the charge of not being, as they call it, *objective*. And yet the truth is that their history and their criticism are saturated with their philosophy, and that their historico-critical conclusions are the natural outcome of their philosophical principles. This will be patent to anyone who reflects. Their three first laws are contained in those three principles of their philosophy already dealt with: the principle of *agnosticism,* the theorem of the *transfiguration* of things by faith, and that other which may be called the principle of *disfiguration.* Let us see what consequences flow from each of these. *Agnosticism* tells us that history, like science, deals entirely with phenomena, and the consequence is that God, and every intervention of God in human affairs, is to be relegated to the domain of faith as belonging to it alone. Wherefore in things where there is combined a double element, the divine and the human, as, for example, in Christ, or the Church, or the sacraments, or the many other objects of the same kind, a division and separation must be made and the human element must be left to history while the divine will be assigned to faith. Hence we have that distinction, so current among the Modernists, between the Christ of history and the Christ of faith; the Church of history and the Church of faith; the sacraments of history and the sacraments of faith, and so in similar matters. Next we find that the human element itself, which the historian has to work on, as it appears in the documents, is to be considered as having been transfigured by faith, that is to say, raised above its historical conditions. It becomes necessary, therefore, to eliminate also the accretions which faith has added, to relegate them to faith itself and to the history of faith. Thus, when treating of Christ, the historian must set aside all that surpasses man in his natural condition, according to what psychology tells us of him, or according to what we gather from the place and period of his existence. Finally, they require, by virtue of the third principle, that even those things which are not outside the sphere of history should pass through the sieve, excluding all and relegating to faith everything which, in their judgment, is not in harmony with what they call the *logic* of facts or not in character with the persons of whom they are predicated. Thus, they will not allow that Christ ever uttered those things which do not seem to be within the capacity of the multitudes that listened to Him. Hence they delete from His *real* history and transfer to faith all the allegories found in His discourses. We may peradventure inquire on what principle they make these divisions? Their reply is that they argue from the character of the man, from his condition of life, from his education, from the complexus of the circumstances under which the facts took place; in short, if We understand them aright, on a principle which in the last analysis is merely *subjective.* Their method is to put themselves into the position and person of Christ, and then to attribute to Him what they would have done under like circumstances. In this way, absolutely *a priori* and acting on philosophical principles which they hold but which they profess to ignore, they proclaim that Christ, according to what they call His *real* history, was not God and never did anything divine, and that as man He did and said only what they, judging from the time in which He lived, consider that He ought to have said or done.

The Modernist as critic. 31. As history takes its conclusions from philosophy, so too criticism takes its conclusions from history. The critic on the data furnished him by the historian, makes two parts of all his documents. Those that remain after the triple elimination above described go to form the *real* history; the rest is attributed to the history of the faith or, as it is styled, to *internal* history. For the Modernists distinguish very carefully between these two kinds of history, and it is to be noted that they oppose the history of the faith to *real* history precisely as real. Thus, as we have already said, we have a twofold Christ: a real Christ, and a Christ, the one of faith, who never really existed; a Christ who has lived at a given time and in a given place, and a Christ who never lived outside the pious meditations of the believer—the Christ, for instance, whom we find in the Gospel of St. John, which, according to them, is mere meditation from beginning to end.

His principles of criticism. 32. But the dominion of philosophy over history does not end here. Given that division, of which We have spoken, of the documents into two parts, the philosopher steps in again with his dogma of *vital immanence,* and shows how everything in the history of the Church is to be explained by *vital emanation*. And since the cause or condition of every vital emanation whatsoever is to be found in some need or want, it follows that no fact can be regarded as antecedent to the need which produced it—historically the fact must be posterior to the need. What, then, does the historian do in view of this principle? He goes over his documents again, whether they be contained in the Sacred Books or elsewhere, draws up from them his list of the particular needs of the Church, whether relating to dogma, or liturgy, or other matters which are found in the Church thus related, and then he hands his list over to the critic. The critic takes in hand the documents dealing with the history of faith and distributes them, period by period, so that they correspond exactly with the list of needs, always guided by the principle that the narration must follow the facts, as the facts follow the needs. It may at times happen that some parts of the Sacred Scriptures, such as the Epistles, themselves constitute the fact created by the need. Even so, the rule holds that the age of any document can only be determined by the age in which each need has manifested itself in the Church. Further, a distinction must be made between the beginning of a fact and its development, for what is born in one day requires time for growth. Hence the critic must once more go over his documents, ranged as they are through the different ages, and divide them again into two parts, separating those that regard the origin of the facts from those that deal with their development, and these he must again arrange according to their periods.

Modernist confusion. 33. Then the philosopher must come in again to enjoin upon the historian the obligation of following in all his studies the precepts and laws of evolution. It is next for the historian to scrutinise his documents once more, to examine carefully the circumstances and conditions affecting the Church during the different periods, the conserving force she has put forth, the needs both internal and external that have stimulated her to progress, the obstacles she has had to encounter, in a word, everything that helps to determine the manner in which the laws of evolution have been fulfilled in her. This done, he finishes his work by drawing up a history of the development in its broad lines. The critic follows and fits in the rest of the documents. He sets himself to write. The history is finished. Now We ask here: Who is the author of this history? The historian? The critic? Assuredly neither of these but the philosopher. From beginning to end everything in it is *a priori,* and an apriorism that reeks of heresy. These men are certainly to be pitied, of whom the Apostle might well say: "They became vain in their thoughts . . . professing themselves to be wise, they became fools." [18] At the same time, they excite resentment when they accuse the Church of arranging and confusing the texts after her own fashion, and for the needs of her cause. In this they are accusing the Church of something for which their own conscience plainly reproaches them.

Modernist treatment of the Bible. 34. The result of this dismembering of the records, and this partition of them throughout the centuries is naturally that the Scriptures can no longer be attributed to the authors whose names they bear. The Modernists have no hesitation in affirming generally that these books, and especially the Pentateuch and the first three Gospels, have been gradually formed from a primitive brief narration, by additions, by interpolations of theological or allegorical interpretations, or parts introduced only for the purpose of joining different passages together. This means, to put it briefly and clearly, that in the Sacred Books we must admit a *vital evolution,* springing from and corresponding with the evolution of faith. The traces of this evolution, they tell us, are so visible in the books that one might almost write a history of it. Indeed, this history they actually do write, and with such an easy assurance that one might believe them to have seen with their own eyes the writers at work through the ages amplifying the Sacred Books. To aid them in this they call to their assistance that branch of criticism which they call *textual,* and labor to show that such a fact or such a phrase is not in its right place, adducing other arguments of the same kind. They seem, in fact, to have constructed for themselves certain types of narration and discourses, upon which they base their assured verdict as to whether a thing is or is not out of place. Let him who can judge how far they are qualified in this way to make such distinctions. To hear them descant of their works on the Sacred Books, in which they have been able to discover so much that is defective, one would imagine that before them nobody ever even turned over the pages of Scripture. The truth is that a whole multitude of Doctors, far superior to them in genius, in erudition, in sanctity, have sifted the Sacred Books in every way, and so far from finding in them anything blameworthy have thanked God more and more heartily the more deeply they have gone into them, for His divine bounty in having vouchsafed to speak thus to men. Unfortunately, these great Doctors did not enjoy the same aids to study that are possessed by the Modernists for they did not have for their rule and guide a philosophy borrowed from the negation of God, and a criterion which consists of themselves.

Contrary to Catholic teaching. We believe, then, that We have set forth with sufficient clearness the historical method of the Modernists. The philosopher leads the way, the historian follows, and then in due order come the internal and textual critics. And since it is characteristic of the primary cause to communicate its virtue to causes which are secondary, it is quite clear that the criticism with which We are concerned is not any kind of criticism, but that which is rightly called *agnostic, immanentist, and evolutionist* criticism. Hence anyone who adopts it and employs it makes profession thereby of the errors contained in it, and places himself in opposition to Catholic teaching. This being so, it is much a matter for surprise that it should have found acceptance to such an extent among certain Catholics. Two causes may be assigned for this: first, the close alliance which the historians and critics of this school have formed among themselves independent of all differences of nationality or religion; second, their boundless effrontery by which, if one then makes any utterance, the others applaud him in chorus, proclaiming that science has made another step forward, while if an outsider should desire to inspect the new discovery for himself, they form a coalition against him. He who denies it is decried as one who is ignorant, while he who embraces and defends it has all their praise. In this way they entrap not a few, who, did they but realise what they are doing, would shrink back with horror. The domineering overbearance of those who teach the errors, and the thoughtless compliance of the more shallow minds who assent to them, create a corrupted atmosphere which penetrates everywhere, and carries infection with it. But let Us pass to the apologist.

The Modernist as apologist. 35. The Modernist apologist depends in two ways on the philosopher. First, *indirectly,* inasmuch as his subject-matter is history—history dictated, as we have seen, by the philosopher; and, secondly, *directly,* inasmuch as he takes both his doctrines and his conclusions from the philosopher. Hence that common axiom of the Modernist school that in the new apologetics controversies in religion must be determined by psychological and historical research. The Modernist apologists, then, enter the arena, proclaiming to the rationalists that, though they are defending religion, they have no intention of employing the data of the sacred books or the histories in current use in the Church, and written upon the old lines, but *real* history composed on modern principles and according to the modern method. In all this they assert that they are not using an *argumentum ad hominem,* because they are really of the opinion that the truth is to be found only in this kind of history. They feel that it is not necessary for them to make profession of their own sincerity in their writings. They are already known to and praised by the rationalists as fighting under the same banner, and they not only plume themselves on these encomiums, which would only provoke disgust in a real Catholic, but use them as a counter-compensation to the reprimands of the Church.

Modernist apologetic methodology. Let us see how the Modernist conducts his apologetics. The aim he sets before himself is to make one who is still without faith attain that *experience* of the Catholic religion which, according to the system, is the sole basis of faith. There are two ways open to him, the *objective* and the *subjective.* The first of them starts from agnosticism. It tends to show that religion, and especially the Catholic religion, is endowed with such vitality as to compel every psychologist and historian of good faith to recognise that its history hides some element of the *unknown.* To this end it is necessary to prove that the Catholic religion, as it exists today, is that which was founded by Jesus Christ; that is to say, that it is nothing else than the progressive development of the germ which He brought into the world. Hence it is imperative first to all to establish what this germ was, and this the Modernist claims to be able to do by the following formula: Christ announced the coming of the kingdom of God, which was to be realised within a brief lapse of time and of which He was to become the Messias, the divinely-given founder and ruler. Then it must be shown how this germ, always *immanent* and *permanent* in the Catholic religion, has gone on slowly developing in the course of history, adapting itself successively to the different circumstances through which it has passed, borrowing from them by *vital* assimilation all the doctrinal, cultural, ecclesiastical forms that served its purpose; whilst, on the other hand, it surmounted all obstacles, vanquished all enemies, and survived all assaults and all combats. Anyone who well and duly considers this mass of obstacles, adversaries, attacks, combats, and the vitality and fecundity which the Church has shown throughout them all, must admit that if the laws of evolution are visible in her life they fail to explain the whole of her history—the *unknown* rises forth from it and presents itself before us, Thus do they argue, not perceiving that their determination of the primitive germ is only an *a priori* assumption of agnostic and evolutionist philosophy, and that the germ itself has been gratuitously defined so that it may fit in with their contention.

Modernist confusion. 36. But while they endeavor by this line of reasoning to prove and plead for the Catholic religion, these new apologists are more than willing to grant and to recognise that there are in it many things which are repulsive. Nay, they admit openly, and with ill-concealed satisfaction, that they have found that even its dogma is not exempt from errors and contradictions. They add also that this is not only excusable but—curiously enough—that it is even right and proper. In the Sacred Books there are many passages referring to science or history where, according to them, manifest errors are to be found. But, they say, the subject of these books is not science or history, but only religion and morals. In them history and science serve only as a species of covering to enable the religious and moral experiences wrapped up in them to penetrate more readily among the masses. The masses understood science and history as they are expressed in these books, and it is clear that the expression of science and history in a more perfect form would have proved not so much a help as a hindrance. Moreover, they add, the Sacred Books, being essentially religious, are necessarily quick with life. Now life has its own truths and its own logic—quite different from rational truth and rational logic, belonging as they do to a different order, viz., truth of adaptation and of proportion both with what they call the *medium* in which it lives and with the end for which it lives. Finally, the Modernists, losing all sense of control, go so far as to proclaim as true and legitimate whatever is explained by life.

The simplicity of Truth. We, Venerable Brethren, for whom there is but one and only one truth, and who hold that the Sacred Books, "written under the inspiration of the Holy Ghost, have God for their author" [19] declare that this is equivalent to attributing to God Himself the lie of utility or officious lie, and We say with St. Augustine: "In an authority so high, admit but one officious lie, and there will not remain a single passage of those apparently difficult to practise or to believe, which on the same most pernicious rule may not be explained as a lie uttered by the author wilfully and to serve a purpose." [20] And thus it will come about, the holy Doctor continues, that "everybody will believe and refuse to believe what he likes or dislikes in them," namely, the Scriptures. But the Modernists pursue their way eagerly. They grant also that certain arguments adduced in the Sacred Books in proof of a given doctrine, like those, for example, which are based on the prophecies, have no rational foundation to rest on. But they defend even these as artifices of preaching, which are justified by life. More than that. They are ready to admit, nay, to proclaim that Christ Himself manifestly erred in determining the time when the coming of the Kingdom of God was to take place; and they tell us that we must not be surprised at this since even He Himself was subject to the laws of life! After this what is to become of the dogmas of the Church? The dogmas bristle with flagrant contradictions, but what does it matter since, apart from the fact that vital logic accepts them, they are not repugnant to symbolical truth. Are we not dealing with the infinite, and has not the infinite an infinite variety of aspects? In short, to maintain and defend these theories they do not hesitate to declare that the noblest homage that can be paid to the Infinite is to make it the object of contradictory statements! But when they justify even contradictions, what is it that they will refuse to justify?

Subjective arguments. 37. But it is not solely by *objective* arguments that the non-believer may be disposed to faith. There are also those that are *subjective,* and for this purpose the modernist apologists return to the doctrine of *immanence.* They endeavor, in fact, to persuade their non-believer that down in the very depths of his nature and his life lie hidden the need and the desire for some religion, and this not a religion of any kind, but the specific religion known as Catholicism, which, they say, is absolutely *postulated* by the perfect development of life. And here again We have grave reason to complain that there are Catholics who, while rejecting *immanence* as a doctrine, employ it as a method of apologetics, and who do this so imprudently that they seem to admit, not merely a capacity and a suitability for the supernatural, such as has at all times been emphasised, within due limits, by Catholic apologists, but that there is in human nature a true and rigorous need for the supernatural order. Truth to tell, it is only the moderate Modernists who make this appeal to an exigency for the Catholic religion. As for the others, who might be called *integralists,* they would show to the non-believer, as hidden in his being, the very germ which Christ Himself had in His consciousness, and which He transmitted to mankind. Such, Venerable Brethren, is a summary description of the apologetic method of the Modernists, in perfect harmony with their doctrines—methods and doctrines replete with errors, made not for edification but for destruction, not for the making of Catholics but for the seduction of those who are Catholics into heresy; and tending to the utter subversion of all religion.

The Modernist as reformer. 38. It remains for Us now to say a few words about the Modernist as reformer. From all that has preceded, it is abundantly clear how great and how eager is the passion of such men for innovation. In all Catholicism there is absolutely nothing on which it does not fasten. They wish philosophy to be reformed, especially in the ecclesiastical seminaries. They wish the scholastic philosophy to be relegated to the history of philosophy and to be classed among absolute systems, and the young men to be taught modern philosophy which alone is true and suited to the times in which we live. They desire the reform of theology: rational theology is to have modern philosophy for its foundation, and positive theology is to be founded on the history of dogma. As for history, it must be written and taught only according to their methods and modern principles. Dogmas and their evolution, they affirm, are to be harmonised with science and history. In the Catechism no dogmas are to be inserted except those that have been reformed and are within the capacity of the people. Regarding worship, they say, the number of external devotions is to be reduced, and steps must be taken to prevent their further increase, though, indeed, some of the admirers of symbolism are disposed to be more indulgent on this head. They cry out that ecclesiastical government requires to be reformed in all its branches, but especially in its disciplinary and dogmatic departments. They insist that both outwardly and inwardly it must be brought into harmony with the modern conscience, which now wholly tends towards democracy; a share in ecclesiastical government should therefore be given to the lower ranks of the clergy, and even to the laity, and authority, which is too much concentrated, should be decentralised. The Roman Congregations, and especially the *Index* and the *Holy Office,* must be likewise modified. The ecclesiastical authority must alter its line of conduct in the social and political world; while keeping outside political organizations, it must adapt itself to them, in order to penetrate them with its spirit. With regard to morals, they adopt the principle of the Americanists, that the active virtues are more important than the passive, and are to be more encouraged in practice. They ask that the clergy should return to their primitive humility and poverty, and that in their ideas and action they should admit the principles of Modernism; and there are some who, gladly listening to the teaching of their Protestant masters, would desire the suppression of the celibacy of the clergy. What is there left in the Church which is not to be reformed by them and according to their principles?

Modernism, synthesis of all heresies. 39. It may, perhaps, seem to some, Venerable Brethren, that We have dealt at too great length on this exposition of the doctrines of the Modernists. But it was necessary that We should do so, both in order to meet their customary charge that We do not understand their ideas, and to show that their system does not consist in scattered and unconnected theories, but, as it were, in a closely connected whole, so that it is not possible to admit one without admitting all. For this reason, too, We have had to give to this exposition a somewhat didactic form, and not to shrink from employing certain unwonted terms which the Modernists have brought into use. And now with Our eyes fixed upon the whole system, no one will be surprised that We should define it to be the synthesis of all heresies. Undoubtedly, were anyone to attempt the task of collecting together all the errors that have been broached against the faith and to concentrate into one the sap and substance of them all, he could not succeed in doing so better than the Modernists have done. Nay, they have gone farther than this, for, as We have already intimated, their system means the destruction not of the Catholic religion alone, but of all religion. Hence the rationalists are not wanting in their applause, and the most frank and sincere among them congratulate themselves on having found in the Modernists the most valuable of all allies.

Let us turn for a moment, Venerable Brethren, to that most disastrous doctrine of *agnosticism*. By it every avenue to God on the side of the intellect is barred to man, while a better way is supposed to be opened from the side of a certain sense of the soul and action. But who does not see how mistaken is such a contention? For the sense of the soul is the response to the action of the thing which the intellect or the outward senses set before it. Take away the intelligence, and man, already inclined to follow the senses, becomes their slave. Doubly mistaken, from another point of view, for all these fantasies of the religious sense will never be able to destroy common sense, and common sense tells us that emotion and everything that leads the heart captive proves a hindrance instead of a help to the discovery of truth. We speak of truth in itself—for that other purely *subjective* truth, the fruit of the internal sense and action, if it serves its purpose for the play of words, is of no benefit to the man who wants above all things to know whether outside himself there is a God into whose hands he is one day to fall. True, the Modernists call in *experience* to eke out their system, but what does this *experience* add to that sense of the soul? Absolutely nothing beyond a certain intensity and a proportionate deepening of the conviction of the reality of the object. But these two will never make the sense of the soul into anything but sense, nor will they alter its nature, which is liable to deception when the intelligence is not there to guide it; on the contrary, they but confirm and strengthen this nature, for the more intense the sense is the more it is really sense. And as we are here dealing with religious sense and the experience involved in it, it is known to you, Venerable Brethren, how necessary in such a matter is prudence, and the learning by which prudence is guided. You know it from your own dealings with souls, and especially with souls in whom sentiment predominates; you know it also from your reading of works of ascetical theology—works for which the Modernists have but little esteem, but which testify to a science and a solidity far greater than theirs, and to a refinement and subtlety of observation far beyond any which the Modernists take credit to themselves for possessing. It seems to Us nothing short of madness, or at the least consummate temerity to accept for true, and without investigation, these incomplete experiences which are the vaunt of the Modernist. Let us for a moment put the question: If experiences have so much force and value in their estimation, why do they not attach equal weight to the experience that so many thousands of Catholics have that the Modernists are on the wrong path? Is it that the Catholic experiences are the only ones which are false and deceptive? The vast majority of mankind holds and always will hold firmly that sense and experience alone, when not enlightened and guided by reason, cannot reach to the knowledge of God. What, then, remains but atheism and the absence of all religion? Certainly it is not the doctrine of *symbolism* that will save us from this. For if all the intellectual elements, as they call them, of religion are nothing more than mere symbols of God, will not the very name of God or of divine personality be also a symbol, and if this be admitted, the personality of God will become a matter of doubt and the gate will be opened to pantheism? And to pantheism pure and simple that other doctrine of the *divine immanence* leads directly. For this is the question which We ask: Does or does not this *immanence* leave God distinct from man? If it does, in what does it differ from the Catholic doctrine, and why does it reject the doctrine of external revelation? If it does not, it is pantheism. Now the doctrine of *immanence* in the Modernist acceptation holds and professes that every phenomenon of conscience proceeds from man as man. The rigorous conclusion from this is the identity of man with God, which means pantheism. The distinction which Modernists make between science and faith leads to the same conclusion. The object of science, they say, is the reality of the knowable; the object of faith, on the contrary, is the reality of the unknowable. Now, what makes the unknowable unknowable is the fact that there is no proportion between its object and the intellect—a defect of proportion which nothing whatever, even in the doctrine of the Modernist, can suppress. Hence the unknowable remains and will eternally remain unknowable to the believer as well as to the philosopher. Therefore if any religion at all is possible, it can only be the religion of an unknowable reality. And why this might not be that soul of the universe, of which certain rationalists speak, is something which certainly does not seem to Us apparent. These reasons suffice to show superabundantly by how many roads Modernism leads to atheism and to the annihilation of all religion. The error of Protestantism made the first step on this path; that of Modernism makes the second; atheism makes the next.

The danger of curiosity. 40. To penetrate still deeper into the meaning of Modernism and to find a suitable remedy for so deep a sore, it behooves Us, Venerable Brethren, to investigate the causes which have engendered it and which foster its growth. That the proximate and immediate cause consists in an error of the mind cannot be open to doubt. We recognise that the remote causes may be reduced to two: curiosity and pride. Curiosity by itself, if not prudently regulated, suffices to account for all errors. Such is the opinion of Our predecessor, Gregory XVI, who wrote: "A lamentable spectacle is that presented by the aberrations of human reason when it yields to the spirit of novelty, when against the warning of the Apostle it seeks to know beyond what it is meant to know, and when relying too much on itself it thinks it can find the truth outside the Catholic Church wherein truth is found without the slightest shadow of error." [21]

Pride sits in the Modernist house. But it is pride which exercises an incomparably greater sway over the soul to blind it and lead it into error, and pride sits in Modernism as in its own house, finding sustenance everywhere in its doctrines and lurking in its every aspect. It is pride which fills

Modernists with that self-assurance by which they consider themselves and pose as the rule for all. It is pride which puffs them up with that vainglory which allows them to regard themselves as the sole possessors of knowledge, and makes them say, elated and inflated with presumption, "We are not as the rest of men," and which, lest they should seem as other men, leads them to embrace and to devise novelties even of the most absurd kind. It is pride which rouses in them the spirit of disobedience and causes them to demand a compromise between authority and liberty. It is owing to their pride that they seek to be the reformers of others while they forget to reform themselves, and that they are found to be utterly wanting in respect for authority, even for the supreme authority. Truly there is no road which leads so directly and so quickly to Modernism as pride. When a Catholic layman or a priest forgets the precept of the Christian life which obliges us to renounce ourselves if we would follow Christ and neglects to tear pride from his heart, then it is he who most of all is a fully ripe subject for the errors of Modernism. For this reason, Venerable Brethren, it will be your first duty to resist such victims of pride, to employ them only in the lowest and obscurest offices. The higher they try to rise, the lower let them be placed, so that the lowliness of their position may limit their power of causing damage. Examine most carefully your young clerics by yourselves and by the directors of your seminaries, and when you find the spirit of pride among them reject them without compunction from the priesthood. Would to God that this had always been done with the vigilance and constancy which were required!

Ignorance of the Modernists. 41. If we pass on from the moral to the intellectual causes of Modernism, the first and the chief which presents itself is ignorance. Yes, these very Modernists who seek to be esteemed as Doctors of the Church, who speak so loftily of modern philosophy and show such contempt for scholasticism, have embraced the one with all its false glamour, precisely because their ignorance of the other has left them without the means of being able to recognise confusion of thought and to refute sophistry. Their whole system, containing as it does errors so many and so great, has been born of the union between faith and false philosophy.

Methods of propagandism. 42. Would that they had but displayed less zeal and energy in propagating it! But such is their activity and such their unwearying labor on behalf of their cause, that one cannot but be pained to see them waste such energy in endeavoring to ruin the Church when they might have been of such service to her had their efforts been better directed. Their artifices to delude men's minds are of two kinds, the first to remove obstacles from their path, the second to devise and apply actively and patiently every resource that can serve their purpose. They recognise that the three chief difficulties which stand in their way are the scholastic method of philosophy, the authority and tradition of the Fathers, and the magisterium of the Church, and on these they wage unrelenting war. Against scholastic philosophy and theology they use the weapons of ridicule and contempt. Whether it is ignorance or fear, or both, that inspires this conduct in them, certain it is that the passion for novelty is always united in them with hatred of scholasticism, and there is no surer sign that a man is tending to Modernism than when he begins to show his dislike for the scholastic method. Let the Modernists and their admirers remember the proposition condemned by Pius IX: "The method and principles which have served the ancient doctors of scholasticism when treating of theology no longer correspond with the exigencies of our time or the progress of science." [22] They exercise all their ingenuity in an effort to weaken the force and falsify the character of tradition, so as to rob it of all its weight and authority. But for Catholics nothing will remove the authority of the second Council of Nicea, where it condemns those "who dare, after the impious fashion of heretics, to deride the ecclesiastical traditions, to invent novelties of some kind . . . or endeavor by malice or craft to overthrow any one of the legitimate traditions of the Catholic Church"; nor that of the declaration of the fourth Council of Constantinople: "We therefore profess to preserve and guard the rules bequeathed to the Holy Catholic and Apostolic Church, by the Holy and most illustrious Apostles, by the orthodox Councils, both general and local, and by every one of those divine interpreters, the Fathers and Doctors of the Church." Wherefore the Roman Pontiffs, Pius IV and Pius IX, ordered the insertion in the profession of faith of the following declaration: "I most firmly admit and embrace the apostolic and ecclesiastical traditions and other observances and constitutions of the Church."

Modernist contempt for the Fathers. The Modernists pass judgment on the holy Fathers of the Church even as they do upon tradition. With consummate temerity they assure the public that the Fathers, while personally most worthy of all veneration, were entirely ignorant of history and criticism, for which they are only excusable on account of the time in which they lived. Finally, the Modernists try in every way to diminish and weaken the authority of the ecclesiastical magisterium itself by sacrilegiously falsifying its origin, character, and rights, and by freely repeating the calumnies of its adversaries. To the entire band of Modernists may be applied those words which Our predecessor sorrowfully wrote: "To bring contempt and odium on the mystic Spouse of Christ, who is the true light, the children of darkness have been wont to cast in her face before the world a stupid calumny, and perverting the meaning and force of things and words, to depict her as the friend of darkness and ignorance, and the enemy of light, science, and progress." [23] This being so, Venerable Brethren, there is little reason to wonder that the Modernists vent all their bitterness and hatred on Catholics who zealously fight the battles of the Church. There is no species of insult which they do not heap upon them, but their usual course is to charge them with ignorance or obstinacy. When an adversary rises up against them with an erudition and force that renders them redoubtable, they seek to make a conspiracy of silence around him to nullify the effects of his attack. This policy towards Catholics is the more invidious in that they belaud with admiration which knows no bounds the writers who range themselves on their side, hailing their works, exuding novelty in every page, with a chorus of applause. For them the scholarship of a writer is in direct proportion to the recklessness of his attacks on antiquity, and of his efforts to undermine tradition and the ecclesiastical magisterium. When one of their number falls under the condemnations of the Church the rest of them, to the disgust of good Catholics, gather round him, loudly and publicly applaud him, and hold him up in veneration as almost a martyr for truth. The young, excited and confused by all this clamor of praise and abuse, some of them afraid of being branded as ignorant, others ambitious to rank among the learned, and both classes goaded internally by curiosity and pride, not infrequently surrender and give themselves up to Modernism.

The temerity of the Modernists. 43. And here we have already some of the artifices employed by Modernists to exploit their wares. What efforts do they not make to win new recruits! They seize upon professorships in the seminaries and universities, and gradually make of them chairs of pestilence. In sermons from the pulpit they disseminate their doctrines, although possibly in utterances which are veiled. In congresses they express their teachings more openly. In their social gatherings they introduce them and commend them to others. Under their own names and under pseudonyms they publish numbers of books, newspapers, reviews, and sometimes one and the same writer adopts a variety of pseudonyms to trap the incautious reader into believing in a multitude of Modernist writers. In short, with feverish activity they leave nothing untried in act, speech, and writing. And with what result? We have to deplore the spectacle of many young men, once full of promise and capable of rendering great services to the Church, now gone astray. It is also a subject of grief to Us that many others who, while they certainly do not go so far as the former, have yet been so infected by breathing a poisoned atmosphere, as to think, speak, and write with a degree of laxity which ill becomes a Catholic. They are to be found among the laity, and in the ranks of the clergy, and they are not wanting even in the last place where one might expect to meet them, in religious communities. If they treat of biblical questions, it is upon Modernist principles; if they write history, they carefully, and with ill-concealed satisfaction, drag into the light, on the plea of telling the whole truth, everything that appears to cast a stain upon the Church. Under the sway of certain *a priori* conceptions they destroy as far as they can the pious traditions of the people, and bring into disrespect certain relics highly venerable from their antiquity. They are possessed by the empty desire of having their names upon the lips of the public, and they know they would never succeed in this were they to say only what has always been said by all men. Meanwhile it may be that they have persuaded themselves that in all this they are really serving God and the Church. In reality they only offend both, less perhaps by their works in themselves than by the spirit in which they write, and by the encouragement they thus give to the aims of the Modernists.

Calls for vigilance. 44. Against this host of grave errors, and its secret and open advance, Our predecessor Leo XIII, of happy memory, worked strenuously, both in his words and his acts, especially as regards the study of the Bible. But, as we have seen, the Modernists are not easily deterred by such weapons. With an affectation of great submission and respect, they proceeded to twist the words of the Pontiff to their own sense, while they described his action as directed against others than themselves. Thus the evil has gone on increasing from day to day. We, therefore, Venerable Brethren, have decided to suffer no longer delay, and to adopt measures which are more efficacious. We exhort and conjure you to see to it that in this most grave matter no one shall be in a position to say that you have been in the slightest degree wanting in vigilance, zeal, or firmness. And what We ask of you and expect of you, We ask and expect also of all other pastors of souls, of all educators and professors ot clerics, and in a very special way of the superiors of religious communities.

Scholastic philosophy. 45. In the first place, with regard to studies, We will and strictly ordain that scholastic philosophy be made the basis of the sacred sciences. It goes without saying that "if anything is met with among the scholastic doctors which may be regarded as something investigated with an excess of subtlety, or taught without sufficient consideration; anything which is not in keeping with the certain results of later times; anything, in short, which is altogether destitute of probability, We have no desire whatever to propose it for the imitation of present generations." [24] And let it be clearly understood above all things that when We prescribe scholastic philosophy We understand chiefly that which the Angelic Doctor has bequeathed to us, and We, therefore, declare that all the ordinances of Our predecessor on this subject continue fully in force, and, as far as may be necessary, We do decree anew, and confirm, and order that they shall be strictly observed by all. In seminaries where they have been neglected it will be for the Bishops to exact and require their observance in the future; and let this apply also to the superiors of religious orders. Further, We admonish professors to bear well in mind that they cannot set aside St. Thomas, especially in metaphysical questions, without grave disadvantage.

Promotion of sound theology. 46. On this philosophical foundation the theological edifice is to be carefully raised. Promote the study of theology, Venerable Brethren, by all means in your power, so that your clerics on leaving the seminaries may carry with them a deep admiration and love of it, and always find in it a source of delight. For "in the vast and varied abundance of studies opening before the mind desirous of truth, it is known to everyone that theology occupies such a commanding place, that according to an ancient adage of the wise it is the duty of the other arts and sciences to serve it, and to wait upon it after the manner of handmaidens." [25] We will add that We deem worthy of praise those who with full respect for tradition, the Fathers, and the ecclesiastical magisterium, endeavor, with well-balanced judgment, and guided by Catholic principles (which is not always the case), to illustrate positive theology by throwing upon it the light of true history. It is certainly necessary that positive theology should be held in greater appreciation than it has been in the past, but this must be done without detriment to scholastic theology; and those are to be disapproved as Modernists who exalt positive theology in such a way as to seem to despise the scholastic.

The role of profane studies. 47. With regard to secular studies, let it suffice to recall here what Our predecessor has admirably said: "Apply yourselves energetically to the study of natural sciences: in which department the things that have been so brilliantly discovered, and so usefully applied, to the admiration of the present age, will be the object of praise and commendation to those who come after us." [26] But this is to be done without interfering with sacred studies, as Our same predecessor prescribed in these most weighty words: "If you carefully search for the cause of those errors you will find that it lies in the fact that in these days when the natural sciences absorb so much study, the more severe and lofty studies have been proportionately neglected—some of them have almost passed into oblivion, some of them are pursued in a half-hearted or superficial way, and, sad to say, now that the splendor of the former estate is dimmed, they have been disfigured by perverse doctrines and monstrous errors." [27] We ordain, therefore, that the study of natural sciences in the seminaries be carried out according to this law.

Practical application. 48. All these prescriptions, both Our own and those of Our predecessor, are to be kept in view whenever there is question of choosing directors and professors for seminaries and Catholic Universities. Anyone who in any way is found to be tainted with Modernism is to be excluded without compunction from these offices, whether of government or of teaching, and those who already occupy them are to be removed. The same policy is to be adopted towards those who openly or secretly lend countenance to Modernism either by extolling the Modernists and excusing their culpable conduct, or by carping at scholasticism, and the Fathers, and the magisterium of the Church, or by refusing obedience to ecclesiastical authority in any of its depositaries; and towards those who show a love of novelty in history, archaeology, biblical exegesis; and finally towards those who neglect the sacred sciences or appear to prefer to them the secular. In all this question of studies, Venerable Brethren, you cannot be too watchful or too constant, but most of all in the choice of professors, for as a rule the students are modelled after the pattern of their masters. Strong in the consciousness of your duty, act always in this matter with prudence and with vigor.

"Do not lay hands hastily . . ." 49. Equal diligence and severity are to be used in examining and selecting candidates for Holy Orders. Far, far from the clergy be the love of novelty! God hateth the proud and the obstinate mind. For the future the doctorate of theology and canon law must never be conferred on anyone who has not first of all made the regular course of scholastic philosophy; if conferred, it shall be held as null and void. The rules laid down in 1896 by the Sacred Congregation of Bishops and Regulars for the clerics, both secular and regular, of Italy, concerning the frequenting of the Universities, We now decree to be extended to all nations.[28] Clerics and priests inscribed in a Catholic Institute or University must not in the future follow in civil Universities those courses for which there are chairs in the Catholic Institutes to which they belong. If this has been permitted anywhere in the past, We ordain that it be not allowed for the future. Let the Bishops who form the Governing Board of such Catholic Institutes or Universities watch with all care that these Our commands be constantly observed.

Examine publications carefully. 50. It is also the duty of the Bishops to prevent writings of Modernists, or whatever savors of Modernism or promotes it, from being read when they have been published, and to hinder their publication when they have not. No books or papers or periodicals whatever of this kind are to be permitted to seminarists or university students. The injury to them would be not less than that which is caused by immoral reading—nay, it would be greater, for such writings poison Christian life at its very fount. The same decision is to be taken concerning the writings of some Catholics, who, though not evilly disposed themselves, are ill-instructed in theological studies and imbued with modern philosophy, and strive to make this harmonise with the faith, and, as they say, to turn it to the profit of the faith. The name and reputation of these authors cause them to read without suspicion, and they are, therefore, all the more dangerous in gradually preparing the way for Modernism.

Imprimatur and Nihil Obstat. 51. To add some more general directions, Venerable Brethren, in a matter of such moment, We order that you do everything in your power to drive out of your dioceses, even by solemn interdict, any pernicious books that may be in circulation there. The Holy See neglects no means to remove writings of this kind, but their number has now grown to such an extent that it is hardly possible to subject them all to censure. Hence it happens sometimes that the remedy arrives too late, for the disease has taken root during the delay. We will, therefore, that the Bishops putting aside all fear and the prudence of the flesh, despising the clamor of evil men, shall, gently, by all means, but firmly, do each his own part in this work, remembering the injunctions of Leo XIII in the Apostolic Constitution *Officiorum:* "Let the Ordinaries, acting in this also as Delegates of the Apostolic See, exert themselves to proscribe and to put out of reach of the faithful injurious books or other writings printed or circulated in their dioceses." [29] In this passage the Bishops, it is true, receive an authorization, but they have also a charge laid upon them. Let no Bishop think that he fulfills his duty by denouncing to Us one or two books, while a great many others of the same kind are being published and circulated. Nor are you to be deterred by the fact that a book has obtained elsewhere the permission which is commonly called the *Imprimatur,* both because this may be merely simulated, and because it may have been granted through carelessness or too much indulgence or excessive trust placed in the author, which last has perhaps sometimes happened in the religious orders. Besides, just as the same food does not agree with everyone, it may happen that a book, harmless in one place, may, on account of the different circumstances, be hurtful in another. Should a Bishop, therefore, after having taken the advice of prudent persons, deem it right to condemn any of such books in his diocese, We give him ample faculty for the purpose and We lay upon him the obligation of doing so. Let all this be done in a fitting manner, and in certain cases it will suffice to restrict the prohibition to the clergy; but in all cases it will be obligatory on Catholic booksellers not to put on sale books condemned by the Bishop. And while We are treating of this subject, We wish the Bishops to see to it that booksellers do not, through desire for gain, engage in evil trade. It is certain that in the catalogs of some of them the books of the Modernists are not infrequently announced with no small praise. If they refuse obedience, let the Bishops, after due admonition, have no hesitation in depriving them of the title of Catholic booksellers. This applies, and with still more reason, to those who have the title of Episcopal booksellers. If they have that of Pontifical booksellers, let them be denounced to the Apostolic See. Finally, We remind all of Article XXVI of the above-mentioned Constitution *Officiorum:* "All those who have obtained an apostolic faculty to read and keep forbidden books, are not thereby authorized to read and keep books and periodicals forbidden by the local Ordinaries unless the apostolic faculty expressly concedes permission to read and keep books condemned by anyone whomsoever."

Censorship. 52. It is not enough to hinder the reading and the sale of bad books—it is also necessary to prevent them from being published. Hence, let the Bishops use the utmost strictness in granting permission to print. Under the rules of the Constitution *Officiorum,* many publications require the authorization of the Ordinary, and in certain dioceses (since the Bishop cannot personally make himself acquainted with them all) it has been the custom to have a suitable number of official censors for the examination of writings. We have the highest esteem for this institution of censors, and We not only exhort, but We order that it be extended to all dioceses. In all episcopal Curias, therefore, let censors be appointed for the revision of works intended for publication, and let the censors be chosen from both ranks of the clergy—secular and regular—men whose age, knowledge, and prudence will enable them to follow the safe and golden mean in their judgments. It shall be their office to examine everything which requires permission for publication according to Articles XLI and XLII of the above-mentioned Constitution. The censor shall give his verdict in writing. If it be favorable, the Bishop will give the permission for publication by the word *Imprimatur,* which must be preceded by the *Nihil obstat* and the name of the censor. In the Roman Curia official censors shall be appointed in the same way as elsewhere, and the duty of nominating them shall appertain to the Master of the Sacred Palace, after they have been proposed to the Cardinal Vicar and have been approved and accepted by the Sovereign Pontiff. It will also be the office of the Master of the Sacred Palace to select the censor for each writing. Permission for publication will be granted by him as well as by the Cardinal Vicar or his Vicegerent, and this permission, as above prescribed, must be preceded by the *Nihil obstat* and the name of the censor. Only on a very rare and exceptional occasion, and on the prudent decision of the Bishop, shall it be possible to omit mention of the censor. The name of the censor shall never be made known to the authors until he shall have given a favorable decision, so that he may not have to suffer inconvenience either while he is engaged in the examination of a writing or in case he should withhold his approval. Censors shall never be chosen from the religious orders until the opinion of the Provincial, or in Rome, of the General, has been privately obtained, and the Provincial or the General must give a conscientious account of the character, knowledge, and orthodoxy of the candidate. We admonish religious superiors of their most solemn duty never to allow anything to be published by any of their subjects without permission from themselves and from the Ordinary. Finally, We affirm and declare that the title of censor with which a person may be honored has no value whatever, and can never be adduced to give credit to the private opinions of him who holds it.

Priests as editors. 53. Having said this much in general, We now ordain in particular a more careful observance of Article XLII of the above-mentioned Constitution *Officiorum,* according to which "it is forbidden to secular priests, without the previous consent of the Ordinary, to undertake the editorship of papers or periodicals." This permission shall be withdrawn from any priest who makes a wrong use of it after having received an admonition thereupon. With regard to priests who are *correspondents* or *collaborators* of periodicals, as it happens not infrequently that they contribute matter infected with Modernism to their papers or periodicals, let the Bishops see to it that they do not offend in this manner; and if they do, let them warn the offenders and prevent them from writing. We solemnly charge in like manner the superiors of religious orders that they fulfil the same duty, and should they fail in it, let the Bishops make due provision with authority from the Supreme Pontiff. Let there be, as far as this is possible, a special censor for newspapers and periodicals written by Catholics. It shall be his office to read in due time each number after it has been published, and if he find anything dangerous in it let him order that it be corrected as soon as possible. The Bishop shall have the same right even when the censor has seen nothing objectionable in a publication.

Congresses. 54. We have already mentioned congresses and public gatherings as among the means used by the Modernists to propagate and defend their opinions. In the future, Bishops shall not permit congresses of priests except on very rare occasions. When they do permit them it shall only be on condition that matters appertaining to the Bishops or the Apostolic See be not treated in them, and that no resolutions or petitions be allowed that would imply a usurpation of sacred authority, and that absolutely nothing be said in them which savors of Modernism, presbyterianism, or laicism. At congresses of this kind, which can only be held after permission in writing has been obtained in due time and for each case, it shall not be lawful for priests of other dioceses to be present without the written permission of their Ordinary. Further, no priest must lose sight of the solemn recommendation of Leo XIII: "Let priests hold as sacred the authority of their pastors, let them take it for certain that the sacerdotal ministry, if not exercised under the guidance of the Bishops, can never be either holy, or very fruitful, or worthy of respect." [30]

Diocesan Vigilance Committees. 55. But of what avail, Venerable Brethren, will be all Our commands and prescriptions if they be not dutifully and firmly carried out? In order that this may be done it has seemed expedient to us to extend to all dioceses the regulations which the Bishops of Umbria, with great wisdom, laid down for theirs many years ago. "In order," they say, "to extirpate the errors already propagated and to prevent their further diffusion, and to remove those teachers of impiety through whom the pernicious effects of such diffusion are being perpetuated, this sacred Assembly, following the example of St. Charles Borromeo, has decided to establish in each of the dioceses a Council consisting of approved members of both branches of the clergy, which shall be charged with the task of noting the existence of errors and the devices by which new ones are introduced and propagated, and to inform the Bishop of the whole, so that he may take counsel with them as to the best means for suppressing the evil at the outset and preventing it spreading for the ruin of souls or, worse still, gaining strength and growth."[31] We decree, therefore, that in every diocese a council of this kind, which We are pleased to name the "Council of Vigilance," be instituted without delay. The priests called to form part in it shall be chosen somewhat after the manner above prescribed for the censors, and they shall meet every two months on an appointed day in the presence of the Bishop. They shall be bound to secrecy as to their deliberations and decisions, and in their functions shall be included the following: they shall watch most carefully for every trace and sign of Modernism both in publications and in teaching, and to preserve the clergy and the young from it they shall take all prudent, prompt, and efficacious measures. Let them combat novelties of words, remembering the admonitions of Leo XIII: "It is impossible to approve in Catholic publications a style inspired by unsound novelty which seems to deride the piety of the faithful and dwells on the introduction of a new order of Christian life, on new directions of the Church, on new aspirations of the modern soul, on a new social vocation of the clergy, on a new Christian civilization, and many other things of the same kind."[32] Language of the kind here indicated is not to be tolerated either in books or in lectures. The Councils must not neglect the books treating of the pious traditions of different places or of sacred relics. Let them not permit such questions to be discussed in journals or periodicals destined to foster piety, either with expressions savoring of mockery or contempt, or by dogmatic pronouncements, especially when, as is often the case, what is stated as a certainty either does not pass the limits of probability or is based on prejudiced opinion. Concerning sacred relics, let this be the rule: if Bishops, who alone are judges in such matters, know for certain that a relic is not genuine, let them remove it at once from the veneration of the faithful; if the authentications of a relic happen to have been lost through civil disturbances, or in any other way, let it not be exposed for public veneration until the Bishop has verified it. The argument of prescription or well-founded presumption is to have weight only when devotion to a relic is commendable by reason of its antiquity, according to the sense of the Decree issued in 1896 by the Congregation of Indulgences and Sacred Relics: "Ancient relics are to retain the veneration they have always enjoyed except when in individual instances there are clear arguments that they are false or supposititious." In passing judgment on pious traditions let it always be borne in mind that in this matter the Church uses the greatest prudence, and that she does not allow traditions of this kind to be narrated in books except with the utmost caution and with the insertion of the declaration imposed by Urban VIII; and even then she does not guarantee the truth of the fact narrated; she simply does not forbid belief in things for which human evidence is not wanting. On this matter the Sacred Congregation of Rites, thirty years ago, decreed as follows: "These apparitions or revelations have neither been approved nor condemned by the Holy See, which has simply allowed them to be believed on purely human faith, on the tradition which they relate, corroborated by testimony and documents worthy of credence." [33] Anyone who follows this rule has no cause to fear. For the devotion based on any apparition, in so far as it regards the fact itself, that is to say, in so far as the devotion is *relative,* always implies the condition of the fact being true; while in so far as it is *absolute,* it is always based on the truth, seeing that its object is the persons of the saints who are honored. The same is true of relics. Finally, We entrust to the Councils of Vigilance the duty of overlooking assiduously and diligently social institutions as well as writings on social questions so that they may harbor no trace of Modernism, but obey the prescriptions of the Roman Pontiffs.

Triennial returns. 56. Lest what We have laid down thus far should pass into oblivion, We will and ordain that the Bishops of all dioceses, a year after the publication of these letters and every three years thenceforward, furnish the Holy See with a diligent and sworn report on the things which have been decreed in this Our Letter, and on the doctrines that find currency among the clergy, and especially in the seminaries and other Catholic institutions, those not excepted which are not subject to the Ordinary, and We impose the like obligation on the Generals of religious orders with regard to those who are under them.

Conclusion. 57. This, Venerable Brethren, is what We have thought it Our duty to write to you for the salvation of all who believe. The adversaries of the Church will doubtless abuse what We have said to refurbish the old calumny by which We are traduced as the enemy of science and of the progress of humanity. As a fresh answer to such accusations, which the history of the Christian religion refutes by never-failing evidence, it is Our intention to establish by every means in our power a special Institute in which, through the co-operation of those Catholics who are most eminent for their learning, the advance of science and every other department of knowledge may be promoted under the guidance and teaching of Catholic truth. God grant that We may happily realise Our design with the assistance of all those who bear a sincere love for the Church of Christ. But of this We propose to speak on another occasion.

Apostolic Blessing. Meanwhile, Venerable Brethren, fully confident in your zeal and energy, We beseech for you with Our whole heart the abundance of heavenly light, so that in the midst of this great danger to souls from the insidious invasions of error upon every hand, you may see clearly what ought to be done, and labor to do it with all your strength and courage. May Jesus Christ, the author and finisher of our faith, be with you in His power; and may the Immaculate Virgin, the destroyer of all heresies, be with you by her prayers and aid. And We, as a pledge of Our affection and of the Divine solace in adversity, most lovingly grant to you, your clergy and people, the Apostolic Benediction.

58. Given at St. Peter's, Rome, September 8, 1907, in the fifth year of Our Pontificate.

PIUS X, POPE

REFERENCES

1. Acts 20:30.
2. Titus 1:10.
3. II Tim. 3:13.
4. *De Revelatione, can.* 1.
5. *Ibid., can.* 2.
6. *De Fide, can.* 3.
7. *De Revelatione, can.* 3.
8. Gregory XVI, encyclical of June 25, 1834, *Singulari Nos.*
9. Brief to the Bishop of Breslau, June 15, 1857.
10. Gregory IX, *Epist. ad Magistros theol. paris.*, July 7, 1223.
11. Proposition 29, condemned by Leo X in the bull of May 16, 1520, *Exsurge Domine: "Via nobis facta est enervandi auctoritatem Conciliorum, et libere contradicendi eorum gestis, et iudicandi eorum decreta, at confidenter confitendi quidquid verum videtur, sive probatum fuerit, sive reprobatum a quocumque Concilio."*
12. *Sess. VII, De Sacramentis in genere, can.* 5.
13. Proposition 2: *"Propositio, quae statuit, potestatem a Deo datam Ecclesiae ut communicaretur Pastoribus, qui sunt eius ministri pro salute animarum; sic intellecta, ut a communitate fidelium in Pastores derivetur ecclesiastici, ministerii ac regiminis potestas: haeretica."* Proposition 3: *"Insuper, quae statuit Romanum Pontificem esse caput ministeriale; sic explicata ut Romanus Pontifex non a Christo in persona beati Petri, sed ab Ecclesia potestatem ministerii accipiat, qua velut Petri successor, verus Christi vicarius ac totius Ecclesiae caput pollet in universa Ecclesia: haeretica."*
14. Pius IX, encyclical of November 9, 1846, *Qui pluribus.*
15. Syllabus, Prop. 5.
16. Constitution *Dei Filius,* cap. 4.
17. *Loc. cit.*
18. Rom. 1:21–22.
19. Vatican Council, *De Revelatione,* can. 2.
20. *Epist.* 28.
21. Gregory XVI, encyclical of June 25, 1834, *Singulari Nos.*
22. Syllabus, Prop. 13.
23. *Motu Proprio* of March 14, 1891, *Ut mysticam.*
24. Leo XIII, encyclical of August 4, 1879, *Aeterni Patris.*
25. Leo XIII, Apostolic letter of December 10, 1889, *In magna.*
26. Leo XIII, allocution of March 7, 1880.

27. *Loc. cit.*
28. Cf. *ASS*, 29:359 ff.
29. Cf. *ASS*, 30:39 ff.
30. Leo XIII, encyclical of February 10, 1884, *Nobilissima Gallorum*.
31. Acts of the Congress of the Bishops of Umbria, November, 1849, *tit.* 2, *art.* 6.
32. Instruction of the Sacred Congregation of Extraordinary Ecclesiastical Affairs, January 27, 1902.
33. Decree of May 2, 1877.

CHAPTER 9

Communium Rerum *April 21, 1909, The Eighth Centenary of Saint Anselm of Aosta*

ON APRIL 21, 1909, Saint Pius X published his second commemorative encyclical, *Communium Rerum,* on the eighth centenary of Saint Anselm of Aosta. He used the occasion, as he mentioned elsewhere, to discuss "those points of Christian doctrine and morals found in the example and teaching of these saints which We thought were best suited to our times." He chose Saint Anselm because he "is even more brilliant in the sense that he is closer to us in time, place, temperament and studies. Moreover, our days are very similar to his by reason of the kind of battles he waged, the pastoral activity he exercised, and the method of teaching he followed and promoted either through his own writings or his disciples."

The encyclical draws upon the life and example of Saint Anselm in order to teach a lesson to the present age. After pointing out Anselm's devotion to the Holy See and his prominence in civil affairs (5–12), Pius describes the evils of the present and the manner of the internal and external attacks launched against the Church. The former attacks were directed by the Modernists; the latter by the anti-clerical governments of Europe (13–17).

The encyclical continues by showing how Anselm met the external attacks by ardently loving the Church (18–22) and the internal attacks by incessantly preaching Truth (23–25). The life and activities of Anselm are a model for every Catholic Bishop who loves and has the interests of the Church at heart (26–29). The loyal Bishop must be as firm, as charitable, as obedient, and as humble as Anselm (30–43) if he would steer clear of the temerity of the bold and the timidity of the cowardly (44–48). Moreover, following Anselm, he must foster Scholasticism, by extolling and maintaining the proper relationship between philosophy and theology (49–53).

Invoking Anselm "to beseech God to deliver the Church and Us, her unworthy ruler, from the oppression of heretics and lead them back from their errors to the path of truth," the Pope concludes with the conferring of the Apostolic Blessing.

Through such letters as this Saint Pius X urged the flock committed to his care to emulate and imitate "the virtue and wisdom of the saints God brought forth in other centuries to withstand the fury of the Church's persecutors and the propagation of iniquity in the world."

Communium Rerum *Encyclical Letter of Our Holy Father Pius X to the Patriarchs, Primates, Archbishops, Bishops and Other Ordinaries in Peace and Communion with the Apostolic See*

VENERABLE BRETHREN, HEALTH AND THE APOSTOLIC BLESSING:

Gratitude for filial devotion. 1. Surrounded as We are by the usual troubles of Our time as well as by the recent local disasters, We are consoled and comforted by the recent manifestations of filial devotion on the part of the Christian people. This display continues to be "a spectacle to the world, and to angels, and to men." [1] Even if recent misfortunes have hastened this manifestation, its primary cause is to be sought chiefly in the charity of Our Lord Jesus Christ. Since Christ is and can be the only source of any genuine charity in the world, He alone is the cause of its various manifestations. Men of little faith or the avowed enemies of religion are indebted to the civilization Christ established (which they have not yet succeeded in repudiating and expelling from human society) for any vestiges of charity which they still might possess.

Expression of gratitude. 2. Words fail Us when We try to express Our gratitude towards all those who have consoled their Father and aided their brethren in these public and personal sufferings. Although We have frequently expressed Our gratitude to various individuals, We now wish publicly to thank you, above all, Venerable Brethren, and through you the faithful committed to your care.

Other causes for gratitude. 3. We also wish to thank Our beloved children throughout the world for the many striking tokens of affection and reverence they offered Us on the occasion of Our sacerdotal jubilee. These we especially appreciate not so much because they honor Us but because they honor religion and the Church. By reverencing him whom the Lord has chosen to lead His family, these professions of undaunted faith are really public demonstrations of respect for Christ and His Church. Other similar manifestations have also increased our joy. There are, for example, the centenary celebrations of several North American dioceses, throughout which prayers of thanksgiving rise up to God because of the growing number of Catholics. There is another illustrious example in the British Isles. There a huge crowd gathered about Our Venerable Brethren and the Papal Legate to pay their public homage in a wondrous display of faith (so long abandoned!) to the Holy Eucharist. In France also the Church, even though undergoing a persecution, dried her tears to witness the brilliant triumphs of the Blessed Sacrament, especially at Lourdes, where We were happy to witness the solemn commemoration of the fiftieth anniversary of the apparitions. Let everyone see in these and similar manifestations—and let the Church's enemies be convinced—that both the ceremonial splendor and devotion paid to the Blessed Mother of God and the filial homage offered the Supreme Pontiff are ultimately destined for the glory of God. In such a way "Christ is all things and in all," [2] the Kingdom of God is established on earth, and eternal salvation is provided for mankind.

Purpose of Pontificate. 4. This individual and social triumph of God on earth is nothing more than the return of the wayward to God through Christ, and to Christ through the Church. We have proposed this triumph as the program of Our Pontificate in Our first Apostolic letter, *E Supremi Apostolatus,*[3] and on many other occasions. We have confidence in this return. Our every plan and hope is directed to bringing it about so that the troubles of this life will come to rest as the storms subside in the port. For that reason We appreciate the homage offered the Church in Our humble person. We take this as a sign—God willing!—of the return of the nations to Christ and to closer union with Peter and the Church.

The eighth centenary of Saint Anselm. 5. This loving union with the Apostolic See varies in intensity according to time and place and differs in its manner of expression. According to the designs of Providence, however, this union seems to grow stronger whenever the safeguarding of sound teaching, sacred discipline, and ecclesiastical liberty becomes more difficult. We have examples of this fact in the virtue and wisdom of the saints God brought forth in other centuries to withstand the fury of the Church's persecutors and the propagation of iniquity in the world. In this letter We desire to commemorate one of these men, since the eighth centenary of his death is now being solemnly celebrated. We refer to the learned Anselm of Aosta. Both as monk and abbot in France and later as Archbishop of Canterbury and Primate of England he proved to be a valiant teacher of Catholic truth and defender of Church rights. It is no more than right, We believe, after commemorating with unusual solemnity the centenaries of those other two Doctors of the Church, Saint Gregory the Great, the light of the West, and

Saint John Chrysostom, the light of the East, to consider this other star. Although he "differs . . . in glory"[4] from the other two, he still is comparable to them in the course he followed and the salutary light of doctrine and example he cast about him. In fact, We might say that Anselm is even more brilliant in the sense that he is closer to us in time, place, temperament and studies. Moreover, our days are very similar to his by reason of the kind of battles he waged, the pastoral activity he exercised, and the method of teaching he followed and promoted either through his own writings or his disciples. He composed all his works "in defense of the Christian religion, for the welfare of souls and the benefit of theologians who would adopt the scholastic method in teaching sacred sciences."[5] Just as some stars set in the middle of the night when others rise to enlighten the earth, so the sons succeed the fathers in illuminating the Church. Saint Anselm was one of the most brilliant of these latter stars.

Anselm, confidant of Popes. 6. Saint Anselm's contemporaries considered him a leader in sanctity and learning amid the iniquity and ignorance of his age. He was "a prince of the faith, an honor to the Church . . . the glory of the episcopate, a man excelling all the great men of his time."[6] He was "wise and good, eloquent in speech and brilliant in mind."[7] His reputation was so outstanding that it was well written that no contemporary in the whole world "would dare say, 'Anselm is not as good as I,' or, 'I am like Anselm.' "[8] For that reason he had the ear of lords and kings, and even of the Supreme Pontiffs. "He was loved" not only by his confreres and his people, "but even by his enemies."[9] When Anselm was still an abbot, the illustrious Pope Gregory VII wrote him tender and respectful letters, "recommending the Catholic Church and himself to his prayers."[10] Urban II also wrote him, acknowledging that he was "outstanding in piety and learning."[11] Paschal II likewise addressed many affectionate letters to him, praising his "reverent devotion, burning faith, pious and persevering zeal, and renown in religion and learning."[12] Such qualities easily led the Pontiff to grant all his requests and unhesitatingly call him the most learned and holy Bishop in England.

Anselm, a humble man. 7. Anselm, however, considered himself nothing but a despicable, unknown, ignorant and sinful man. But his excessive modesty and sincere humility did not in the least prevent him from thinking lofty thoughts. Although depraved men might think contrariwise, recall that Scripture says "the sensual man does not perceive the things that are of the Spirit of God."[13] What is even more remarkable is the fact that Anselm combined generosity and constancy (so often tested by troubles, attacks and exiles) with a gentleness and charm that calmed the raging passions and won the hearts of his enemies. Consequently, "even his enemies praised his goodness."[14]

Anselm, an exemplary man. 8. Simplicity and dexterity, humility and magnanimity, strength and suavity, learning and piety—qualities the world calls contradictory—were admirably blended in Anselm's character. Through his religious life "everyone looked upon him as an exceptional model of holiness and learning."[15]

Anselm, man of the world. 9. These remarkable qualities of Anselm were not confined to monastic or scholastic circles. They came forth, as from a military tent, into the open field since, as We have already mentioned, Anselm lived in trying times and was forced to battle fiercely for the cause of truth and justice. Although by nature he was inclined to lead a life of contemplation and study, he was forced to assume many important tasks, some of them concerning the government of the Church. Thus he was drawn into the most bitter battles. Even though he was of meek and gentle temperament, he was compelled to surrender a life of peace for the sake of sound doctrine and the holiness of the Church. He sacrificed the friendship of the world's nobles, the favor of the world's great, the mutual affection (which at first he enjoyed) of even his religious and episcopal brothers in order to be continually surrounded by trouble. In a hateful and danger-strewn England he had to withstand kings and princes who usurped and dominated the Church and the people. He had to reprimand weak and unworthy ministers who had betrayed their sacred trust. He had to struggle against the ignorance and vice of all classes of society. He proved himself to be the valiant defender of the Faith and morals, the discipline and liberty of the Church. For that reason he was the preserver of her sanctity and integrity of doctrine. No one questioned his worthiness. How deserving he was of Pope Paschal's praise: "Thank God that you have maintained the Bishop's authority! Even though surrounded by barbarians, neither tyrant's force nor noble's favor, neither executioner's fire nor warrior's spears can stop you from preaching the truth. We rejoice because by the grace of God neither threats disturb you nor promises sway you."[16]

Anselm, the light of the Church. 10. Considering these things, Venerable Brethren, it is no more than right that after eight centuries We also, like Our Predecessor Paschal, return thanks to God. We take great pleasure in exhorting you to fasten your gaze on this light of learning and holiness. He rose here in Italy, enlightened France for over thirty years and England over fifteen years. In time the whole Church looked upon him as a tower of strength and beauty.

Anselm's greatness lies in Christ. 11. Anselm was mighty *in word and deed*. He brought glorious triumphs to the Church and singular benefits to civil society in learning and living, in contemplation and activity, in peace and battle. This he could do, however, only because of his unbroken union with Christ and the Church throughout his entire life and ministry.

Anselm—a source of Consolation. 12. As We recall all these things in a special way during the great Doctor's centenary, We find, Venerable Brethren, many wonderful examples for admiration and imitation. More than that! They will be a source of strength and consolation for us in the arduous work of governing the Church and saving souls. They will help us persevere in our duty of fully cooperating in restoring all things in Christ, "until Christ is formed" [17] in all things, especially in those who are the hope of the priesthood. These examples will help us to be inflexible in maintaining the Church's doctrine and indomitable in defending the liberty of the Spouse of Christ. The Sacred Pontificate demands that We protect the inviolability of her divine rights and all their ramifications.

The evils of the present day. 13. You well know, Venerable Brethren, and have often lamented with Us the evil days in which we live and the criminal conditions imposed on us. Even though We experienced tremendous sorrow in the recent public disaster, Our wounds were re-opened when some shamefully charged that the clergy were tardy in offering their assistance. Our sorrow was full to the brim when obstacles were raised to conceal the relief the Church offered the afflicted, or when her maternal vigilance and care met with open contempt. We pass over the many other injustices against the Church. They were devised with treacherous cunning. They were executed contrary to all the laws of public right. They completely ignore all natural equity and justice. To think this could happen in those countries whose stream of civilization has flowed most copiously from the Church! What could be more unnatural than to see those very children whom the Church nourished and cherished as her first-born, her flower and strength, thrust their weapons into the very bosom of their most loving mother? Nor do some other countries give Us any more consolation. There also the same struggle (perhaps the form is a bit different) has either already broken out or is at least in the planning stage. Countries which have gained the most from Christian civilization are scheming how to deprive the Church of her rights, to treat her as though she were not the perfect society she is by right and by nature (for Christ Himself, the Redeemer of our nature, instituted her), and to destroy her influence which is as beneficial to human society as for eternal salvation. All kinds of attempts are being made to supplant the Kingdom of God for the reign of license which conceals itself under the name of liberty. The cry rises on all sides: "We do not wish this man to be king over us." [18] In such a way the hideous slaveries of vice and lust triumph and the people rush madly into ruin, for "sin maketh nations miserable." [19] For that reason the religious orders, the strength and honor of the Church and nurseries of learning and culture among civilized and uncivilized alike, have been expelled from Catholic countries. Works of Christian charity have been reduced and curtailed as much as possible. Ministers of religion have been despised and ridiculed and made as ineffectual as possible. By gradually depriving them of their right to instruct and teach youth, it is either altogether impossible or at least morally impossible for them to seek higher education or occupy professorial chairs. It has become impossible to undertake any Catholic work that would benefit the common good. Those distinguished laymen who boldly profess their Catholic Faith have been ridiculed, persecuted and trodden upon as if they belong to an inferior and outcast class. The day is quickly approaching when, by means of unjust laws, they will be completely ostracized from public affairs. The authors of this cunning and merciless law go about bragging that they are moved out of love of liberty, civilization, progress and (would you believe it!) patriotism. Thus they imitate their father, the avowed enemy of God and the human race, who "was a murderer from the beginning . . . When he tells a lie he speaks from his very nature, for he is a liar." [20] These shameless men try to confuse and ensnare the unlearned by their deceitful words. Neither patriotism nor love for the people, neither noble motives nor the common good have inspired them to engage in this ferocious war. Blind hatred is the fuel that keeps their fanatical designs burning. In their desire to weaken the Church and exclude her from social life, they audaciously assume that she is dead, even though they continually wage battle against her. In fact, first they rob her of her liberty and then boldly ridicule her because she is unable to assist mankind or the civil government. The same hatred brings forth vile calumnies or complete silence or suspicion about the services of the Church and the Apostolic See. They deceitfully twist and turn everything the Church says or does in such a way that they trick the masses into believing that Our acts carry with them some imminent danger to society. In reality, however, the progress of real liberty and lasting civilization flow chiefly from Christ through His Church.

The Church is attacked from without. 14. Venerable Brethren, We have frequently called your attention to this war the enemy is waging from without. "In this struggle the Church seems to be attacked from every side, sometimes as if by an army in the battle-field and sometimes by cunning underhanded methods." This fact We underscored in Our consistorial allocution of December 16, 1907.

The Church is attacked from within. 15. With equal severity and sorrow We must denounce another kind of war. This war is internal and domestic. The more hidden it is, the more dangerous it is. This war is directed against the very foundation and soul of the Church by those unnatural children who hide in the bosom of the Church herself in order to bring about her ruin without being detected. So they cast their spears at the very soul of the Church in order to destroy her, just as the axe is laid at the roots of the tree in order to fell it. Their efforts, however, are easily detected. They pollute the springs of Christian life and doctrine. They ignore the deposit of Faith. They undermine her divinely instituted foundations by boldly despising Papal and Episcopal authority, by attributing a new structure to the Church, by proposing new laws and obligations according to the teachings of their absurd philosophy. In a word, they would exchange the beauty of the Spouse of Christ for the deceptive glamour of a new culture which is falsely called scientific. The Apostle frequently warns us about this deception: "See to it that no one deceives you by philosophy and vain deceit, according to human traditions, according to the elements of the world and not according to Christ." [21]

Confusion of the Modernists. 16. The fallacious tenets of this kind of philosophy and foolish erudition when allied with an extremely outspoken criticism induced some men to "become vain in their reasonings" [22] and by rejecting a good conscience "have made shipwreck of the faith." [23] They are miserably tossed to and fro on the waves of doubt, not even knowing themselves where they are going to land. Others waste so much time and diligence on obscure technicalities that they alienate themselves from theology and the true fonts of doctrine. This poisonous disease (which is called *Modernism* because of its consuming passion for startling novelties) has not only been denounced on several occasions but has also been unmasked by its disciples' extravagances. It is still, however, a serious danger to Christian society. It has stealthily crept into the very warp and woof of modern society, which has cut itself off from Christ and the Church. Like a cancerous growth it gnaws away at the younger generation, which by its very nature lacks experience and caution. Its success does not rest upon the foundation of serious and accurate study (since there can be no real conflict between reason and faith),[24] but is rather built on that intellectual pride and poisonous mentality which results from ignorance or confusion about religious truth as well as from a foolish arrogance. When the spirit of incredulity and rebellion against God are added, the infection spreads. Thus those who are possessed with the desire for novelty come to think they are sufficient in themselves. They are free to abandon openly or secretly their duty of obedience to divine authority. Then they begin to construct, according to their own feelings, a vague, naturalistic, individualistic religion which bears the names and has some accidentals of Christianity but lacks its life and truth.

Their attempt to do the impossible. 17. One can easily see in all this one of the phases of the eternal struggle against divine truth. This battle, however, is by far more dangerous than the others. In the present case the weapons are cunningly hid under the cloak of false piety, simplicity and stubbornness, and wielded by men who seek to reconcile the irreconcilable. For example, they try to harmonize the excesses of fickle human science with the principles of divine faith, and the frivolity of the world with the dignity and constancy of the Church.

Anselm's struggle is our hope. 18. However, the knowledge of these things, Venerable Brethren, should not cause you to lose hope. You are acquainted with the tremendous struggles (even though they were different than ours) that faced the Christians of other ages. We need only recall the age in which Anselm lived. Indeed, Church history recalls for us the numberless difficulties he faced. He had to fight for the altar and the home, that is, the preservation of public order. He had to defend the liberty, culture, and truth which the Church defended and taught to all nations. He had to restrain the princes' power which was infringing on most sacred liberties. He had to blot out vice and ignorance by recalling men to a sense of common decency and love of learning. He had to recall some clerics to their sense of duty inasmuch as they had become, to say the least, imprudent or remiss. This was especially so since frequently they were chosen according to that infamous system of royal election which reduced the clergy to mere vassals of the nobles.

Anselm's field of labor. 19. Such was the state of affairs especially in those countries where Anselm labored. In the one he was the doctor who taught others, in the other, the religious who led others by his example, in the third, the primatial Archbishop who ruled others by his constant vigilance and many-sided activities. He labored principally among the people of France and England. Only a few centuries previously the former was invaded by the Normans and the latter was converted. Both countries had been so shaken by internal revolutions and external attacks that moral depravity had crept into the lives of rulers and subjects, clergy and people.

The Church was humiliated by the rulers. 20. Such abuses brought forth bitter laments from the great men of the time, as, for example, from Lanfranc, Anselm's master and predecessor in the See of Canterbury, and especially from the Roman Pontiffs. Suffice it to mention the name of that courageous and zealous champion of justice, staunch defender of Church rights, and vigilant guardian of priestly holiness, Pope Gregory VII. Following their example and rivaling their zeal, Anselm also condemned these same abuses. For instance, Anselm addressed the following words to a prince of his people who liked to call himself Anselm's relative both by reason of blood and affection. "You see, my dearest lord, how wicked princes humiliate the Church of God, our Mother, whom God calls His beautiful friend and beloved spouse. You see how she fears the eternal perdition of those very persons whom God commanded to be her protector and defender. You see how they have boldly stolen her property, reduced her to slavery, despised her holiness and violated her rights. In refusing obedience to the Supreme Pontiff's decrees (which he issues for the good of the Christian religion), they are actually disobeying the Apostle Peter, whom the Pope represents. In fact, they disobey Christ Himself since He entrusted His Church to Peter. . . . Those who disobey God's law can only be numbered among God's enemies."[25] Imagine what it would be like today if Anselm's words had been treasured by the successor and descendants of that mighty prince! Imagine what it would be like today if the other sovereigns and people Anselm loved, admonished and served would have heeded his words!

Anselm's devotion to the Church. 21. Neither persecution nor exile, neither deprivation nor hardship could destroy Anselm's devotion to the Church and the Apostolic See. They only served, on the contrary, to increase that affection. "I fear," he wrote, "neither exile nor poverty, sufferings nor death. As long as God strengthens me, I am prepared to endure everything out of obedience to the Apostolic See and for the liberty of the Church of Christ, my Mother."[26] During his greatest sufferings he wrote the following words to Pope Paschal, revealing his reason for turning to Peter's Chair for counsel and assistance and at the same time leaving Us an example of pastoral fortitude and dignity: "I would prefer death or, if I live, the extreme penury of an exile, rather than see the glory of God's Church dimmed in any way through my fault."[27]

Anselm's labor for the Church. 22. Day and night this holy man labored on behalf of the Church's liberty, honor, and integrity. He begged God by his prayers, tears and sacrifices to preserve her inviolability; he wore himself out by firmly and patiently defending her in all his words, actions and writings.

Bishop's duty to preach the truth. 23. These noble appeals for sacred liberty take on a special significance in our days when they are uttered by those whom "the Holy Spirit has placed . . . as bishops, to rule the Church of God."[28] They are timely, We repeat, even if men of lifeless faith, immoral manners, or prejudiced ideas fail to heed them. You fully realize, Venerable Brethren, that the following divine admonition was addressed in a special way to Us: "Cry, cease not, lift up thy voice like a trumpet."[29] "The Highest gave his voice"[30] through natural signs and catastrophes. The voice of the Lord shakes the earth, recalling to our minds that all material things shall pass, "for here we have no permanent city, but we seek for the city that is to come."[31] Although His voice warns of divine justice, it is also a merciful reminder to those nations who have gone astray and trampled all righteousness and goodness underfoot. These public misfortunes demand that We cry out and preach the great truths of faith not only to the humble and afflicted but also to the powerful and rich, as well as those who formulate and execute national policies. We must let every creature hear the great religious truths which history confirms through many calamities. The following are examples of such truths: "Sin maketh nations miserable."[32] "The mighty shall be mightily tormented."[33] "And now, O ye kings, understand: receive instruction, you that judge the earth. Serve ye the Lord with fear. . . . Embrace discipline: lest at any time the Lord be angry, and you perish from the just way."[34] The more frequently these social sins are committed, the more serious shall be the consequences these threats foretell. This will especially be the ending of those rulers and people who criminally exclude God and rebel against the Church of Christ. This dual social apostasy is the terrible source of anarchy, corruption, and misery for both individuals and states.

Anselm's example in preaching truth. 24. Silence or slothfulness is unfortunately an all too common occurrence among good men. God forbid that we will ever be accused of it! Let every sacred pastor take to heart for the protection of his flock and the necessary admonition of others the following words which Anselm addressed to the powerful prince of Flanders: "You are my liege and dearly beloved in the Lord. Therefore I earnestly beseech you as your spiritual counselor not to consider your exalted position lowered if you cherish and defend God's Spouse and your Mother, the Church. Do not think you humble yourself when you exalt her. Do not believe you are weakened when she is strengthened. Look around and see the examples of those princes who attack or mistreat her. What did they gain? What did they achieve? The matter is so clear that we need no longer dwell upon it."[35] The same truth he expresses with his customary gentle persuasiveness in a letter to the powerful Baldwin, King of Jerusalem. "As your faithful friend I beseech you (just as I beseech God Himself) to live according to God's law and at all times submit your will to His will. Only when you rule according to God's law do you rule for your own welfare. Do not fall into that mentality of many bad kings who think God's Church is their servant. Rather bear well in mind that you are called to be her advocate and defender. *In this world God loves nothing better than His Church's liberty.* Those who would rather rule than obey her are undoubtedly God's enemies. He does not want His Spouse to be a slave; He wills her freedom. Those who treat her with filial honor prove themselves worthy of being numbered among her sons and the sons of God. Those who lord it over her, like a ruler over his subject, are not her children. They are strangers and will not receive her heritage and dowry."[36] Thus Anselm manifested his tremendous love for the Church. At the same time the illustrious Doctor shows his zeal in defending her liberty (as necessary for harmony among the Christian people as it is cherished by God) in those emphatic words: "In this world God loves nothing better than His Church's liberty." The best way We can reveal Our intention, Venerable Brethren, is to make that powerful expression Our Own.

Anselm's advice to the rulers. 25. The advice the Saint directed to the rulers of his day has equal merit for our own day. Take, for example, his letter to Matilda, the Queen of England. "If you really wish to express your heartfelt gratitude to God, do not overlook that Queen whom God chose as His Spouse in this world. . . . Imitate her and praise her, so that through her intercession you will please God on earth and reign with her in unending happiness." [37] When you happen to meet some son who, drunk with worldly power, either forgets or rebels against his mother, remember that "you must frequently suggest—regardless of circumstances—these and similar admonitions. You must exhort him to act at all times as the defender and son (not the master and stepson) of the Church." [38] We should also take to heart that other saying of Saint Anselm: "When I hear you did something displeasing to God and unworthy of your dignity, I would betray both God and your friendship if I did not correct you." [39] When We hear that "you have treated the churches committed to your charge unworthily" We must imitate Anselm's example by renewing our prayers, counsels, and admonitions "so that you seriously consider the matter and if your conscience tells you that something should be corrected, you will correct it immediately." [40] "Nothing," the Saint adds, "should be neglected that can be corrected. God demands an account not only of the evil that one does but also of the evil he could remedy but fails to. If men in higher positions must make corrections, the more strictly does God oblige them to do so, since He always gives the grace of prudent thought and action. . . . If you cannot attend to everything immediately, it is no excuse for not trying to do better. In His goodness God customarily perfects good intentions and noble efforts by rewarding them with an abundant harvest." [41]

Bishops should follow Anselm's example. 26. The pastors and princes of the Church, who are obliged to defend truth, justice and religion, would do well to restate today these and similar wise and holy admonitions Anselm directed to the lords and princes of his day. Undoubtedly, in recent times so many obstacles have been set up that it is not only difficult to do so but also exceedingly dangerous. License reigns supreme, and the Church lies disgracefully bound in chains. The very notion of liberty has become ridiculous. New technicalities are constantly being invented to restrict your ministry and your clergy's ministry. The correction of the erring, the suppression of abuses, the promotion of truth and good morals, and the lessening of the evils afflicting the Church are all matters of your concern. Little wonder that "you cannot attend to everything immediately!"

The Church is in via. 27. However, We do not lack consolation. The Lord lives and He shall see to it "that for those who love God all things work together unto good." [42] He will draw good out of these evils. Shattering the scheming of fallen nature He will crown His work and His Church with magnificent triumph. Behold the marvellous designs and "unsearchable ways" [43] of Providence in the present order of affairs! "My thoughts are not your thoughts: nor your ways my ways, saith the Lord." [44] The Church of

Christ will ever renew in herself the life of her Divine Founder. Since He suffered much, she will also, in a certain way, be called upon to fill up "what is lacking of the sufferings of Christ."[45] According to the Divine Will she must be militant on earth, that is to say, surrounded by struggles, troubles, and dissensions. "Through many tribulations" she "must enter the kingdom of God."[46] Only then will she be united with the Church triumphant in heaven.

The Boat tossed on the waves. 28. Anselm's commentary on that passage in Saint Matthew, "Jesus made his disciples get into the boat," can profitably be recalled at this point. "These words," he writes, "mystically summarize the state of the Church from the Saviour's coming until the end of the world. Just as the boat was 'buffeted by the waves' as long as Jesus remained on the mountain top, so also ever since Our Saviour's ascension into heaven the Church has been cast to and fro by tribulations and buffeted by the storms of persecution, disturbed by the fickleness of the wicked and assailed by the vices of the vicious. 'For the wind was against them': that is, desiring to prevent her from reaching the port of salvation, malicious forces are constantly lined up against her. Thus they try to sink her under the waves of the world and place as many obstacles as possible in her course."[47]

The actions of cowardly men. 29. How mistaken they are who lose faith during the storm and desire a permanent state of perfect tranquility, universal prosperity, and practical, unanimous recognition of sacred authority for themselves and the Church! More serious, however, is the error of those who deceive only themselves when they think they can gain peace (illusory though it be) by watering down the rights and interests of the Church. Hoping to reconcile the modernists and bring them back to the Church, they will either sacrifice the Church's rights for personal interests, or unjustly minimize those rights, or even completely surrender them to the world which is completely "in the power of the evil one."[48] Is it possible to reconcile light and darkness, Christ and Belial? This deception is as old as the world. Yet, as long as there are timid or traitorous soldiers, it will always be modern and present in the world. Such soldiers are the first to lay down their weapons and negotiate with the enemy, even if it be, as in this case, the irreconcilable enemy of God and man.

Firmness mingled with charity. 30. You, Venerable Brethren, whom Divine Providence has chosen to be the pastors and leaders of the Christian people, must valiantly resist this deadly tendency which lulls modern society into a shameful indolence during this open war against religion. It aims at a cowardly neutrality built upon specious schemes and compromises which is not only injurious to divine and human rights but is also completely forgetful of Christ's emphatic statement: "He who is not with me is against me."[49] It is no more than right, however, that the ministers of Christ be filled with paternal charity since Paul's words especially apply to them: "I became all things to all men, that I might save all." [50] Accordingly there may be times when prudence would dictate that we relinquish our rights whenever that is lawful and the good of souls demands it. Nor could such action be considered a defect in you when motivated by the charity of Christ. It is a reasonable gesture, and can most assuredly be done without the slightest prejudice to duty or the immutable principles of truth and justice.

Anselm's example of charity. 31. We find examples of such actions on the part of Anselm (or rather, on behalf of God and the Church for whom Anselm endured long and arduous sufferings). When he finally settled the wearisome conflict, Our Predecessor, Paschal II, whom We frequently mentioned, wrote him the following words: "We believe your charity and incessant prayers have persuaded the divine mercy to look favorably upon the people committed to your care." Then referring to the paternal kindness of the Supreme Pontiff towards the guilty, Paschal continues: "Our condescension is the daughter of love and compassion. In such a way We feel We can best lift up the fallen. The strong man will never be able to raise the weak man by merely stretching out his hand; only when the former bends a little will he be able to lift the latter. Even though this condescension may seem a bit like fraternization, it never goes to the extent of violating the dictates of prudence." [51]

Anselm balances the two extremes. 32. In borrowing the words Our holy Predecessor wrote for Anselm's consolation, We also express Our fear of that danger which faces even the best of the Church's pastors. We refer to the danger of transgressing the reasonable boundaries of indulgence on the one hand, and resistance on the other. The fact that they realize this danger is readily seen from the anxiety, fear and sorrow with which these holy men have borne the terrible responsibility of governing souls. On many important occasions Anselm experienced the same danger. When torn from the solitary life of study to be elevated to the highest dignity amid the most trying circumstances, he was beset with torments of the acutest anxiety. His greatest fear was that he might not do enough for his own and others' salvation and the honor of God and His Church. In spite of all these worries (and the sorrow he experienced when others, even his fellow bishops, said the trouble was his own fault), his great solace was his confidence in God and the secure refuge he found in the bosom of the Church. Thus he found shelter in the arms of his Mother, the Church, "when the raging storm threatened shipwreck," and from the Roman Pontiff he received "loving and immediate assistance and comfort." [52] Perhaps God permitted this wise and holy man to endure such extreme sufferings in order that he might be our comfort and example in the weighty problems and trials of the pastoral ministry. In such a way Paul's saying would be realized in each one of us:

"Gladly . . . I will glory in my infirmities, that the strength of Christ may dwell in me. Wherefore I am satisfied, for Christ's sake, with infirmities. . . . For when I am weak, then I am strong." [53] Anselm expressed the same thought in a letter to Urban II. "Holy Father," he wrote, "I am sorry to say that I am no longer what I used to be. I am sorry that I am a Bishop because my sins prevent me from exercising the office of a Bishop. When I was in a humble position I thought I was doing something worth while. Now when I am given an exalted rank and heavily burdened, I am of value neither to myself nor others. I am crushed under this burden because of my extreme poverty in the strength, virtue, zeal and knowledge this lofty office demands. I wish I could escape this unbearable anxiety and leave the burden behind me. On the other hand, I fear that such action would offend God. Fear of God forced me to accept this burden, and now that same fear compels me to retain it. Since I cannot fathom God's Will, I do not know what to do. I wander aimlessly about, not even knowing how it all shall end." [54]

Obedience is the foundation. 33. In such a way God makes very holy men conscious of the fact that even their natural strength comes from above. By giving them a humble and true estimation of their individual insufficiency, He preserves in a more perfect manner their obedience to the Church's authority. This bears itself out both in Anselm's life as well as in his contemporaries who fought under the direction of the Apostolic See for the liberty and integrity of the Church. Their obedience bore the fruit of victory. Their example confirmed that divine saying: "An obedient man shall speak of victory." [55] Hope of the same reward is open for all those who obey the Vicar of Christ in those matters which pertain to the direction of souls or the government of the Church, and things pertaining to these objects. "The Church's sons shall take their directives and counsels under the authority of the Apostolic See." [56]

Anselm's obedience to the Holy See. 34. Without a doubt Anselm has merited this praise. The devotedness and faithfulness which bound him to the Chair of Peter can be gathered from the following words he addressed to Pope Paschal II: "The many grievous tribulations of my heart (which only God and I know) are witnesses of my determination to cling reverently and obediently to the Apostolic See. . . . I hope to God that nothing will ever be able to separate me from this union. I therefore desire whenever possible to submit all my actions to the judgment of this same authority for its direction and, if necessary, correction." [57]

His writings manifest his obedience. 35. He displays the same degree of intense determination in all his actions and writings, especially in his letters, which Our Predecessor Paschal II described as "written with the pen of charity." [58] In writing to the Supreme Pontiff, however, he is not satisfied with merely "asking for assistance and comfort." In language of filial affection and undaunted faith he promises that he will be incessant in his prayers on behalf of the Holy Father. For example, when he was Abbot of Bec he wrote the following words to Pope Urban II: "We are continually beseeching God to bring these evil days to an end in which you and the Roman Church (as well as ourselves and all the devoted faithful) are being persecuted. And we shall persevere in our prayers until the offender receives his just punishment. Even though the Lord seems to be tarrying, we are confident that He will not permit the sinner to triumph over the saint. We most certainly know that He will never forsake His heritage nor allow the gates of hell to prevail against her." [59]

Anselm's letters are Our comfort. 36. We find a constant source of comfort in Anselm's letters. They not only remind Us of a saint devoted to the Apostolic See, but also, Venerable Brethren, they call to Our mind the letters and other numerous signs of affection you yourselves have offered Us in similar sorrows and struggles.

The greater the trial, the stronger the union. 37. Without a doubt, whenever the storms raged most fiercely against Christianity throughout the ages, the Bishops and faithful have always been marvelously drawn into the closest bonds of unity with the Roman Pontiff. In these present times this union has been so firm and affectionate that one can easily perceive its divine character. This union of love and obedience is Our strongest consolation and most powerful defense. The stronger it is, the more it incurs the devil's envy and the world's hatred. It cannot be compared with any other human society; it cannot be explained in any political or human terms. It is simply the fulfillment of Christ's sublime prayer at the Last Supper.

The need of unity. 38. It is Our duty, Venerable Brethren, to do everything We can to make this union of the members with the head even more binding. Therefore, We must set aside human considerations and employ all the divine motives We have at Our disposal. In such a way *we all will be one in Christ.* In pursuing this noble aim We shall even better fulfill Our sublime vocation of continuing and spreading the work and Kingdom of Christ on earth. For that reason the Church has constantly been repeating throughout the ages this loving prayer (which is also the most ardent desire of Our heart): "Holy Father, keep in thy name those whom thou hast given me, that they may be one even as we are." [60]

Unity, the strongest defense. 39. This unity must be our aim if we wish to withstand both the external attacks of those who boldly seek to destroy the liberty and rights of the Church, as well as those internal dangers which arise from that other kind of warfare We have mentioned above. These latter misguided souls, through their deceitful systems, are trying to undermine the very constitution and essence of the Church, destroy the integrity of her doctrine, and ruin her entire discipline. This poison is still in the air. It has infected many people, even some of the clergy, and especially the junior clergy. Their capricious desiring for novelty has not only dragged them down and completely stifled them, but also, as We have already mentioned, completely clouded their mentality.

The danger of intellectual pride. 40. Many weak and intemperate minds (who are regretably deceiving only themselves) have made the progress (good in itself) of positive science and material prosperity the occasion for displaying an intolerable arrogance towards divinely revealed truth. Such people, however, should recall the many mistakes and frequent contradictions the devotees of hasty novelties have already made in dealing with those speculative or practical questions which are of vital importance to mankind. They should bear well in mind that human pride is punished by confusion and shipwreck even before the port of truth is sighted. Their own experience never seems to teach these people to be humble and destroy the "reasoning . . . of every lofty thing that exalts itself against the knowledge of God" and bring "every mind into captivity to the obedience of Christ." [61]

Pride leads to agnosticism. 41. As a matter of fact, their arrogance has led them straight into the opposite extreme. Their philosophy, which doubts everything, has enveloped them in a cloak of darkness. As a result they profess *agnosticism* and an almost infinite number of other errors and opinions which are, strange to say, contradictory. Such conflicting opinions have made them "vain in their reasonings. . . . For while professing to be wise, they have become fools." [62]

Pascendi Dominici Gregis. 42. Unfortunately, their pompous phrases and specious promises of a new wisdom (fallen, as they say, from heaven!) as well as their new methodology have won over many young men just as the Manicheans enticed Augustine. Consequently these young men have more or less unconsciously fallen from the right path. However, We have already discussed these dangerous teachers of mad knowledge as well as their aims, illusions, and disastrous errors in Our encyclical letter of September 8, 1907, *Pascendi Dominici Gregis.*

Anselm, a comfort and an example. 43. At this point We should add, however, that even if the dangers We have described are more serious and threatening today, they are not altogether different from those that menaced the Church in Anselm's days. We can find in Anselm's labors as a teacher the same counsels and comfort in Our cause of protecting truth as We found in his apostolic firmness in Our cause of defending the liberty and rights of the Church.

The excesses of Anselm's days. 44. Without going into detail about the intellectual state of the clergy and people of that distant age, We can readily see that their minds were exposed to the danger of a twofold excess.

The temerity of some. 45. In those days some unqualified and foolish teachers of a superficial knowledge became so incredibly conceited because of their little learning that they allowed themselves to be tricked by a deceptive philosophy and dialectics. In their conceited fallacies (which they called science) "they despised sacred authority and boldly called into question the dogmas of the Catholic faith. . . . Blinded by their pride, they declared everything impossible they could not understand instead of humbly admitting, as a truly wise person would, that there may be many things beyond their comprehension. . . . As soon as some of these men developed the horns of this presumptuous knowledge (not being able to distinguish between knowing something and the manner of knowing it), and had not yet acquired the wings of the spirit through a firm faith, they immediately proceeded to delve into the deepest questions of faith. Although they tried to ascend the heights by means of their own intelligence, the very lack of understanding threw them down into many obvious errors." [63] Today there are many sad examples of such men among us!

The timidity of others. 46. On the other hand, there were some timid souls in those days who were so alarmed by so many losing their faith that they became suspicious of this infatuated science to such an extent that they denounced the use of philosophy and, for that matter, every rational discussion of sacred doctrines.

The Catholic golden mean. 47. Catholic thought stands in the middle of these two extremes. It loathes the presumption of the former who, according to the expression of Gregory IX in a succeeding age, "are inflated like balloons with the air of vanity and, in their desire to establish the Faith by natural reasoning, transgress fixed boundaries by adulterating God's word with philosophers' fictions." [64] On the other hand, it condemns the slothfulness of the latter, who, in their excessive and avowed neglect of true investigations, refuse "to perfect the intellect by using the principles of faith." [65] This mentality especially merits condemnation when found in those who are duty-bound to defend the Catholic Faith against the errors that spring up on every side.

Anselm, the trail-blazer. 48. It would seem that God sent Anselm to be an example by his speech and writings to show us the safe road. His mission seems to have been to stir up the springs of Christian wisdom for the common good and to point out the right path for those Catholic teachers who would follow him in teaching "sacred doctrine according to the Scholastic method." [66] Without a doubt, he deserves to be called and honored as their precursor.

Anselm's place in Scholasticism. 49. We do not wish to imply that the Doctor of Aosta had attained the heights of theological and philosophical speculation or the renown of the other two supreme masters, Thomas and Bonaventure. These latter harvested the fruit of wisdom only after time and the labors of many teachers had ripened it. Anselm himself possessed that modesty so characteristic of the truly wise. Consequently, in spite of his learning and brilliance, he published only those writings which circumstances demanded or some authority commanded. Even in the works he did publish he hastens to note that "if anything needs correction, he readily stands corrected." [67] In fact, when the question is debatable and not one of faith, he gives the following advice to his disciples: "You must not hold our teaching so tenaciously that you would refuse to give it up when others disprove it with solid arguments and propose contrary opinions. When that happens you will at least concede that what we have taught was useful in carrying out the controversy." [68]

Anselm's glory endures forever. 50. Anselm accomplished far more than he or others expected of him. He attained a position which not even the glory of his successors could dim. Even if the noble Thomas did not accept all his conclusions and proceeded to treat questions he already treated with greater clarity and accuracy, Anselm deserves the distinction of blazing the trail of speculation. He removed the timid's doubts, the foolhardy's dangers, and the quarrelsome sophist's mistakes. He calls the last mentioned "the heretical dialecticians" [69] whose reason is the slave of imagination and vanity.

Anselm's contempt for the dialecticians. 51. Concerning these latter he makes the following observation: "While it is true that anyone who discusses problems concerning Sacred Scripture should be warned to act with the greatest prudence, these dialecticians of our day should be altogether forbidden to discuss spiritual questions." His reason for this statement can be applied with equal force to those who imitate their errors today: "Reason, which should be the leader and judge of all human activity, is so confused in their souls with material imaginations that it is impossible to separate the one from the other. More than that, their reason cannot distinguish the object of its contemplation from the objects of the senses." [70] The following words, in which he ridicules false philosophers, are also appropriate for our times: "Since these men cannot understand what they believe, they call into question the truth of the Faith itself which the holy Fathers confirmed. They are like owls and bats (who see the sky only at night) arguing with eagles (who look straight into the sun at high noon) about the length of the sun's rays." [71]

Relation of philosophy and theology. In this same treatise as well as elsewhere [72] he condemns that erroneous opinion which grants philosophy the privilege of invading the field of theology. In refuting this foolish theory he clearly defines the boundaries of the two sciences and adequately points out the role of reason in regard to divinely revealed truths. "Our faith," he says, "must be defended by reason against scoffers." He then proceeds to explain the manner and extent of this defense in the following sentence: "It must show them the reasonableness of our position and the unreasonableness of their contempt."[73] Philosophy's primary duty is to show *the reasonableness of faith* and our subsequent obligation of believing that divine authority which proposes these sublime mysteries. Add to this many motives of credibility and one can readily see that these truths are eminently worthy of belief. The proper function of Christian theology is entirely different from this. Based on the fact of divine revelation, it strengthens the Faith in those who already enjoy the honor of being Christians. "Consequently no true Christian would call into question those things which the Catholic Church firmly believes and openly teaches. On the contrary, firmly holding to that Faith and lovingly living according to it, he must seek as far as he can the reason for these truths. If he understands, let him be grateful. If he cannot understand, let him not sharpen his horns for battle, but reverently bow his head."[74]

Reasonableness of the faith. 52. When theologians search for, and the faithful inquire about, reason for our faith, they are not seeking a foundation for the Faith, since its foundation is the authority of God revealing. Rather, however, as Anselm says, "just as prudence obliges us to believe the profundities of the Christian Faith [which we call mysteries] before we begin to discuss them, so it seems to me that we would act negligently if, after being confirmed in the Faith, we do not try to understand our Faith."[75] Here Anselm is speaking of that understanding which the Vatican Council discussed.[76] He explains this in that other passage where he writes: "Ever since the time of the Apostles the holy Fathers and Doctors have said many great things about the reasonableness of the Faith. . . . At that, however, they have not said everything that could be said on the subject had they lived longer, simply because the reasonableness of the Faith has so many ramifications that mortals will never be able to exhaust them. Furthermore, the Lord never ceases distributing the gifts of grace in His Church since He promised to be with her till the end of the world. Passing over the other texts of Sacred Scripture which invite us to investigate the reasonableness of things, there is one that says you will not believe if you do not understand. Scripture plainly both urges us to increase our intellectual comprehension and tells us how to profit from it." This last mentioned reason is not to be neglected since the intellectual comprehension we achieve in this life stands midway between faith and vision. The more perfect our intellectual comprehension is here, the more perfect our vision will be hereafter."[77]

Renewal of past directives. 53. Anselm laid the foundations of sound philosophical and theological studies on such principles. Other very learned men, the princes of Scholasticism (especially the Doctor from Aquin), followed and developed, illustrated and perfected them for the honor and defense of the Church. We have been anxious to eulogize the distinctive merits of Saint Anselm, Venerable Brethren, in order to take one more opportunity for urging you to lead your young men (and especially the junior clergy) to the abundant springs of Christian wisdom which the Doctor of Aosta discovered and the Doctor of Aquin enriched. In this matter always bear in mind the instructions of Our Predecessor, Leo XIII, of happy memory [78] as well as those We Ourselves have issued many times, especially in the above-mentioned encyclical, *Pascendi Dominici Gregis.* Experience is a daily testimony to the great loss and harm that follows upon the neglect of these studies or the pursuance of them without logical and certain methodology. On the other hand, many unqualified or unprepared men "dare to discuss the most profound question of faith." [79] As Anselm did, so We also lament this evil and repeat his strong recommendations: "Let no one rush headlong into discussing intricate questions concerning divine things until he has first acquired a firm faith, upright conduct and mature wisdom. Otherwise his imprudent and frivolous discussions will be interspersed with many contradictory sophistries and lead him into the inescapable snare of error." [80] This same imprudence and thoughtlessness, when kindled by the flames of passion, destroys both serious study and the integrity of doctrine. Spurred on by pride (which Anselm lamented in the "heretical dialecticians" of his day), these souls come to despise the sacred authority of Scripture, the Fathers, and the Doctors of the Church. A more humble genius would gladly make his own the respectful words of Anselm concerning Sacred Scripture, the Fathers, and Doctors of the Church: "We can never hope to find their equal in contemplation of the truth either in our own time or in any future time." [81]

Disobedience leads to confusion. Nor are they any more respectful to the authority of the Church and the Supreme Pontiff when attempts are made to recall them to their sense of duty. Of course they are lavish in uttering promises of submission whenever they can hide behind them and gain recognition and protection through them. Their contempt, however, practically destroys any well-founded hope of their conversion. All the while they refuse to obey him "whom Divine Providence has commissioned to guard Christian life, doctrine and government as the lord and father of the Church universal during its pilgrimage on earth. For that reason, whenever a question of faith arises in the Church, it can lawfully be referred only to his authority for correction. After having prudently examined the case, he, more than anyone else, has been enlightened so as to hand down a certain answer." [82] If only these poor wanderers who frequently utter such delightful words as "sincerity," "conscience," "religious experience," "faith that is felt and lived" and such like—oh, if only they would learn their lesson from Anselm! If only they would understand his holy teachings! If only they would imitate his holy example! If only they would take to heart these words he wrote: "Before one can be truly wise, his heart must be purified by faith, his eyes must be opened through observance of the Lord's commands . . . and he must be humbly obedient to the Scriptures. . . . Moreover, when the dictates of conscience are ignored, intellectual ability is frequently removed and faith destroyed." [83]

Prayers for protection. 54. If the erring, however, obstinately continue to sow seeds of dissension and error, demolish the deposit of sacred doctrine, attack discipline, despise venerable customs, and destroy ("which is a species of heresy" Saint Anselm says [84]) the constitution of the Church, then, Venerable Brethren, We must be all the more vigilant. We must keep this deadly disease away from the Christian people and especially the young of the flock. We are continually imploring God for grace. We are constantly invoking the assistance of the august Mother of God and the intercession of the other saintly citizens of the Church triumphant. We prayerfully turn to Saint Anselm, the shining light of Christian wisdom and the valiant guardian and protector of the Churchs sacred rights. In conclusion We address him in the same words Our holy Predecessor, Gregory VII, wrote him during his lifetime: "The sweet odor of your good works has reached us and, thanking God for them, We warmly embrace you in the love of Christ. We firmly believe that your example has been a source of many blessings for God's Church. Through your prayers and the prayers of men like you, she may even be freed from the threatening dangers, and the mercy of Christ will come to Our assistance. . . . Therefore We beg you and your brothers to beseech God to deliver the Church and Us, her unworthy ruler, from the heretics' oppression and lead them back from their errors to the path of truth." [85]

Apostolic Blessing. 55. We are supported by this mighty protection and We trust in your cooperation. As a pledge of heavenly grace, and a testimony of Our good will, from the bottom of Our heart We bestow, Venerable Brethren, on you and the clergy and people entrusted to your care, the Apostolic Blessing.

56. Given at Saint Peter's, Rome, on the Feast of Saint Anselm, April 21, 1909, in the eighth year of Our Pontificate.

PIUS X, POPE

REFERENCES

1. I Cor. 4:9.
2. Col. 3:11.
3. Cf. pp. 3–13 of this volume.
4. I Cor. 15:41.
5. *Breviarium Romanum,* April 21.
6. *Epicedion in obitum Anselmi.*
7. Epitaph of Saint Anselm.
8. *Epicedion in obitum Anselmi.*
9. *Ibid.*
10. *Breviarium Romanum,* April 21.
11. *In libro II Epist. S. Anselmi, ep.* 32.
12. *In libro III Epist. S. Anselmi, ep.* 74 & 42.
13. I Cor. 2:14.

14. *Epicedion in obitum Anselmi.*
15. *Breviarium Romanum,* April 21.
16. *In libro II Epist. S. Anselmi, ep.* 44 & 74.
17. Gal. 4:19.
18. Luke 19:14.
19. Prov. 14:34.
20. John 8:44.
21. Coloss. 2:8.
22. Rom. 1:21.
23. I Tim. 1:19.
24. Vatican Council, *Constit. Dei filius, cap.* 4.
25. *In libro III Epist. S. Anselmi, ep.* 65.
26. *Ibid., ep.* 73.
27. *In libro IV Epist. S. Anselmi, ep.* 47.
28. Acts 20:28.
29. Is. 58:1.
30. Ps. 17:14.
31. Heb. 13:14.
32. Prov. 14:34.
33. Wisd. 6:7.
34. Ps. 2:10–12.
35. *In libro IV Epist. S. Anselmi, ep.* 12.
36. *Ibid., ep.* 8.
37. *In libro III Epist. S. Anselmi, ep.* 57.
38. *Ibid., ep.* 59.
39. *In libro IV Epist. S. Anselmi, ep.* 52.
40. *Ibid., ep.* 52.
41. *In libro III Epist. S. Anselmi, ep.* 142.
42. Rom. 8:28.
43. *Ibid.,* 11:33.
44. Is. 55:8.
45. Col. 1:24.
46. Acts 14:21.
47. *Hom.* III.
48. I John 5:19.
49. Math. 12:30.
50. I Cor. 9:22.
51. *In libro III Epist. S. Anselmi, ep.* 140.
52. *Ibid., ep.* 37.
53. II Cor. 12:9–10.
54. *In libro III Epist. S. Anselmi, ep.* 37.
55. Prov. 21:28.
56. *In libro IV Epist. S. Anselmi, ep.* 1.
57. *Ibid., ep.* 5.
58. *In libro III Epist. S. Anselmi, ep.* 74.
59. *In libro II Epist. S. Anselmi, ep.* 33.
60. John 17:11.
61. II Cor. 10:4–5.
62. Rom. 1:21–22.
63. *De fide Trinitatis, cap.* 2.
64. Gregory IX, *Epist. Tacti dolore cordis, ad theologos Parisiensos,* July 7, 1228.
65. *In libro II Epist. S. Anselmi, ep.* 41.
66. *Breviarium Romanum,* April 21.
67. *Cur Deus homo?* 1. *II, cap.* 23.
68. *De Grammatico, cap.* 21, *sub finem.*
69. *De fide, Trinitatis, cap.* 2.
70. *Ibid.*
71. *Ibid.*
72. *In libro II Epist. S. Anselmi, ep.* 41.
73. *Ibid.*
74. *De fide Trinitatis, cap.* 2.
75. *Cur Deus homo?* 1. *I, cap.* 2.
76. *Constit. Dei filius, cap.* 4.
77. *De fide Trinitatis, Praefatio.*
78. Encyclical letter of August 4, 1879, *Aeterni Patris.*
79. *De fide Trinitatis, cap.* 2.
80. *Ibid.*
81. *Ibid., Praefatio.*
82. *Ibid.*
83. *Ibid., cap.* 2.
84. *S. Anselm, De nuptiis consanguineorum, cap.* 1.
85. *In libro II Epist. S. Anselmi, ep.* 31.

CHAPTER 10

Editae Saepe *May 26, 1910, The Tercentenary of Saint Charles Borromeo*

SEVERAL years previous to 1910 the people of Milan were making elaborate plans for the celebration of the tercentenary of their holy Archbishop.* On May 26, 1910, Saint Pius X issued his thirteenth encyclical letter, *Editae Saepe,* commemorating the tercentenary of Saint Charles Borromeo.

The importance Saint Pius X attached to the example of Saint Charles Borromeo can be readily seen. The former set up the purpose of his Pontificate in the motto *Instaurare omnia in Christo;* the latter fulfilled that motto most perfectly in his own life and work. Thus in the encyclical's very lengthy introduction Saint Pius X takes pains to show that since the Church is divine she is the mother of holiness, holding up for her children the example of Christ and His saints as the path to be followed in restoring all things in Christ (1–8). Just as God "set a great light on the Apostolic rock when he singled Charles out of the heart of the Roman Church as the faithful priest and good servant to be a model for the pastors and their flocks," so Saint Pius X chose the tercentenary of his canonization as the occasion to contemplate "the glory (and even more the example and teaching) of the saints" so that "the Church's enemies will be humiliated and thrown into confusion."

The encyclical describes the times in which Charles lived, their errors and depravity, their true and false reformers (9–10). It shows how Charles' quiet life of preparation, adherence to and support of the decrees of the Papacy and the Council of Trent, and zeal to labor for all without tiring set him in perfect accord with "the mystery of the Divine Will, which is . . . to re-establish all things in Christ" (11–16). These very virtues distinguished him from the false reformers of his time just as they distinguish the true reformer today from his Modernist opponent (17–20).

* As far back as 1908 there appeared in Milan the richly illustrated periodical entitled, *San Carlo Borromeo nell terzo Centenario della Canonizzatione.*

Like Charles, the true reformer (in counter-distinction to the false reformer) will always insist on the importance of teaching and preaching Christian doctrine by being faithful to the Word of God (18–29), and ardently love and follow the Church's directives as they come forth from the Apostolic See (30–35). Again, like Charles, the true reformer will do everything possible to urge the faithful to receive frequently and treat reverently the two Sacraments of Divine Love, will subordinate the natural to the supernatural, will foster Catholic Action on every possible occasion, and clearly distinguish between the temporal and spiritual power (36–44). Praying that God will let "Charles now assist by his patronage the Church he loved so ardently and aided so greatly by his merits and example, thus making peace for us in the day of wrath," the Pope concludes with the Apostolic Blessing (45–46).

Even such a cursory outline clearly shows the purpose of the encyclical. As a writer in 1910 remarks,

> . . . the Pope had a very definite reason for laying stress upon the evils generated by the false teachers of the sixteenth century, because it was part of his design to contrast the principles of sham reformers with those of the true reformers, to insist that a moral renovation of the same kind is needed in our own day, and to urge that the example of St. Charles in doing battle against the heresy of Luther and Calvin ought to serve as a lesson and an encouragement to modern Catholics in dealing with the yet more insidious religious errors of the twentieth century.†

At the time of its publication *Editae Saepe* caused quite a stir. In Germany many journalists loudly protested the *"Borromaus-Encyclica"* as a sectarian attack against the religious leaders of their country. In many English circles it was considered as "a glorification of Catholic intolerance." Both camps of critics, however, had completely missed the point of the encyclical. As the above-quoted author rightly mentions,

> . . . the language of the Holy Father is singularly guarded as regards anything which might seem to touch upon the Church's present relations with Protestantism. It is not the severity of St. Charles in dealing with the heretics of his own time that the Pope puts forward as matter for thankfulness and imitation. It is the ascetic ideal, the boundless self-sacrifice, the watchfulness which is shown in bringing religious instruction to the doors of all, the charity which made him alive to the needs of the poor, the true desire to improve social conditions, a desire proved, as the Encyclical says, "not by a vain display of words, after the fashion

† "St. Charles Borromeo and the Recent Encyclical," by Herbert Thurston, S.J., in *The Month,* 116:392.

of the rebellious reformers, but by acts, by a long and sustained effort even to the sacrifice of goods and health and life." ‡

Saint Pius X merely holds up Saint Charles Borromeo as an example to be followed in restoring all things in Christ. He was mainly preoccupied with the doings of the enemies of the Church in our own day, and . . . his strictures upon the leaders of the revolt against Papal authority in the sixteenth century were altogether subordinate to his purpose of pointing out the fallacy of anti-clerical and Modernist schemes of reform. If the work of restoring all things in Christ is to be successfully carried through, it must be, he urges, on the lines indicated by the example of St. Charles, not by unfurling the standard of rebellion. §

Editae Saepe *Encyclical Letter of Our Holy Father Pius X to the Patriarchs, Primates, Archbishops, Bishops and Other Ordinaries in Peace and Communion with the Apostolic See*

VENERABLE BRETHREN, HEALTH AND THE APOSTOLIC BLESSING:

The Church, the mother of holiness. 1. Sacred Scripture records the divine word as saying that men will remember the just man forever, for even though he is dead, he yet speaks.[1] Both in word and deed the Church has for a long time verified the truth of that saying. She is the mother and the nurse of holiness, ever renewed and enlivened by the breath of the Spirit Who dwells in us.[2] She alone conceives, nourishes, and educates the noble family of the just. Like a loving mother, she carefully preserves the memory of and affection for the saints. This remembrance is, as it were, a divine comfort which lifts her eyes above the miseries of this earthly pilgrimage so that she finds in the saints "her joy and her crown." Thus she sees in them the sublime image of her heavenly Spouse. Thus she shows her children in each age the timeliness of the old truth: "For those who love God all things work together unto good, for those who, according to his purpose, are saints through his call."[3] The glorious deeds of the saints, however, do more than

‡ *Ibid.*, p. 395.
§ *Ibid.*, p. 393.

afford us comfort. In order that we may imitate and be encouraged by them, one and all the saints echo in their own lives the saying of Saint Paul, "I beg you, be imitators of me, as I am of Christ." [4]

Christ and His saints are our examples. 2. For that reason, Venerable Brethren, immediately after Our elevation to the Supreme Pontificate We stated in Our first encyclical that We would labor without ceasing "to restore all things in Christ." [5] We begged everyone to turn their eyes with Us to Jesus, "the apostle and high priest of our confession . . . the author and finisher of faith." [6] Since the majesty of that Model may be too much for fallen human nature, God mercifully gave Us another model to propose for your imitation, the glorious Virgin Mother of God. While being as close to Christ as human nature permits, she is better suited to the needs of our weak nature.[7] Over and above that, We made use of several other occasions to recall the memory of the saints. We emulated these faithful servants and ministers of God's household (each in his own way enjoying the friendship of God), "who by faith conquered kingdoms, wrought justice, obtained promises." [8] Thus encouraged by their example, we would be "now no longer children, tossed to and fro and carried about by every wind of doctrine devised in the wickedness of men, in craftiness, according to the wiles of error. Rather are we to practise the truth in love, and so grow up in all things in him who is the head, Christ." [9]

Previous encyclicals. 3. We have already pointed out how Divine Providence was perfectly realized in the lives of those three great doctors and pastors of the Church, Gregory the Great, John Chrysostom and Anselm of Aosta. Although they were separated by centuries, the Church was beset by many serious dangers in each of their respective ages. In recent years We celebrated all of their solemn centenaries. In a very special way, however, We commemorated Saint Gregory the Great in the encyclical of March 12, 1904, and Saint Anselm in the encyclical of April 21, 1909. In these documents We treated those points of Christian doctrine and morals found in the example and teaching of these saints which We thought were best suited to our times.

The third centenary of St. Charles Borromeo. 4. As We have already mentioned,[10] We are of the opinion that the shining example of Christ's soldiers has far greater value in the winning and sanctifying of souls than the words of profound treatises. We therefore gladly take this present opportunity to teach some very useful lessons from the consideration of the life of another holy pastor whom God raised up in more recent times and in the midst of trials very similar to those We are experiencing today. We refer to Saint Charles Borromeo, Cardinal of the Holy Roman Church and Archbishop of Milan, whom Paul V, of holy memory, raised to the altar of the saints less than thirty years after his death. The words of Our Predecessor are to the point: "The Lord alone performs great wonders and in recent times He has accomplished marvelous things among Us. In His wonderful dispensation He has set a great light on the Apostolic rock when He singled Charles out of the heart of the Roman Church as the faithful priest and good servant to be a model for the pastors and their flock. He enlightened the whole Church from the light diffused by his holy works. He shone forth before priests and people as innocent as Abel, pure as Enoch, tireless as Jacob, meek as Moses, and zealous as Elias. Surrounded by luxury, he exhibited the austerity of Jerome, the humility of Martin, the pastoral zeal of Gregory, the liberty of Ambrose, and the charity of Paulinus. In a word, he was a man we could see with our eyes and touch with our hands. He trampled earthly things underfoot and lived the life of the spirit. Although the world tried to entice him, he lived crucified to the world. He constantly sought after heavenly things, not only because he held the office of an angel but also because even on earth he tried to think and act as an angel." [11]

The purpose of this celebration. 5. Such are the words of praise Our Predecessor wrote after Charles' death. Now, three centuries after his canonization, "we can rightly rejoice on this day when We solemnly confer, in the name of the Lord, the sacred honors on Charles, Cardinal Priest, thereby crowning his own Spouse with a diadem of every precious stone." We agree with Our Predecessor that the contemplation of the glory (and even more, the example and teaching of the saints) will humiliate the enemy and throw into confusion all those who "glory in their specious errors." [12] Saint Charles is a model for both clergy and people in these days. He was the unwearied advocate and defender of the true Catholic reformation, opposing those innovators whose purpose was not the restoration, but the effacement and destruction of faith and morals. This celebration of the third centenary of his canonization should prove to be not only a consolation and lesson for every Catholic but also a noble incentive for everyone to cooperate wholeheartedly in that work so dear to Our heart of restoring all things in Christ.

God draws good out of evil. 6. You know very well, Venerable Brethren, that even when surrounded by tribulation the Church still enjoys some consolation from God. "Christ also loved the Church, and delivered himself up for her, that he might sanctify her . . . in order that he might present to himself the Church in all her glory, not having spot or wrinkle or any such thing, but that she might be holy and without blemish." [13] When vice runs wild, when persecution hangs heavy, when error is so cunning that it threatens her destruction by snatching many children from her bosom (and plunges them into the whirlpool of sin and impiety)—then, more than ever, the Church is strengthened from above. Whether the wicked will it or not, God makes even error aid in the triumph of Truth, whose guardian and defender is the Church. He puts corruption in the service of sanctity, whose mother and nurse is the Church. Out of persecution He brings a more wondrous "freedom from our enemies." For these reasons, when worldly men think they see the Church buffeted and almost capsized in the raging storm, then she really comes forth fairer, stronger, purer, and brighter with the lustre of distinguished virtues.

The divinity of the Church. 7. In such a way God's goodness bears witness to the divinity of the Church. He makes her victorious in that painful battle against the errors and sins that creep into her ranks. Through this victory He verifies the words of Christ: "The gates of hell shall not prevail against it." [14] In her day-to-day living He fulfills the promise, "Behold, I am with you all days, even unto the consummation of the world." [15] Finally, He is the witness of that mysterious power of the other Paraclete (Who Christ promised would come immediately after His ascension into heaven), Who continually lavishes His gifts upon her and serves as her defender and consoler in all her sorrows. This is the Spirit Who will "dwell with you forever, the Spirit of truth whom the world cannot receive, because it neither sees him nor knows him . . . he will dwell with you and be in you." [16] The life and strength of the Church flows forth from this font. As the ecumenical Vatican Council teaches, this divine power sets the Church above every other society by those obvious notes which mark her "as a banner raised up among the nations." [17]

Proof of her divinity. 8. In fact, only a miracle of that divine power could preserve the Church, the Mystical Body of Christ, from blemish in the holiness of her doctrine, law, and end in the midst of the flood of corruption and lapses of her members. Her doctrine, law and end have produced an abundant harvest. The faith and holiness of her children have brought forth the most salutary fruits. Here is another proof of her divine life: in spite of a great number of pernicious opinions and great variety of errors (as well as the vast army of rebels) the Church remains immutable and constant, "as the pillar and foundation of truth," in professing one identical doctrine, in receiving the same Sacraments, in her divine constitution, government, and morality. This is all the more marvellous when one considers that the Church not only resists evil but even "conquers evil by doing good." She is constantly blessing friends and enemies alike. She is continually striving and ardently desiring to bring about the social and individual Christian restoration which is her particular mission in the world. Moreover, even her enemies benefit from it.

Conditions in the days of St. Charles. 9. This wonderful working of Divine Providence in the Church's program of restoration was seen with the greatest clarity and was given as a consolation for the good especially in the century of Saint Charles Borromeo. In those days passions ran riot and knowledge of the truth was almost completely twisted and confused. A continual battle was being waged against errors. Human society, going from bad to worse, was rushing headlong into the abyss. Then those proud and rebellious men came on the scene who are "enemies of the cross of Christ. . . . Their god is the belly . . . they mind the things of earth." [18] These men were not concerned with correcting morals, but only with denying dogmas. Thus they increased the chaos. They dropped the reins of law, and unbridled licentiousness ran wild. They despised the authoritative guidance of the Church and pandered to the whims of the dissolute princes and people. They tried to destroy the Church's doctrine, constitution and discipline. They were similar to those sinners who were warned long ago: "Woe to you that call evil good, and good evil." [19] They called this rebellious riot and perversion of faith and morals a reformation, and themselves reformers. In reality, they were corrupters. In undermining the strength of Europe through wars and dissensions, they paved the way for those modern rebellions and apostasy. This modern warfare has united and renewed in one attack the three kinds of attack which have up until now been separated; namely, the bloody conflicts of the first ages, the internal pests of heresies, and finally, in the name of evangelical liberty, the vicious corruption and perversion of discipline such as was unknown, perhaps, even in medieval times. Yet in each of these combats the Church has always emerged victorious.

False and true reformers. 10. God, however, brought forth real reformers and holy men to arrest the onrushing current, to extinguish the conflagration, and to repair the harm caused by this crowd of seducers. Their many-sided zealous work of reforming discipline was especially consoling to the Church since the tribulation afflicting her was so great. Their work also proves the truth that "God is faithful and . . . with the temptation will also give you a way out. . . ." [20] In these circumstances God provided a pleasing consolation for the Church in the outstanding zeal and sanctity of Charles Borromeo.

The mission of Saint Charles. 11. God ordained that his ministry would be the effective and special means of checking the rebels' boldness and teaching and inspiring the Church's children. He restrained the former's mad extravagances by the example of his life and labor, and met their empty charges with the most powerful eloquence. He fanned the latter's hopes and kindled their zeal. Even from his youth he cultivated in a remarkable manner all the virtues of the true reformer which others possessed only in varying degrees. These virtues are fortitude, counsel, doctrine, authority, ability, and alacrity. He put them all in the service of Catholic truth against the attacks of error (which is precisely the mission of the Church). He revived the faith that had either become dormant or almost extinct in many by strengthening it with many wise laws and practices. He restored that discipline which had been overthrown by bringing the morals of clergy and people alike back to the ideals of Christian living. In executing all the duties of a reformer he also fulfilled the functions of the "good and faithful servant." Later he performed the works of the high priest who "pleased God in his days and was found just." He is, therefore, a worthy example for both clergy and laity, rich and poor. He can be numbered among those whose excellence as a bishop and prelate is eulogized by the Apostle Peter when he says that he became "from the heart a pattern to the flock."[21] Even before the age of twenty-three and although elevated to the highest honors and entrusted with very important and difficult ecclesiastical matters, Charles made truly wonderful daily progress in the practice of virtue through the contemplation of divine things. This sacred retirement perfected him, prepared him for later days, and caused him to shine forth as "a spectacle to the world, and angels, and men."

Charles and the Council of Trent. 12. Then (again borrowing the words of Our Predecessor, Paul V), the Lord began to work His wonders in Charles. He filled him with a wisdom, justice, and burning zeal for promoting His glory and the Catholic cause. Above all, the Lord filled him with a great concern for restoring the faith in the Church universal according to the decrees of the renowned Council of Trent. That Pontiff himself, as well as all future generations, attributed the success of the Council to Charles, since even before carrying its decrees into action he was its most ardent promoter. In fact, his many vigils, trials, and labors brought its work to its ultimate completion.

Preparation is necessary for greatness. 13. All these things, however, were only a preparation or sort of novitiate where he trained his heart in piety, his mind in study, and his body in work (always remaining a modest and humble youth) for that life in which he would be as clay in the hands of God and His Vicar on earth. The innovators of that time despised just that kind of life of preparation. The same folly leads the modern innovators also to spurn it. They fail to see that God's wondrous works are matured in the obscurity and silence of a soul dedicated to obedience and contemplation. They cannot see that just as the hope of the harvest lies in the sowing, so this preparation is the germ of future progress.

Charles' reform in Milan. 14. As We have already hinted, this sanctity and industry prepared under such conditions in due time came to produce a truly marvellous fruit. When Charles, "good laborer that he was, left the convenience and splendor of the city for the field (Milan) he was to cultivate, he discharged his duties better and better from day to day. Although the wickedness of the time had caused that field to become overrun with weeds and rank growths, he restored it to its pristine beauty. In time the Milanese Church became an example of ecclesiastical discipline."[22] He effected all these outstanding results in his work of reformation by adopting the rules the Council of Trent had only recently promulgated,

The zeal of the true reformer. 15. The Church knows very well that "the imagination and thought of man's heart are prone to evil."[23] Therefore she wages continual battle against vice and error "in order that the body of sin may be destroyed, that we may no longer be slaves to sin."[24] Since she is her own mistress and is guided by the grace which "is poured forth in our hearts by the Holy Spirit," she is directed in this conflict in thought and action by the Doctor of the Gentiles, who says, "Be renewed in the spirit of your mind. . . . And be not conformed to this world, but be transformed in the newness of your mind, that you may discern what is the good and acceptable and perfect will of God."[25] The true son of the Church and reformer never thinks he has attained his goal. Rather, with the Apostle, he acknowledges that he is only striving for it: "Forgetting what is behind, I strain forward to what is before, I press on towards the goal, to the prize of God's heavenly call in Christ Jesus."[26]

All things in Christ. 16. Through our union with Christ in the Church we grow up "in all things in him who is the head, Christ. For from him the whole body . . . derives its increase to the building up of itself in love. . . ."[27] For that reason Mother Church daily fulfills the mystery of the Divine Will which is "to be dispensed in the fulness of the times: to re-establish all things in Christ."[28]

Old errors, new labels. 17. The reformers that Borromeo opposed did not even think of this. They tried to reform faith and discipline according to their own whims. Venerable Brethren, it is no better understood by those whom We must withstand today. These moderns, forever prattling about culture and civilization, are undermining the Church's doctrine, laws, and practices. They are not concerned very much about culture and civilization. By using such high-sounding words they think they can conceal the wickedness of their schemes.

New reformers are more dangerous. 18. All of you know their purpose, subterfuges, and methods. On Our part We have denounced and condemned their scheming. They are proposing a universal apostasy even worse than the one that threatened the age of Charles. It is worse, We say, because it stealthily creeps into the very veins of the Church, hides there, and cunningly pushes erroneous principles to their ultimate conclusions.

Activities of the two reformations. 19. Both these heresies are fathered by the "enemy" who "sowed weeds among the wheat"[29] in order to bring about the downfall of mankind. Both revolts go about in the hidden ways of darkness, develop along the same line, and come to an end in the same fatal way. In the past the first apostasy turned where fortune seemed to smile. It set rulers against people or people against rulers only to lead both classes to destruction. Today this modern apostasy stirs up hatred between the poor and the rich until, dissatisfied with their station, they gradually fall into such wretched ways that they must pay the fine imposed on those who, absorbed in worldly, temporal things, forget "the kingdom of God and His justice." As a matter of fact, this present conflict is even more serious than the others. Although the wild innovators of former times generally preserved some fragments of the treasury of revealed doctrine, these moderns act as if they will not rest until they completely destroy it. When the foundations of religion are overthrown, the restraints of civil society are also necessarily shattered. Behold the sad spectacle of our times! Behold the impending danger of the future! However, it is no danger to the Church, for the divine promise leaves no room for doubt. Rather, this revolution threatens the family and nations, especially those who actively stir up or indifferently tolerate this unhealthy atmosphere of irreligion.

Charles, our model. 20. This impious and foolish war is waged and sometimes supported by those who should be the first to come to Our aid. The errors appear in many forms and the enticements of vice wear different dresses. Both cause many even among our own ranks to be ensnared, seducing them by the appearance of novelty and doctrine, or the illusion that the Church will accept the maxims of the age. Venerable Brethren, you are well aware that we must vigorously resist and repel the enemy's attacks with the very weapons Borromeo used in his day.

The chief duty of pastors. 21. Since they attack the very root of faith either by openly denying, hypocritically undermining, or misrepresenting revealed doctrine, we should above all recall the truth Charles often taught. "The primary and most important duty of pastors is to guard everything pertaining to the integral and inviolate maintenance of the Catholic Faith, the Faith which the Holy Roman Church professes and teaches, without which it is impossible to please God." [30] Again: "In this matter no diligence can be too great to fulfill the certain demands of our office." [31] We must therefore use sound doctrine to withstand "the leaven of heretical depravity," which, if not repressed, will corrupt the whole. That is to say, we must oppose these erroneous opinions now deceitfully being scattered abroad, which, when taken all together, are called *Modernism*. With Charles we must be mindful "of the supreme zeal and excelling diligence which the Bishop must exercise in combatting the crime of heresy." [32]

The Bishop's duty. 22. We need not mention the Saint's other words (echoing the sanctions and penalties decreed by the Roman Pontiffs) against those prelates who are negligent or remiss in purging the evil of heresy out of their dioceses. It is fitting, however, to meditate on the conclusions he draws from these papal decrees. "Above everything else," he says, "the Bishop must be eternally on guard and continually vigilant in preventing the contagious disease of heresy from entering among his flock and removing even the faintest suspicion of it from the fold. If it should happen to enter (the

Lord forbid!), he must use every means at his command to expel it immediately. Moreover, he must see to it that those infected or suspected be treated according to the Pontifical canons and sanctions." [33]

The teaching of Christian doctrine. 23. Liberation or immunity from this disease of heresy is possible only when the clergy are properly instructed, since "faith . . . depends on hearing, and hearing on the word of Christ." [34] Today we must heed the words of truth. We see this poison penetrating through all the veins of the State (from sources where it would be the least expected) to such an extent that the causes are the same as those Charles records in the following words: "If those who associate with heretics are not firmly rooted in the Faith there is reason to fear that they will easily be seduced by the heretics into the trap of impiety and false doctrine." [35] Nowadays facility in travel and communication has proven just as advantageous for error as for other things. We are living in a perverse society of unbridled license of passions in which "there is no truth . . . and there is no knowledge of God," [36] in "all the land made desolate, because there is none that considereth in the heart." [37] For that reason, borrowing the words of Charles, "We have already emphasized the importance of having all the faithful of Christ well instructed in the rudiments of Christian doctrine" [38] and have written a special encyclical letter on that extremely important subject.[39] However, We do not wish to repeat the lamentation Borromeo was moved to utter because of his burning zeal, namely, that "up until now We have received very little success in a matter of such importance." Rather, moved like him "by the enormity and danger of the task," We would once again urge everyone to make Charles his model of zeal so that he will contribute in this work of Christian restoration according to his position and ability. Fathers and employers should recall how the holy Bishop frequently and fervently taught that they should not only afford the opportunity but even consider it their duty to see that their children, servants, and employees study Christian doctrine. Clerics should remember that they must assist the parish priests in the teaching of Christian doctrine. Parish priests should erect as many schools for this same purpose as the number and needs of the people demand. They should further take care that they have upright teachers, who will be assisted by men and women of good morals according to the manner the holy Archbishop of Milan prescribed.[40]

Schools of Christian doctrine. 24. Obviously the need of this Christian instruction is accentuated by the decline of our times and morals. It is even more demanded by the existence of those public schools, lacking all religion, where everything holy is ridiculed and scorned. There both teachers' lips and students' ears are inclined to godlessness. We are referring to those schools which are unjustly called *neutral* or *lay*. In reality, they are nothing more than the stronghold of the powers of darkness. You have already, Venerable

Brethren, fearlessly condemned this new trick of mocking liberty especially in those countries where the rights of religion and the family have been disgracefully ignored and the voice of nature (which demands respect for the faith and innocence of youth) has been stifled. Firmly resolved to spare no effort in remedying this evil caused by those who expect others to obey them (although they refuse to obey the Supreme Master of all things themselves), We have recommended that schools of Christian doctrine be erected in those cities where it is possible. Thanks to your efforts, this work has already made good progress. It is, however, very much to be desired that this work spread even more widely, with many such religious schools established everywhere and teachers of sound doctrine and good morals provided.

The preacher is also a teacher. 25. The preacher (whose duty is closely allied to the teacher of the fundamentals of religion) should also have those same qualities of sound doctrine and good morals. For that reason, when drawing up the statutes of the provincial and diocesan synods, Charles was most careful to provide preachers full of zeal and holiness to exercise "the ministry of the word." We are convinced that this care is even more urgent in our times when so many men are wavering in the Faith and some vainglorious men, filled with the spirit of the age, "adulterate the word of God" and deprive the faithful of the food of life.

Fidelity to the word of God. 26. We must spare no pains, Venerable Brethren, in seeing that the flock does not feed on this air of foolish empty-headed men. Rather, it should be nourished with the life-giving food of "the ministers of the word." These can truly say, "On behalf of Christ . . . we are acting as ambassadors, God, as it were, appealing through us . . . be reconciled to God . . . we avoid unscrupulous conduct, we do not corrupt the word of God; but making known the truth, we commend ourselves to every man's conscience in the sight of God . . ." We are workmen "that cannot be ashamed, rightly handling the word of truth." [41] Those very holy and fruitful rules the Bishop of Milan frequently laid down for his people have a similar value for us. They can best be summarized in these words of Saint Paul: "When you heard and received from us the word of God, you welcomed it not as the word of men, but, as it truly is, the word of God, who works in you who have believed." [42]

Faith without works is dead. 27. "The word of God is living and efficient and keener than any two-edged sword." [43] It will not only preserve and defend the faith but also effectively motivate us to do good works since "faith . . . without works is dead." [44] "For it is not they who hear the Law that are just in the sight of God; but it is they who follow the Law that will be justified." [45]

Natural and supernatural. 28. Now in this also we see the immense difference between true and false reform. The advocates of false reform, imitating the fickleness of the foolish, generally rush into extremes. They either emphasize faith to such an extent that they neglect good works or they canonize nature with the excellence of virtue while overlooking the assistance of faith and divine grace. As a matter of fact, however, merely naturally good acts are only a counterfeit of virtue since they are neither permanent nor sufficient for salvation. The work of this kind of a reformer cannot restore discipline. On the contrary, it ruins faith and morals.

The true reformer. 29. On the other hand, the sincere and zealous reformer will, like Charles, avoid extremes and never overstep the bounds of true reform. He will always be united in the closest bonds with the Church and Christ, her Head. There he will find not only strength for his interior life but also the directives he needs in order to carry out his work of healing human society. The function of this divine mission, which has from time immemorial been handed down to the ambassadors of Christ, is to "make disciples of all nations" both the things they are to believe as well as the things they are to do since Christ Himself said, "Observe all that I have commanded you." [46] He is "the way, and the truth, and the life," [47] coming into the world that man "may have life, and have it more abundantly." [48] The fulfillment of these duties, however, far surpasses man's natural powers. The Church alone possesses together with her magisterium the power of governing and sanctifying human society. Through her ministers and servants (each in his own station and office), she confers on mankind suitable and necessary means of salvation.

The true reformer is no innovator. True reformers understand this very clearly. They do not kill the blossom in saving the root. That is to say, they do not divorce faith from holiness. They rather cultivate both of them, enkindling them with the fire of charity, "which is the bond of perfection." [49] In obedience to the Apostle, they "keep the deposit." [50] They neither obscure nor dim its light before the nations, but spread far and wide the most saving waters of truth and life welling up from that spring. They combine theory and practice. By the former they are prepared to withstand the "masquerading of error" and by the latter they apply the commandments to moral activity. In such a way they employ all the suitable and necessary means for attaining the end, namely, the wiping out of sin and the perfecting "the saints for a work of ministry, for building up the body of Christ." [51] This is the purpose of the statutes, canons, and laws of the Fathers and Councils. This is the purpose of every kind of instruction, government, and munificence. In a word, this is the ultimate purpose of every discipline and action of the Church. When the true son of the Church sets out to reform himself and others, he fixes his eyes and heart on matters of faith and morals. On just such matters Borromeo based his reformation of ecclesiastical discipline. Thus he often referred to them in his writings, as, for example, when he says, "Following the ancient custom of the holy Fathers and sacred Councils, especially the ecumenical Synod of Trent, we have decreed many regulations on these very matters in our preceding provincial Councils." [52] In the same way, when providing for the suppression of public scandals, he declares that he is following "both the law and sacred sanctions of the sacred canons, and especially the decrees of the Council of Trent." [53]

Charles, supporter of the Papacy. 30. However, he did not stop at that. In order to assure as much as possible that he would never depart from this rule, he customarily concluded the statutes of his provincial Synods with the following words: "We are always prepared to submit everything we have done and decreed in this provincial Synod to the authority and judgment of the Roman Church, the Mother and Mistress of all the churches." [54] The more quickly he advanced in the perfection of the active ministry, the more firmly was he rooted in this resolve, not only when the Chair of Peter was occupied by his uncle, but also during the Pontificates of his successors, Pius V and Gregory XIII. He wielded his influence in having these latter elected; he was tireless in supporting their great endeavors; and he fulfilled in a perfect manner whatever they expected of him.

Charles, executor of Papal reform. 31. Moreover, he seconded every one of their acts with the practical means needed to realize the end in view, namely, the real reform of sacred discipline. In this respect also he proved that in no wise he resembled those false reformers who concealed their obstinate disobedience under the cloak of zeal. He began "the judgment . . . with the household of God." [55] He first of all restored discipline among the clergy by making them conform to certain definite laws. With this same end in view he built seminaries, founded a congregation of priests known as the Oblates, unified both the ancient and modern religious families, and convoked Councils. By these and other provisions he assured and developed the work of reform. Then he immediately set a vigorous hand to the work of reforming the morals of the people. He considered the words spoken to the Prophet as addressed to himself: "Lo, I have set thee this day . . . to root up and to pull down, and to waste and to destroy, and to build and to plant." [56] Good shepherd that he was, he personally set out on the wearisome visitation of the churches of the province. Like the Divine Master "he went about doing good and healing." He spared no efforts in suppressing and uprooting the abuses he met everywhere either because of ignorance or neglect of the laws. He checked the rampant perversion of ideas and corruption of morals by founding schools for the children and colleges for youth. After seeing their early beginnings in Rome, he promoted the Marian societies. He founded orphanages for the fatherless, shelters for girls in danger, widows, mendicants, and men and women made destitute by sickness or old age. He opened institutions to protect the poor against tyrannical masters, usurers, and the enslavement of children. He accomplished all these things by completely ignoring the methods of those who think human society can be restored only by utter destruction, revolution, and noisy slogans. Such persons have forgotten the divine words: "The Lord is not in the earthquake." [57]

Self-interest of false reformers. 32. Here is another difference between true and false reformers which you, Venerable Brethren, have often encountered. The latter "seek their own interests, not those of Jesus Christ." [58] They listen to the deceitful invitation once addressed to the Divine Master, "Manifest thyself to the world." [59] They repeat the ambitious words, "Let us also get us a name" and in their rashness (which We unfortunately have to deplore in these days) "some priests fell in battle, while desiring to do manfully, they went out unadvisedly to fight." [60]

Disinterest of true reformers. 33. On the other hand, the true reformer "seeks not his own glory, but the glory of the one who sent him." [61] Like Christ, his Model, "he will not wrangle, nor cry aloud, neither will anyone hear his voice in the streets . . . He shall not be sad nor troublesome" [62] but he shall be "meek and humble of heart." [63] For that reason he will please the Lord and bring forth abundant fruit for salvation.

Self-confidence and confidence in God. 34. They are distinguished one from the other in yet another way. The false reformer "trusteth in man and maketh flesh his arm." [64] The true reformer places his trust in God and seeks His supernatural aid for all his strength and virtue, making his own the Apostle's words: "I can do all things in him who strengthens me." [65]

Love and hatred for the Church. 35. Christ lavishly communicates these aids, among which are especially prayer, sacrifice and the Sacraments, which "become . . . a fountain of water, springing up unto life everlasting." [66] Since the Church has been endowed with them for the salvation of all men, the faithful man will look for them in her. False reformers, however, despise these means. They make the road crooked and, so wrapped up in reforming that they forget God, they are always trying to make these crystal springs so cloudy or arid that the flock of Christ will be deprived of their waters. In this respect the false reformers of former days are even surpassed by their modern followers. These latter, wearing the mask of religiosity, discredit and despise these means of salvation, especially the two Sacraments which cleanse the penitent soul from sin and feed it with celestial food. Let every faithful pastor, therefore, employ the utmost zeal in seeing that the benefits of such great value be held in the highest esteem. Let them never permit these two works of divine love to grow cold in the hearts of men.

St. Charles and Holy Communion. 36. Borromeo conducted himself in precisely that way. Thus we read in his writings: "Since the fruit of the Sacraments is so abundantly effective, its value can be explained with no little difficulty. They should, therefore, be treated and received with the greatest preparation, deepest reverence, and external pomp and ceremony." [67] His exhortations (which We have also made in Our decree, *Tridentina Synodus* [68]) to pastors and preachers concerning the ancient practice of frequent Holy Communion is most worthy of notice. "Pastors and preachers," the holy Bishop writes, "should take every possible opportunity to urge the people to cultivate the practice of frequently receiving Holy Communion. In this they are following the example of the early Church, the recommendations of the most authoritative Fathers, the doctrine of the Roman Catechism (which treats this matter in detail), and, finally, the teaching of the Council of Trent. The last mentioned would have the faithful receive Communion in every Mass, not only spiritually but sacramentally." [69] He describes the intention and affection one should have in approaching the Sacred Banquet in the following words: "The people should not only be urged to receive Holy Communion frequently, but also how dangerous and fatal it would be to approach the Sacred Table of Divine Food unworthily." [70] It would seem that our days of wavering faith and coldness need this same fervor in a special way so that frequent reception of Holy Communion will not be accompanied by a decrease in reverence toward this great mystery. On the contrary, by this frequency a man should "prove himself, and so let him eat of that bread and drink of the cup." [71]

First things first. 37. An abundant stream of grace will flow from these fonts, strengthening and nourishing even natural and human means. By no means will a Christian neglect those useful and comforting things of this life, for these also come from the hands of God, the Author of grace and nature. In seeking and enjoying these material and physical things, however, he will be careful not to make them the end and quasi-beatitude of this life. He will use them rightly and temperately when he subordinates them to the salvation of souls, according to Christ's words: "Seek first the kingdom of God and His justice, and all these things shall be given you besides." [72]

The supernatural aids the natural. 38. This wise evaluation and use of means is not in the least opposed to the happiness of that inferior ordering of means in civil society. On the contrary, the former promotes the latter's welfare—not, of course, by the foolish prattle of quarrelsome reformers, but by acts and heroic efforts, even to the extent of sacrificing property, power, and life itself. We have many examples of this fortitude during the Church's worst days in the lives of many bishops who, equalling Charles' zeal, put into practice the Divine Master's words: "The good shepherd lays down his life for his sheep." [73] Neither vainglory, party spirit, nor private interest is their motive. They are moved to spend themselves for the common good by that charity "which never fails." This flame of love cannot be seen by the eyes of the world. It so enkindled Borromeo, however, that, after endangering his own life in caring for the victims of the plague, he did not rest with merely warding off present evils but began to provide for the dangers the future might have in store. "It is no more than right that a good and loving father will provide for his children's future as well as their present by setting aside the necessities of life for them. In virtue of our duty of paternal love, we are also prudently providing for the faithful of our province by setting aside those aids for the future which the experience of the plague has taught us are most effective." [74]

Catholic Action. 39. These same loving plans and considerations can be put into practice, Venerable Brethren, in that Catholic Action We have so often recommended. The leaders of the people are called to engage in this very noble apostolate which includes all the works of mercy [75] which will be prepared and ready to sacrifice all they have and are for the cause. They must bear envy, contradiction, and even the hatred of many who will repay their labors with ingratitude. They must conduct themselves as "good soldiers of Jesus Christ." [76] They must "run with patience to the fight set before us; looking towards the author and finisher of faith, Jesus Christ." [77] Without a doubt, this is a very difficult contest. Nevertheless, even though a total victory will be slow in coming, it is a contest that serves the welfare of civil society in a most worthy manner.

Charles' example in the apostolate. 40. In this work we have the splendid example of Saint Charles. From his example each one of us can find much for imitation and consolation. Even though his outstanding virtue, his marvelous activity, his never failing charity commanded much respect, he was nonetheless subject to that law which reads, "All who want to live piously in Christ Jesus will suffer persecution." [78] His austere life, his defense of righteousness and honesty, his protection of law and justice only led to his being hated by rulers and tricked by diplomats and, later, distrusted by the nobility, clergy and people until he was eventually so hated by wicked men that they sought his very life. In spite of his mild and gentle disposition he withstood all these attacks with unflinching courage.

Charles and the two powers. 41. He yielded no ground on any matter that would endanger faith and morals. He admitted no claim (even if it was made by a powerful monarch who was always a Catholic) that was either contrary to discipline or burdensome to the faithful. He was always mindful of Christ's words: "Render . . . to Ceasar the things that are Caesar's, and to God the things that are God's." [79] He never forgot the Apostles' declaration: "We must obey God rather than men." [80] Thus he was religion's and society's chief benefactor. In his time civil society was paying the price of almosts certain destruction because of its worldly prudence. It was practically shipwrecked in the seditious storms it had stirred up.

Duties of Catholic citizens. 42. The Catholics of our days, together with their leaders, the Bishops, will deserve the same praise and gratitude as

Charles as long as they are faithful to their duties of good citizenship. They must be as faithful in their loyalty and respect to "wicked rulers" when their commands are just, as they are adamant in resisting their commands when unjust. They must remain as far from the impious rebellion of those who advocate sedition and revolt as they are from the subservience of those who accept as sacred the obviously wicked laws of perverse men. These last mentioned wicked men uproot everything in the name of a deceitful liberty, and then oppress their subjects with the most abject tyranny.

The modern tyranny. 43. This is precisely what is happening today in the sight of the whole world and in the broad light of modern civilization. Especially is this the case in some countries where "the powers of darkness" seem to have made their headquarters. This domineering tyranny has suppressed all the rights of the Church's children. These rulers' hearts have been closed to all feelings of generosity, courtesy and faith which their ancestors, who gloried in the name of Christians, manifested for so long a time. It is obvious that everything quickly lapses back into the ancient barbarism of license whenever God and the Church are hated. It would be more correct to say that everything falls under that most cruel yoke from which only the family of Christ and the education it introduced has freed us. Borromeo expressed the same thought in the following words: "It is a certain, well-established fact that no other crime so seriously offends God and provokes His greatest wrath as the vice of heresy. Nothing contributes more to the downfall of provinces and kingdoms than this frightful pest." [81] Although the enemies of the Church completely disagree among themselves in thought and action (which is a sure indication of error), they are nevertheless united in their obstinate attacks against truth and justice. Since the Church is the guardian and defender of both these virtues, they close their ranks in a unified attack against her. Of course, they loudly proclaim (as is the custom) their impartiality and firmly maintain they are only promoting the cause of peace. In reality, however, their soft words and avowed intentions are only the traps they are laying, thus adding insult to injury, treason to violence. From this it should be evident that a new kind of warfare is now being waged against Christianity. Without a doubt it is far more dangerous than those former conflicts which crowned Borromeo with such glory.

Charles is our strength. 44. His example and teaching will do much to help us wage a valiant battle on behalf of the noble cause which will save the individual and society, faith, religion, and the inviolability of public order. Our combat, it is true, will be spurred on by bitter necessity. At the same time, however, we will be encouraged by the hope that the omnipotent God will hasten the victory for the sake of those who wage so glorious a contest. This hope increases through the fruitfulness of the work of Saint Charles even down to our own times. His work humbles the proud and strengthens us in the holy resolve to restore all things in Christ.

Prayer to Saint Charles. 45. We can now conclude, Venerable Brethren, with the same words with which Our Predecessor, Paul V (whom We already mentioned several times), concluded the letter conferring the highest honors on Charles. "In the meantime," he wrote, "it is only right that we return honor, glory, and benediction to Him Who lives for all ages, for He blessed Our fellow servant with every spiritual gift in order to make him holy and spotless in His sight. The Lord gave him to us as a star shining in the darkness of these sins which are Our affliction. Let us beseech the Divine Goodness both in word and deed to let Charles now assist by his patronage the Church he loved so ardently and aided so greatly by his merits and example, thus making peace for us in the day of wrath, through Christ Our Lord." [82]

Apostolic Blessing. 46. May the fulfillment of our mutual hope be granted through this prayer. As a token of that fulfillment, Venerable Brethren, from the depth of Our heart We impart to you and the clergy and people committed to your care, the Apostolic Blessing.

47. Given at Saint Peter's, Rome, on May 26, 1910, in the seventh year of Our Pontificate.

PIUS X, POPE

REFERENCES

1. Cf. Ps. 111:7; Prov. 10:7; Heb. 11:4.
2. Rom. 8:11.
3. Rom. 8:28.
4. I Cor. 4:16.
5. Cf. pp. 3–13 of this volume.
6. Heb. 3:1; 12:2.
7. Cf. pp. 15–27 of this volume.
8. Heb. 11:33.
9. Eph. 4:11 ff.
10. Cf. encyclical *E Supremi Apostolatus.*
11. Paul V, Papal bull of November 15, 1610, *Unigenitus.*
12. *Ibid.*
13. Eph. 5:25 ff.
14. Matt. 16:18.
15. Matt. 28:20.
16. John 14:16 ff., 26, 59; 16:7 ff.
17. *Sessio III, c.* 3.
18. Phil. 3:18–19.
19. Is. 5:20.
20. I Cor. 10:13.
21. I Pet. 5:3.
22. Paul V, Papal bull *Unigenitus.*
23. Gen. 8:21.
24. Rom. 6:6.
25. Eph. 4:23; Rom. 12:2.
26. Phil. 3:13–14.
27. Eph. 4:15–16.
28. Eph. 1:10.
29. Matt. 13:25.
30. *Conc. Prov. I, sub initium.*
31. *Conc. Prov. V, Pars I.*
32. *Ibid.*
33. *Conc. Prov. V, Pars I.*
34. Rom. 10:17.
35. *Conc. Prov. V, Pars I.*
36. Osee 4:1.
37. Jer. 12:11.
38. *Conc. Prov. V, Pars I.*
39. Cf. pp. 44–55 of this volume.

40. *Conc. Prov. V, Pars I.*
41. II Cor. 5:20; 4:2; II Tim. 2:15.
42. I Thess. 2:13.
43. Heb. 4:12.
44. James 2:26.
45. Rom. 2:13.
46. Matt. 28:18, 20.
47. John 14:6.
48. John 10:10.
49. Col. 3:14.
50. I Tim. 4:20.
51. Eph. 4:12.
52. *Conc. Prov. V, Pars I.*
53. *Ibid.*
54. *Conc. Prov. VI, sub finem.*
55. I Pet. 4:17.
56. Jer. 1:10.
57. III Kings 19:11.
58. Phil. 2:21.
59. John 7:4.
60. I Mac. 5:57, 67.
61. Cf. John 7:18.
62. Matt. 12:19; Is. 42:2 ff.
63. Matt. 11:29.
64. Jer. 17:5.
65. Phil. 4:13.
66. John 4:14.
67. *Conc. Prov. I, Pars II.*
68. Cf. pp. 215–216 of this volume.
69. *Conc. Prov. III, Pars I.*
70. *Conc. Prov. IV, Pars II.*
71. I Cor. 11:28.
72. Matt. 6:33; Luke 12:31.
73. John 10:11.
74. *Conc. Prov. V, Pars II.*
75. Cf. Matt. 25:34 ff.
76. II Tim. 2:3.
77. Heb. 12:1–2.
78. II Tim. 3:12.
79. Matt. 22:21.
80. Acts 5:29.
81. *Conc. Prov. V, Pars I.*
82. Paul V, Papal bull *Unigenitus.*

CHAPTER 11

Iamdudum *May 24, 1911, The Separation of Church and State in Portugal*

ON FEBRUARY 1, 1908, King Carlos of Portugal, his wife and the Crown Prince were assassinated in the streets of Lisbon. The world knew very well that the assassination was backed by the anti-clerical republican party. The same partisan papers kept alive the revolutionary spirit through the next three years in the pages of such Lisbon papers as the *Mundo, Seculo,* and *Os Ridiculos.*

Finally, backed with funds that poured over the border from the coffers of the French Masonic lodges, the anarchical republican party of Portugal plotted the overthrow of the government behind the closed doors of Masonic lodges. The date was set for October 10, 1910. But revolution prematurely broke out in the streets of Lisbon on October 3. The republicans seized the opportunity and on October 6 proclaimed the establishment of a provisional republican government of Portugal. Legislative acts, as thoughtless as hasty, were promulgated out of hatred for all things Catholic by the republican government headed by President Theophilus Braga. The religious congregations were expelled on moment's notice. All hereditary privileges and titles were abolished. The religious oath was abandoned in the law courts; the name of God erased from all public documents; and holy days were expunged from the calendar. Employees were no longer bound to observe the Sunday rest, and the most extreme divorce law, allowing married people to separate at will, was hastily passed. "In short, the policy of the republic has been in the last degree not only anti-Catholic but even anti-Christian." *

A few days after the revolution the notorious anti-clerical and Freemason, Dr. Afonso Costa, the newly created Minister of Justice, made the following remarks in a public address:

> The Church had no such thing as five million followers in Portugal. It had some adherents, but the State which comprised all the citizens was

* "Separation of Church and State in Portugal," by Francis McCullagh, in *The Catholic World,* 93:377.

> greater than the Church. The Church worked inside the State like any other commercial company. The State possessed, therefore, the right of controlling the Church. This grave duty could not be neglected. The Church must be controlled exactly like any other joint-stock company. . . . The Government . . . must be informed of all the ecclesiastical regulations and must forbid such regulations as were intended to coerce the mind of any man. . . .†

On April 20, 1911, the decree of separation of Church and State was passed and ordered to be effective as of June 1. On June 19 the monarchy was abolished. The anti-clericals had their day. For them separation was not a "complete divorce but a *separacao na oppressao*—a subjection of the Church to servitude." Their revolution, so bloody and treacherous, opened the door to one of the most bitter and hostile persecutions of the Church in modern times.

In the encyclical *Iamdudum* Saint Pius X vehemently objected to this oppression which the minority (at most 40,000) of Portuguese anti-clericals imposed on the Catholic majority (at least 5,000,000). After recounting the swift succession of events in Portugal (1–2), he points out the injustices of the separation, both concerning the material and spiritual organization of the Portuguese Church as well as its interference in clerical studies and discipline (3–5). It condemns the Law of Separation on the count that "it tries to tear her away from Catholic unity and the bosom of the Roman Church" (6). It declares "that any part of it that violates the inalienable rights of the Church is, and should be considered, null and void" (7). After revealing the sorrow this persecution causes the common Father, it urges the Catholics of Portugal to remain firm in their unity (8). The encyclical concludes, as usual, with the Apostolic Blessing (9).

Subsequent history ‡ has shown that ever since the proclamation of the Republic on October 6, 1910 Portugal has been torn by internal revolutions. Doubtlessly, these domestic troubles result in no small way from the godless policies of that government which ruled a country whose population is almost totally Catholic. Striking, too, is the fact that such a country was honored by the Apparitions of the Virgin of Fatima in 1917. However, the mighty in Lisbon and in the luxurious, corrupt coastal resorts saw no light, heard no voice. The faithful of Fatima, the poor and oppressed peasant class were filled with the joy and peace of the Lady. Theophilus Braga and Afonso Costa are forgotten names; Saint Pius X is honored and revered by millions. "My thoughts are not your thoughts: nor your ways my ways, saith the Lord!" §

† *Ibid.*, pp. 375–376.
‡ See "Portugal," *Catholic Encyclopedia,* Suppl., pp. 596–597.
§ Isaias 55:8.

Iamdudum *Encyclical Letter of Our Holy Father Pius X to the Patriarchs, Primates, Archbishops, Bishops and Other Ordinaries in Peace and Communion with the Apostolic See*

VENERABLE BRETHREN, HEALTH AND THE APOSTOLIC BLESSING:

Recent events in Portugal. 1. We think all of you, Venerable Brethren, are already quite familiar with the incredible course of events in Portugal. The Church is being persecuted by all kinds of savage deeds. Everyone knows that as soon as the government of that State was changed into a Republic measures inspired out of irreconcilable hatred for the Catholic religion were sanctioned one after the other. We have seen the religious communities harshly and mercilessly banished from Portugal. Because of an obstinate desire to secularize every civil regulation and abolish every trace of religion in public life, We have seen the Church's feast days erased from the list of public holidays, the juridical oath deprived of its religious character, a divorce law hastily passed, and the teaching of religious doctrine banished from the public schools. Passing over other things (since it would take too long to discuss the problem in detail), We have seen some people openly attacking the Bishops. Two of them in particular, the Bishops of Oporto and Beja, men distinguished for their integrity of life and many services to their country and Church, have been expelled from their Sees.

Law of Separation. In spite of the many extraordinary examples of malicious tyranny on the part of the new rulers of Portugal, you know only too well how patiently and gently the Holy See has acted toward the Republic. We had hoped that these men would sooner or later come to their senses and enter into an agreement with the Church after satisfying for the wrongs they have committed. We were, however, altogether deceived. They have now completed their evil work by promulgating a most insidious and dangerous Law of Separation of Church and State. Our Apostolic duty demands that We vehemently protest this very serious transgression of the rights and dignity of the Catholic religion. For that reason, Venerable Brethren, We are writing this letter to denounce these shameful actions before the whole Catholic world.

The injustices of this separation. 2. Obviously, this law is as foolish as it is shocking. In the first place it declares that the State is in no way bound to preserve public worship (as if it does not depend on Him Who is the

Founder and Preserver of all things, both of individuals and society in general). Moreover, it absolves Portugal from the duty of observing Catholic worship. Yet that religion has always been the chief support and glory of the Portuguese people and nearly all of them profess that Faith. But let us go on. The Government capriciously severs that union of Church and State which has been confirmed in solemn agreements. After this separation, however, it was no more than right to allow her those rights and liberties which every citizen and honorable society of citizens enjoyed by law. Quite the contrary has taken place. Although they call this a law of separation, in reality it reduces the Church in external matters to utter poverty. In spiritual matters the Republic through the means of this law has hung the chains of persecution about her neck.

Material restrictions. 3. Let us now consider the external affairs. The Republic of Portugal separated itself from the Church in such a way that it leaves her absolutely nothing to provide for the dignity of the house of God, to support the sacred ministers, and to discharge her many duties of charity and piety. This law not only dispossesses the Church of all her movable and immovable possessions (even though justly acquired), but also takes away all her power of acquiring anything in the future. Although the law states that corporate bodies of citizens should have authority over public worship, their power of receiving anything offered for that purpose is narrowly circumscribed. Moreover, the law abolishes the customary obligation which bound Catholic citizens to contribute to the support of their clergy. It even forbids any demand of the kind to be made. Although the law permits Catholics to provide for the expense of divine worship through voluntary donations, it demands that a third of the contribution be devoted to works of civil beneficence. Now this is the greatest injustice! In the future, buildings which are bought or erected for the purpose of religion are, after a certain number of years, to be taken away from their legitimate owners and used by the State without any indemnity being made.

Spiritual travesties. 4. Now let us pass over to those matters which belong in a special way to the sacred province of the Church. In these affairs this contemptuous separation is more serious and ruinous since, as We have already said, it reduces the Church to the condition of a slave. First of all, the hierarchy is completely ignored. If the clergy are mentioned, it is only in order to forbid them to partake in the organizations of religious worship. That duty is entrusted to lay associations. These associations have been established according to State law by the authority of the Republic and are in no way dependent on the ecclesiastical power. If clerics and laymen disagree over what association should discharge which duty, the Republic, not the Church, is the sole power that can render a decision in the case. The priest has no role in the regulating of divine worship. The law plainly states that no minister of religion can be chosen to serve on the above-mentioned parochial committees. They can neither be associated with the administration nor join in the activities of the associations. No more unjust and intolerable arrangement than this could ever be introduced, for it makes the priest inferior to the other citizens in the very work he especially is qualified to fulfill.

Further injustices of the law. 5. This Portuguese law shackles the liberty of the Church with almost unbelievable chains. This state of affairs is not only a reproach to modern institutions and popular ideas of public liberties, but also most unworthy of any civilized human beings. For instance, the law seriously forbids under any circumstance any kind of printed communication from the Bishops. Furthermore, it even forbids its reading to the people, even in the churches, without the Republic's first granting permission. Moreover, all external ceremonies, all pomp at any religious function, sacred vestments, and even the wearing of the cassock, are absolutely forbidden unless the Republic grants permission. The erection of public religious monuments, even if they be on a person's own house, is also forbidden. On the other hand, it is not forbidden to erect monuments offensive to Catholics. It is forbidden to form societies promoting religion or piety; in fact, such societies are treated like those whose evil purpose is the promotion of crime. Notwithstanding the fact that every citizen can distribute his goods according to his own liking, this right is restricted in the case of Catholics. Contrary to every law of justice, Catholic citizens do not have full liberty in disposing of their goods for the sake of the faithful departed and the welfare of religious worship. Furthermore, in violation of the testaments and desires of the donors, bequests previously made for these purposes have been impiously converted into other uses.

Interference with seminary order. Another painfully serious matter is the Republic's interference in the very realm of Church authority. It boldly promulgates a number of regulations regarding the discipline and teaching of seminarians. Since, however, these matters concern the very foundation of the clerical life, the Church jealously claims this matter subject to her exclusive care. The State, however, obliges these students to take those studies in science and literature which precede theology in the public schools, where there is very serious danger to the loss of faith since these subjects are divorced from God and the Church. Moreover, the Republic even dares to interfere with the domestic life and government of the seminaries. It claims as its own the right of appointing professors, approving books, and directing the curriculum of studies.

Interference with the clerical life. This, in effect, is a revival of the ancient so-called royal privileges. Even when there was peace between Church and State these claims were exceedingly arrogant. Now when the State wants nothing to do with the Church, can they savor of any other spirit than of warfare and complete insanity? In fact, who would deny that this law was promulgated for any other reason than to corrupt the clergy and stir up rebellion in their ranks against their superiors? The following concessions which the law makes only go to prove the validity of that conclusion. The law grants a certain pension to those who have been suspended by their Bishops and special favors to those blackguards who, forgetful of their dignity, presume to enter a marriage union. What is even more shameful, these benefits are extended to the surviving women and children!

Attempts to destroy the Church's unity. 6. Finally, as was to be expected, the Republic not only despoiled and subjected the Portuguese Church almost to the extent of veritable slavery, but it even tries to tear her away from Catholic unity and the bosom of the Roman Church. Moreover, it even tries to interfere with the Apostolic See's authority and vigilance over religious affairs in Portugal. Thus the law forbids the publication of the Roman Pontiff's orders without first obtaining the civil authority's permission. By the same measure a priest who might have taken a theological degree from any Pontifical college, even though he already made his theological studies at home, is not allowed to exercise his ministry. In this matter the Republic's intention is obvious. It prevents these priests, desirous of perfecting and polishing themselves in the higher studies, from going to Rome (the center of Christianity), where more certainly than in any other place they can strengthen their minds on the truths of Christian doctrine and inflame their souls in sincere faith and piety toward the Apostolic See. Overlooking the other no less iniquitous acts, these are the principal points of this infamous law.

Condemnation of the Law of Separation. 7. In view of this brazen insolence of God's enemies and conscious of Our Apostolic duty, which demands that We jealously guard the dignity and honor of religion and preserve the rights of the Holy Catholic Church, by Our Apostolic authority We disapprove, condemn and reject the Portuguese law of separation of Church and State. It neglects God, rejects the Catholic faith, and in violation of natural and international law, breaks the solemn concordat between Portugal and the Apostolic See. It robs the Church of the legal possession of her own property; it suppresses her liberty; it destroys her divine constitution. Finally, it heaps insolent insult upon the majesty of the Roman Pontiff, the Episcopacy, the clergy and people of Portugal, and, for that matter, on all Catholics throughout the world. We are overwhelmed with sorrow that such a law should even be passed, sanctioned and promulgated. At the same time We most severely rebuke those who prepared or carried out the work. Unhesitatingly We declare that any part of it that violates the inalienable rights of the Church is, and should be considered, null and void.

Sorrow of the Holy Father. 8. Believe Us when We say that these trying times in which Portugal has publicly declared war against religion fill Our heart with great anxiety and sorrow. We are filled with sadness when We behold the people We love very dearly suffering persecution. We are worried about the even greater sufferings that will come to pass if the rulers do not quickly recall their sense of duty. However, your outstanding fortitude, Venerable Brethren, the rulers of the Church in Portugal, as well as your clergy's zeal, is a source of tremendous consolation and confidence for Us. Such qualities will surely, in God's own good time, improve the situation in your country. Without a doubt, all of you, forgetful of personal security and convenience, were influenced by the duty and dignity of your office to denounce freely this law of separation. You unanimously declared that you would rather sacrifice material goods than forsake the freedom to exercise your sacred office. You chose rather to pay a small price than be reduced to the state of slavery. Finally, you frankly stated that neither craftiness nor persecution could ever separate you from the Roman Pontiff.

Words of encouragement. Rest assured that these striking examples of your faith, constancy, and magnanimity, witnessed as they are by the whole Church, bring joy to all good men, honor to yourselves, and glory to suffering Portugal. Persevere in your good resolve. Defend with all your might the cause of religion, which is the salvation of your country. Above all, see to it that both yourselves and all the Christian people remain united in the closest bonds with this See of Blessed Peter. Well do you know the purpose the authors had in mind when framing this despicable law. Even though they wish to create the impression that they are merely separating the Portuguese Church from the Republic by means of spoliation and oppression, in reality they are trying to separate her from the Vicar of Jesus Christ. If you firmly resist the criminal designs of these men, you will be making safe provision for the future of Catholic Portugal. Because We love you all so tenderly, We shall never cease beseeching God to look with mercy upon your untiring zeal. Further, We beg the prelates of the whole Catholic world to discharge the same duty by joining in prayer on behalf of their suffering Portuguese Brethren in their time of need.

Apostolic Blessing. 9. As a pledge of divine blessings and a testimony of Our Own good will, We lovingly impart to you, Venerable Brethren, your clergy and people, the Apostolic Blessing.

10. Given at Saint Peter's, Rome, on the Feast of Our Lady Help of Christians, May 24, 1911, in the eighth year of Our Pontificate.

PIUS X, POPE

CHAPTER 12

Lacrimabili Statu *June 7, 1912, The Conditions of the South American Indians*

IN 1911 Saint Pius X addressed a letter to the Archbishop of Caracas-Santiago de Venezuela concerning the reform of the clergy of South America. Among other things, he penned the following words:

> The reform of the clergy will go far towards promoting a truly Christian life among the generality of the people. Doubtless we know that among your priests many live correctly as becomes their sacred ministry; but at the same time we have to deplore, in the highest degree, that many behave in a way that degrades their priestly character; and this is the more painful to us inasmuch as the good effected by the edifying life of the former is less than the evil caused by the bad example of the latter. . . . You ought not to put up any longer with this perversion of the right order of things in the House of the Lord, when no father of a family would tolerate it within the walls of his home. You are admonished to do this by the statutes of the sacred canons; and to this gently exhorted by the constitutions of the Plenary Council of Latin America, never to be forgotten; to these must be added the recent prescriptions of this Apostolic See. Fix your attention on this and take in hand the remedy without delay.*

The following year, on June 7, he addressed his fifteenth and shortest encyclical letter "to the Archbishops and Bishops of Latin America" on the pitiful condition of the Indians of South America. It is brief and to the point. The Pope recalls the serious abuses the whites are inflicting on the natives, praises the rulers for leaving "no stone unturned in banishing this evil from their States," implores the Bishops "to devote particular attention and care to this cause," recalls the efforts of the Holy See in alleviating these racial abuses, condemns the slave-traders, and confers the Apostolic Blessing.

* "Pius X on the Reform of the Latin-American Clergy," *Fortnightly Review*, 18:244.

The encyclical points out three traits of Saint Pius X. The editor of the *Fortnightly Review* phrases the first characteristic in these words: "Pope Pius X is not of the number of those . . . who regard it as their duty to deny the existence of and to gloss over notorious evils. He knows that a malignant abscess must be cut open lest it poison the whole organism." †

The second is his love for the poor and the oppressed. This man who prefaced his will with the statement "I was born poor, I lived poor, and I die poor" deserved in a very special way to be "the Father of the poor." With the peasants of Riese he worked and played as a boy; with the laborers of Mantua he joined as a fellow member of the Workingmen's Union by founding a weekly paper, *The Citizen of Mantua*. Now the poor and oppressed of another continent received his assistance through one of the most solemn pronouncements of statecraft.

The third characteristic is the universality of his thinking. Although his person was a veritable prisoner of the Vatican, his mind and heart were world-wide. The needs and dangers of his children, wherever they be, were always his chief concern. His interests were as universal as the Church.

Lacrimabili Statu *Encyclical Letter of Our Holy Father Pius X to the Archbishops and Bishops of Latin America*

VENERABLE BRETHREN, HEALTH AND THE APOSTOLIC BLESSING:

Sad condition of the Indians. 1. Deeply moved by the pitiful condition of the Indians of South America, Our illustrious Predecessor, Benedict XIV, earnestly pleaded for them, as you know, in his letter of December 22, 1741, *Immensa Pastorum*. Since We lament almost the same things that he did, We wish to remind you of his letter. In it Benedict complains, among other things, that even though the Holy See has done a great deal to alleviate their sad condition, there were even then "men who, entirely insensitive to the feelings of charity the Holy Spirit poured into our hearts, presume not only in the case of Indians who are deprived of the light of faith, but even of

† *Ibid.*, p. 243.

those who have been bathed in the sacred waters of regeneration either to make them slaves, or sell them as slaves to others, or rob them of their possessions, or treat them so cruelly that they prevent them altogether from embracing the faith of Christ, or confirm them all the more in their hatred for it."

Slavery abolished. The worst of these indignities—slavery in the strict sense of the word—was by the mercy of God soon afterward abolished. The material entreaties of the Church directed to the distinguished rulers of these States greatly contributed to its public abolition in Brazil and other countries. We readily admit that their designs would have better results had not many serious difficulties of place and circumstance confronted them.

Crimes against the natives. Even though something has already been accomplished on behalf of the Indians, there still remains a great deal more to be done. When We consider the crimes and injustices still inflicted upon that unhappy race, We are horror-stricken and filled with compassion. What is more cruel and barbarian than, for oftentimes trivial reasons and frequently only for the mere pleasure of inflicting torture, to put men to death by scourging or with red-hot irons? By surprise they are attacked and massacred. At one and the same time hundreds and thousands of them are killed. Their towns and villages are sacked; the natives are slaughtered. We have learned that in the past few years some tribes have been almost exterminated.

Pagan depravity renewed. Certainly greed largely contributes in making minds so savage. The climate and the situation of those countries, however, are factors that also must be considered. These countries are situated in a torrid zone, thus affecting the blood with a certain lassitude which breaks down strength of character. It can easily happen that if persons of good morals go there, they will soon become strangers to every religious practice, being far removed from the vigilance of the State and almost completely deprived of civil society. Then in a short time they will become depraved and, with all restraints of duty and law removed, will gradually plunge into every sinful excess. Thus they spare neither sex nor age. One would blush if he were going to record all the crimes and evils they perpetrate. They acquire and traffic in women and children. There is no exaggeration in saying that they have surpassed the most heinous examples of pagan depravity.

Rumors confirmed. In fact, rumors of these atrocities seemed so incredible that when We first heard them, We were inclined to be skeptical. However, after we received the testimony of many of you, Venerable Brethren, as well as the Apostolic Delegates, missionaries, and other trustworthy persons, We can no longer doubt the truth of these rumors. Already for a long time We have resolved to do everything possible to remedy these serious abuses. In humble and suppliant prayer We begged the merciful Lord to show Us the best means for uprooting these evils. Since the most loving Creator and Redeemer of all men has inspired Us to labor for the salvation of the Indians, He will certainly offer the means We need to carry out Our purpose.

Praise for the State. In the meantime We are greatly consoled by the knowledge that the rulers of these Republics are leaving no stone unturned in banishing this disgraceful stain from their States. We can find no suitable words of approval and praise for their endeavor. There are areas, however, far removed from the capitals and, because either evil men craftily cross the frontier or public officials continue to be apathetic and perfidious, for the most part they remain inaccessible. Consequently, the efforts of the civil authorities sometimes have only little effect and sometimes none at all. If the efforts of State and Church were united, the desired results would be more fruitful.

Directives for the Bishops. Therefore, Venerable Brethren, We beseech you before all others to devote particular attention and care to this cause which is so worthy of your pastoral office and ministry. You have, to be sure, other matters that demand your concern and zeal. Before everything else, however, We earnestly exhort you to promote all those institutions in your dioceses which labor for the sake of the Indians. Try to establish others which will serve the same purpose. Strive to impress the faithful with their sacred duty of assisting the missions among the natives, since they were the first inhabitants of America. Let them know that they must collaborate in this work through alms and prayer. The welfare of both religion and the fatherland places this obligation on their shoulders. In centers of religious education, namely, the seminaries, institutions for the young, schools for girls, and, above all, the churches, you must see to it that no one waters down in his teaching or preaching that obligation of Christian charity which looks upon all men as brothers, regardless of nationality or color. This charity must be manifested not only in words but also in actions. Do not allow any opportune occasion to pass without pointing out the great dishonor inflicted on Christianity by these reprehensible actions.

Efforts of the Apostolic See. Since We have reason to believe that We enjoy the favor and consent of the public authorities, Our chief aim shall be to extend the field of the apostolate in those vast regions by instituting more missionary stations where the Indians can find refuge and a place of safety. To be sure, the Catholic Church has always possessed apostolic men, urged by the charity of Jesus Christ, who were ready and willing to surrender even life itself for their brethren. Even today, when so many turn against the Faith or renounce it, zeal for spreading the Gospel among the pagans has not died out in the ranks of religious or secular priests and holy nuns. In fact, it increases, diffusing itself far and wide through the power of the Holy Spirit, Who comes to the aid of His Spouse according to the needs of the age. We believe Our duty demands that We make abundant use of the means at our disposal for freeing the Indians from the slavery of Satan and evil men since their needs are so much the greater. Moreover, since these countries were bedewed by not only the sweat but also the blood of the preachers of the Gospel, We are confident that their labors will produce an abundant harvest of Christian civilization and ultimately bring forth good fruit.

Condemnation of slave-traders. May whatever you are about to do on behalf of the Indians either through your own initiative or our exhortation be productive of the greatest good. For that reason, following the example of Our Predecessor whom We already mentioned, We condemn and declare guilty of a heinous crime all those who, as he says, "dare or presume to reduce the Indians to slavery; to sell, buy, exchange, or donate them; to separate them from their wives and children; to take away their possessions; to carry or transport them elsewhere; to deprive them in any way of their liberty or treat them as slaves; similarly, to counsel, aid or support on any kind of pretext or plea those who do these things or to teach and proclaim that all this is lawful; or, in a word, to cooperate in these things which have already been mentioned." We reserve the power of absolving penitents from such crimes in the sacred tribunal or penance to the local Ordinaries.

Apostolic Blessing. 2. We thought it best to write you, Venerable Brethren, on behalf of the Indians. In this, We are following not only the promptings of Our own paternal heart but also the example of Our Predecessors, of whom Leo XII of happy memory is worthy of particular mention. You must strive with all your might to put Our desires into practice. The rulers of these Republics will surely support you in this work. The priests, and especially those attached to the missions, will also assist you by work and advice. Without a doubt, all good people will collaborate with you; those who can, with money, and everyone by charity. They will not fail a work which involves at one and the same time these matters which concern both religion and the dignity of the human being. Above all else, however, Almighty God will assist you with His grace. As a token of that grace and a testimony of Our paternal benevolence, We impart with all Our heart to you, Venerable Brethren, and to your flocks, the Apostolic Blessing.

3. Given at Saint Peter's, Rome, on June 7, 1912, in the ninth year of Our Pontificate.

PIUS X, POPE

CHAPTER 13

Singulari Quadam *September 24, 1912, German Labor Organizations*

SINGULARI QUADAM stands midway between the two great labor encyclicals: nineteen years after *Rerum Novarum,* twenty-one years before *Quadragesimo Anno.* It offers its own particular contribution to Catholic social thought. In its own day it was given to German Catholics as a solution of an exceedingly complex problem; in our day it also serves as an outstanding Papal document concerning a similarly complex problem.

The encyclical letter concerns the famous *Gewerkschaftsstreit* among German Catholics in the early years of the century. The discussion reached such a peak that the Holy See was called upon to render its decision. This Saint Pius X gave in the encyclical letter of September 24, 1912.

The problem of the German labor organization resolved itself into two schools of thought. The one school, centered in the Catholic regions of the Rhineland, was outspoken on behalf of the interdenominational Christian trade unions. The other school, centered in the non-Catholic area around Berlin, opined that Catholics could join only confessional Catholic unions.

"The Rhineland idea was followed in Bavaria, and at first it won approval also in the North and East. But the 1900 Fulda Pastoral of the Prussian Episcopate came out against it, and favored the development of strictly Catholic occupational groups (*Fachabteilungen*) within the Catholic *Arbeitervereine,* whose history, filled with many vicissitudes, went back to von Ketteler. No stand was directly taken against interconfessional cooperation as such, but simply against the Rhineland mode of its organization.

"The dispute which ensued lasted more than a decade; it was waged, at times with lamentable bitterness, in speeches and in the spate of trade-union periodicals that deluged the country." *

Saint Pius X opens the encyclical with a summary of the problem as he has heard it from both the reports of the German hierarchy, "as well as

* "Inter-credal Cooperation: Theory and Organization," by John C. Murray, S. J., in *Theological Studies,* 4:265.

qualified and respected representatives of both viewpoints" (1). After reiterating fundamental Christian social principles (2–3), he turns to a discussion of workingmen's organizations in general, stating that "those associations are to be most approved and considered as most useful for the genuine and permanent advantage of their members which are established chiefly on the foundation of the Catholic religion and openly follow the directives of the Church" (4). Consequently, he lavishes praise and encouragement on the Catholic unions in Germany (5). However, "in view of the particular circumstances of Catholic affairs in Germany," he declares that mixed labor organizations "can be tolerated and Catholics may be permitted to join them" if two necessary precautions are taken (6–7). Finally, reminding the Bishops of their duty "to observe carefully the conduct of all these associations" and exhorting the Catholics of Germany to live in "fraternal charity and perfect obedience," he closes with the Apostolic Blessing (8–10).

In *Singulari Quadam* Saint Pius X drew a fundamental distinction between religious cooperation and sociological cooperation. The former would be no more than "a vague and indefinite form of the Christian religion. . . . This amounts to nothing more than an empty recommendation of a generalized Christianity. Obviously, nothing is more contrary to the teachings of Jesus Christ." That latter, however, namely, "an interconfessional agreement on certain necessary religious and moral bases of a just social order," in the words of Saint Pius X, "can be tolerated and Catholics may be permitted to join" as long as a good reason exists and necessary precautions be adopted. Although Leo XIII set up the principle of intercredal cooperation,† it was the task of Saint Pius X to elucidate and apply these principles to a given situation. By his action in the case of the German labor organizations he set out on a practical policy of cooperation that has guided the Holy See throughout the past forty years. Father Murray, S. J., aptly remarks that "the Holy See has taken hold of the social end of the problem, and has asked for agreement on the natural religious and ethical principles which are the basic structural elements of right order in human society, and for sincere cooperation towards their realization in social institutions. This solution, therefore, reduces religious pluralism to unity on the social plane. And consequently, it opens a way to a practical solution at least of the social problem, which is all it pretends to do." ‡

In this encyclical Saint Pius X manifests the same intellectual grasp of circumstances in Protestant Germany that he previously manifested in the case of Catholic France. In both cases, although the solutions were so different, he exercised that practical pastoral wisdom and simplicity that always strikes at the very root of the problem.

† See "Inter-Credal Cooperation in the Papal Documents," by Wilfred Parsons, S. J., in *Theological Studies,* 4:159–182.

‡ John C. Murray, S. J., *op. cit.*

Singulari Quadam *Encyclical Letter of Our Holy Father Pius X to Our Beloved Son, George Kopp, Cardinal Priest of the Holy Roman Church, Bishop of Breslau, and to the Other Archbishops and Bishops of Germany*

Beloved Son and Venerable Brethren, Health and the Apostolic Blessing:

Problem of workers' associations. 1. We are moved by particularly affectionate and benevolent sentiments toward the Catholics of Germany, who are most loyally and obediently devoted to the Apostolic See and accustomed to battle generously and courageously on behalf of the Church. We therefore feel compelled, Venerable Brethren, to devote Our full strength and attention to the discussion of that issue which has arisen among them about workingmen's associations. Concerning this problem several of you, as well as qualified and respected representatives of both viewpoints, have already informed Us repeatedly during the past few years. Conscious of Our Apostolic Office, We have studied this problem most diligently. We fully realize that Our sacred duty is to labor unceasingly that Our beloved sons may preserve the Catholic teaching unadulterated and unimpaired, in no way allowing their Faith to be endangered. If they are not in time urged to be on guard, they would obviously, gradually and inadvertently, fall into the danger of being satisfied with a vague and indefinite form of the Christian religion which has lately been designated as *intercredal.* This amounts to nothing more than an empty recommendation of a generalized Christianity. Obviously, nothing is more contrary to the teachings of Jesus Christ. Moreover, since Our most ardent desire is the promotion and fortification of concord among Catholics, We constantly try to remove all those occasions of quarrels which dissipate the strength of men of good will and are advantageous only for the enemies of religion. Finally, We desire and intend that the faithful live with their non-Catholic fellow citizens in that peace without which neither the order of human society nor the welfare of the State can endure.

Consultation of the Bishops. If, however, as We have already said, the existence of this question was known to Us, We nevertheless thought it wise to obtain each of your opinions, Venerable Brethren, before announcing Our decision. You have answered Our questions with that conscientiousness and diligence which the seriousness of the question demands.

Duty of all Catholics. 2. Accordingly, We first of all declare that all Catholics have a sacred and inviolable duty, both in private and public life, to obey and firmly adhere to and fearlessly profess the principles of Christian truth enunciated by the teaching office of the Catholic Church. In particular We mean those principles which Our Predecessor has most wisely laid down in the encyclical letter *Rerum Novarum*. We know that the Bishops of Prussia followed these most faithfully in their deliberations at the Fulda Congress of 1900. You yourselves have summarized the fundamental ideas of these principles in your communications regarding this question.

Fundamental principles. 3. These are fundamental principles: No matter what the Christian does, even in the realm of temporal goods, he cannot ignore the supernatural good. Rather, according to the dictates of Christian philosophy, he must order all things to the ultimate end, namely, the Highest Good. All his actions, insofar as they are morally either good or bad (that is to say, whether they agree or disagree with the natural and divine law), are subject to the judgment and judicial office of the Church. All who glory in the name of Christian, either individually or collectively, if they wish to remain true to their vocation, may not foster enmities and dissensions between the classes of civil society. On the contrary, they must promote mutual concord and charity. The social question and its associated controversies, such as the nature and duration of labor, the wages to be paid, and workingmen's strikes, are not simply economic in character. Therefore they cannot be numbered among those which can be settled apart from ecclesiastical authority. "The precise opposite is the truth. It is first of all moral and religious, and for that reason its solution is to be expected mainly from the moral law and the pronouncements of religion." [1]

Complete approbation of Catholic societies. 4. Now, concerning workingmen's associations, even though their purpose is to obtain earthly advantages for their members, nonetheless those associations are to be most approved and considered as most useful for the genuine and permanent advantage of their members which are established chiefly on the foundation of the Catholic religion and openly follow the directives of the Church. We have repeated this declaration on several previous occasions in answer to questions from various countries. Consequently, such so-called confessional Catholic associations must certainly be established and promoted in every way in Catholic regions as well as in all other districts where it can be presumed that they can sufficiently assist the various needs of their members. However, when there is a question about associations which directly or indirectly touch upon the sphere of religion and morality, it would not be permitted to foster and spread mixed organizations, that is, associations composed of Catholics and non-Catholics, in the areas just mentioned. Over and above other matters, in such organizations there are or certainly can be for our people serious dangers to the integrity of their faith and their due obedience to the commandments and precepts of the Catholic Church. Venerable Brethren, you yourselves have also openly called attention to this question in several of your answers which We have read.

Preference for Catholic societies. 5. We therefore lavish praise upon each and every one of the strictly Catholic workingmen's associations existing in Germany. We wish them every success in all their endeavors on behalf of the laboring people, hoping they will enjoy a constant increase. However, in saying this We do not deny that Catholics, in their efforts to improve the workers' living conditions, more equitable distribution of wages, and other justified advantages, have a right, provided they exercise due caution, to collaborate with non-Catholics for the common good. For such a purpose, however, We would rather see Catholic and non-Catholic associations unite their forces through that new and timely institution known as the *cartel.*

Toleration of interconfessional societies. 6. Not a few of you, Venerable Brethren, have asked Us whether it is permissible to tolerate the so-called Christian Trade Unions that now exist in your dioceses, since, on the one hand, they have a considerably larger number of members than the purely Catholic associations and, on the other hand, if permission were denied serious disadvantages would result. In view of the particular circumstances of Catholic affairs in Germany, We believe that We should grant this petition. Furthermore, We declare that such mixed associations as now exist within your dioceses can be tolerated and Catholics may be permitted to join them, as long as such toleration does not cease to be appropriate or permissible by reason of new and changed conditions. Necessary precautions, however, must be adopted in order to avoid the dangers which, as has already been mentioned, follow upon such associations.

Precautions must be taken. The following are the most important of these precautions: In the first place, provision should be made that Catholic workers who are members of the trade unions must also belong to those Catholic associations which are known as *Arbeitervereine.* In the event that they must make some sacrifice for this cause, even in a monetary way, We are convinced that they will readily do so for the sake of safeguarding the integrity of their Faith. As has been happily demonstrated, the Catholic workingmen's associations, aided by the clergy and by its leadership and alert direction, are able to achieve very much toward preserving the truths of religion and the purity of morals among their members, and nourish the religious spirit through frequent practices of piety. Therefore, the leaders of such associations, clearly recognizing the needs of the age, are undoubtedly prepared to instruct the workers about their duties in justice and charity, especially regarding all those commandments and precepts in which an accurate knowledge is needed or useful in order to enable them to take an active part in their trade unions according to the principles of Catholic doctrine.

Further precautions. 7. Furthermore, if Catholics are to be permitted to join the trade unions, these associations must avoid everything that is not in accord, either in principle or practice, with the teachings and commandments of the Church or the proper ecclesiastical authorities. Similarly, everything is to be avoided in their literature or public utterances or actions which in the above view would incur censure.

Duty of the Bishops. The Bishops, therefore, should consider it their sacred duty to observe carefully the conduct of all these associations and to watch diligently that the Catholic members do not suffer any harm as a result of their participation. The Catholic members themselves, however, should never permit the unions, whether for the sake of material interests of their members or the union cause as such, to proclaim or support teachings or to engage in activities which would conflict in any way with the directives proclaimed by the supreme teaching authority of the Church, especially those mentioned above. Therefore, as often as problems arise concerning matters of justice or charity, the Bishops should take the greatest care to see that the faithful do not overlook Catholic moral teaching and do not depart from it even a finger's breadth.

The Holy See is the supreme judge. 8. We are convinced, Venerable Brethren, that you will diligently take care to see that all these directives of Ours are conscientiously and exactly fulfilled, carefully and constantly reporting to Us concerning this very serious problem. Since We have taken this matter under Our jurisdiction and, after hearing the views of the Bishops, since the decision rests with Us, We hereby command all Catholics of good will to desist from all disputes among themselves concerning this matter. We are confident that with fraternal charity and perfect obedience they will completely and gladly carry out Our command. If any further difficulty arises among them, they should seek its solution in the following manner: Let them first turn to their Bishops for counsel, and then submit the matter to the Apostolic See for its decision.

Relation between the two types of societies. There is one more point to consider, and it was already implied in what has been said. On the one hand, no one could accuse of bad faith and, under such a pretext, bear ill will toward those who, while firmly defending the teachings and rights of the Church, nonetheless for good reasons have joined or wish to join mixed labor associations in those places where, under certain safeguards, ecclesiastical authority has permitted them in view of local conditions. On the other hand, it would likewise be most reprehensible to oppose or attack the purely Catholic associations (this type of association must, on the contrary, be supported and promoted in every possible manner), and to demand that the so-called *intercredal* associations be introduced and force their establishment on the grounds that all Catholic associations in every diocese ought to be set up along one and the same pattern.

Apostolic Blessing. 9. While expressing Our desire that Catholic Germany may make great progress in religion and civil life, and in order that this wish may be happily fulfilled, We beseech for the beloved German people the special help of Almighty God and the protection of the Virgin Mother of God, the Queen of Peace. As a pledge of the divine graces and also as a sign of Our particular love, We impart, most lovingly, to you, Beloved Son and Venerable Brethren, to your clergy and people, the Apostolic Blessing.

10. Given at Saint Peter's, Rome, on September 24, 1912, the tenth year of Our Pontificate.

PIUS X, POPE

REFERENCES

1. Encyclical letter of Leo XIII, *Graves de communi,* of January 18, 1901.

Part Two

SELECTED DOCUMENTS

Introduction

ALREADY during his lifetime, Saint Pius X was recognized as "the Reform Pope." Within a few months after his elevation to the Papacy he remarked to the distinguished Swiss Catholic layman, M. Decurtins, "that he had ten *Motu Proprios,* each of them effecting a reform, ready in his desk." * The directives and regulations embodied in these reforming decrees have largely overshadowed the beauty, simplicity, and warmth of his encyclicals. Even the titles posterity has conferred on him have been to a great extent evoked because of the reforms his directives inaugurated. Thus, for example, we call him "the Pope of the Catechism," "the Pope of Christian Doctrine," "the Pope of Holy Communion," and "the Pope of Priests."

In the very beginning of 1904, less than six months after his election, the Rome correspondent of the *Freeman's Journal* grasped the reforming spirit of Saint Pius X and penned the following words:

> Pope Pius X . . . has applied a new and rigorous system for the election of Italian bishops, by transferring the charge to the Holy Office; he has provided for the decorum of the temple by suppressing the most objectionable of the practices which have hitherto defied both decency and authority; he has begun the reorganization of the Roman Congregations; he has instituted a severe investigation into the supposed sacred character of many bodies supposed to be those of early martyrs of the Church, and has ordered one of these about which the evidence was not conclusive as to martyrdom, to be removed from a church where it had been kept for centuries; he has abolished all secular interference in papal elections; he has appointed a commission to undertake the enormous work of codifying all the laws of the Church; he has foreshadowed a complete reform of the Breviary; he has removed all ambiguities from the path of Christian social action in Italy. . . . Everybody knows just what he means and he is nothing if not practical.†

In editing the encyclical letters of the saintly Pontiff, I was, admittedly, prevailed upon by my associates to include one or the other of his reform decrees. "By way of an appendix," they said. Their requests, when joined to my own desires, produced an appendix which gradually took on the proportions of another section.

* Quoted in *The Review,* XI, 154.
† Quoted in *The Review,* 11:127–128.

In this second section I have selected ten documents. When taken together, I believe they represent the scope and depth of the Saint's sacramental, intellectual, Biblical, and social restoration. Striking is the fact that each of these documents finds its counterpart in the encyclical letters. The *Motu Proprio* on the *Restoration of Sacred Music* is foreshadowed in *E Supremi Apostolatus* and echoed in *Iucunda Sane.* The reforming zeal of Borromeo in enacting rules and regulations to meet the challenge of the Reformation is imitated in Saint Pius X's zeal in publishing the *Motu Proprio* on the codification of Canon Law. The *Motu Proprio* on Popular Christian Action is a delineation of *Il Fermo Proposito;* the Eucharistic decrees are elaborated and restated in *Editae Saepe.* The Biblical decree and the Syllabus are the practical conclusions following upon *Pascendi Dominici Gregis. Haerent Animo* is the crown of all the priestly exhortations and directives that run like a golden thread throughout all the encyclicals; the Apostolic constitution on the rearrangement of the Psalter takes its inspiration from the prayer-life of Saint Gregory in *Iucunda Sane* and the need of prayer from the sad example of the Polish priests in *Tribus Circiter.* The *Motu Proprio* on the study of Thomistic Philosophy is the logical successor to *Pieni L'Animo.*

These and similar documents, and especially the results they produced, moved Pope Benedict XV to write the following eulogy:

> . . . We find a source of no small consolation in the remarkable fruits of the active foresight of Our Predecessor, Pope Pius X, who shed upon the Apostolic Chair the lustre of a most holy life. For We see as a result of his efforts a revival of religious spirit in the clergy throughout the whole world; the piety of the Christian people revived; activity and discipline stimulated in Catholic associations; the foundation and increase of episcopal sees; provision made for the education of ecclesiastical students in harmony with the canonical requirements and in so far as necessary with the needs of the times; the saving of the teaching of sacred science from the dangers of rash innovations; musical art brought to minister worthily to the dignity of sacred functions; the Faith spread far and wide by new missions of heralds of the Gospel. Well, indeed, has Our Predecessor merited of the Church, and grateful posterity will preserve the memory of his deeds. . . . ‡

‡ Pope Benedict XV, encyclical letter *Ad Beatissimi Apostolorum,* November 1, 1914 (in *The Pope and the People;* London: Catholic Truth Society, 1932, p. 211).

CHAPTER 1

Inter Plurimas Pastoralis* *November 22, 1903, Motu Proprio on the Restoration of Sacred Music*

ONE of the principal duties of the pastoral office, both of this Supreme Chair which We, though unworthy, occupy through the unsearchable designs of Divine Providence, as well as every local church is, undoubtedly, maintaining and fostering the decorum of the House of God. The Christian people gather there to receive the grace of the Sacraments, assist at the Holy Sacrifice of the Altar, adore the Most Blessed Sacrament of the Lord's Body, and join in the common prayer of the Church during the public and solemn liturgical services. Nothing, therefore, should take place in the church which would disturb or even diminish the piety and devotion of the faithful. Nothing should be there which would be a reasonable cause for disgrace or scandal. Above all, nothing should take place which would directly violate the decorum and holiness of the sacred functions and thus be unworthy of the House of Prayer and the Majesty of God.

We do not intend to treat every one of the abuses which can arise in this matter. Today We wish to discuss only one of these abuses which is very common and very difficult to abolish. Even when everything else merits the highest praise, such as the beauty and richness of the church, the splendor and accurate order of the ceremonies, the attendance of the clergy, and the seriousness and piety of those officiating, even then, this abuse must be deplored. We refer to the abuse of sacred chant and music. As a matter of fact, there is an ever-constant tendency to depart from the right norm. This may be due to the very nature of this art which fluctuates and varies or the succession of changes in taste and custom through the course of centuries. It may result from that regrettable influence which profane and theatrical art have exercised on sacred art or from that pleasure which music directly produces and which is kept in bounds with no little difficulty. Finally, it may result from the many prejudices which are springing up in this art even

* This translation is taken from the Latin version as found in *Acta Sanctae Sedis,* 36:387–395.

among some very responsible and pious people. This right norm, however, is determined by that purpose which permits art to play a role in the sacred services. It is very clearly stated in the ecclesiastical canons, the regulations of the general and provincial councils, and the directives handed down by the Sacred Roman Congregations and Our Predecessors, the Roman Pontiffs.

We are most happy to single out for praise the tremendous good accomplished in this field during recent times. This has been done not only in Our Own city and in many churches of Our Italy, but especially in some countries where men distinguished by their zeal for the worship of God, after obtaining the Holy See's approval, have banded together under the direction of their Bishops into flourishing societies in order to restore sacred music to its highest honor in almost all of their churches and chapels. This good work, however, is far from being universal. If We consider Our Own personal experience in this regard, as well as the numerous complaints that have come to Us from all over the world even in this short time since the Lord willed to elevate Our humble person to the heights of the Roman Pontificate, We feel now that Our first duty is to denounce and condemn everything in the sacred ceremonies which violates that correct norm We mentioned above. We are filled with a burning desire to see the true Christian spirit flourish in every respect and be preserved by all the people. We therefore are of the opinion that before everything else it is necessary to provide for the sanctity and dignity of the temple where the faithful assemble for no other purpose than that of acquiring this spirit from its primary and indispensable fount, that is, the active participation in the most sacred mysteries and in the public and solemn prayer of the Church. It is sheer folly to expect an abundant showering of heavenly blessings upon us when our homage to the Most High places once again in the Lord's hand the scourges with which the Divine Redeemer once drove the unworthy profaners from the temple. Rather, it should rise in the odor of sweetness.

Therefore, in order that no one in the future may be able to make ignorance of his duty an excuse, and in order to erase all vagueness in interpreting what has already been commanded, We have decided to point out briefly the principles governing sacred music and to draw up a single list of the Church's rules against the commoner abuses in this regard. Hence, of Our Own accord and with deliberate knowledge We publish this *Instruction*. We will with the fullness of Our Apostolic authority that it shall have the force of law as a juridical code of sacred music. Finally, We command that every Christian observe it to the very letter.

Instruction on Sacred Music

I. *General Principles*

1. Sacred music, as an essential part of solemn worship, shares its general purpose of giving glory to God and at the same time of edifying and making the faithful holy. It increases the decorum and beauty of the Church's ceremonies. Its chief duty is to adorn the words of the liturgy with suitable melody. These very words, then, should become more intelligible and more easily enkindle the faithful's faith and devotion. In such a way they will then be able to receive many more of the graces associated with the sacred mysteries.

2. Sacred music, therefore, should possess all the qualities of the liturgy; especially, *holiness, good form,* and, following upon these, *universality.*

It must be *holy.* All profanity, therefore, either in itself or in the manner of the performers' presentation, must be excluded.

It must be *true art.* If it is not, it cannot achieve the effect on its listeners which the Church intends by associating music with the liturgy.

It must be *universal.* That is to say, every nation can use in its ecclesiastical compositions those special forms, as it were, which mark its music as native. Nevertheless, these forms must be so subordinated to the general laws of sacred music that, when heard by a foreigner, they would still create a good impression.

II. *Kinds of Sacred Music*

3. These qualities are especially found in Gregorian Chant. It is, therefore, the chant proper to the Roman Church and the only chant she has inherited from antiquity. Throughout the centuries she has jealously preserved it in her liturgical codices and, as is right, offered it as her own to the faithful. She commands that it alone be used in some parts of the liturgy. Finally, recent studies have restored its pristine integrity and purity.

For these reasons Gregorian Chant has always been considered the finest example of sacred music. Consequently, we can set up the following safe rule: *The closer a musical composition approaches Gregorian Chant in its composition, the more sacred and liturgical it is; the further it departs from that supreme model, the less worthy it is of the temple.*

Gregorian Chant, therefore, which has been handed down from antiquity, must be totally restored in the sacred rites. The sacred liturgy loses none of its solemnity when only this type of music is used. Gregorian Chant should especially be restored to the people so that, as in former times, th faithful may once again more fully participate in the sacred liturgy.

4. The above-mentioned qualities are found for the most part in th classical polyphony, especially of the Roman School. During the sixteent century Pierluigi da Palestrina crowned it with perfection, and so it con tinued to flourish during the following years. Since classical polyphony is s close to Gregorian Chant, the supreme model of all sacred music, it deserve to be used together with the latter in the solemn services of the Church such as the services in the Pontifical chapel. Therefore it should also be re stored to the greater basilicas, cathedrals, seminary and other conventua chapels where suitable means are at hand.

5. The Catholic Church has always favored the progress of the arts Anything good and beautiful which genius has discovered throughout th centuries She has always admitted, according to the liturgical laws, to th service of the Altar. Since modern music has compositions so suitable tha they are not in the least unworthy of the sacred liturgy, it may also be per mitted in the churches. It must be admitted, however, that music of today ha a profane purpose. Therefore, this music which is written in a moder style must be carefully watched when permitted to be used in the churche so that it savors of nothing profane or theatrical. Neither should it imitat the forms of these profane pieces.

6. Of all the different kinds of modern music the theatrical style, whic was especially popular in Italy during the previous century, seems to be th least suitable for the sacred functions. By its very nature this type is the exac opposite of Gregorian Chant and classical polyphony, and thus also is oppose to the laws of sacred music. Finally, the very structure, rhythm, and wha they call *conventionalism* of this style correspond badly to the rules of sacre music.

III. *The Liturgical Text*

7. Latin is the language of the Church. It is forbidden, therefore, to sin anything in the vernacular during the sacred services. It is especially for bidden to sing the ordinary or common of the Mass and the Office in th vernacular.

8. Since the texts to be sung and the order to be followed are determine for every liturgical function, it is permitted neither to change that order, no to substitute one's own choice of texts, nor to omit them entirely or partially unless the rubrics of the liturgy permit the organ to accompany some verse of the text while the choir simply recites them. According to the custom o the Roman Church, however, it is permissible to sing a short motet to th Blessed Sacrament after the *Benedictus* of a Solemn Mass. It is also permitte

fter singing the Offertory of the Mass to sing a short motet to words which he Church has approved.

9. The liturgical text must be sung as it is in the books. The words hould neither be altered, inverted nor unduly repeated; the syllables should ot be broken. It should, on the other hand, always be rendered in such a vay that it is intelligible to the faithful who are listening.

V. *External Form of Sacred Compositions*

10. The various parts of the Mass and Office must even musically pre- erve the form that ecclesiastical tradition has given them and which is so dmirably expressed in Gregorian Chant. Therefore the *Introit, Gradual, Antiphon, Psalm, Hymn, Gloria,* and so forth, will each be composed dif- erently.

11. More specifically, the following norms must be observed:

(a) The *Kyrie, Gloria* and *Credo* of the Mass should have a unity of omposition in conformity with their text. It is not allowed, therefore, to ompose them as individual pieces in such a way that they would be distinct nusical compositions which could be separated from each other or substi- uted by others.

(b) In the solemn recitation of Vespers the *Caeremoniale Episcoporum* nust be followed. This demands that Gregorian Chant be used for the salmody and permits figured music only for the verses of the *Gloria Patri* nd the hymn. Nevertheless, on the greater feasts it may be permitted to al- ernate Gregorian Chant with what they call *falso-bordone* or other verses omposed in a similar manner. Sometimes it is permissible to sing individual salms completely in (figured) music, as long as in such compositions that orm proper to psalmody is preserved. That is to say, it is permitted as long s the singers seem to be reciting alternately with new melodies or themes ither taken from Gregorian Chant or based on it. We therefore forbid those salms which are termed *di concerto*.

(c) The traditional form of a hymn should be preserved in the hymns f the Church. Thus it is not allowed, for example, to compose a *Tantum Ergo* in such a way that the first verse would be a *romanza* or an *adagio* and he *Genitori* an *allegro*.

(d) The antiphons of Vespers as a rule must be sung in Gregorian Chant. If, however, on special occasions they are going to be sung to figured nusic, they should have neither the form of concert melody nor the length f a motet.

I. The Singers

12. All liturgical chant, excepting the melodies of the celebrant and min-

isters at the altar (which must always be sung only in Gregorian Chant and without the accompaniment of an organ), belongs to the choir of clerics. The Church's singers, therefore, even when they are laymen, are in reality substitutes for the ecclesiastical choir. Hence at least the greater part of the music they sing should have the character of choral music. This, however, is not meant to exclude all solo work. Yet it should never be so prominent that the greater part of the liturgical chant would be performed in that way. Rather, it should be more like emphasis of the melody and remain closely connected to the rest of the composition in choral form.

13. According to this same principle the singers in the church hold a true liturgical office. Therefore, since women cannot exercise any such office they cannot be admitted to the choir. Thus, when a person wishes to use the high voices of sopranos or contraltos, he should follow the very ancient custom of the Church and call upon boys to execute these parts.

14. Finally, only men of solid piety and good morals should be allowed to join the church's choir. These men should prove their worthiness of the holy office they hold by their piety and devotion during the sacred services. When the singers are singing in church it would be appropriate if they wore ankle-length garments and surplices. When the choir is too conspicuous to the congregation it should be concealed behind grills.

VI. *The Organ and Instruments*

15. Although purely vocal music is the music proper to the Church, music with organ accompaniment is also permitted. Sometimes, with prudence and circumspection other musical instruments may be permitted, provided the Ordinary's permission is obtained, as the *Caeremoniale Episcoporum* demands.

16. Since the singing should occupy the chief place, the organ and musical instruments should only sustain, and not overpower it.

17. The chant should neither be preceded by long preludes nor interrupted by interludes.

18. When the organ accompanies the chant in preludes, interludes and the like, it must conform both to the peculiar nature of the instrument as well as participate in all the qualities of sacred music which We have already explained.

19. The piano, drum, cymbals, bells and such like are forbidden in church.

20. Band music is strictly forbidden in the churches. Nevertheless, with the Bishop's permission, a limited number of wind instruments can be employed, provided the composition and accompaniment has a serious style and is almost the same as the style of the organ.

21. In public processions the Bishop can permit a band, provided no profane pieces are played. In such cases it would be highly desirable if the band would limit itself to accompany some spiritual hymns sung either in Latin or the vernacular by the singers or pious associations which take part in the processsion.

VII. *The Length of Liturgical Music*

22. It is not permissible to keep the priest at the altar waiting because of the singing longer than the liturgical ceremony demands. According to a decree of the Church the *Sanctus* of the Mass should be finished before the Elevation. The priest, therefore, must respect the singing. According to the Gregorian tradition, the *Gloria* and *Credo* should be comparatively short.

23. Generally speaking, it must be condemned as a serious abuse to make the liturgy appear inferior, or like a handmaid, to the music in sacred functions. On the contrary, music is only a part of the liturgy.

VIII. *The Principal Means*

24. In order that these decrees may be correctly observed, the Bishops should appoint for their dioceses (unless they have already done so) a commission of men trained in sacred music. According to the ways they judge best, the Bishops should entrust this commission with the responsibility of watching over the music sung in their churches. This commission should see to it not only that the music is good but also that it is not beyond the singers' ability and is always rendered according to the canons of good taste.

25. According to the decrees of the Council of Trent, the traditional Gregorian Chant should be studiously and zealously cultivated in seminaries and ecclesiastical institutions. The superiors, too, should lavish praise upon the young students. Wherever it is possible, a *Schola Cantorum* should be formed among the clerics which will perform sacred polyphony and the best liturgical music.

26. In the daily lessons of liturgy, moral and canon law the professors should be sure to discuss with the students of theology those things pertaining to sacred music. They should also point out for the students the beauty of sacred art so that when their course is finished the students will have an appreciation of those subjects which are necessary for a thorough ecclesiastical culture.

27. At least in the more important churches efforts should be taken to restore the ancient *Scholas Cantorum*. This has actually been done already in many places. As a matter of fact, even in the smaller churches in rural areas a zealous clergy can establish these *Scholas*. Such a work, moreover, will

prove a ready means for uniting both young and old with the priest, both for their own advancement and the people's edification.

28. Every possible support and assistance should be given the higher schools of sacred music where they already exist and everything should be done to found them where they do not yet exist. The Church herself must support and provide for the culture and training of her choirmasters and singers according to the principles of sacred music.

IX. *Conclusion*

29. Finally, We command all choirmasters, singers, clerics, superiors of seminaries, ecclesiastical institutions, and religious communities, parish priests and rectors of churches, canons of collegiate churches and cathedrals, and especially the Bishops to be zealous in carrying out these wise reforms. For a long time already they have been desired and sought by all the faithful. Now labor zealously on their behalf, lest the Church's authority, which has so often previously proposed and now again proposes them, be despised.

Given at the Vatican Palace, on the feast of the Virgin-Martyr, Saint Cecilia, November 22, in the first year of Our Pontificate.

PIUS X, POPE

CHAPTER 2

Fin Dalla Prima *December 18, 1903, Motu Proprio on Popular Christian Action*

IN OUR first encyclical to the Bishops of the world We restated all that Our glorious Predecessors had laid down concerning the Catholic Action of the laity. We declared that this action was not only most praiseworthy, but, as a matter of fact, necessary in the present state of the Church and civil society. We lavishly praised the zeal of the many distinguished persons who have for a long time already dedicated themselves to this glorious task, as well as the enthusiasm of the many brilliant young people who have unselfishly aided in this work. The recent Nineteenth Catholic Congress of Bologna which We have encouraged and promoted [1] has strikingly shown everyone the virile strength of the Catholic forces. Moreover, it has demonstrated how many useful and beneficial results will come to a believing people when their action is properly directed and disciplined and unity in thought, affection, and work reigns supreme in the hearts of the members.

At the same time We were sorry to hear that certain disagreements among the members gave rise to some bitter disputes. If these differences are not immediately repressed, they may divide these forces and lessen their effectiveness. Now We cannot remain silent, since We were so insistent before the Congress that above everything else peace and harmony should motivate every decision concerning the practical execution of Catholic Action. Since practical differences of opinion have their origin and foundation in the realm of theory, We must restate the principles which should animate every work of Catholic Action.

Our illustrious Predecessor, Leo XIII, of holy memory, brilliantly outlined the rules that should direct Popular Christian Action in the following documents: the encyclicals *Quod Apostolici Muneris* of December 28, 1878; *Rerum Novarum* of May 15, 1891; *Graves de Communi* of January 18, 1901; and the special instruction of the Sacred Congregation of Extraordinary Ecclesiastical Affairs of January 27, 1902.[2]

Like Our Predecessor, We realize how important it is that Popular

Christian Action be properly guided and directed. We desire that these very prudent directives be exactly and faithfully observed. In order that no one may dare depart from them in the least, We have decided to gather them together in the following articles (abridged from the original documents) as the fundamental regulations of Popular Christian Action. In such a way they should be more vital and ready at hand.

Fundamental Regulations of Popular Christian Action

1. Just as the members of the human body are unequal, so also human society as established by God consists of unequal elements. It is impossible to try to make them equal. To do so would only lead to the destruction of society. (Encyclical *Quod Apostolici Muneris.*)

2. The various members of society are equal in this: All men are created by God, redeemed by Jesus Christ, and will be judged by God, rewarded or punished exactly according to their merits or demerits. (Encyclical *Quod Apostolici Muneris.*)

3. Accordingly, in the order of human society as established by God there are rulers and ruled, employers and employees, rich and poor, learned and ignorant, nobility and proletariat. United in a bond of love, all should strive to help one another attain their final end in heaven and their material and moral welfare here on earth. (Encyclical *Quod Apostolici Muneris.*)

4. Concerning the goods of this earth, man has not merely their use, like the animals, but also the right of permanent ownership. This applies to goods that are consumable as well as non-consumable. (Encyclical *Rerum Novarum.*)

5. Private property is an indisputable natural right. Whether it be the result of labor or industry, or a donation from others, every one can reasonably dispose of it as he pleases. (Encyclical *Rerum Novarum.*)

6. In healing the breach between rich and poor, one must necessarily distinguish between justice and charity. One can lodge a claim only when justice has been violated. (Encyclical *Rerum Novarum.*)

7. These are the obligations of justice binding the poor and the worker: They must fully and faithfully perform the work that has been freely and equitably agreed upon; they must not injure the master's property or person; they must not resort to violence, even in defending their own rights; they must refrain from turning their demands into riots. (Encyclical *Rerum Novarum.*)

8. These are the obligations of justice binding capitalists and employers: They must pay their workers a just wage; they must not injure the latter's just savings by violence, fraud, or open or hidden usury; they must allow their workers to fulfill their religious duties freely; they must protect them from corrupting allurements and the danger of scandal; they must not alienate their love of family life and thriftiness; they must not assign them work beyond their strength, age, or sex. (Encyclical *Rerum Novarum.*)

9. The wealthy and those of considerable means have an obligation of charity to help the poor and needy according to the Gospel's precept. Christ Himself tells us that this obligation is so serious that on the Day of Judgment a particular account of its fulfillment will be demanded.[3] (Encyclical *Rerum Novarum.*)

10. The poor, on the other hand, should neither be ashamed of their poverty nor disdain the charity of the wealthy. They should consider that Jesus the Redeemer, although He could have been born in luxury, willed to be poor in order to ennoble poverty with an endowment of incomparable merit for Heaven. (Encyclical *Rerum Novarum.*)

11. Capitalists and workers can do a great deal themselves in solving the labor question. They can form institutions to aid the needy and draw the two classes together in closer bonds of unity. Such organizations are the mutual aid societies, many private insurance companies, orphanages for the young, and especially workingmen's unions. (Encyclical *Rerum Novarum.*)

12. This solution of the labor question is the special aim of Popular Christian Action, or Christian Democracy, in all its various branches. This Christian Democracy, however, must be taken in the sense already defined by authority. It is totally different from the movement called "Social Democracy." It is based on the principles of Catholic faith and morality, especially on the principle of never attacking in any way the sacred right of private property. (Encyclical *Graves de Communi.*)

13. Christian Democracy, moreover, should never mix in politics or be made the tool of party purposes or political aims. That is not its purpose. It should be a beneficent movement for all the people, founded on the natural law and evangelical precepts. (Encyclical *Graves de Communi* and instruction of the Sacred Congregation of Extraordinary Ecclesiastical Affairs.) Christian Democrats in Italy must completely refrain from any kind of participation in political action. In the present circumstances this is forbidden to every Catholic *for reasons of the highest good.* (Instruction of the Sacred Congregation.)

14. Christian Democracy is strictly bound in the carrying out of its work to depend on ecclesiastical authority by complete submission and obedience to the Bishops and their representatives. There is neither meritorious zeal nor sincere piety in starting works (albeit good in themselves) which have not been approved by the lawful pastor. (Encyclical *Graves de Communi.*)

15. The actions of the Christian Democrats in Italy must be under the direction of the Association of Catholic Congresses and Committees so that their efforts will be united. For many years this Association has faithfully and excellently served the Church. Pius IX and Leo XIII, of holy memory, entrusted it with the care of directing the whole Catholic movement, always, of course, under the auspices and guidance of the Bishops. (Encyclical *Graves de Communi.*)

16. When treating anything concerning religious interests or the Church's action in society, Catholic writers, like the rest of the faithful, should submit with their whole mind and heart to their Bishops and the Roman Pontiff. Above all, in any matter of consequence they should take care not to anticipate the judgment of the Apostolic See. (Instruction of the Sacred Congregation.)

17. In virtue of the Constitution *Officiorum et Munerum,* Article 41, Christian Democratic writers must submit, like all Catholic writers, all their writings concerning religion, Christian morality, and natural ethics to the previous examination of the Ordinary. In virtue of the same Constitution, Article 42, clerics also must obtain permission of their Ordinary previous to the publication of writings of even a purely technical nature. (Instruction of the Sacred Congregation.)

18. They should also make every effort and sacrifice to preserve charity and harmony among themselves, carefully avoiding all abusive and reproachful language. When causes of disagreement arise, before publishing anything in the newspapers they should refer the matter to ecclesiastical authority, which will then render a just decision. If they happen to be censured by authority, let them promptly obey without evasion or public complaints. Of course, exception is made in the case of a proper appeal to higher authority when the matter seems to require it. (Instruction of the Sacred Congregation.)

19. Finally, Catholic writers, when defending the cause of the people and the poor, should not use language which may inspire the masses with hatred for the upper classes of society. As We have already explained, let them refrain from talking of just claims when it is only a question of charity. Let them remember that Christ wills to unite all men in a mutual bond of love (the perfection of justice), which implies the duty of working for each other's welfare. (Instruction of the Sacred Congregation.)

* * * * * * *

Of Our own will and with certain knowledge, We renew by Our apostolic authority and order the foregoing fundamental norms in all their details to be sent to all Catholic committees, circles, and unions of every kind. All these societies should keep them posted in their meeting rooms and frequently read them at their meetings. We further command all Catholic newspapers to publish them in their entirety, to promise and, in fact, religiously to observe them. If they do not, they must be seriously admonished and if, after such an admonition, they do not correct their ways, they must be banned by ecclesiastical authority.

Strong words and actions, however, are of no avail unless constantly preceded, accompanied, and followed by example. Therefore the fundamental characteristic of all the members of every Catholic association should be a public manifestation of their faith by a holy life, irreproachable morals, and scrupulous observance of divine and ecclesiastical laws. This is the duty of every Christian. By it "anyone opposing may be put to shame, having nothing bad to say of us."[4]

Because of Our solicitude for the welfare of Catholic Action, especially in Italy, We hope, with the divine blessing, to reap plenteous and precious fruits.

Given at Saint Peter's, Rome, December 18, 1903, in the first year of Our Pontificate.

PIUS X, POPE

REFERENCES

1. Cf. *ASS,* 36:285–286.
2. Cf. *ASS,* 11:569 ff.
   ASS, 23:641 ff.
   ASS, 33:385 ff.
   ASS, 34:401 ff.
3. Cf. Matt. chapter 25.
4. Titus 2:8.

CHAPTER 3

Arduum Sane Munus *March 19, 1904, Motu Proprio on the Codification of Canon Law*

AS SOON as We received, in the hidden designs of Divine Providence, the extremely difficult charge of ruling the Universal Church, Our chief desire and resolve was, to the best of Our ability, to restore all things in Christ. We revealed this program of restoration to the Bishops of the world in Our first encyclical letter. So far We have directed all Our resources toward its fulfillment. We have constantly tried to conform Our undertakings in line with that principle. Since We rightly understand ecclesiastical discipline to have the purpose of ordering everything properly and producing the best results, it should, then, above everything else, bring about this restoration of all things in Christ. For that reason We have been most interested in it.

The Apostolic See, also, whether in ecumenical council or not, has never ceased to foster ecclesiastical discipline. It has always passed laws which would be best suited for the various conditions of time and needs of men. Laws, however, even the most wise, if they remain unorganized, can not only be easily ignored by those who are bound to obey them but also cannot be put into practice as they should. In order to overcome this problem of regulating ecclesiastical discipline, various collections of the sacred canons have been drawn up. Passing over the more ancient canonists, We wish to single out Gratian, who, in his famous *Decretals,* both gathered the sacred canons together as well as harmonized and synthesized them. Following him, Our Predecessors, Innocent III, Honorius III, Gregory IX, Boniface VIII, Clement V, and John XXII, imitating what Justinian did for Roman law, edited and promulgated authentic collections of *Decretals.* The works of the last three mentioned Pontiffs, together with the *Decretals* of Gratian, today is called the *Corpus Juris Canonici.* However, the Council of Trent and the promulgation of new laws rendered this work obsolete. Thus the Roman Pontiffs, Gregory XIII, Sixtus V, Clement VIII and Benedict XIV, either published new editions of the *Corpus Juris Canonici* or prepared other collections of the sacred canons. To these must be added the recent authentic collections of the decrees of some of the Sacred Roman Congregations.

Such work was done in order to diminish the difficulties that time introduces. Nevertheless, the objective was far beyond reach. The very number of collections produced no little difficulty. The succeeding centuries passed many laws and these, too, were published in many volumes. Not a few of these laws, formerly suitable for their time, have either been abrogated or become obsolete. Finally, changes in the course of time have brought about their neglect either because they were too difficult to fulfill or because they scarcely contributed to the common good of souls.

Our Predecessors, especially Pius IX and Leo XIII, of holy memory, sought to abolish the ambiguities in some of those parts of the law which demanded immediate attention. The former modified the censures *latae sententiae* in the constitution *"Apostolicae Sedis"*;[1] the latter established the laws governing the publication and prohibition of books in the constitution *"Officiorum et munerum"*[2] and set up the norms governing religious Congregations with simple vows in the constitution *"Conditae a Christo."*[3] Now distinguished members of the hierarchy as well as many of the Cardinals have earnestly requested that all the laws of the Church, published up until the present day, be arranged in a logical order and published in a single volume. Moreover, they have asked that everything obsolete or abrogated be removed and other things, where needed, be better adapted to the conditions of our times. (Many Bishops made the same request at the Vatican Council.)

Since We heartily approved of and openly received these worthy petitions, We finally asked about to find the best means for accomplishing this work. We did this, first of all, because We did not in the least underestimate the tremendous task it would be. Now, after examining the matter with certain knowledge and mature deliberation, We command, by Our own authority, that this procedure be followed:

1. We have appointed a Council, or, as they say, a Pontifical Commission, which shall govern and direct the whole work. It shall consist of some of the Cardinals of the Holy Roman Church whom the Pope shall individually designate.[4]

2. The Pope shall be the chairman of this Commission. In his absence, the senior Cardinal shall be chairman *pro tem.*

3. Furthermore, there shall be a suitable number of Consultors whom the Cardinals, with the Pope's approval, shall select from the ranks of the most distinguished canonists and theologians.

4. We desire, moreover, that every Bishop, according to the rules that shall presently be published, shall wholeheartedly cooperate in this very important undertaking.

5. Whenever a canonical problem arises which demands further investigation, the Consultors should prepare the matter and present their opinion about it in session. He shall be the chairman whom the Pope has appointed after consulting the commission of Cardinals. The Cardinals shall then examine their studies and opinions. Finally, the whole matter shall be submitted to the Pope for his lawful approbation.

We have decreed these things by this letter and We will that they be considered as ratified and binding, notwithstanding anything to the contrary, no matter how worthy it is of special mention.

Given at Saint Peter's, Rome, March 19, on the feast of Saint Joseph, the Spouse of the Blessed Virgin Mary, 1904, in the first year of Our Pontificate.

PIUS X, POPE

REFERENCES

1. Cf. *ASS,* 5:287 ff.
2. Cf. *ibid.,* 29:588 ff.
3. Cf. *ibid.,* 33:241 ff.
4. His Holiness has appointed the following Cardinals to serve as members of this Pontifical Commission: Serafino Vannutelli, Antonio Agliardi, Vincent Vannutelli, Francis Satolli, Mario Rampolla del Tindaro, Jerome M. Gotti, Dominic Ferrata, Francis de Paula Cassetta, Francis Desideratus Mathieu, Casimir Gennari, Benjamin Cavicchioni, Raphael Merry del Val, Andrew Steinhuber, Francis Segna, Joseph Calasanctius Vives y Tuto, and Felix Cavagnis. At the same time His Holiness has appointed the Most Reverend Peter Gasparri, Archbishop of Caesarea, as Secretary of the abovementioned Pontifical Commission and President of the Committee of Consultors.

CHAPTER 4

Sacra Tridentina Synodus* *December 20, 1905,*

Decree on the Necessary Dispositions for Frequent and Daily Reception of Holy Communion

THE Holy Council of Trent, having in view the ineffable riches of grace which are offered to the faithful who receive the Most Holy Eucharist, makes the following declaration: "The Holy Council wishes indeed that at each Mass the faithful who are present should communicate, not only in spiritual desire, but sacramentally, by the actual reception of the Eucharist." [1] These words declare plainly enough the wish of the Church that all Christians should be daily nourished by this heavenly banquet and should derive therefrom more abundant fruit for their sanctification.

The wish of the Council fully conforms to that desire wherewith Christ our Lord was inflamed when He instituted this Divine Sacrament. For He Himself, more than once, and in clarity of word, pointed out the necessity of frequently eating His Flesh and drinking His Blood, especially in these words: "This is the bread that has come down from heaven; not as your fathers ate the manna, and died. He who eats this bread shall live forever." [2] From this comparison of the Food of angels with bread and with the manna, it was easily to be understood by His disciples that, as the body is daily nourished with bread, and as the Hebrews were daily fed with manna in the desert, so the Christian soul might daily partake of this heavenly bread and be refreshed thereby. Moreover, we are bidden in the Lord's Prayer to ask for "our daily bread" by which words, the holy Fathers of the Church all but unanimously teach, must be understood not so much that material bread which is the support of the body as the Eucharistic bread which ought to be our daily food.

* *Sacra Tridentina Synodus* was translated by Joseph Collins, S.S., D.D., Ph.D., and appears in *Catechetical Documents of Pope Pius X* (Paterson, N. J., St. Anthony Guild Press).

Moreover, the desire of Jesus Christ and of the Church that all the faithful should daily approach the sacred banquet is directed chiefly to this end, that the faithful, being united to God by means of the Sacrament, may thence derive strength to resist their sensual passions, to cleanse themselves from the stains of daily faults, and to avoid those graver sins to which human frailty is liable; so that its primary purpose is not that the honor and reverence due to our Lord may be safe-guarded, or that it may serve as a reward or recompense of virtue bestowed on the recipients.[3] Hence the Holy Council calls the Eucharist "the antidote whereby we may be freed from daily faults and be preserved from mortal sins."[4]

The will of God in this respect was well understood by the first Christians; and they daily hastened to this Table of life and strength. "They continued steadfastly in the teaching of the apostles and in the communion of the breaking of the bread."[5] The holy Fathers and writers of the Church testify that this practice was continued into later ages and not without great increase of holiness and perfection.

Piety, however, grew cold, and especially afterward because of the widespread plague of Jansenism, disputes began to arise concerning the dispositions with which one ought to receive frequent and daily Communion; and writers vied with one another in demanding more and more stringent conditions as necessary to be fulfilled. The result of such disputes was that very few were considered worthy to receive the Holy Eucharist daily, and to derive from this most health-giving Sacrament its more abundant fruits; the others were content to partake of it once a year, or once a month, or at most once a week. To such a degree, indeed, was rigorism carried that whole classes of persons were excluded from a frequent approach to the Holy Table, for instance, merchants or those who were married.

Some, however, went over to the opposite view. They held that daily Communion was prescribed by divine law and that no day should pass without communicating, and besides other practices not in accord with the approved usage of the Church, they determined that the Eucharist must be received even on Good Friday and in fact so administered it.

Toward these conditions, the Holy See did not fail in its duty. A Decree of this Sacred Congregation, which begins with the words *Cum ad aures,* issued on February 12, 1679, with the approbation of Pope Innocent XI, condemned these errors, and put a stop to such abuses; at the same time it declared that all the faithful of whatsoever class, merchants or married persons not at all excepted, could be admitted to frequent Communion according to the devotion of each one and the judgment of his confessor. Then on December 7, 1690, by the Decree of Pope Alexander VIII, *Sanctissimus Dominus noster,* the proposition of Baius was condemned, which required a most pure love of God, without any admixture of defect, on the part of those who wished to approach the Holy Table.

The poison of Jansenism, however, which, under the pretext of showing due honor and reverence to the Eucharist, had infected the minds even of good men, was by no means a thing of the past. The question as to the dispositions for the proper and licit reception of Holy Communion survived the declarations of the Holy See, and it was a fact that certain theologians of good repute were of the opinion that daily Communion could be permitted to the faithful only rarely and subject to many conditions.

On the other hand, there were not wanting men endowed with learning and piety who offered an easier approach to this practice, so salutary and so pleasing to God. They taught, with the authority of the Fathers, that there is no precept of the Church which prescribed more perfect dispositions in the case of daily than of weekly or monthly Communion; while the fruits of daily Communion will be far more abundant than those of Communions received weekly or monthly.

In our own day the controversy has been continued with increased warmth, and not without bitterness, so that the minds of confessors and the consciences of the faithful have been disturbed, to the no small detriment of Christian piety and fervor. Certain distinguished men, themselves pastors of souls, have as a result of this urgently begged His Holiness, Pope Pius X, to deign to settle, by his supreme authority, the question concerning the dispositions required to receive the Eucharist daily; so that this practice, so salutary and so pleasing to God, not only might suffer no decrease among the faithful, but rather that it increase and everywhere be promoted, especially in these days when religion and the Catholic faith are attacked on all sides, and the true love of God and piety are so frequently lacking. His Holiness, being most earnestly desirous, out of his solicitude and zeal, that the faithful should be invited to the sacred banquet as often as possible, even daily, and should benefit by its most abundant fruits, committed the aforesaid question to this Sacred Congregation, to be studied and decided definitely (*definiendam*).

Accordingly, the Sacred Congregation of the Council, in a Plenary Session held on December 16, 1905, submitted this matter to a very careful study; and, after sedulously examining the reasons adduced on either side, determined and declared as follows:

1. Frequent and daily Communion, as a practice most earnestly desired by Christ our Lord and by the Catholic Church, should be open to all the faithful, of whatever rank and condition of life; so that no one who is in the state of grace, and who approaches the Holy Table with a right and devout intention (*recta piaque mente*) can be prohibited therefrom.

2. A right intention consists in this: that he who approaches the Holy Table should do so, not out of routine, or vain-glory, or human respect, but

that he wish to please God, to be more closely united with Him by charity, and to have recourse to this divine remedy for his weaknesses and defects.

3. Although it is especially fitting that those who receive Communion frequently or daily should be free from venial sins, at least from such as are fully deliberate, and from any affection thereto, nevertheless, it is sufficient that they be free from mortal sin, with the purpose of never sinning in the future; and if they have this sincere purpose, it is impossible but that daily communicants should gradually free themselves even from venial sins, and from all affection thereto.

4. Since, however, the Sacraments of the New Law, though they produce their effect *ex opere operato,* nevertheless produce a greater effect in proportion as the dispositions of the recipient are better, therefore, one should take care that Holy Communion be preceded by careful preparation, and followed by an appropriate thanksgiving, according to each one's strength, circumstances and duties.

5. That the practice of frequent and daily Communion may be carried out with greater prudence and more fruitful merit, the confessor's advice should be asked. Confessors, however, must take care not to dissuade anyone from frequent or daily Communion, provided he is found to be in a state of grace and approaches with a right intention.

6. But since it is plain that by the frequent or daily reception of the Holy Eucharist union with Christ is strengthened, the spiritual life more abundantly sustained, the soul more richly endowed with virtues, and the pledge of everlasting happiness more securely bestowed on the recipient, therefore, parish priests, confessors and preachers, according to the approved teaching of the Roman Catechism [6] should exhort the faithful frequently and with great zeal to this devout and salutary practice.

7. Frequent and daily Communion is to be promoted especially in religious Institutes of all kinds; with regard to which, however, the Decree *Quemadmodum* issued on December 17, 1890, by the Sacred Congregation of Bishops and Regulars, is to remain in force. It is to be promoted especially in ecclesiastical seminaries, where students are preparing for the service of the altar; as also in all Christian establishments which in any way provide for the care of the young (*ephebeis*).

8. In the case of religious Institutes, whether of solemn or simple vows, in whose rules, or constitutions, or calendars, Communion is assigned to certain fixed days, such regulations are to be considered as *directive* and not *preceptive*. The prescribed number of Communions should be regarded as a minimum but not a limit to the devotion of the religious. Therefore, access to the Eucharistic Table, whether it be rather frequently or daily, must always be freely open to them according to the norms above laid down in this Decree. Furthermore, in order that all religious of both sexes may clearly un-

derstand the prescriptions of this Decree, the Superior of each house will provide that it be read in community, in the vernacular, every year within the octave of the Feast of Corpus Christi.

9. Finally, after the publication of this Decree, all ecclesiastical writers are to cease from contentious controversy concerning the dispositions requisite for frequent and daily Communion.

All this having been reported to His Holiness, Pope Pius X, by the undersigned Secretary of the Sacred Congregation in an audience held on December 17, 1905, His Holiness ratified this Decree, confirmed it, and ordered its publication, anything to the contrary notwithstanding. He further ordered that it should be sent to all local Ordinaries and regular prelates, to be communicated by them to their respective seminaries, parishes, religious institutes, and priests; and that in their reports on the state of their dioceses or institutes they should inform the Holy See concerning the execution of the prescriptions therein enacted.

Given at Rome, the 20th day of December, 1905.

VINCENT, *Cardinal Bishop of Palestrina, Prefect*
CAJETAN DE LAI, *Secretary*

REFERENCES

1. *Sess. XXII, cap.* 6.
2. John 6:59.
3. St. Augustine, *Serm.* 57 *in St. Matt., De Orat. Dom., n.* 7.
4. *Sess. XIII, cap.* 2.
5. Acts 2:42.
6. *Pars II, cap.* 4, *n.* 60.

CHAPTER 5

Quoniam in Re Biblica* *March 26, 1906,*

Apostolic Letter on the Study of Holy Scriptures in Clerical Seminaries

THE Biblical Question has, perhaps, never been of such importance as it is today, and it is therefore absolutely necessary that young clerics should be assiduously trained in the knowledge of the Scriptures, so that they may not only know and understand the force and character and teaching of the Bible, but that they may be skillfully and rightly trained in the ministry of the Divine Word, and able to defend the books written by the inspiration of God from the attacks of those who deny that anything has been divinely handed down to us. To this end Our illustrious Predecessor in his encyclical *Providentissimus* decreed: "Let our first care be to see that in seminaries and academical institutions the study of Holy Scripture be placed on such a footing as its own importance and the circumstances of the time demand." On this same subject, then, We now lay down the following rules which We regard as of the greatest utility:

1. The instruction in Sacred Scripture to be imparted in every seminary should embrace, first, the principal ideas concerning inspiration, the canon of the Scripture, the original text and the most important versions, the laws of hermeneutics; secondly, the history of both Testaments; and, thirdly, the analysis and exegesis of the different books according to the importance of each.

2. The curriculum of Biblical studies is to be divided over the entire period during which ecclesiastical students pursue their course of sacred studies within the walls of the seminary; so that when the course is finished each student may have gone through the entire curriculum.

3. The chairs of Scripture shall be organized according to the condition and the means of the different seminaries, but always in such a way that no student shall be deprived of the means of learning those things of which a priest may not lawfully be ignorant.

* This translation of *Quoniam in Re Biblica* appears in the booklet *Rome and the Study of Scripture* (St. Meinrad, Ind., The Grail Press).

4. Since, on the one hand, it is not possible to have a detailed exposition of the whole of Scripture given in school, and, on the other, it is necessary that the whole of Scripture should be in some sense known to the priest, the professor shall take care to have special treatises or introductions for each of the books to prove their authority,when occasion requires, to teach the analysis of them, but he will, at the same time, dwell at greater length on the more important books and parts of books.

5. With regard to the Old Testament, he will make use of the latest results of research in illustrating the history of the Hebrew people and their relations with other Oriental nations; he will treat of the main features of the Mosaic Law; and he will explain the principal prophecies.

6. He will take special pains to imbue his students with zeal to study and understand those Psalms which they recite daily in the Divine Office; he will select some of those Psalms for interpretation in order to show by way of example the method to be followed by the students in their private studies to interpret the others.

7. Treating of the New Testament, he will explain briefly and clearly the special characteristics of each of the four Gospels, and the proofs of their authenticity; he will also illustrate the general characters of the entire Gospel story, and the doctrine in the Epistles and the other books.

8. He will pay special attention in treating of those parts of both Testaments, which concern Christian faith and morals.

9. He will always remember, especially in treating of the New Testament, to conform to the precepts he explains to those who are afterwards by their words and their example to teach the people the doctrine of salvation. He will, therefore, in the course of his instruction explain to his students the best way of preaching the Gospel, and will stimulate them, as occasion may offer, to observe diligently the commands of the Lord Jesus Christ and the Apostles.

10. The more promising students are to be instructed in the Hebrew tongue, in Biblical Greek, and whenever possible, in some other Semitic language, such as Syriac or Arabic. "It is most proper that Professors of Sacred Scripture and theologians should master those tongues in which the sacred books were originally written; and it would be well that ecclesiastical students also should cultivate them, more especially those who aspire to academic degrees. And endeavors should be made to establish in all academic institutions chairs of the other Oriental languages, especially the Semitic" (*Providentissimus Deus*).

11. In seminaries which enjoy the right of conferring academical degrees it will be necessary to increase the number of lectures on Sacred Scripture and consequently to go more deeply into general and special questions, and to devote more time and study to Biblical exegesis, archaeology, geography, chronology, theology and history.

12. Special diligence is to be shown in preparing select students for the academical degrees in Sacred Scripture according to the rules laid down by the Biblical Commission—a matter of no small importance for securing suitable professors for Scripture for the seminaries.

13. Every doctor in Sacred Scripture will be most careful never to swerve in the least in his teaching from the doctrine and tradition of the Church; he will of course make use of the real additions to our knowledge with modern research supplies, but he will avoid the rash commentaries of innovators; so, too, he will confine himself to the treatment of those questions which contribute to the elucidation and defence of the Sacred Scriptures; and finally he will be guided in his plan of teaching by those rules, full of prudence, contained in the Encyclical *Providentissimus*.

14. Students should endeavor to make up by private study what the schools fail to supply in this branch of sacred learning. As lack of time will render it impossible for the professor to go over the whole of Scripture in detail, they will by themselves devote a certain portion of time every day to a careful perusal of the Old and New Testaments—and in this they will be greatly helped by the use of some brief commentary to throw light on obscure passages and explain the more difficult ones.

15. Students are to undergo an examination in Scripture, as well as in other parts of theology, to show the profit they have derived from the lessons, before they are allowed to pass into another class or to be initiated in sacred orders.

16. In all academies every candidate for academical degrees in theology will be asked certain questions on Scripture relating to the historical and critical introduction as well as to exegesis; and will prove by examination that he is sufficiently acquainted with the Hebrew tongue and has knowledge of Biblical Greek.

17. The students of Sacred Scripture are to be exhorted to read not only interpretations of the Scripture, but good authors who treat of subjects connected with this study—for instance, the history of both Testaments, the life of Our Lord and the Apostles, and books of travel in Palestine—from all of which they will easily acquire knowledge of Biblical places and customs.

18. To further this object efforts will be made to supply each seminary, as far as circumstances will permit, with a small library in which books of this kind will be at the disposal of the students.

This is Our will and Our command, everything to the contrary notwithstanding.

Given at Rome at St. Peter's on the 27th of March, 1906, the third year of Our Pontificate.

A. CARDINAL MACCHI

CHAPTER 6

Lamentabili Sane *July 3, 1907, Syllabus Condemning the Errors of the Modernists*

WITH truly lamentable results, our age, casting aside all restraint in its search for the ultimate causes of things, frequently pursues novelties so ardently that it rejects the legacy of the human race. Thus it falls into very serious errors, which are even more serious when they concern sacred authority, the interpretation of Sacred Scripture, and the principal mysteries of Faith. The fact that many Catholic writers also go beyond the limits determined by the Fathers and the Church herself is extremely regrettable. In the name of higher knowledge and historical research (they say), they are looking for that progress of dogmas which is, in reality, nothing but the corruption of dogmas.

These errors are being daily spread among the faithful. Lest they captivate the faithful's minds and corrupt the purity of their faith, His Holiness, Pius X, by Divine Providence, Pope, has decided that the chief errors should be noted and condemned by the Office of this Holy Roman and Universal Inquisition.

Therefore, after a very diligent investigation and consultation with the Reverend Consultors, the Most Eminent and Reverend Lord Cardinals, the General Inquisitors in matters of faith and morals have judged the following propositions to be condemned and proscribed. In fact, by this general decree, they are condemned and proscribed.

* * * * *

1. The ecclesiastical law which prescribes that books concerning the Divine Scriptures are subject to previous examination does not apply to critical scholars and students of scientific exegesis of the Old and New Testament.

2. The Church's interpretation of the Sacred Books is by no means to be rejected; nevertheless, it is subject to the more accurate judgment and correction of the exegetes.

3. From the ecclesiastical judgments and censures passed against free and more scientific exegesis, one can conclude that the Faith the Church proposes contradicts history and that Catholic teaching cannot really be reconciled with the true origins of the Christian religion.

4. Even by dogmatic definitions the Church's magisterium cannot determine the genuine sense of the Sacred Scriptures.

5. Since the deposit of Faith contains only revealed truths, the Church has no right to pass judgment on the assertions of the human sciences.

6. The "Church learning" and the "Church teaching" collaborate in such a way in defining truths that it only remains for the "Church teaching" to sanction the opinions of the "Church learning."

7. In proscribing errors, the Church cannot demand any internal assent from the faithful by which the judgments she issues are to be embraced.

8. They are free from all blame who treat lightly the condemnations passed by the Sacred Congregation of the Index or by the Roman Congregations.

9. They display excessive simplicity or ignorance who believe that God is really the author of the Sacred Scriptures.

10. The inspiration of the books of the Old Testament consists in this: The Israelite writers handed down religious doctrines under a peculiar aspect which was either little or not at all known to the Gentiles.

11. Divine inspiration does not extend to all of Sacred Scriptures so that it renders its parts, each and every one, free from every error.

12. If he wishes to apply himself usefully to Biblical studies, the exegete must first put aside all preconceived opinions about the supernatural origin of Sacred Scripture and interpret it the same as any other merely human document.

13. The Evangelists themselves, as well as the Christians of the second and third generation, artificially arranged the evangelical parables. In such a way they explained the scanty fruit of the preaching of Christ among the Jews.

14. In many narrations the Evangelists recorded, not so much things that are true, as things which, even though false, they judged to be more profitable for their readers.

15. Until the time the canon was defined and constituted, the Gospels were increased by additions and corrections. Therefore there remained in them only a faint and uncertain trace of the doctrine of Christ.

16. The narrations of John are not properly history, but a mystical contemplation of the Gospel. The discourses contained in his Gospel are theological meditations, lacking historical truth concerning the mystery of salvation.

17. The fourth Gospel exaggerated miracles not only in order that the extraordinary might stand out but also in order that it might become more suitable for showing forth the work and glory of the Word Incarnate.

18. John claims for himself the quality of witness concerning Christ. In reality, however, he is only a distinguished witness of the Christian life, or of the life of Christ in the Church at the close of the first century.

19. Heterodox exegetes have expressed the true sense of the Scriptures more faithfully than Catholic exegetes.

20. Revelation could be nothing else than the consciousness man acquired of his relation to God.

21. Revelation, constituting the object of the Catholic faith, was not completed with the Apostles.

22. The dogmas the Church holds out as revealed are not truths which have fallen from heaven. They are an interpretation of religious facts which the human mind has acquired by laborious effort.

23. Opposition may, and actually does, exist between the facts narrated in Sacred Scripture and the Church's dogmas which rest on them. Thus the critic may reject as false facts the Church holds as most certain.

24. The exegete who constructs premises from which it follows that dogmas are historically false or doubtful is not to be reproved as long as he does not directly deny the dogmas themselves.

25. The assent of faith ultimately rests on a mass of probabilities.

26. The dogmas of the Faith are to be held only according to their practical sense; that is to say, as preceptive norms of conduct and not as norms of believing.

27. The divinity of Jesus Christ is not proved from the Gospels. It is a dogma which the Christian conscience has derived from the notion of the Messias.

28. While He was exercising His ministry, Jesus did not speak with the object of teaching He was the Messias, nor did His miracles tend to prove it.

29. It is permissible to grant that the Christ of history is far inferior to the Christ Who is the object of faith.

30. In all the evangelical texts the name "Son of God" is equivalent only to that of "Messias." It does not in the least way signify that Christ is the true and natural Son of God.

31. The doctrine concerning Christ taught by Paul, John, and the Councils of Nicea, Ephesus and Chalcedon is not that which Jesus taught but that which the Christian conscience conceived concerning Jesus.

32. It is impossible to reconcile the natural sense of the Gospel texts with the sense taught by our theologians concerning the conscience and the infallible knowledge of Jesus Christ.

33. Everyone who is not led by preconceived opinions can readily see that either Jesus professed an error concerning the immediate Messianic coming or the greater part of His doctrine as contained in the Gospels is destitute of authenticity.

34. The critics can ascribe to Christ a knowledge without limits only on a hypothesis which cannot be historically conceived and which is repugnant to the moral sense. That hypothesis is that Christ as man possessed the knowledge of God and yet was unwilling to communicate the knowledge of a great many things to His disciples and posterity.

35. Christ did not always possess the consciousness of His Messianic dignity.

36. The Resurrection of the Saviour is not properly a fact of the historical order. It is a fact of merely the supernatural order (neither demonstrated nor demonstrable) which the Christian conscience gradually derived from other facts.

37. In the beginning, faith in the Resurrection of Christ was not so much in the fact itself of the Resurrection as in the immortal life of Christ with God.

38. The doctrine of the expiatory death of Christ is Pauline and not evangelical.

39. The opinions concerning the origin of the Sacraments which the Fathers of Trent held and which certainly influenced their dogmatic canons are very different from those which now rightly exist among historians who examine Christianity.

40. The Sacraments had their origin in the fact that the Apostles and their successors, swayed and moved by circumstances and events, interpreted some idea and intention of Christ.

41. The Sacraments are intended merely to recall to man's mind the ever-beneficent presence of the Creator.

42. The Christian community imposed the necessity of Baptism, adopted it as a necessary rite, and added to it the obligation of the Christian profession.

43. The practice of administering Baptism to infants was a disciplinary evolution, which became one of the causes why the Sacrament was divided into two, namely, Baptism and Penance.

44. There is nothing to prove that the rite of the Sacrament of Confirmation was employed by the Apostles. The formal distinctiton of the two Sacraments of Baptism and Confirmation does not pertain to the history of primitive Christianity.

45. Not everything which Paul narrates concerning the institution of the Eucharist (I Cor. 11:23–25) is to be taken historically.

46. In the primitive Church the concept of the Christian sinner reconciled by the authority of the Church did not exist. Only very slowly did the Church accustom herself to this concept. As a matter of fact, even after Penance was recognized as an institution of the Church, it was not called a Sacrament since it would be held as a disgraceful Sacrament.

47. The words of the Lord, "Receive the Holy Spirit; whose sins you shall forgive, they are forgiven them; and whose sins you shall retain, they are retained" (John 20:22–23), in no way refer to the Sacrament of Penance, in spite of what it pleased the Fathers of Trent to say.

48. In his Epistle (Ch. 5:14–15) James did not intend to promulgate a Sacrament of Christ but only commend a pious custom. If in this custom he happens to distinguish a means of grace, it is not in that rigorous manner in which it was taken by the theologians who laid down the notion and number of the Sacraments.

49. When the Christian supper gradually assumed the nature of a liturgical action those who customarily presided over the supper acquired the sacerdotal character.

50. The elders who fulfilled the office of watching over the gatherings of the faithful were instituted by the Apostles as priests or bishops to provide for the necessary ordering of the increasing communities and not properly for the perpetuation of the Apostolic mission and power.

51. It is impossible that Matrimony could have become a Sacrament of the new law until later in the Church since it was necessary that a full theological explication of the doctrine of grace and the Sacraments should first take place before Matrimony should be held as a Sacrament.

52. It was far from the mind of Christ to found a Church as a society which would continue on earth for a long course of centuries. On the contrary, in the mind of Christ the kingdom of heaven together with the end of the world was about to come immediately.

53. The organic constitution of the Church is not immutable. Like human society, Christian society is subject to a perpetual evolution.

54. Dogmas, Sacraments and hierarchy, both their notion and reality, are only interpretations and evolutions of the Christian intelligence which have increased and perfected by an external series of additions the little germ latent in the Gospel.

55. Simon Peter never even suspected that Christ entrusted the primacy in the Church to him.

56. The Roman Church became the head of all the churches, not through the ordinance of Divine Providence, but merely through political conditions.

57. The Church has shown that she is hostile to the progress of the natural and theological sciences.

58. Truth is no more immutable than man himself, since it evolved with him, in him, and through him.

59. Christ did not teach a determined body of doctrine applicable to all times and all men, but rather inaugurated a religious movement adapted or to be adapted to different times and places.

60. Christian Doctrine was originally Judaic. Through successive evolutions it became first Pauline, then Joannine, finally Hellenic and universal.

61. It may be said without paradox that there is no chapter of Scripture, from the first of Genesis to the last of the Apocalypse, which contains a doctrine absolutely identical with that which the Church teaches on the same matter. For the same reason, therefore, no chapter of Scripture has the same sense for the critic and the theologian.

62. The chief articles of the Apostles' Creed did not have the same sense for the Christians of the first ages as they have for the Christians of our time.

63. The Church shows that she is incapable of effectively maintaining evangelical ethics since she obstinately clings to immutable doctrines which cannot be reconciled with modern progress.

64. Scientific progress demands that the concepts of Christian doctrine concerning God, creation, revelation, the Person of the Incarnate Word, and Redemption be re-adjusted.

65. Modern Catholicism can be reconciled with true science only if it is transformed into a non-dogmatic Christianity; that is to say, into a broad and liberal Protestantism.

* * * * *

The following Thursday, the fourth day of the same month and year, all these matters were accurately reported to our Most Holy Lord, Pope Pius X. His Holiness approved and confirmed the decree of the Most Eminent Fathers and ordered that each and every one of the above-listed propositions be held by all as condemned and proscribed.

PETER PALOMBELLI,
Notary of the Holy Roman and Universal Inquisition

CHAPTER 7

Haerent Animo* *August 4, 1908, Apostolic Exhortation to the Catholic Clergy*

BELOVED SONS, HEALTH AND APOSTOLIC BENEDICTION!

DEEPLY engraven upon Our hearts are the words of warning which the Apostle of the Gentiles addresses to the Hebrews when he reminds them of the obedience due to their superiors, saying, "for they keep watch as having to render an account of your souls" (Heb. 13:17). For, whilst these words apply to all those who exercise authority in the Church of Christ, yet do they apply in an especial manner to Us, who, however unworthily, have received from God the supreme authority. Wherefore, with deep and insistent solicitude have We sought, night and day, to devise ways and means to foster the well-being and growth of Christ's flock. Above all else has the desire been dominant in Our mind, that those who have been raised to the high station of the sacred ministry might be found to walk worthily of the great dignity of their office, since We are convinced that the hope of a healthy religious activity lies mainly in this work of reform.

Hence it has been Our aim, from the very outset of Our Pontificate, to exhort Our Venerable Brothers of the Episcopate, despite the general impression that the clergy in most places enjoy a reputation for zeal and virtue, to expend their chief energy and thought upon the formation of those whose vocation it is to form Christ in others. We are well aware of the earnest good will established in this direction by Bishops devoted to their holy office. We know with what scrupulous care they seek to train up their clergy in the ways of virtue; and for this We are glad not only to express our approbation, but to render to them public thanks.

But whilst, as a result of this care on the part of the Bishops, many priests are imbued with heavenly fervor by which they kindle ever anew and preserve the grace of God received through the imposition of hands in the sacred

* This translation of *Haerent Animo* appears in *A Papal Symposium on the Priesthood* (St. Meinrad, Ind., The Grail Press).

priesthood, We are forced to complain that there are others to be found in different parts of the world who are not so disposed as to lead the Christian people who observe them to the faithful imitation of them. To these, then, We wish to lay open Our heart in this letter, the heart as it were of a father, which beats with anxious love at the sight of his sick child. Therefore, with this intent We add to the Bishops' exhortations Our entreaties, which, though addressed particularly to those who in their torpor are straying from the right road that We may lead them back to the better path, are intended also to encourage others. We point out the way by which each one should carefully strive day after day to be in truth what the Apostle has neatly expressed, a "man of God" (1 Tim. 6:11), and thus fulfill the just expectation of the Church. We have nothing to say to you that is absolutely new or unknown to anyone, but We repeat simply those truths which should be in the constant remembrance of all. God inspires us with the hope that Our voice will bear no meagre fruit. This, indeed, We earnestly desire, that you "Be renewed in the spirit of your mind, and put on the new man, which has been created according to God in justice and holiness of truth" (Eph. 4:23–24) and this will be a most excellent and acceptable gift from you on the fiftieth anniversary of Our priesthood, and while We "in a contrite heart and humble spirit" (Dan. 3:39) consider before God the years spent in the priesthood, We shall appear to expiate in some way at least whatever frailty is to be condoned, by admonishing and exhorting you to "walk worthily of God and please him in all things" (Col. 1:10). We shall regard, nevertheless, in this exhortation *not only your utility,* but the *common advantage of the Catholic people,* since the one cannot be divorced from the other. For the *priest is not a person who can be good or bad in himself alone:* his mode of living and his conduct have a consequent effect on the people. Where the priest is really good, what a great blessing he becomes!

Sanctity of our priesthood. Wherefore, beloved sons, We speak to you in the first place that We may incite you to that sanctity of life which the dignity of your office demands. For, whoever becomes a priest, is a priest, not for himself alone but for others: "for every high priest taken from among men is appointed for men in the things pertaining to God" (Heb. 5:1). This Christ indicated when, to show what should be the priest's conduct, He used to compare him to salt and to light. The priest, then, is the salt of the earth and the light of the world. Surely all know that he becomes this by teaching the truths of Christ, but who does not likewise know that his instruction is almost for nothing, unless he proves by his works what he preaches. His auditors insolently, indeed, yet deservedly reply: "They profess to know God, but by their works they disown him" (Tit. 1:16), and they refuse his doctrine and are not illumined by his light. Wherefore, Christ Himself, once He became the exemplar of priests, first taught by deeds and then by words. "Jesus did and taught" (Acts 1:1). Likewise, without sanctity, the priest can never be the salt of the earth, for what is corrupt and contaminated is by no means fit to confer health, and where there is no sanctity, there corruption must dwell. Wherefore, Christ insisting on the same similitude calls such priests salt that has lost its savor, which "is no longer of any use but to be thrown out and trodden underfoot by men" (Matt. 5:13).

This is all the more evident from the fact that we exercise the priestly office not in our own name, but in Christ's. "Let a man so account us," says the Apostle, "as servants of Christ and stewards of the mysteries of God" (1 Cor. 4:1); "on behalf of Christ, therefore, we are acting as ambassadors" (2 Cor. 5:20). It is for this reason that Christ Himself has enrolled us, not among His servants but His friends. "No longer do I call you servants. . . . But I have called you friends, because all things that I have heard from my Father I have made known to you. . . . I have chosen you, and have appointed you that you should go and bear fruit" (John 15:15–16). Therefore, We are to act the part of Christ and the ministry given by Him is to be carried on in such a way that we accomplish precisely what He intends. And since durable friendship consists in having the same will in all things, we are bound as friends to feel within ourselves what Jesus Christ felt, who is "holy, innocent, undefiled" (Heb. 7:26); as legates, we must win the faith of men to His doctrine and His laws, observing them ourselves first; as the participants of His power to lighten souls weighed down with sin, we must strive with every care lest we ourselves be burdened also. But particularly in that excellent sacrifice which is renewed with perennial grace for the life of the world, must we possess that conformity of spirit in which He offered Himself an immaculate victim to God on the altar of the Cross. For, if formerly, while yet the sacrifice was in shadow and figure only, such sanctity was demanded of the priests, what from us, when the victim is Christ? "Who should be purer than the one offering such a sacrifice? Are the sun's rays more glorious than the hand that divides this flesh? than the mouth that is filled with heavenly fire, or the tongue that is red with the terrible blood?"[1] St. Charles Borromeo in his sermons to the clergy thus aptly speaks:

> If we should remember, dearly beloved brethren, what great and wonderful gifts the Lord God has placed in our hands, what influence this thought would exert in impelling us to lead lives worthy of ecclesiastical men! What has the Lord not placed in my hand, when He has put there His only begotten Son, co-eternal and co-equal to Himself? In my hand He has placed all His riches, His graces, His sacraments; He has placed there souls which He preferred in His love to Himself and redeemed with His Blood; He has placed heaven in my hand, which I can both open and close to others. How, then, can I be so ungrateful

after such condescension and love, as to sin against Him, to offend His honor? to pollute this body which is His? to defile this dignity, this life consecrated to His service.

The Church with vigilant and unceasing care seeks this sanctity of life, about which it is advantageous to speak somewhat at length; for this, her sacred seminaries have been instituted where those who are to be the future priests, while they are grounded in the Scriptures and doctrines of the Church, should be especially trained from their tender years in every form of piety. And then, while she promotes her candidates gradually and at long intervals, like a prudent mother, she never ceases to exhort her sons to sanctity. It is pleasant, indeed, to recall her exhortations. When she first receives us into the sacred militia she wishes us to profess, "the Lord is the portion of my inheritance and of my cup: it is thou that wilt restore my inheritance to me" (Ps. 15:5). By these words, says St. Jerome, "the cleric is warned in order that he, who is the portion of the Lord, or has the Lord for his portion, should so conduct himself that he may possess the Lord and be in turn possessed by Him." [2] How impressively she speaks to those who are about to be made subdeacons! "Think seriously and repeatedly on the heavy burden, which you desire today. But if you receive this order you cannot hereafter revoke your decision, but must forever belong to God and observe with His assistance chastity." Then, finally, she adds: "If up to the present you have been tardy in regard to the Church, now you must be constant; if up to the present you have been careless, now you must be vigilant; if up to the present unchaste, now you must be pure. Behold! whose ministry is delivered to you." Then for those who are to be promoted to the diaconate she thus implores God through the mouth of the Bishop: "May the form of every virtue abound in them, modest authority, constant chastity, purity of innocence, and the spiritual observance of discipline. May their precepts shine forth in their actions, so that the people by the example of their chastity may in holy imitation follow them." But still more impressive is the warning that she gives to those approaching the sacred priesthood: "With great fear must one ascend to this high dignity, and it must be an object of care that heavenly wisdom, sound morals and continual observance of what is just commend those chosen for it. Let the odor of your life be the joy of Christ's Church, that by preaching and example you may build the House of God, that is, His people." And then too she adds most solemnly this important admonition, "Imitate what you do," which agrees in full with the precept of Paul, "that we may present every man perfect in Christ Jesus."

Since this is the mind of the Church concerning the sacerdotal life, no one can wonder if the Holy Fathers and Doctors are so unanimous on this point that one might think them too severe; yet if we consider them prudently, we find that they have taught nothing save what is right and just. In a word, this is their teaching: that there should be as much difference between the priest and the good layman, as there is between heaven and earth, and therefore the priest's life should be free not only of the graver defects, but even of the least. The Tridentine Synod was of the same mind when it warned clerics to avoid "even light faults, which in them are very serious," [3] not in themselves, but with regard to the one that sins, to whom with better right than to material edifices the words of Scripture apply: "Holiness becometh thy house" (Ps. 92:5).

The quality of priestly perfection. Let us see in what sanctity of this kind, which the priest cannot lack, consists; for he who does not know this or accepts it perversely is surely exposed to great danger. There are those, indeed, who think, nay even profess that the priest's glory should be founded entirely on the fact that he gives himself wholly to others; wherefore, neglecting the cultivation of those virtues by which man perfects himself (and, therefore, these they call passive), they contend that all effort and study should be directed to the cultivation and exercise of active virtues. This doctrine has a strange mixture of fallacy and ruin. On this subject Our Predecessor of happy memory has wisely said: [4]

> He alone wishes to fit the Christian virtue to changing times who forgets the words of the Apostle, "for those whom he has foreknown he has also predestined to become conformed to the image of his son" (Rom. 8:29). The Master and exemplar of all sanctity is Christ, and all who desire to take their place among the seats of the blessed must adapt themselves to the rule He has given. Christ, however, does not change as the ages roll on, but is the same "yesterday and today, yes, and forever" (Heb. 13:8).

"Learn from me, for I am meek and humble of heart" (Matt. 11:29), and at all times Christ shows Himself as "becoming obedient to death, even to death on a cross" (Phil. 2:8). In every age the saying of the Apostle holds true: "They who belong to Christ have crucified their flesh with its passions and desires" (Gal. 5:24).

And if these truths are applicable to each of the faithful, more properly do they apply to the priests; and let them before all others regard as addressed to themselves those words which Our same Predecessor added in his apostolic zeal:

> Would that there were more in the present age who cultivate those virtues which the example of holy men of past centuries has set for us, who by their humility, obedience, abstinence were a power both in word and deed, and of the greatest possible assistance, not only in religious matters but in public and civil life also.

And here it would not be inopportune to note that this prudent Pontiff has made special mention of abstinence, which in the words of the gospel we call self-abnegation, and deservedly; for under this head, beloved sons, the constancy and virtue and fruit of every priestly duty are included, and when this is neglected, there springs forth whatever may offend the eyes and hearts of the faithful in the life of the priest. For, if one acts for the sake of filthy lucre, or involves himself in worldly affairs or seeks promotions and despises others, or yields to flesh and blood, or endeavors to please men, or trusts in the fickle words of human wisdom, all these are the result of neglecting the mandate of Christ and refusing the condition laid down by Him: "If anyone wishes to come after me, let him deny himself" (Matt. 16:24).

While We inculcate these truths, We would at the same time warn the priest that he must live holily not for himself alone; he is the laborer whom Christ "went out . . . to hire . . . for his vineyard" (Matt. 20:1). Therefore, he must uproot the seeds of error, and plant those of truth; he must care and watch lest the enemy sow cockle over them. Besides, he must be on his guard, lest through some imprudent desire for high perfection he neglect any of those duties conducive to the welfare of others. These are to preach the Word of God, hear confessions, visit the sick, especially the dying, instruct those ignorant of their faith, comfort the sorrowful, lead back the wanderers, and in every way imitate Christ (Acts 10:38). And in performing these duties let the famous admonition of Paul be always before his mind: "So then neither he who plants is anything, nor he who waters, but God who gives the growth" (1 Cor. 3:7). It may be that going and weeping they cast their seeds; it may be that with anxious care they nourished it; but to make it sprout and bring forth the cherished fruit, this is the work of God alone and His powerful assistance.

This, also, is to be well considered, that men are nothing more than instruments which God uses for the saving of souls and that these instruments must be fit, therefore, to be handled by God. By what means, indeed, are they made fit? Do we think that God is moved to join our resources to the greatness of His glory by any excellence on our part, either inborn or obtained by study? By no means, for it is written: "The foolish things of the world has God chosen to put to shame the 'wise,' and the weak things of the world has God chosen to put to shame the strong, and the base things of the world and the despised has God chosen, and the things that are not, to bring to naught the things that are" (1 Cor. 1:27–28).

There is one quality which indisputably links man with God and makes him the pleasing and not unworthy "dispenser" of His mercy, namely, sanctity of life and morals. If this, which is but the supereminent knowledge of Jesus Christ, be lacking in a priest, all things are lacking. For when not united with sanctity, that supply of carefully acquired learning (which We

Ourselves are striving to promote in the clergy), and that dexterity and skill n exercising it, even if they may be able to bestow some advantage either upon the Church or upon individuals, are often the lamentable cause of harm o their possessors. But how many wonderfully salutary works can he, though he humblest, attempt and accomplish for the "people of God," if he is graced and adorned by sanctity, the testimonies of every age bear witness; among them John Baptist Vianny, of recent memory, the exemplary pastor of souls, to whom We are happy to have given the honors of the Blessed in Heaven. Sanctity alone makes us what our divine vocation demands, namely, men crucified to the world and to whom the world is crucified; men walking n the newness of life, who, as Paul tells us, show themselves to be the ministers of God "in labors, in sleepless nights, in fastings; in innocence, in knowledge, in long-sufferings; in kindness, in the Holy Spirit, in unaffected love; in he word of truth" (2 Cor. 6:5–7), who seek heavenly things alone and strive in every way to lead others to them.

Necessity of cultivating a love of prayer. But since, as everyone knows, sanctity of life results from proper exercise of the will, provided that it is supported by the help of God's grace, God Himself has provided for us abundantly, lest we should lack at any time the help of His grace, if we desire it, and this we obtain especially through prayer. Indeed, there is a necessary union between prayer and holiness, so that one cannot be had without he other. Wherefore, in perfect consonance with this truth are the words of Chrysostom, "I think it clear to all that it is simply impossible to live virtuously without the aid of prayer";[5] and Augustine keenly concludes: "He truly knows how to live rightly, who rightly knows how to pray." [6] These words Christ Himself both by frequent exhortation and example confirmed. It was to pray that He withdrew to the desert; that He went into the mountains alone; that He passed whole nights in meditation; that He made frequent visits to the temple; nay, even to the astonishment of the crowd He prayed aloud with eyes raised to heaven, and finally nailed to the Cross He supplicated in the agony of death His Father with cries and with tears. Therefore, let us hold this as absolutely certain, that the priest, to maintain worthily his office and his calling, must be devoted in a singular manner to the love of prayer. More frequently must we lament that he prays from habit rather than from devotion, who recites the Psalms at stated periods in a negligent manner, or says a few short prayers and gives no part of his day to conversing with God, speaking to Him through gratitude and devotion. For the priest more than others should obey exactly the precept of Christ; "that hey must always pray" (Luke 18:1), to which St. Paul adds: "Be assiduous n prayer, being wakeful therein with thanksgiving" (Col. 4:2); "pray without ceasing" (1 Thess. 5:17). How many opportunities to turn to God offer themselves during the day to the soul that desires its own sanctity as well as the salvation of others! Anguish of spirit, the onslaught and persistency of temptations, the lack of virtues, the poverty and sterility of our works, our frequent offences and negligences, the fear of God's judgments: all these incite us to pray, and with the aid that we seek make for ourselves in heaven a treasury of our good deeds and merits. Nor must we weep for ourselves alone; in the deluge of crimes, which has spread far and wide, we must implore and pray for divine clemency; we must solicit Christ, who is most benignly lavish with all grace in His wonderful sacrament. Spare, O Lord, spare Thy people!

The principal point is to devote a certain space of time daily to the meditation of things eternal. There is no priest who can omit this without a grave mark of neglect and without harm to his soul. The most holy Abbot Bernard, when writing to Eugene III, his foster-son, but then the Roman Pontiff, admonishes him freely and strongly never to fail in his daily meditation of divine things, admitting none of the many and very great cares which the supreme Apostle had, as an excuse. And he asserted that he was demanding this with justice, thus enumerating with the greatest foresight the advantages of this practice:

> Meditation purifies the very spring, that is, the mind, from which it arises. Then it rules our affections, guides our actions, corrects our excesses, arranges our habits, regulates and rectifies our life; finally it gives a knowledge of human and divine truths. This is the knowledge which separates those things that are confused, puts together those that are loosely connected, gathers those that are scattered, searches those that are hidden, traces those that are true, examines those that are probable, explores those that are feigned and counterfeited. This is the knowledge which sets in order those things which are to be done, which considers those already performed, so that nothing remains in the mind uncorrected or needing correction. This is the knowledge which feels adversity in prosperity, and in adversity, is, as it were, without feeling. One of these is fortitude, the other prudence.[7]

Thus the chief advantages which meditation produces is to teach and urge upon us not only how salutary, but also how necessary it is in every way.

Dangers to guard against. For, although the different duties of the priesthood are sacred and wont to inspire reverence, nevertheless, through frequent contact, those performing them do not treat them with that respect which is due them. Hence, as ardor diminishes, the descent to neglect and even to loathing of most sacred objects is easy. Let me add that it is necessary for the priest to live day by day in the midst of a corrupt nation, as it were; and that often in every performance of his pastoral charity he must be constantly alert against the plots and snare of hell that lie in wait for him. What is more easy than for even religious hearts to become soiled by the filth of the world? Therefore, the fact is made apparent how great is the necessity of turning daily to the contemplation of things eternal, in order that the mind and will may presently take on new strength to persevere against allurements. Furthermore, it befits every priest to acquire a disposition to desire and strive after heavenly things. He should know, preach, and recommend heavenly things; and he should guide his whole life in a superhuman course so that whatever he does for his sacred office, he does according to God, at the inspiration and guidance of faith. But it is the habit of daily meditation that effects and preserves this state of mind and this quasi-natural union with God; a truth that is so evident to anyone gifted with prudence, that it is necessary to pursue it no longer.

A confirmation, sad indeed, of these words we may find in the lives of those priests who give little time to the meditation of divine truths or openly dislike it. For, behold; men, in whom the spirit of Christ, that inestimable good, has grown languid, busy with the things of this world entirely, seeking varieties, desiring novelties, and performing sacred duties carelessly, coldly, perhaps unworthily. Formerly these very men, imbued with the still fresh chrism of their priestly unction prepared diligently their souls for prayer, lest they should be like those who tempted God; they sought opportune moments and convenient places away from distraction; they sought to know the divine sense they praised, and sighed, rejoiced and poured forth their spirit with their psalmody. But now, how changed! In like manner, hardly a trace of that quick devotion remains in them which they once felt toward the divine mysteries. How beautiful were those tabernacles formerly! The soul loved to be present at the table of the Lord and to call other devoted hearts there also. What cleanliness before the altar, and what prayers of a thirsting soul! their reverence in the Mass itself, the smallest ceremonies properly observed. What blessings poured forth from the heart! How the good odor of Christ diffused itself happily among the people! "Call to mind," we beseech you, beloved son, "call to mind the days gone by" (Heb. 10:32); then the soul was warm because it was nourished with holy meditation.

But among those who refuse or neglect "to consider in heart" (Jer. 12:11), there are some who do not conceal the consequent sterility of their souls and excuse themselves, offering as a reason that they are given entirely to the cares of the ministry to the manifold advantage of others. They are deceived miserably. For, unaccustomed to speak with God, they lack the divine fire when they speak to men about Him or impart the principles of Christian living, so that the gospel message seems to be lifeless in them. Their voice, whatever praise may be given to it for its facility and eloquence, does not echo the voice of the Good Shepherd, which the sheep hear to their safety: it roars and sounds empty, and sometimes it is pregnant with dangerous examples that bring shame to religion and offence to the faithful; nor is it different in the other duties of the active life, for there can be no fruits of lasting good, or even of short duration, when the dew of heaven is lacking, which the prayer of him that humbleth himself brings down in abundance (Ecclus. 35:21). We cannot at this place refrain from grieving for those who, carried away by pestilential novelties, do not fear to think otherwise and regard the work given to meditation and prayer lost.

Alas, unhappy blindness! Would that they themselves should consider it justly and that some time they should know to what point the neglect and contempt of prayer lead. From these were born pride and arrogance; whence arose those so bitter fruits which Our paternal mind both shrinks from mentioning and desires most earnestly to forget. May God be favorable to Our desires; may He look down benignly upon the wayward and pour out upon them the spirit of grace and prayer in so great an abundance that repenting their error they may willingly seek out, to the joy of all, the ways which they in their evil have deserted, and continue with more caution. Let God Himself be Our witness, as He was once to the Apostle (Phil. 1:8), how We long after them all in the bowels of Jesus Christ. Therefore, O beloved sons, may Our exhortation, "Take heed, watch and pray" (Mark 13:33), which is that of Christ Our Lord, sink deeply into their hearts and yours. Especially let the industry of each and every one be exerted in the zeal for pious meditation; let also your confidence of soul be exercised, asking again and again: "Lord, teach us to pray" (Luke 11:1).

There is one reason in particular which should urge us to the practice of meditation, namely the assistance it gives us in properly caring for souls, which is a very difficult task for us all. While on this matter, the pastoral address of St. Charles is worthy of mention:

> Understand, brethren, that nothing is so necessary to ecclesiastical vigor as mental prayer, preceding, accompanying and following all our actions. "I will sing," says the prophet, "and I will understand" (Ps. 100:2). If you administer the Sacraments, brother, meditate on what you are doing; if you celebrate Mass, meditate on what you are offering; if you pray, meditate on what you say and to whom you are speaking; if you are directing souls, think in what Blood they have been washed.[8]

Wherefore, with justice the Church commands us to repeat frequently the words of David, "Blessed is the man who hath not walked in the counsel of the ungodly . . . his will is in the law of the Lord: and on his law he shall meditate day and night . . . and all whatsoever he shall do shall prosper" (Ps. 1:1–3). For all that We have said, let there be one great incentive that sums up in itself all others. For, if a priest is called another Christ and is the recipient of His power, should he not both become and be considered so, even by the imitation of His deeds? "Let it then be our chief study to meditate on the life of Jesus Christ." [9]

Spiritual reading. It is of great import that a priest assiduously combine together with his daily consideration of divine things the reading of pious books, and especially those which are divinely inspired. So Paul commands Timothy, "be diligent in reading" (1 Tim. 4:13). Likewise Jerome, when instructing Nepotian about the priestly life, inculcates the following: "Never let sacred reading fall from your hands," and he adds the reason: "Learn what you teach, obtain that faithful truth which is according to doctrine, that you may be able to exhort in sane doctrine and convince those that contradict you." And how much, indeed, those priests advance who accustom themselves to this habit; how wisely they preach Christ, and how they impel the minds and hearts of their listeners to better things and direct them to heavenly desires, rather than soothing and appeasing them. But also for another reason, and that profitable to your work, beloved sons, the precept of St. Jerome applies: "Let your hands be always occupied with sacred reading"; [10] for who does not know that the greatest influence that one friend exerts over another is the influence of him who gives candid advice, who aids by his counsel, who corrects, encourages, and recalls from error? "Blessed is the man that findeth a true friend and he that hath found him hath found a treasure" (Ecclus. 25:12; 6:14). Now we ought to make pious books our faithful friends.

They tell us of our duties and they give rules of legitimate discipline; they arouse the heavenly voices that are silent in our souls; they chastise the idleness of our designs; they disturb our deceitful tranquility; they throw into a clear light our less worthy affections that are sometimes disguised; they show the dangers that lie before the imprudent. All these favors they show us with such silent benevolence that we may regard them not only as friends, but as the best of friends. For, indeed, we have them whenever we wish, clinging as it were to our side, ready at any time to assist us in our immediate necessities—whose voice is never harsh, whose advice never partial, and whose words are never timid or deceitful. Many illustrious examples prove the wholesome efficiency of pious books; but the example of Augustine stands forth among others, whose marvelous deeds for the Church received their guidance thence: "Take and read, take and read." "I snatched [the Epistles of Paul the Apostle], opened, read in silence." "As if the light of faith was infused into my heart, the shadows of every doubt rolled away." [11] But, alas! it often happens in our day, that members of the clergy are gradually affected by the shadows of doubts and the strangeness of the age, precisely because they prefer other books and every kind and species of periodicals to divine and pious writings, and those which they prefer are filled with tempting errors and deceptions. Beware, beloved sons, trust not your mature and advanced age, and do not allow yourselves to be deluded by the deceitful hope that you can better provide for the common good. Let those exact limits be observed which the laws of the Church determine, and which prudence and love of self suggest; for if poison of this kind is once admitted into the soul, rarely can the evils of destruction thus conceived be avoided.

Besides, the advantages gained from pious reading and the meditation of heavenly doctrines will certainly be more abundant, if the priest should form some scheme by which he may know whether he is religiously striving to carry out in his life what he has read and meditated.

Examination of conscience. There is a certain document of Chrysostom's especially suited to the priest, which applies most fittingly to the matter at hand. Every night before going to sleep, "Examine your conscience, demand a reckoning from it and whatever evil plans you began during the day, tear to pieces, dissect, and from these take your punishment." [12] How good this practice is and how productive of Christian virtue, those who are more advanced in the love of the Master succeed most excellently in teaching, by their admonitions and exhortations. We are pleased to refer to that well-known passage from the teaching of St. Bernard: "Examine your life daily, as a curious explorer of your own integrity. Weigh carefully how much you are advancing, or how much you are receding. Strive to know yourself. Put all your transgressions before your eyes; place yourself before yourself as before another and thus weep over yourself." [13] Even in this regard, it would be truly disgraceful, if this sentence of Christ's should come to pass, "the children of this world . . . are more prudent than the children of the light" (Luke 16:8). You can see with what vigilance men care for their worldly affairs; how often they look over their accounts and receipts; how accurately and closely they make their calculations; how they grieve over the losses they sustain, and how eagerly they strive to repair them. But, we whose souls burn perhaps to acquire honors, to foster some private interests, to obtain some unique commendation and praise by our knowledge, we oftentimes pursue our greatest and most difficult business, that of acquiring sanctity, in a half-hearted, languid manner. For we scarcely collect our senses and explore the depths of our souls; and these, therefore, grow like the vine of the sluggish man of which it is written: "I passed by the field of the slothful man, and by the vineyard of the foolish man: And behold, it was all filled with nettles and thorns had covered the face thereof, and the stone wall was broken down" (Prov. 24: 30–31).

The matter becomes serious since it is surrounded with ever-increasing bad examples, which are harmful in the greatest degree to priestly virtue, so that there is need of proceeding more cautiously, day by day, and of striving more earnestly. Now, it is known by experience that he who censured himself often for his thoughts, words and deeds is stronger in soul, both for hating and fleeing evil and for desiring and loving good. It has all been the result of experience that these misfortunes and losses occur to the one who declines that tribunal where equity sits in judgment and conscience stands accused and accusing. In him you may desire in vain that circumspection of conduct, so much approved in the life of every Christian, of avoiding even less serious faults, and the soul's dread of wrong-doing, which is especially befitting a priest, who should fear even the slightest offense to God. Moreover, indifference and neglect of himself sometimes go so far as not to heed the sacrament of penance, which is the greatest gift that Christ in His unbounded mercy has bestowed upon human weakness. It certainly cannot be denied, and the fact is greatly to be deplored, which often happens, that he who deters others from sinning by the lightning force of his sacred eloquence, should feel no such fear for himself, and become insensible to sin; that he who exhorts and encourages others not to delay in cleansing their souls of the defilements of sin by acts of due religion, should himself do this so slothfully and delay even for months; that he knows how to pour the salutary oil and wine into the wounds of others, while he himself lies wounded by the way and will not seek, in prudence, the saving hand of a brother, though it be almost within his grasp. Alas! how many evils have happened far and wide, and are happening today, unworthy of God and His Church, a menace to the Christian flocks and a detriment to the priestly character. While We, beloved sons, from a conscientious sense of duty, consider these evils, Our soul is oppressed with grief and in Our groaning We cry out: Woe to the priest who cannot maintain his dignity, but pollutes the name of the holy God, before whom he ought to be holy. The corruption of those who are in the highest places is the most abject of all others. "Great is the dignity of priests, but great their fall if they sin. We rejoice at their dignity, but we tremble at their ruin; there is not so much joy for having obtained the highest honors as there is sorrow for having fallen from the most sublime." [14] Woe, then, to the priest, who, forgetful of himself, forsakes the pursuit of prayer; who refuses the food of spiritual reading; who never enters his own heart to hear the voice of his accusing conscience. Neither the callousness of his seared conscience, nor the laments of Mother Church will move him until those terrible judgments come upon him: "Blind the heart of this people, and make their ears heavy, and shut their eyes: lest they see with their eyes and hear with their ears and understand with their heart and be converted, and I heal them" (Isa. 6:10). May the God who is rich in mercy avert this sad omen from each of you, beloved sons, He who sees Our heart, that is filled with bitterness toward no one, but inflamed with the charity of pastor and father toward all. "For what is our hope, or joy, or crown of glory, if not you before our Lord Jesus Christ at his coming?" (1 Thess. 2:19).

But you yourself know, wherever you are, into what times the Church in the hidden designs of God has fallen. Behold, likewise, and consider what a holy office you possess, that, since you have been given such honor and such dignity, you will strive to be equal to it and assist it in distress. And so there is need, especially now, if ever, of ripe virtue, virtue that shines in example, vigilant, industrious, ready to do for Christ and to suffer. Nor is there anything which We desire more earnestly and ask of you all. Let purity, the choicest ornament of our order, flourish among you in honor undefiled, by the splendor of which the priest is made like to the angels and becomes more venerated among the Christian people and more fruitful in holy works. May reverence and obedience flourish with perpetual increase, the reverence and obedience promised in solemn rite to those whom the Divine Spirit has elected the rulers of the Church: and especially let your minds and spirits be fettered by the ever closer bonds of fidelity in that allegiance which is most justly due this Apostolic See. May charity abound in all—charity, which never seeks what belongs to itself, so that you may check the incentives of envious contention and greedy ambition which goad on humanity, and may all your desires unite in fraternal rivalry to the one end of increasing God's glory.

Priestly charity. The benefits of your charity, "the great multitude of languishing, blind, lame, poor," in the greatest misery await you; or in other words, great numbers of young men, the dearest hope of the state and religion await you, surrounded as they are on all sides by deceits and corruptions. Be zealous, therefore, not only in imparting the sacred truths of the catechism, which we commend again and again, but strive also with whatever resources of wisdom and skill you may have at your command, to merit well and highly from all men. Assisting, defending, remedying, peacemaking, you will, at length, desire and almost thirst for the winning or the retaining of souls to Christ. But alas; how energetically, how laboriously, how fearlessly is work inaugurated and pressed forward by His enemies for the immeasurable destruction of souls! On account of this glory of her charity, the Catholic Church rejoices and glories in her clergy, which is preaching the gospel of Christianity and is bringing salvation and culture even to the barbarous races, where, by their great labors consecrated by the shedding of no little blood, the realm of Christ is extended, day by day, and the holy faith is ornamented more richly by new decorations. But if, beloved sons, contention, wrangling and calumny be the only response to the acts of charity which you have performed, as is often the case, do not on that account succumb to sadness. "Do not grow tired of well-doing" (2 Thess. 3:13). Before your eyes may be seen phalanxes of those who, remarkable in numbers as well as in deeds, and following the example of the Apostles, went rejoicing in the midst of the harshest calumnies for Christ's sake, and blessed those who cursed them. And, indeed, we are the sons and brothers of the Saints, whose names shine in the book of life, whose praises the Church sings. "Let us not stain our glory" (1 Mach. 9:10).

Renewal of the priestly spirit. And with a renewed and increased spirit of priestly grace in the ranks of the clergy, Our proposals for further improvement, no matter how great they are, will, with God's help, be of far more avail. Wherefore, it seems proper to add a few words to what We have before said as a convenient assistance for retaining and fostering this grace. First, the plan which is known and approved by some, but surely has not been tried by all, namely, the pious retreat of the soul to spiritual exercises, as they are called; this should be done yearly, if it is possible, without violating the commands of the Bishops, either alone or together with others, and the latter plan is preferred as it has been productive of better results. We Ourselves have already sufficiently extolled the advantages of this system, since We have published many decrees of the same nature which pertain to the training of the Roman Clergy.[15]

Nor will it be of less profit to souls, if a monthly retreat, for a few hours, is held either privately or in common, and We are glad to see this custom already introduced in some places, the Bishops favoring the plan and sometimes presiding.

Besides, it is in Our heart to commend another suggestion: a closer union among priests, as befits brothers, which the authority of the Bishop should strengthen and moderate. This, indeed, is to be commended, that they form a society to help one another in adversity, to defend their name and office against hostile attacks and to promote other such objects. But surely it is of more profit to enter an association to cultivate sacred doctrine and especially to retain by means of greater solicitude the holy intention of their vocation, and to promote the interests of souls by comparing together their plans and forces. The annals of the Church bear witness to the fact that in those times in which the priests lived a certain common life, innumerable good results were derived from such companionship. Why not recall something like this to our own age, fitted to the different places and duties of the priests. May We not hope surely for those former results, to the joy of the Church? And there are, indeed, societies of this kind formed with the approbation of the Bishops, and all the more beneficial, the sooner one enters them at the very beginning of his priesthood. We Ourselves fostered one in our episcopal office, having known its worth by experience, and the same one even now and others We regard with special benevolence. These helps to sacerdotal grace and those also which the watchful prudence of your Bishops may suggest, as opportunity offers, so esteem and so cherish, beloved sons, that more and more day by day, you may "walk in a manner worthy of the calling with which you were called" (Eph. 4:1), honoring your ministry, and fulfilling the will of God in you, which is "your sanctification."

Thus Our principal thoughts and anxieties are laid before you; therefore with Our eyes raised to heaven as suppliants, We frequently repeat in the voice of Christ the Lord over the universal clergy, "Holy Father . . . sanctify them!" (John 17:11, 17). We rejoice that many of the faithful, solicitous for your common good and that of the Church, are praying with us; nay, even it is a joy to feel that there are many souls of a more generous spirit, not only in the sacred cloisters, but in the midst of the busy world, who for the same reason offer themselves in never ending combat votive victims to God. May God in heaven receive their pure and excellent prayers in the odor of sweetness, and not refuse these Our most humble supplications. May He favor Us, We pray, in His clemency and foresight, and may He pour forth upon the entire clergy the treasures of grace, of charity, and of every virtue, from the most sacred Heart of His Blessed Son. Lastly, We are most happy to give you Our heartfelt thanks, beloved sons, for the prayers for happiness, which you eagerly and with increased piety have offered up for Us, on this anniversary of the fiftieth year of Our priesthood and We wish to entrust Our prayers for you to the care of the great Virgin Mother, Queen of the Apostles, so that they may be more powerful. For she taught by her example those first happy fruits of the sacred order how to persevere united in prayer, until they were clothed with heavenly virtue; and she made that virtue much more abundant in them with the aid of her prayers, and she strengthened and fortified them with counsel, so that their labors were most happily fruitful. We desire, furthermore, beloved sons, that your hearts rejoice in the peace of Christ and in the joy of the Holy Spirit, by favor of the Apostolic Benediction, which We now bestow upon you all with deepest affection.

Given at Rome, at St. Peter's, on the fourth of August, 1908, at the beginning of the sixth year of Our Pontificate.[16]

Pius X, Pope

REFERENCES

1. St. John Chrysostom, *Hom.* 82 *in Mt., n.* 5.
2. *Epist.* 52, *ad Nepotianum, n.* 5.
3. *Sess. XXII, de Reform., c. i.*
4. Leo XIII, *Testem benevolentiae,* Jan. 22, 1899.
5. *De precatione,* 1.
6. *Hom.* 4, *ex.* 50.
7. *De Consideratione, I,* 7.
8. *Ex orationibus ad clerum.*
9. *De imit. Chr., I,* 1.
10. *Epist.* 58, *ad Paulinum, n.* 6.
11. *Conf.,* VIII, 12.
12. *Exposit. in Ps.* 4.
13. *Meditationes piissimae, c. V.*
14. St. Jerome, *in Ez.* 12:44.
15. *Epist. Experiendo, ad Card. in Urbe Vicarium,* Dec. 27, 1904.
16. *ASS,* 41:555–577.

CHAPTER 8

Quam Singulari* *August 8, 1910, Decree on the Age of Children Who Are to be Admitted to First Holy Communion*

THE PAGES of the Gospel show clearly how special was that love for children which Christ showed while He was on earth. It was His delight to be in their midst; He was wont to lay His hands on them; He embraced them; and He blessed them. At the same time He was not pleased when they would be driven away by the disciples, whom He rebuked gravely with these words: "Let the little children come to me, and do not hinder them, for of such is the kingdom of God." [1] It is clearly seen how highly He held their innocence and the open simplicity of their souls on that occasion when He called a little child to Him and said to the disciples: "Amen, I say to you, unless you turn and become like little children, you will not enter into the kingdom of heaven. . . . And whoever receives one such little child for my sake, receives me." [2]

The Catholic Church, bearing this in mind, took care even from the beginning to bring the little ones to Christ through Eucharistic Communion, which was administered even to nursing infants. This, as was prescribed in almost all ancient Ritual books, was done at Baptism until the thirteenth century, and this custom prevailed in some places even later. It is still found in the Greek and Oriental Churches. But to remove the danger that infants might eject the Consecrated Host, the custom obtained from the beginning of administering the Eucharist to them under the species of wine only.

Infants, however, not only at the time of Baptism, but also frequently thereafter were admitted to the sacred repast. In some churches it was the custom to give the Eucharist to the children immediately after the clergy; in others, the small fragments which remained after the Communion of the adults were given to the children.

This practice later died out in the Latin Church, and children were not

* *Quam Singulari* was translated by Joseph Collins, SS., DD., Ph.D., and appears in *Catechetical Documents of Pope Pius X* (Paterson, N. J., Saint Anthony Guild Press).

permitted to approach the Holy Table until they had come to the use of reason and had some knowledge of this august Sacrament. This new practice, already accepted by certain local councils, was solemnly confirmed by the Fourth Council of the Lateran, in 1215, which promulgated its celebrated Canon XXI, whereby sacramental Confession and Holy Communion were made obligatory on the faithful after they had attained the use of reason, in these words: "All the faithful of both sexes shall, after reaching the years of discretion, make private confession of all their sins to their own priest at least once a year, and shall, according to their capacity, perform the enjoined penance; they shall also devoutly receive the Sacrament of Holy Eucharist at least at Easter time unless on the advice of their own priest, for some reasonable cause, it be deemed well to abstain for a while."

The Council of Trent,[3] in no way condemning the ancient practice of administering the Eucharist to children before they had attained the use of reason, confirmed the Decree of the Lateran Council and declared anathema those who held otherwise: "If anyone denies that each and all Christians of both sexes are bound, when they have attained the years of discretion, to receive Communion every year at least at Easter, in accordance with the precept of Holy Mother Church, let him be anathema."[4]

In accord with this Decree of the Lateran Council, still in effect, the faithful are obliged, as soon as they arrive at the years of discretion, to receive the Sacraments of Penance and Holy Eucharist at least once a year.

However, in the precise determination of "the age of reason or discretion" not a few errors and deplorable abuses have crept in during the course of time. There were some who maintained that one age of discretion must be assigned to reception of the Sacrament of Penance and another to the Holy Eucharist. They held that for Confession the age of discretion is reached when one can distinguish right from wrong, hence can commit sin; for Holy Eucharist, however, a greater age is required in which a fuller knowledge of matters of faith and a better preparation of the soul can be had. As a consequence, owing to various local customs and opinions, the age determined for the reception of First Communion was placed at ten years or twelve, and in places fourteen years or even more were required; and until that age children and youth were prohibited from Eucharistic Communion.

This practice of preventing the faithful from receiving on the plea of safeguarding the august Sacrament has been the cause of many evils. It happened that children in their innocence were forced away from the embrace of Christ and deprived of the food of their interior life; and from this it also happened that in their youth, destitute of this strong help, surrounded by so many temptations, they lost their innocence and fell into vicious habits even before tasting of the Sacred Mysteries. And even if a thorough instruction and a careful Sacramental Confession should precede Holy Communion, which does not everywhere occur, still the loss of first innocence is always to be deplored and might have been avoided by reception of the Eucharist in more tender years.

No less worthy of condemnation is that practice which prevails in many places of prohibiting from Sacramental Confession children who have not yet made their First Holy Communion, or of not giving them absolution. Thus it happens that they, perhaps having fallen into serious sin, remain in that very dangerous state for a long time.

But worse still is the practice in certain places which prohibits children who have not yet made their First Communion from being fortified by the Holy Viaticum, even when they are in imminent danger of death; and thus, when they die they are buried with the rites due to infants and are deprived of the prayers of the Church.

Such is the injury caused by those who insist on extraordinary preparations for First Communion, beyond what is reasonable; and they doubtless do not realize that such precautions proceed from the errors of the Jansenists who contended that the Most Holy Eucharist is a reward rather than a remedy for human frailty. The Council of Trent indeed teaches otherwise when it calls the Eucharist, "An antidote whereby we may be freed from daily faults and be preserved from mortal sins." [5] This doctrine was not long ago strongly emphasized by a Decree of the Sacred Congregation of the Council given on December 20, 1905. It declared that daily approach to Communion is open to all, old and young, and two conditions only are required; the state of grace and a right intention.

Moreover, the fact that in ancient times the remaining particles of the Sacred Species were even given to nursing infants seems to indicate that no extraordinary preparation should now be demanded of children who are in the happy state of innocence and purity of soul, and who, amidst so many dangers and seductions of the present time, have a special need of this heavenly food.

The abuses which we are condemning are due to the fact that they who distinguished one age of discretion for Penance and another for the Eucharist did so in error. The Lateran Council required one and the same age for reception of either Sacrament when it imposed the one obligation of Confession and Communion. Therefore, the age of discretion for Confession is the time when one can distinguish between right and wrong, that is, when one arrives at a certain use of reason, and so similarly, for Holy Communion is required the age when one can distinguish between the Bread of the Holy Eucharist and ordinary bread—again the age at which a child attains the use of reason.

The principal interpreters of the Lateran Council and contemporaries of that period had the same teaching concerning this Decree. The history of the Church reveals that a number of synods and episcopal decrees beginning with the twelfth century, shortly after the Lateran Council, admitted children of seven years of age to First Communion. There is moreover the word of St. Thomas Aquinas, who is an authority of the highest order, which reads: "When children begin to have some use of reason, so that they can conceive a devotion toward this Sacrament (the Eucharist), then this Sacrament can be given to them." [6] Ledesma thus explains these words: "I say, in accord with common opinion, that the Eucharist is to be given to all who have the use of reason, and just as soon as they attain the use of reason, even though at the time the child may have only a confused notion of what he is doing." [7] Vasquez comments on the same words of St. Thomas as follows: "When a child has once arrived at the use of reason he is immediately bound by the divine law from which not even the Church can dispense him." [8] The same is the teaching of St. Antoninus, who wrote: "But when a child is capable of doing wrong, that is of committing a mortal sin, then he is bound by the precept of Confession and consequently of Communion." [9] The Council of Trent also forces us to the same conclusion when it declares: "Children who have not attained the use of reason are not by any necessity bound to Sacramental Communion of the Eucharist." [10] It assigns as the only reason the fact that they cannot commit sin: "they cannot at that age lose the grace of the sons of God already acquired." From this it is the mind of the Council that children are held to Communion by necessity and by precept when they are capable of losing grace by sin. The words of the Roman Synod, held under Benedict XIII, are in agreement with this in teaching that the obligation to receive the Eucharist begins, "after boys and girls attain the age of discretion, that is, at the age in which they can distinguish this Sacramental food, which is none other than the true Body of Jesus Christ, from common and ordinary bread; and that they know how to receive it with proper religious spirit." [11] The Roman Catechism adds this: "At what age children are to receive the Holy Mysteries no one can better judge than their father and the priest who is their confessor. For it is their duty to ascertain by questioning the children whether they have any understanding of this admirable Sacrament and if they have any desire for it." [12] From all this it is clear that the age of discretion for receiving Holy Communion is that at which the child knows the difference between the Eucharistic Bread and ordinary, material bread, and can therefore approach the altar with proper devotion. Perfect knowledge of the things of faith, therefore, is not required, for an elementary knowledge suffices—some knowledge (*aliqua cognitio*); similarly full use of reason is not required, for a certain beginning of the use of reason, that is, some use of reason (*aliqualis usus rationis*) suffices. To postpone Communion, therefore, until later and to insist on a more mature age for its reception must be absolutely discouraged, and indeed such practice was condemned more than once by the Holy See. Thus Pope Pius IX, of happy memory, in a Letter of Cardinal Antonelli to the Bishops of France, March 12, 1866, severely condemned the growing custom existing in some dioceses of postponing the First Communion of children until more mature years, and at the same time sharply disapproved of the age limit which had been assigned. Again, the Sacred Congregation of the Council, on March 15, 1851, corrected a prescription of the Provincial Council of Rouen, which prohibited children under twelve years of age from receiving First Communion. Similarly, this Sacred Congregation of the Discipline of the Sacraments, on March 25, 1910, in a question proposed to it from Strasburg whether children of twelve or fourteen years could be admitted to Holy Communion, answered: "Boys and girls are to be admitted to the Holy Table when they arrive at the years of discretion or the use of reason."

After careful deliberation on all these points, this Sacred Congregation of the Discipline of the Sacraments, in a general meeting held on July 15, 1910, in order to remove the above-mentioned abuses and to bring about that children even from their tender years may be united to Jesus Christ, may live His life, and obtain protection from all dangers of corruption, has deemed it needful to prescribe the following rules which are to be observed everywhere for the First Communion of children.

1. The age of discretion, both for Confession and for Holy Communion, is the time when a child begins to reason, that is about the seventh year, more or less. From that time on begins the obligation of fulfilling the precept of both Confession and Communion.

2. A full and perfect knowledge of Christian doctrine is not necessary either for First Confession or for First Communion. Afterwards, however, the child will be obliged to learn gradually the entire Catechism according to his ability.

3. The knowledge of religion which is required in a child in order to be properly prepared to receive First Communion is such that he will understand according to his capacity those Mysteries of faith which are necessary as a means of salvation (*necessitate medii*) and that he can distinguish between the Bread of the Eucharist and ordinary, material bread, and thus he may receive Holy Communion with a devotion becoming his years.

4. The obligation of the precept of Confession and Communion which binds the child particularly affects those who have him in charge, namely, parents, confessor, teachers and the pastor. It belongs to the father, or the person taking his place, and to the confessor, according to the Roman Catechism, to admit a child to his First Communion.

5. The pastor should announce and hold a General Communion of the children once a year or more often, and he should on these occasions admit

not only the First Communicants but also others who have already approached the Holy Table with the above-mentioned consent of their parents or confessor. Some days of instruction and preparation should be previously given to both classes of children.

6. Those who have charge of the children should zealously see to it that after their First Communion these children frequently approach the Holy Table, even daily if possible, as Jesus Christ and Mother Church desire, and let this be done with a devotion becoming their age. They must also bear in mind that very grave duty which obliges them to have the children attend the public Catechism classes; if this is not done then they must supply religious instruction in some other way.

7. The custom of not admitting children to Confession or of not giving them absolution when they have already attained the use of reason must be entirely abandoned. The Ordinary shall see to it that this condition ceases absolutely, and he may if necessary use legal measures accordingly.

8. The practice of not administering the Viaticum and Extreme Unction to children who have attained the use of reason, and of burying them with the rite used for infants is a most intolerable abuse. The Ordinary should take very severe measures against those who do not give up the practice.

His Holiness, Pope Pius X, in an audience granted on the seventh day of this month, approved all the above decisions of this Sacred Congregation, and ordered this Decree to be published and promulgated. He furthermore commanded that all the Ordinaries make this Decree known not only to the pastors and the clergy, but also to the people; and he wishes that it be read in the vernacular every year at the Easter time. The Ordinaries shall give an account of the observance of this Decree together with other diocesan matters every five years. All things to the contrary notwithstanding.

Given at Rome, from the Office of the aforesaid Sacred Congregation, August 8, 1910.

D. Cardinal Ferrata, *Prefect*
Ph. Giustini, *Secretary*

REFERENCES

1. Mark 10:14.
2. Matt. 18:3–5.
3. *Sess. XXI, de Communione, cap.* 4.
4. *Sess. XIII, de Eucharistia, cap.* 8, *can.* 9.
5. *Idem, cap.* 2.
6. *Summa Theol., III, q.* 80, *a.* 9, *ad* 3.
7. *In St. Thom. III, q.* 80, *a.* 9, *dub.* 6.
8. *In III P., S. Thom., disp.* 214, *n.* 43.
9. *Pars III, tit.* 14, *cap.* 2, 5.
10. *Sess. XXI, cap.* 4.
11. *Istruzione per quei che debbono la prima volta ammettersi alla S. Communione (Append. XXX, Pars* 11).
12. *Pars II, De Sacr. Euchar., n.* 63.

CHAPTER 9

Divino Afflatu *November 1, 1911, Apostolic Constitution on the New Arrangement of the Psalter in the Roman Breviary*

WITHOUT a doubt the Psalms, composed under Divine Inspiration and gathered together in the Sacred Books, have from the very beginning of the Church not only contributed wonderfully to foster the piety of the faithful, who offer up "a sacrifice of praise always to God, that is, fruit of lips praising His name," [1] but also, according to a custom dating from the time of the Old Law, have played an outstanding role in the Sacred Liturgy and Divine Office. Basil calls these "the natural voice of the Church," [2] and Our Predecessor, Urban VIII, calls psalmody "the daughter of her hymnody which is constantly sung before the throne of God and the Lamb." [3] This, according to Athanasius, teaches men (whose chief duty is to perform acts of divine worship) "how to glorify God and what words they can best use in praising Him." [4] On this subject Augustine makes the beautiful remark: "God has praised Himself to show man how to praise Him well. Since God first chose to praise Himself, man has found a way to praise Him." [5]

Moreover, the Psalms possess a very remarkable power for arousing men's minds to strive after every virtue. Although "all our Scripture, both Old and New, is divinely inspired and useful for doctrine, as is written; nevertheless the Book of Psalms is like a paradise adorned with the fruits of all the other books. It sends forth joyful music, mingling its own songs in psalmody with the others." Such are the words of Athanasius.[6] In the same place he rightly adds, "It seems to me that the Psalms are like a mirror in which the singer contemplates himself and the movements of his soul and then in such a spirit recites them." [7] Thus Augustine remarks in his *Confessions,* "I wept at the beauty of Your hymns and canticles, and was powerfully moved at the sweet sound of Your Church's singing. Those sounds flowed into my ears, and the truth streamed into my heart: so that my feeling of devotion overflowed, and the tears ran from my eyes, and I was happy in them." [8] Who can remain unmoved by the numerous passages of the Psalms which loudly proclaim the tremendous majesty, omnipotence, unspeakable justice, goodness, or clemency of God, as well as His other infinite praises? Who can fail to be inspired by those thanksgivings for benefits received from God, or by those confident prayers for benefits desired, or those cries of the penitent soul for his sins? Who does not admire the Psalmist's accounting of the acts of Divine Goodness toward the people of Israel and the human race when he hands down the teachings of heavenly wisdom? Who is not inflamed with love by the picture of Christ the Redeemer so lovingly depicted? In all the Psalms Saint Augustine heard "His voice, praising or mourning, rejoicing in hope or yearning for fulfillment." [9]

The decrees of the Roman Pontiffs, the canons of the Councils, and the rules of monastic institutes have all wisely provided that the members of both branches of the clergy should chant or recite the entire Psalter every week. Our Predecessors, Saint Pius V, Clement VIII, and Urban VIII religiously observed this venerable law in revising the Roman Breviary. Even at the present time the Psalter should be entirely recited within the week. The changed condition of things, however, has frequently hindered this complete recitation.

In the course of time the number of those whom, after their mortal life, the Church has been accustomed to reckon among the citizens of heaven and to set before the Christian people as patrons and models has been constantly increasing. In their honor the offices of the saints have gradually been lengthened to such an extent that now the Sunday and ferial offices are hardly ever heard. Consequently many Psalms have been neglected. Yet these, as well as the others, are, according to Saint Ambrose, "the people's benediction, God's praise, and humanity's glory: everyone's rejoicing speech and the voice of the Church; a harmonious profession of faith and a total dedication to authority; a joyous liberty, gladsome cry, and joyous echo." [10] More than once prudent and pious men have bitterly complained about this omission. They claim it had deprived those in Sacred Orders of many admirable aids for praising the Lord. They allege that it destroyed that desirable variety in prayer which human weakness needs so very much in order to pray worthily, attentively, and devoutly. Basil expressed this thought in the following words: "Strangely enough, the soul often grows old in monotony. However, by changing and varying the psalms and chant for the different hours, the soul's desire is rekindled and attention restored." [11]

No wonder, then, that many Bishops throughout the world have expressed their opinions on this matter to the Apostolic See. In the Vatican Council especially, they asked, among other things, that the ancient practice of reciting the whole Psalter within the week might be restored as far as possible. However, in such a way, they added, that the burden would not be any heavier for the clergy, whose labors in the vineyard of the sacred ministry are now increased because the number of the laborers has decreased. These petitions were also Our Own before We assumed the Pontificate. Together with these, appeals have since come from others of Our Venerable Brethren and from pious men. We have, therefore, decided to grant that request. That concession, however, must be made so carefully that the recitation of the entire Psalter within the week, on the one hand, will not diminish the cultus of the saints and, on the other hand, will not make the burden of the Divine Office heavier, but actually lighter. Therefore We beseeched the Father of Lights and asked for the aid of holy prayers on its behalf. Then, following the example of Our Predecessor, We appointed a group of learned and zealous men to collaborate by study and consultation in finding some plan of execution which would be in accordance with Our wishes. They have fulfilled the charge entrusted to them and have brought forth a new arrangement of the Psalter. It has already been approved by the Cardinals of the Congregation of Sacred Rites. Since it is in complete harmony with Our Own mind, We have, therefore, ratified it in all its details; that is, regarding the order and partition of the Psalms, the antiphons, versicles, and hymns with their rubrics and rules. Furthermore, We have ordered an authentic edition of it to be set up and published by Our Vatican Printing Press.

Since the arrangement of the Psalter is intimately connected with the whole Divine Office and the Liturgy, everyone can plainly see that this decree is Our first step in correcting the Roman Breviary and Missal. For this work, however, We shall soon appoint a special Council, or, as they say, a Commission of experts. In the meantime, since this occasion presents the opportunity, We have decided to make some changes which are found prescribed in the accompanying rubrics. The first of these changes is as follows: In the recitation of the Divine Office the appointed lessons of Sacred Scripture with the responsories of the season should be restored to their rightful honor by more frequent usage. Secondly, in the Sacred Liturgy those most ancient Sunday and ferial Masses (especially the Lenten ferials) should regain their proper place.

In virtue of this letter, We therefore first of all abolish the order of the Psalter as it now exists in the Roman Breviary. We absolutely forbid its use after January 1, 1913. From that day forward, in all the churches of the secular and regular clergy, in the monasteries, orders, congregations, and religious institutes, each and every one, who by office or custom recite the canonical hours according to the Roman Breviary issued by Saint Pius V and revised by Clement VIII, Urban VIII and Leo XIII, We command the scrupulous observance of the Psalter according to the form We have approved and decreed to be published by the Vatican Printing Press. At the same time We confirm the penalties prescribed by law against all those who neglect their duty of reciting the canonical hours every day. Let such persons understand that they do not fulfill their serious obligation unless they use Our new arrangement of the Psalter.

Therefore, We command all the Patriarchs, Archbishops, Bishops, Abbots, and other prelates of churches (not even excluding the Cardinal Archpriests of the patriarchal basilicas of Rome) to take care to introduce at the appointed time in their respective dioceses, churches, or monasteries the Psalter with the rules and rubrics We have arranged. We order the Psalter, together with its rules and rubrics, to be used and observed without alteration by all others who are under the obligation of reciting or chanting the canonical hours. Meanwhile, it shall be lawful for everybody (the chanters also if the majority of the chapter agree) to use the new order of the Psalter immediately after its publication.

We publish, declare, sanction and decree that this Apostolic letter is and always shall be valid and effective, notwithstanding Apostolic constitutions and ordinances, general and special, or anything else to the contrary. Let no one, therefore, contemptuously ignore or boldly oppose Our abolition, revocation, permission, ordinance, precept, statute, indult, mandate and will. If any one does, let him know that he will incur the indignation of Almighty God and His Apostles, the Blessed Peter and Paul.

Given at Saint Peter's, Rome, November 1, the feast of All Saints, in the year of the Incarnation of Our Lord, 1911, the ninth year of Our Pontificate.

A. CARD. AGLIARDI,
Chancellor of the Holy Roman Church

FR. SEB. CARD. MARTINELLI,
Prefect of the Sacred Congregation of Rites

REFERENCES

1. Heb. 13:15.
2. *Homil. in Ps.*, 1, *n.* 2.
3. Bull *Divinam Psalmodiam.*
4. *Epist. ad Marcellinum in interpret. Psalmor.*, *n.* 10.
5. *In Psalm.* 144, *n.* 1.
6. *Epist. ad Marcell.*, *n.* 2 & *n.* 12.
7. *Lib. IX, cap.* 6.
8. *In Ps.* 42, *n.* 1.
9. *Enarrat. in Ps.* 1, *n.* 9.
10. *Regulae fusius tractatae, interrog.* 37, *n.* 5.

CHAPTER 10

Doctoris Angelici* *June 29, 1914, Motu Proprio on the Study of Thomistic Philosophy in Catholic Schools*

NO TRUE Catholic has ever ventured to call in question the opinion of the Angelic Doctor that: The regulation of studies is the special concern of the authority of the Holy See by which the universal Church is governed and the need is met by the establishment of Universities.[1] We have already discharged this great duty of Our office elsewhere, and more particularly on the 1st September, 1910, when in the Letter *Sacrorum Antistitum,* addressed to all Bishops and Superiors of Religious Orders duly charged with the duty of educating young men for the priesthood, We counselled them in the first place as follows: "So far as studies are concerned, it is Our will and We hereby explicitly ordain that the Scholastic philosophy be considered as the basis of sacred studies. . . . And what is of capital importance in prescribing that Scholastic philosophy is to be followed, We have in mind particularly the philosophy which has been transmitted to us by St. Thomas Aquinas. It is Our desire that all the enactments of Our Predecessor in respect thereto be maintained in full force; and, where need be, We renew and conform them and order them to be strictly observed by all concerned. Let Bishops urge and compel their observance in future in any Seminary in which they may have been neglected. The same injunction applies also to Superiors of Religious Orders."

Now because the word We used in the text of that letter recommending the philosophy of Aquinas was "particularly," and not "exclusively," certain persons persuaded themselves that they were acting in conformity to Our Will or at any rate not actively opposing it, in adopting indiscriminately and adhering to the philosophical opinions of any other Doctor of the School, even though such opinions were contrary to the principles of St. Thomas. They were greatly deceived. In recommending St. Thomas to Our subjects

* This translation of *Doctoris Angelici* appears in *The Angelic Doctor* by Jacques Maritain (New York, Dial Press).

as supreme guide in the Scholastic philosophy, it goes without saying that Our intention was to be understood as referring above all to those principles upon which that philosophy is based as its foundation. For just as the opinion of certain ancients is to be rejected which maintains that it makes no difference to the truth of the Faith what any man thinks about the nature of creation, provided his opinions on the nature of God be sound, because error with regard to the nature of creation begets a false knowledge of God; so the principles of philosophy laid down by St. Thomas Aquinas are to be religiously and inviolably observed, because they are the means of acquiring such a knowledge of creation as is most congruent with the Faith; [2] of refuting all the errors of all the ages, and of enabling man to distinguish clearly what things are to be attributed to God and to God alone.[3] They also marvellously illustrate the diversity and analogy between God and His works, a diversity and analogy admirably expressed by the Fourth Lateran Council as follows: "The resemblance between the Creator and the creature is such that their still greater dissimilarity cannot fail to be observed." [4] For the rest, the principles of St. Thomas, considered generally and as a whole, contain nothing but what the most eminent philosophers and doctors of the Church have discovered after prolonged reflection and discussion in regard to the particular reasons determining human knowledge, the nature of God and creation, the moral order and the ultimate end to be pursued in life.

St. Thomas perfected and augmented still further by the almost angelic quality of his intellect all this superb patrimony of wisdom which he inherited from his predecessors and applied it to prepare, illustrate and protect sacred doctrine in the minds of men.[5] Sound reason suggests that it would be foolish to neglect it and religion will not suffer it to be in any way attenuated. And rightly, because, if Catholic doctrine is once deprived of this strong bulwark, it is useless to seek the slightest assistance for its defence in a philosophy whose principles are either common to the errors of materialism, monism, pantheism, socialism and modernism, or certainly not opposed to such systems. The reason is that the capital theses in the philosophy of St. Thomas are not to be placed in the category of opinions capable of being debated one way or another, but are to be considered as the foundations upon which the whole science of natural and divine things is based; if such principles are once removed or in any way impaired, it must necessarily follow that students of the sacred sciences will ultimately fail to perceive so much as the meaning of the words in which the dogmas of divine revelation are proposed by the magistracy of the Church.

We therefore desired that all teachers of philosophy and sacred theology should be warned that if they deviated so much as a step, in metaphysics especially, from Aquinas, they exposed themselves to grave risk. We now go further and solemnly declare that those who in their interpretations misrepresent or affect to despise the principles and major theses of this philosophy are not only not following St. Thomas but are even far astray from the saintly Doctor. If the doctrine of any writer or Saint has ever been approved by Us or Our Predecessors with such singular commendation and in such a way that to the commendation were added an invitation and order to propagate and defend it, it may easily be understood that it was commended to the extent that it agreed with the principles of Aquinas or was in no way opposed to them.

We have deemed it Our apostolic duty to make this declaration and order so that the clergy, both regular and secular, may clearly know Our will and mind in a matter of the gravest importance and fulfill Our desire with the appropriate alacrity and diligence. Teachers of Christian philosophy and sacred theology will be particularly zealous in this respect, for they must bear in mind that they have not been entrusted with the duty of teaching in order to impart to their pupils whatever opinions they please, but to instruct them in the most approved doctrines of the Church.

As for sacred theology itself, it is Our desire that the study of it be always illuminated by the light of the philosophy before referred to, but in ordinary clerical seminaries, provided suitable teachers are available, there is no objection to the use of text books containing summaries of doctrines derived from the source of Aquinas. There is an ample supply of excellent works of the kind.

But for the more profound study of this science, as it ought to be studied in Universities and Colleges and in all Seminaries and Institutions which are empowered to grant academic degrees, it is of the first importance that the old system of lecturing on the actual text of the *Summa Theologica*—which should never have been allowed to fall into disuse—be revived; for the reason also that prelections on this book make it easier to understand and to illustrate the solemn decrees of the teaching Church and the acts passed in consequence. For ever since the happy death of the saintly Doctor, the Church has not held a single Council, but he has been present at it with the wealth of his doctrine. The experience of so many centuries has shown and every passing day more clearly proves the truth of the statement made by Our Predecessor John XXII: "He [Thomas Aquinas] enlightened the Church more than all the other Doctors together; a man can derive more profit from his books in one year than from a lifetime spent in pondering the philosophy of others."[6] St. Pius V confirmed this opinion when he ordered the feast of St. Thomas as Doctor to be kept by the universal Church: "But inasmuch as, by the providence of Almighty God, the power and truth of the philosophy of the Angelic Doctor, ever since his enrollment amongst the citizens of Heaven, have confounded, refuted and routed many subsequent heresies, as was so often clearly seen in the past and was lately apparent in the sacred decrees of the Council of Trent, We order that the memory of the Doctor by whose valor the world is daily delivered from pestilential errors be cultivated more than ever before with feelings of pious and grateful devotion." [7] To avoid recapitulating the many other resounding praises of Our Predecessors, We may adopt the following words of Benedict XIV as a summary of all the commendations bestowed upon the writings of Thomas Aquinas, more particularly the *Summa Theologica:* "Numerous Roman Pontiffs, Our Predecessors, have borne glorious testimony to his philosophy. We, also, in the books which We have written on various topics, after by diligent examination perceiving and considering the mind of the Angelic Doctor, have always adhered and subscribed with joy and admiration to his philosophy, and candidly confess that whatever good is to be found in Our own writings is in no way to be attributed to Us, but entirely to so eminent a teacher." [8]

Therefore that "the philosophy of St. Thomas may flourish incorrupt and entire in schools, which is very dear to Our heart," and that "the system of teaching which is based upon the authority and judgment of the individual teacher" and therefore "has a changeable foundation whence many diverse and mutually conflicting opinions arise . . . not without great injury to Christian learning" [9] be abolished forever, it is Our will and We hereby order and command that teachers of sacred theology in Universities, Academies, Colleges, Seminaries and Institutions enjoying by apostolic indult the privilege of granting academic degrees and doctorates in philosophy, use the *Summa Theologica* of St. Thomas as the text of their prelections and comment upon it in the Latin tongue, and let them take particular care to inspire their pupils with a devotion for it.

Such is already the laudable custom of many Institutions. Such was the rule which the sagacious founders of Religious Orders, with the hearty approval of Our Predecessors, desired should be observed in their own houses of study; and the saintly men who came after the time of St. Thomas Aquinas took him and no other for their supreme teacher of philosophy. So also and not otherwise will theology recover its pristine glory and all sacred studies be restored to their order and value and the province of the intellect and reason flower again in a second spring.

In future, therefore, no power to grant academic degrees in sacred theology will be given to any institution unless Our present prescription is religiously observed therein. Institutions or Faculties of Orders and Regular Congregations, also, already in lawful possession of the power of conferring such academic degrees or similar diplomas, even within the limits of their own four walls, shall be deprived of such a privilege and be considered to have been so deprived if, after the lapse of three years, they shall not have religiously obeyed for any reason whatsoever, even beyond their control, this Our injunction.

This is Our Order, and nothing shall be suffered to gainsay it.

Given at Rome, at St. Peter's, on the 29th day of June, 1914, the eleventh year of Our Pontificate.

PIUS X, POPE

REFERENCES

1. *Opusc. Contra impugnantes Dei cultum et religionem, iii.*
2. *Contra Gentiles, ii,* 2, 3.
3. *Ibid., iii. Sum. Theol., I xii,* 4; *liv.* 1.
4. *Decretalis iii, Damnamus ergo.* Cf. St. Thomas, *Quaest. disp., De Scientia Dei, ii.*
5. *In Librum Boethii de Trinitate, quaest. ii,* 3.
6. Consistorial Address of 1318.
7. Bull *Mirabilis Deus,* April 11, 1567.
8. *Acta Cap. Gen. O.P., Vol. XI, p.* 196.
9. Leo XIII, *Epist. Qui te,* June 19, 1886.

religiously observed for any reason whatsoever [illegible] of their country. [illegible]

[illegible]

The [illegible] shall be [illegible]

[illegible]

[illegible] Our [illegible]

[illegible]

REFERENCES

1. [illegible]
2. [illegible]
3. [illegible]
4. [illegible]

[illegible]

Bibliography

This bibliography is merely a selection of those references I came across in preparing this book. No attempt was made to do any excluding since they have all aided me in preparing backgound material, some, naturally, more than others. For a detailed bibliography of biographies, collections, and studies in foreign languages on the life and work of Saint Pius X the reader is referred to: *A Symposium on the Life and Work of Pope Pius X,* pp. 297–300, and, *A Guide to the Encyclicals of the Roman Pontiffs,* pp. 119–142.

.I.

1. *Biography*

Bazin, René. *Pius X.* London, Sands & Co., 1928.

Brown-Olf, Lilian. *Their Name is Pius.* Milwaukee, Bruce Publ. Co., 1941.

Burton, Katherine. *The Great Mantle.* New York, Longmans, Green & Co., 1950.

Collins, Joseph. *Pope Pius X.* Washington, Confraternity of Christian Doctrine, 1945.

Farnum, Mabel A. *The White Knight.* Saint Paul, Catholic Library Series, 1937.

Forbes, F. A. *Life of Pius X.* London, Burns, Oates & Washbourne, 1918.

Galloni, G. *Pope Pius X, the Pope of Favors;* trans. by E. Seton. Rochdale, England, 1914.

Life of His Holiness Pope Pius X. New York, Benziger Bros., 1904.

Merry del Val, Rafaelo Cardinal. *Memories of Pope Pius X.* Westminster, Newman Press, 1951.

Schmitz, E. *Life of Pius X.* New York, American Catholic Truth Society.

Belloc, Hilaire. "The Reign of Pope Pius X." *Tablet,* 197:432–433.

Cushing, Richard J., Abp. "The Cause of Pope Pius X and Devotion to the Holy See." *American Ecclesiastical Review,* 120:178–180.

"Death of Pius X." *Catholic Fortnightly Review,* 21:513–514.

Dever, Daniel A. "Pius the Tenth: An Ecclesiastical Pope." *American Catholic Quarterly Review,* 39:361–394.

Diarista, A. "Pius X: From Venice to the Vatican." *Catholic World,* 77:715–722.

Donnelly, F. B. "Miracles Accepted for the Beatification of Pius X." *Homiletic and Pastoral Review,* 51:836.

Ellard, Gerald. "Pius X and a Liturgical Concept." *Orate Fratres,* 2:11–15.

———. "Pius X and the New Liturgy." *Orate Fratres,* 1:241–246.

Hoare, F. R. "Testimony of a Convert." *Tablet,* 197:435–436, 456–457.

Hunter-Blair, D. O. "Memories of Three Popes." *Dublin Review,* 205:27–31.

"Instaurare Omnia in Christo." *Tablet,* 197:431–432.

Ireland, John, Abp. "The Pontificate of Pius X." *North American Review,* 184:233–245.

Johnson, Humphrey J. T. "A Pontificate in Retrospect." *Tablet,* 197:434–435.
Kenkel, F. P. "Blessed Pius X." *Social Justice Review,* 44:65.
Kenny, M. "The People's Pope." *Catholic Mind,* 10:255–267.
Murphy, John T. "The Golden Jubilee of the Priesthood of Pius X." *American Catholic Quarterly Review,* 33:677–686.
"Pius X, Man, Pope, and Priest." *America,* 11:465–466.
Shahan, Thomas J. "Pius the Tenth." *Catholic University Bulletin,* 20:501–504.
Smiddy, T. W. "Blessed Pius X." *Homiletic and Pastoral Review,* 52:157–160.
Smith, M. P. "Pope Pius X." *Catholic World,* 100:90–99.
Stearns, M. G. "Visit to a Friend." *Commonweal,* 13:657–659.
"The Jubilee Gift to Pius X from His Clergy." *American Ecclesiastical Review,* 39:336–342.
"The Jubilee of Pius X." *The Month,* 112:225–241.
Tucker, Dunstan. "The Council of Trent, Gueranger, and Pius X." *Orate Fratres,* 10:538–544.
Ward, Wilfred. "Pope Pius X." *Dublin Review,* 155:217–225.

2. *Collections and Studies*

Acta Apostolicae Sedis. Romae, Typis Polyglottis Vaticanis, 1909–1914.
Acta Sanctae Sedis. Romae, Directio et Administratio, 1903–1908.
Actes de Pie X. Paris, Maison de La Bonne Presse, vol. I–VIII.
Carlen, Sister Mary Claudia. *A Guide to the Encyclicals of the Roman Pontiffs from Leo XIII to the Present Day, 1878–1937*. New York, H. W. Wilson Co., 1939.
Collins, Joseph B. *Catechetical Documents of Pope Pius X*. Paterson, N. J., Saint Anthony Guild Press, 1946.
Koenig, Harry C. *Principles for Peace: Selections from Papal Documents, Leo XIII to Pius XII*. Washington, National Catholic Welfare Conference, 1943.
Mausbach, Joseph. *Catholic Moral Teaching and Its Antagonists;* trans. by A. M. Buchanan. New York, Joseph F. Wagner Co., 1914.
Rome and the Study of Scripture. St. Meinrad, Ind., Abbey Press, 1943.
Symposium on the Life and Work of Pope Pius X. Washington, Confraternity of Christian Doctrine, 1946.
The Pope and the People: Select Letters and Addresses on Social Questions by Pope Leo XIII, Pope Pius X, Pope Benedict XV, and Pope Pius XI; ed. by Rev. A. Keogh, S.J. London, Catholic Truth Society, 1932.
The Popes and the Priesthood: A Symposium of Papal Documents on the Priesthood. St. Meinrad, Ind., Grail Publication, 1947.
Unger, Dominic J. *Mary Mediatrix*. Paterson, N. J., Saint Anthony Guild Press, 1948.

II.

1. *E SUPREMI APOSTOLATUS*

Original Text: *Acta Sanctae Sedis,* 36:129–139.
Previous Translation: *American Catholic Quarterly Review,* 29:10–19.

Ellard, Gerald. "A Papal Motto and Its Meaning." *Orate Fratres,* 1:141–145.
O'Doherty, John. "The Motto of Pius X." *Irish Ecclesiastical Review,* 20:52–60.
"Reform of Pius X." *The Review,* 11:127–128; 551–553.
"The First Encyclical of Pius X." *Ave Maria,* 57:545–550.

2. *AD DIEM ILLUM*

Original Text: *Acta Sanctae Sedis,* 36:449–462.
Previous Translation: *American Catholic Quarterly Review,* 29:209–221.
"A New Encyclical—The Jubilee of the Immaculate Conception." *Ave Maria,* 58:321–326.
"Apostolic Letter of Pope Pius X Announcing the Jubilee of the Immaculate Conception." *American Ecclesiastical Review,* 29:609–610.
Most, William G. "Blessed Pius X and the Blessed Virgin Mary." *Homiletic and Pastoral Review,* 52:331–314.
O'Malley, Austin. "Mediatrix Omnium Gratiarum." *American Ecclesiastical Review,* 73:225–230.

3. *IUCUNDA SANE*

Original Text: *Acta Sanctae Sedis,* 36:513–529.
Previous Translation: *American Catholic Quarterly Review,* 29:588–603.
Dennehy, W. F. "The Greatest of the Gregories." *Ave Maria,* 58:449–453.
Ellard, Gerald. "Gregory and Pius, Fathers of the Liturgy." *Orate Fratres,* 1:12–16.
"The Encyclical on St. Gergory." *The Month,* 103:502–515.
Walsh, Marie Donegan. "The Thirteenth Gregorian Centenary." *Catholic World,* 79:22–38.

4. *ACERBO NIMIS*

Original Text: *Acta Sanctae Sedis,* 37:613–625.
Previous Translation: *American Catholic Quarterly Review,* 30:426–435.
Brady, J. F. "The Teaching of Christian Doctrine." *Catholic World,* 81:671–680.
Collins, J. B. "Blessed Pius X and Religious Education." *Catholic School Journal,* 51:221–222.
Cushing, Richard J., Abp. "Restoring All Things in Christ." Address delivered to the Eighth National Congress of the Confraternity of Christian Doctrine, Boston Garden, Oct. 27, 1946.
Emling, John F. "Exceedingly Harsh beyond Measure." *Journal of Religious Instruction,* 16:298–301.
"Encyclical Letter of Pius X on the Teaching of the Catechism." *Catholic Fortnightly Review,* 12:322–323.
Hogan, J. F. "Encyclical of Pope Pius X." *Irish Ecclesiastical Review,* 17:481–484.
"The Encyclical of Pius X on the Teaching of Christian Doctrine." *American Ecclesiastical Review,* 29:599–611.

5. *IL FERMO PROPOSITO*

Original Text: *Acta Sanctae Sedis,* 37:741–767.
"Fundamentals of 'a Real Apostolate.'" *Social Justice Review,* 39:375–376.
Sommers, J. V. "Pius X and Catholic Action." *Review for Religious,* 5:3–16.

6. *TRIBUS CIRCITER*

Original Text: *Acta Sanctae Sedis,* 39:129–134.
Previous Translation: *Catholic University Bulletin,* 12:391–395.

7. *PIENI L'ANIMO*

Original Text: *Acta Sanctae Sedis,* 39:321–330.
Previous Translation: *American Catholic Quarterly Review,* 31:744–750.
"The Sovereign Pontiff to His Bishops." *American Ecclesiastical Review,* 35:337–344.

8. *PASCENDI DOMINICI GREGIS*

Original Text: *Acta Sanctae Sedis,* 40:593–650.

Previous Translation: *American Catholic Quarterly Review,* 32:705–730.
Burke, Thomas F. "The Errors Condemned." *Catholic World,* 86:524–531.
Currier, Charles W. "Modernism in the Past Year." *American Ecclesiastical Review,* 39:465–472; 618–627.
Daily, Joseph W. "The Causes of Modernism." *Catholic World,* 86:644–650.
Gerard, J. "Papal Encyclical from a Catholic's Point of View." *Hibbert Journal,* 6:256–263.
Harent, Stephane. "Modernism, or Experience and Faith." *Catholic Mind,* 1908:1–39.
Horty, J. M. "Is the Encyclical 'Pascendi Dominici Gregis' an ex cathedra Document?" *Irish Ecclesiastical Record,* 25:408–411.
Hughes, H. G. "Catholic and Modernist Theories of Development." *American Catholic Quarterly Review,* 38:277–290; 385–399.
"Humani Generis and Predecessors." *American Ecclesiastical Review,* 123:152 ff.
Ireland, John, Abp. "The Dogmatic Authority of the Papacy." *North American Review,* 187:486–497.
Keiley, Benjamin J., Bp. "Condemnation of Modernism." *Catholic Mind,* 9:121–146.
MacCaffrey, James. "The Papal Encyclical on Modernism." *Irish Ecclesiastical Record,* 22:561–575.
"Modernism in the Church in America." *American Ecclesiastical Review,* 38:1–10.
Mooney, Joseph F. "The Rights of the Supreme Pontiff." *Catholic World,* 86:519–523.
Moyes, James. "Modernism and the Papal Encyclical." *Nineteenth Century and After,* 62:865–878.
Murphy, John T. "The Pope's Encyclical on Modernism." *American Catholic Quarterly Review,* 33:130–137.

"Pius X on Recent Manifestations of Modernism." *Catholic Mind,* 8:319–350.
Smith, Sydney F. "Newman's Relation to Modernism." *The Month,* 120:1–15.
———. "The Encyclical 'Pascendi Gregis.'" *The Month,* 110:449–468.
———. "What is Modernism?" *The Month,* 111:284–301.
"The Catholic Institute of Paris and the Papal Encyclical." *Tablet,* 110:881–882.
The Doctrines of the Modernists and Modernist Errors; ed. by Lewis Watt, S. J., London, Catholic Truth Society, 1937.
"The Encyclical: A Criticism in *The Times.*" *Tablet,* 110:561–563.
"The Encyclical and Modern Thought." *Tablet,* 111:161–163.
"The Encyclical on the Teaching of Modernists in our Seminaries." *American Ecclesiastical Review,* 37:504–511.
"The Encyclical 'Pascendi.'" *Dublin Review,* 142:1–10.
"The Modernists of the Thirteenth Century." *The Month,* 111:302–307.
"The Modernists and Cardinal Newman." *Tablet,* 110:784.
Turner, William. "'Scholasticism' versus 'Modernism.'" *American Ecclesiastical Review,* 40:129–139.
———. "The Philosophical Bases of Modernism." *Catholic University Bulletin,* 14:443–465.
Vieban, A. "Modernism and Protestantism." *American Ecclesiastical Review,* 41:130–151.
———. "Who are the Modernists in the Encyclical?" *American Ecclesiastical Review,* 38:489–507.

9. *COMMUNIUM RERUM*

Original Text: *Acta Apostolicae Sedis,* 1:333–388.
Previous Translation: *American Catholic Quarterly Review,* 34:347–369.
Moyes, J. "Saint Anselm of Canterbury." *Dublin Review,* 145:107–127; 323–352.

10. *EDITAE SAEPE*

Original Text: *Acta Apostolicae Sedis,* 2:357–380.
Previous Translation: *American Catholic Quarterly Review,* 35:394–412.
"The Latest Encyclical." *Ave Maria,* 71:21–23.
Thurston, Herbert. "St. Charles Borromeo and the Recent Encyclical." *The Month,* 116:379–390.

11. *IAMDUDUM*

Original Text: *Acta Apostolicae Sedis,* 3:217–224.
Previous Translation: *American Catholic Quarterly Review,* 36:551–556.
Allies, Mary H. "The Voltaire of Portugal." *Catholic World,* 96:46–57.
Britten, James. "The Lusitanian Church." *The Month,* 118:2–14.
Cabral, Luiz Gonsaga. "The Portuguese Jesuits." *Catholic Mind,* 9:1–23.
"Horrors of Portuguese Prisons." *Catholic Mind,* 10:73–103.
McCullagh, Francis. "Separation of Church and State in Portugal." *Catholic World,* 93:371–379.

———. "Some Causes of the Portuguese Revolution." *Catholic Mind,* 9:49–69.
"Protest of the Portuguese Bishops." *Catholic Mind,* 9:220–235.
"Portugal." *Catholic Encyclopedia,* Suppl.: 596–597.
Smith, Sydney F. "The Call of Portugal Again." *The Month,* 122:417–420.
———. "The Revolution in Portugal." *The Month,* 116:449–464.
"The Portuguese Revolution." *Catholic Mind,* 9:25–48.
"The Portuguese Separation Law." *Dublin Review,* 149:126–142.
Torrend, Comillo. "Anti-Clerical Policy in Portugal." *Dublin Review,* 150:128–151.

12. *LACRIMABILI STATU*

Original Text: *Acta Apostolicae Sedis,* 4:521–525.
Previous Translation: *American Catholic Quarterly Review,* 37:741–744.
"Pius X on the Reform of the Latin American Clergy." *Catholic Fortnightly Review,* 18:243–244.

13. *SINGULARI QUADAM*

Original Text: *Acta Apostolicae Sedis,* 4:657–662.
Cort, John. "After Sixty Years." *Commonweal,* 54:114–115.
"Declaration of Principles Adopted by the Ninety-Seventh Convention of the Catholic Central Verein of America." Saint Louis, Central Bureau, 1952.
E. W. "Rome Hath Spoken." *Central-Blatt and Social Justice,* 5:217–219; 243–245; 269–272.
Matt, Alphonse. "A Forgotten Encyclical of Pius X." *Wanderer,* May 22, 1952.
Matt, Walter L. "More About the Forgotten Encyclical." *Wanderer,* June 19, 1952.
Murray, John Courtney. "Intercredal Co-Operation: Its Theory and Its Organization." *Theological Studies,* 4:257–286.
Parsons, Wilfrid. "Intercredal Co-Operation in the Papal Documents." *Theological Studies,* 4:159–182.
"Pius X to the Workingmen." *Catholic Fortnightly Review,* 19:642.
Twomey, L. J. "Blessed Pius X: A Great Social Apostle." *Catholic Mind,* 49:694–696.

III.

1. *INTER PLURIMAS PASTORALIS*

Original Text: *Acta Sanctae Sedis,* 36:387–395.
Previous Translation: *American Catholic Quarterly Review,* 29:226–234.
Connerton, J. W. "Forty Years after Motu Proprio." *Ave Maria,* 58:775–777.
deBrant, C. "Forerunners of the Motu Proprio." *Catholic Choirmaster,* 29:6–9.
Donovan, J. P. "Is the Law on Church Music Honored in Its Observance?" *Homiletic and Pastoral Review,* 44:290–292.
Ehmann, B. "Motu Proprio: Fortieth Anniversary." *Catholic Choirmaster,* 29:2.
Finn, William J. "Has Church Music Progressed in a Decade?" *American Ecclesiastical Review,* 49:681–690.

Marier, T. A. "Contemporary Church Music and the Motu Proprio." *Caecilia,* 73:127–129.
McNaspy, C. J. "Singing with the Church." *Review for Religious,* 2:345–353.
"Papal Letter to His Eminence Cardinal Respighi, Vicar General of Rome, Regarding the Regulations for the Restoration of Sacred Music." *American Catholic Quarterly Review,* 29:222–225.
"Pastoral Letter of 1895 to Clergy of Venice Concerning Church Music." *Catholic Choirmaster,* 29:142–143; 187–188.
Rigby, T. "The Reform of Sacred Music." *The Month,* 103:113–118.
Stockley, W. F. P. "The Pope and the Reform in Church Music." *American Ecclesiastical Review,* 30:279–292; 384–401.
Taunton, Ethelred L. "The Old Roman Chant." *Catholic World,* 85:237–246.
Vitry, Ermin. "Reflections on the Twenty-Fifth Anniversary of the Motu Proprio on Church Music." *Orate Fratres,* 2:240–245.
———. "Restore All Things in Christ." *Caecilia,* 78:130–131.
Ward, Justine B. "The Reform of Church Music." *Catholic Mind,* 1906:209–227.

2. *FIN DALLA PRIMA*

Original Text: *Acta Sanctae Sedis,* 36:339–345.
Previous Translation: *American Catholic Quarterly Review,* 29:234–239.
Husselein, Joseph. "Pius X and Catholic Action." *America,* 8:125–126.
"Preaching and Popular Christian Action: Motu Proprio of Pius X." *American Catholic Quarterly Review,* 31:744–750.

3. *ARDUUM SANE MUNUS*

Original Text: *Acta Sanctae Sedis,* 36:549–551.
Cicognani, Amleto Giovanni, Abp. *Canon Law.* Westminster, Newman Press, 1934, pp. 419–423.
Risk, James E. "Arduum Sane Munus: A Retrospect." *Theological Studies,* 5:184–197.

4. *SACRA TRIDENTINA SYNODUS*

Original Test: *Acta Sanctae Sedis,* 38:400–406.
"American Bishops and Daily Communion." *American Ecclesiastical Review,* 37:34–42.
Ellard, Gerald. "Pius X and Christocracy." *Orate Fratres,* 10:8–14.
Hedley, John C., Bp. "The Practice of Holy Communion." *Catholic Mind,* 11:15–26.
Heuser, H. J. "The Holy Father's Wish Regarding Daily Communion." *American Ecclesiastical Review,* 35:60–67.
King, Edward. "Holy Communion in the Early Church." *Catholic Mind,* 4:323–340.
McMahon, Joseph H. "Reactions and By-Products of the Decree on Frequent Communion." *American Ecclesiastical Review,* 47:702–707.

Pernin, Claude J. "The Apostolate of Daily Communion." *American Ecclesiastical Review*, 46:547–564.
Schoenbechler, Roger. "The Decree of Pius X on Frequent Communion." *Orate Fratres*, 10:108–112.

5. *QUONIAM IN RE BIBLIA*

Original Text: *Acta Sanctae Sedis*, 39:77–80.
Previous Translation: *Catholic University Bulletin*, 12:388–390.
"Quoniam in Re Biblia." *Catholic Fortnightly Review*, 13:316–318.

6. *LAMENTABILI*

Original Text: *Acta Sanctae Sedis*, 40:470–478.
Previous Translation: *American Catholic Quarterly Review*, 32:561–566.
"The New Syllabus." *The Month*, 110:113–114.
"The New Syllabus in Its Relation to Bible Study." *American Ecclesiastical Review*, 37:535–541.

7. *HAERENT ANIMO*

Original Text: *Acta Sanctae Sedis*, 41:555–577.
Previous Translation: *American Catholic Quarterly Review*, 32:561–566.
"Pope Pius to His Priests." *Catholic Fortnightly Review*, 15:667.

8. *QUAM SINGULARI*

Original Text: *Acta Apostolicae Sedis*, 2:577–583.
Previous Translation: *American Catholic Quarterly Review*, 36:374–377.
deZulueta, F. M. *Early First Communion*. New York, Benziger Brothers, 1911.
———. "The Control of Children's First Communions." *American Ecclesiastical Review*, 48:21–25.
Husslein, Joseph. "Children's Early and Frequent Communion." *Catholic Mind*, 9:345–360.
McNicholas, John T. "The Age of Children for First Communion." *American Ecclesiastical Review*, 43:482–488.
"The Holy See and the Children." *American Ecclesiastical Review*, 43:479–482.

9. *DIVINO AFFLATU*

Original Text: *Acta Apostolicae Sedis*, 3:633–638.
Previous Translation: *American Catholic Quarterly Review*, 37:166–170.
Ducey, W. M. "Blessed Pius and the Praise of God." *Orate Fratres*, 25:509–514.
Ellard, Gerald. "Pius X and the New Liturgy." *Orate Fratres*, 1:241–246.
Hedrick, John T. "The Office with the New Psalter." *American Ecclesiastical Review*, 46:450–462.
"Motu Proprio on the Recitation of the Divine Office." *Irish Ecclesiastical Record*, 2:650–655.

O'Doherty, Thomas. "The New Method of Reciting the Divine Office." *Irish Ecclesiastical Record,* 1:19–29.
1:19–29.
Storck, Herman I. "The Reform of the Roman Breviary." *American Ecclesiastical Review,* 46:441–449.
Walker, Charlton Benedict. "The Revised Psalter of the Breviary." *Catholic World,* 94:784–791.

10. *DOCTORIS ANGELICI*

Original Text: *Acta Apostolicae Sedis,* 6:336–341.
Egan, J. M. "Blessed Pius X and Theology." *Thomist,* 14:313–322.

Index

I

J

K

L

M

A NOTE ON THE TYPE

IN WHICH THIS BOOK WAS SET

This book has been set in Granjon, a lovely Linotype face, designed by George W. Jones, one of England's great printers, to meet his own exacting requirements for fine book and publication work. Like most useful types, Granjon is neither wholly new nor wholly old. It is not a copy of a classic face nor an original creation, but rather something between the two—drawing its basic design from classic Garamond sources, but never hesitating to deviate from the model where four centuries of type-cutting experience indicate an improvement or where modern methods of punch-cutting make possible a refinement far beyond the skill of the originator. This book was composed and printed by The York Composition Company, Inc. of York, Pa., and bound by Moore and Company of Baltimore. The design and typography are by Howard N. King.

A NOTE ON THE TYPE

IN WHICH THIS BOOK WAS SET

This book has been set in Granjon, a Linotype face designed by George W. Jones, one of England's great printers, to meet his own exacting requirements for fine book and publication work. Like many useful types, Granjon is neither wholly new nor wholly old. It is not a copy of a classic face nor an original creation, but rather something between the two—drawing its basic design from classic Garamond sources, but never hesitating to deviate from the model where four centuries of type-cutting experience indicate an improvement or where modern methods of punch-cutting make possible a refinement far beyond the skill of the originator. This book was composed and printed by The York Composition Company, Inc., of York, Pa., and bound by Moore and Company of Baltimore. The design and typography are by Howard N. King.